Business Development Services

A review of international experience

Edited by
JACOB LEVITSKY

C000165801

INTERMEDIATE TECHNOLOGY PUBLICATIONS 2000

Intermediate Technology Publications
103/105 Southampton Row, London WC1B 4HH, UK

© Intermediate Technology Publications 2000

A CIP catalogue record of this book is available from the British Library

ISBN 1 85339 506 4

Typeset by Dorwyn Ltd, Rowlands Castle, Hants
Printed in UK by Cromwell Press, Trowbridge

Contents

PART VII, BUSINESS LINKAGES

PART VIII, BUSINESS INCUBATORS

PART IX, MARKETING

PART X, TECHNOLOGY

PART XI, VIABILITY AND MEASUREMENT OF BDS

Preface

Introduction and background

The Committee of Donor Agencies for Small Enterprise Development was set up at a meeting of the major donor agencies in October 1979 in Berlin. The committee was created to enhance co-operation between the various donor agencies and to achieve greater harmonization in approaches to supporting SME development. The committee was to provide a forum for exchanging ideas and distilling lessons based on the experience of donor SME support programmes.

The Donor Agency Committee focused on finance in the early 1990s, which led to a publication embodying agreed guiding principles[1] for selecting inter-mediaries for financial support programmes. Since 1995, the committee has turned its attention to non-financial services. The wide range of business de-velopment services (BDS) receiving donor support, the different approaches and the lack of any overall agreement on best practices, made this an important issue. After some years of work, a publication was finally produced by a working group set up by a meeting of the committee in Budapest in June 1995 and subsequently co-ordinated by the International Labour Organisation (ILO). It was decided to prepare an international conference, the findings of which would be used to develop further the working group paper.[2] The Inter-American Development Bank (IADB) offered support and services to organize such a conference in Rio de Janeiro, Brazil for 2-5 march 1999.

Prior to the international meeting in Brazil, a regional conference, dealing with the BDS for SME in Africa was held in Harare in October 1998. A report on the Harare regional meeting, which has since been published, was presented to the Rio conference by the ILO representative. It was also decided to schedule a conference for the Asian region in the Spring of 2000.

The Rio Conference was divided into two parts; the first two days comprising an international meeting with participants mainly from donor agencies, and the second part organized by the IADB for invited Latin American participants. Around 70 attended the first part and over 300 the latter two days.

In all, 32 papers, selected and reviewed at meetings of a working group in Geneva, were presented in plenary and panel sessions. The sessions were de-voted to integrated SME capacity building, establishment and operation of busi-ness centres and advisory services, business linkages, industrial clusters and business incubators, support for marketing services, innovative developments in business training and counselling, entrepreneurship development programmes, distance consulting and strengthening technologies and information services. There were also papers on the viability of business development services and the measurement of indicators to monitor the degree to which the objectives of such services were achieved. The major thrust in all the sessions was new approaches and innovative methods towards the sustainability of BDS services, and ways of achieving greater cost effectiveness in their delivery.

The arrangements and content for the conference were co-ordinated by the World Bank, IADB and the ILO. Other agencies, including UNIDO, UNC-TAD, UNDP, USAID (USA), DFID(UK), SDC (Switzerland) CIDA and IDRC (Canada), GRET (France), NORAD (Norway), Netherlands Aid as well as the Ford and Soros Foundations, also contributed mainly through financing studies and special projects and the preparing of papers. Donors also covered the travel costs of the donor representatives and of the presenters of papers sponsored.

Special mention should be made of two presentations on the potential of using distance consulting methods through the Internet for delivering information and conducting training for SMEs which have not been included. Resumés are given in the summary on the contents of the papers that were not included in this publication for lack of space.

Conference facilities, logistical support and hospitality were provided by FIR-JAN (The Federation of Industries of the State of Rio de Janeiro) and BNDES, the major National Development Bank of Brazil. The Secretaria do Trabalho of the Prefecture of the Rio de Janeiro, Xerox Corporation of Brazil and the Fundacao Roberto Marinho also gave support.

This publication, and the summary given here apply only to the international part of the Rio Conference i.e. the first two days, 2–3 March, 1999. A separate publication will appear of a selection from the second, IADB-organized, part of the Conference, focusing specifically on BDS in Latin America. Regrettably, it has not been possible to publish all the 32 papers presented at the international part of the conference. Some of the African papers prepared have already appeared in a separate ILO publication[3] reporting on the Harare meeting.

Notes

1 *Micro and Small Enterprise Finance Guiding Principles for Selecting and Supporting Intermediaries* — Committee of Donor Agencies for Small Enterprise Development/ Donors' Working Group on Financial Sector Development — October 1995.

2 *Business Development Services for SMEs: Preliminary Guidelines for Donor-Funded Interventions* — Report to Donor Committee for Small Enterprise Development — January 1998.

3 'Business Development Services: How sustainable can they be?' Report on a workshop for African countries, Harare, October 1998. J. Tanburn, Committee of Donor Agencies for Small Enterprise Development/Department for International Development (DFID)/International Small Enterprise Programme, ILO, April 1999.

Contributors

BENAVENTE, J.M.: *Corporacion de Fomento, (Development Corporation) Chile; Advisor, Inter-American Development Bank*

BOTZUNG, Michel: *Consultant, Group de Recherche et d'Echanges Technologiques (GRET), Paris*

CEGLIE, Giovanna: *Industrial Development Officer, Private Sector Development Branch, United Nations Industrial Development Organisation (UNIDO), Vienna*

CRISAFULLI, Daniel: *Private Sector Development, World Bank, Washington DC*

CROMBRUGGHE, André de: *Senior Industrial Development Officer, Private Sector Development Branch, United Nations Industrial Development Organisation (UNIDO), Vienna*

DINI, Marco: *Consultant, United Nations Industrial Development Organisation (UNIDO), Vienna*

GIBSON, Alan: *Consultant, The Springfield Centre for Business in Development, Durham, U.K.*

GOLDMARK, Lara: *Consultant, Inter-American Development Bank, Washington DC*

GRIERSON, John: *Senior Specialist, Enterprise Development, FTP International Consultants, Helsinki*

HALLBERG, Kris: *Private Sector Development, World Bank, Washington DC*

HITCHINS, Robert: *Consultant, The Springfield Centre for Business in Development, Durham, U.K.*

KAKORE, Edward: *Confederation of Zimbabwe Industries, Harare*

KENNEDY, Richard M.: *Industrial Development Officer, Private Sector Development Branch, United Nations Industrial Development Organisation (UNIDO), Vienna*

KOLSHORN, Rainer: *Programme Director, CEFE International, German Agency for Technical Co-operation (GTZ), Eschborn, Germany*

LALKAKA, Rustam: *Program Advisor, United Nations Development Programme (UNDP), New York*

LEVITSKY, Jacob: *Consultant, Donor Agencies Committee for Small Enterprise Development, formerly Small Enterprise Adviser, World Bank, U.K.*

LLISTERRI, Juan José: *Enterprise Development Co-ordinator, Inter-American Development Bank, Washington DC*

LOUCKS, Kenneth E.: *Professor, Faculty of Business, Brock University, Ontario, Canada*

LYNCH, Mary M.: *M.M. Lynch Consultants International, Ottawa, Canada*

McVAY, Mary: *Consultant, Microenterprise Best Practices Project for US Agency for International Development (USAID)*

MEAD, Donald C.: *Professor Emeritus, Department of Agricultural Economics, Michigan State University, USA*

MIKKELSEN, Lene: *Consultant, Inter-American Development Bank, Washington DC*

MONTES, J.C.: *Industrial Development Officer, Private Sector Development Branch, United Nations Industrial Development Organisation (UNIDO), Vienna*

RILEY, Thyra A.: *African Region Private Sector Group, World Bank, Washington DC*

SCHMERTZ, Ida F.S.: *Vice-President and Director, Alliance of American and Russian Women; Chairman, Board of Trustees, Volkov International Business Incubator, Russia*

SCHOLTES, Philippe: *Industrial Development Officer, Private Sector Development Branch, United Nations Industrial Development Organisation (UNIDO), Vienna*

SHAFFER, Daniel: *President, Shaffer and Associates, Inc., Arizona, USA*

SINHA, Sanjay: *Consultant, EDA Rural Systems Limited, Delhi*

SONESSON, Casper: *Programme Officer, United Nations Development Programme (UNDP), New York*

STEEL, William F.: *Adviser, Private Sector Development, African Technical Department, World Bank, Washington DC*

TABUENCA, Antonio Garcia: *Consultant, Inter-American Development Bank (IADB), Washington DC*

TANBURN, Jim: *Senior SED Specialist, International Small Enterprise Programme (ISEP), International Labour Organisation, Geneva, Switzerland*

TOMESEN, Leon: *Consultant, The Springfield Centre for Business in Development, Durham, U.K.*

WEIHERT, Uwe: *Senior Advisor, Department of Economics Development and Employment Promotion, German Corporation; German Agency for Technical Co-operation (GTZ), Eschborn, Germany*

YOUNG-GYAMPO, Kwame: *Consultant, Canadian International Development Agency (CIDA), Ghana*

Acronyms

ALABSUB	Asociación Latino Americana de Bolsas de Subcontractación
AMPIH	Asociación Nacional de Mediana y Pequena Industria de Honduras
ANDI	Asociación Nacional de Industriales
ANPROTEC	National Association of Institutes Promoting Advanced Technology Ventures
APDF	African Project Development Facility
ApproTEC	Appropriate Technology Organisation (Kenya)
APW	Appreciation Workshop
BCS	Business Consultancy Services
BDS	Business Development Services
BESO	British Executive Service Overseas
BNDES	National Development Bank of Brazil
CAPEO	Cellule d'Appui à la Petite Enterprise d'Ouagadougou (Ouagadougou Support Cell for Small Enterprises)
CCI	Chambers of Commerce and Industry
CEEM	Enterprise Extension Centre
CEFE	Competency Based Formation of Enterprises
CEO	Chief Executive Officer
CEPAE	Paraguayan Centre for Assistance to Enterprise
CEPRI	Centro de Productividad Integral (Chile)
CERTEC	Centro de Recursos y Technologia (Honduras)
CIDA	Canadian International Development Agency
CINET	Centro Incubador de Empresas Tecnologicas
CNPq	National Scientific & Technological Centre
COFIDE	Development Finance Corporation (Peru) (Corporacion Financiera de Desarrollo)
CONCAMIN	Confederation of Industrial Chambers
CORFO	Corporaciòn de Fomento de la Producion – Development Corporation (Chile)
CTUP	Cluster Technology Upgrading Programme (India)
CUBOS	Credit Insurance Bonus Coupons (Chile)
CZI	Confederation of Zimbabwean Industries
DCSED	Donor Committee of Small Enterprise Development
DFID	Department for International Development (UK)
DTI	Department of Trade and Industry
EDC	Enterprise Development Centre
EDP	Entrepreneurship Development Programme
EMPRETEC	Combination of EMPRESAS (enterprises) and TECNOLOGIAS (technologies)
EPZDA	Export Processing Zone Development Authority
ESSA	Enterprise Support Services for Africa
EU	European Union

EWW	Enterprise Works Worldwide
FAIDA	Netherlands Aid Project for Small Enterprises (Tanzania)
FAPEMIG	State Funds
FAT	Technical Assistance Funds (Chile)
FINEP	Studies and Projects Financing Agency (Brazil)
FIRJAN	Federation of Industries of the State of Rio de Janiero
FIT	Farm Implements and Tools (see footnote 8, page 40)
FSP	Fondation pour le Secteur Privé
FUNTEC	Fundacion para la Transferencia Tecnologica a la Pequeñas y Medianas Empresas
GESO	Ghana Executive Service Overseas
GMT	Grassroots Management Training (World Bank)
GRET	Group de Recherche et d'Echanges Technologiques (Paris)
GTZ	German Agency for Technical Co-operation
IADB	Inter-American Development Bank
IDA	International Development Association (soft credits arm of World Bank)
IDB	Inter-American Development Bank (also IADB)
IDRC	International Development Research Centre (Ottawa)
IFC	International Finance Corporation
ILO	International Labour Organisation
INFOP	Instituto Nacional de Formacion Profesional
INSOTEC	Instituto de Investigacions Socioeconomicas y Tecnologicas (Socio Economic and Technological Research Institute) (Ecuador)
ISB	Industrial Services Bureau
ISTARN	Informal Sector Training and Resource Network (Zimbabwe)
ITDG	Intermediate Technology Development Group (UK)
JAMPRO	Jamaica Productivity Centre
MBLP	Manicaland Business Linkages Project (Zimbabwe)
MEDA	Mennonite Economic Development Associates
MFI	Micro-finance Institution
MIF	Multilateral Investment Fund (Latin America)
MIIT	Ministry of Industry and Industrial Technology (Chile)
MSE	Micro and Small Enterprise
NBDP	New Business Development Programme (USAID programme in Russia)
NEPC	North Eastern Provincial Council (Sri Lanka)
NET	Network Evaluation Tool
NGO	Non-governmental Organization
NORAD	Norwegian Agency for Development Co-operation
NTSIKA	Agency for Small Enterprise Development (South Africa)
PASI	Programa de Apoyo al Sector Informal
PBEP	Polish-British Enterprise Project
PCO	Project Co-ordination Office

PCS	Promotora de Comercio Social (Colombia)
PEPC	Provincial Enterprise Promotion Centre (Sri Lanka)
PO	Partner Organization
PROARTE	Handicraft Marketing Company (Nicaragua)
PROEXSAL	Sociedad Cooperativa de Productores y Exportadores del Salvador
PROFO	Proyectos de Fomento (Chile)
REDS	Rural Enterprise Development Sector
RHAE	Programme of Human Resources and Technology Development (Brazil)
RIP	Rural Industries Programme (India)
RMA	Rapid Market Appraisal
SBA	Small Business Adviser
SC	Swisscontact
SCORE	Senior Core of Retired Executives
SDC	Swiss Agency for Development and Co-operation
SEBRAE	Services for Support for Micro and Small Enterprises (Brazil)
SED	Small Enterprise Development
SEEDS	Sarvodaya Economic Enterprises Development Services (Sri Lanka)
SEON	Social and Economic Enterprise of Netherlands
SERCOTEC	Servicio de Cooperaction Tecnica (Technical Cooperation Service) (Chile)
SIDBI	Small Industries Development Bank of India
SLBDC	Sri Lanka Business Development Centre
SMED	Small and Medium Enterprise Development
SPX	Subcontracting and Partnership Exchanges
STUP	Skill-cum-Technology Upgradation Programme (India)
TDS	Technology Diffusion Scheme
TOT	Training-of-Trainers
TX	Traidcraft Exchange
ULI	User-led Innovation
UNCTAD	United Nations Conference on Trade and Development
UNCTC	United Nations Centre for Transnational Corporations
UNDP	United Nations Development Programme
UNHCR	United Nations High Commission for Refugees
UNIDO	United Nations Industrial Development Organization
USAID	United States Agency for International Development
VBI	Volkhov Business Incubator
ZOPP	Zimbabwe Oil Press Project

1. Summary Report

JACOB LEVITSKY

Integrated SME capacity building

EMPRETEC's programmes[1]

WHILE MOST OF THE presentations at the conference concerned the establishment and operation of specific BDS support instruments, there were a number of cases which described efforts to develop organizations offering a wider range of services to stimulate business development. These provide an extensive range of training, consultancy and promotional programmes covering the variety of different support products and services. Presentations exemplifying this type of approach included two different cases involving the EMPRETEC programme, started in 1988 in Argentina by the former United Nations Centre for Transnational Corporations (UNCTC). Since the dissolution of the UNCTC, the EMPRETEC programme has been co-ordinated internationally by the UN Conference on Trade and Development (UNCTAD) Division for Investment, Technology and Enterprise Development.

By 1999, the EMPRETEC programme was operating in 10 African and Latin American (LA) countries with varying degrees of success: Argentina, Brazil, Chile, Colombia, Ghana, Morocco, Nigeria, Uruguay, Venezuela and Zimbabwe. UNCTAD presented a paper reviewing EMPRETEC's programme in selected Latin American countries,[2] selecting principally those in Uruguay (1989) and Brazil (1991), with some reference to later programmes in Colombia (1996) and Chile (1990). The second paper, presented by DFID of the UK, covered an account of the most important programme in Africa, that of EMPRETEC in Ghana, started in 1990 but having developed into an independent foundation in 1994.

The varied approach used in the various EMPRETEC programmes was highlighted within the Latin American countries, and more specifically with the independent organizational structure of EMPRETEC in Ghana. From the start, the EMPRETEC programme in Latin America, was developed to enhance the role of the private sector in support for SMEs but encouraged flexibility as to how its organizational framework could be adapted to local conditions and needs. Efforts were made at the time to identify a 'best practice' EMPRETEC model, but experience showed that flexibility was to be preferred. From the early days of the EMPRETEC programme, there have been differences within the organizers as to whether EMPRETEC should be incorporated within an existing functioning BDS organization – as in the case of SEBRAE in Brazil, and with other national organizations in Chile and Colombia – or to build a new separate, independent, self-sustainable operation as in Ghana.

In the two LA programmes described – those of EMPRETEC in Uruguay and Brazil – these followed the approach of incorporation within a strong national counterpart organization, but the type of organization differed. In Uruguay, EMPRETEC chose a bank – the main publicly owned bank in the country,

1

Banco de la República Oriental del Uruguay – while in Brazil, the programme was implemented within SEBRAE – Servicio Brasileiro de Apoio as Micro e Pequenas Empresas – a national organization which already had a long history of providing SME supporting services. In Uruguay, because the counterpart organization, as a bank, was not suitable for organizing SME support activities, EMPRETEC used the bank, at no charge, mainly for the administration and the facilities for its training and consulting activities, while in Brazil, as SEBRAE was already an experienced BDS organization, there was no call on EMPRETEC to operate separately in this respect.

Both in Uruguay and Brazil, EMPRETEC's primary activity was to conduct entrepreneurship development programmes (EDPs) and even now, in both these countries as in the others, the EMPRETEC programme is known mainly for these EDP activities. In both countries, EMPRETEC has since moved into consultancy services, starting with the so-called 'diagnostic health checks' and helps in the preparation of business plans, as follow-up to the EDP workshops.

The Ghanaian EMPRETEC, operating since 1994 as an independent foundation – the EMPRETEC Ghana Foundation (EGF) – has benefited from donor support from the European Union, the World Bank, the UK DFID and UNDP. EGF, which now has a staff of over 60, (mostly) experienced professionals, is also known for its EDP and for specialized training programmes for selected groups of businessmen, but has also provided consultancy services, partly by its own staff and partly through facilitating and subsidizing the services of accredited consultants. Usually, the 'diagnostic health checks' – involving short reviews of the performance of the business, as in the Latin American EMPRETEC services, are carried out by the in-house staff of the organization. A difference between the Ghana operation and those in the Latin American countries is that the 'diagnostic checks' are made for a fee, albeit at a subsidized level.

EMPRETEC in Uruguay, it was claimed, was now recognized as the main source of BDS for SME in the country. It is now becoming increasingly self-sustaining by charging fees for most of its services at a level which gives the programme the prospect of recovering costs from income. The EMPRETEC programme, which is estimated at US$700,000 for three years, a third of which is contributed by the local organization, is working on developing new, marketable products to be financed fully from within the country. It is projected that the cost can be reduced to below US$200,000 by using more local trainers and consultants, and by better control of expenses as well as increasing income from participants' fees. In Brazil, the EMPRETEC programme has stimulated groups of entrepreneurs to take the lead in the creation of business associations, and recently two EMPRETEC Associations have been set up.

The presentations also raised the question of whether the EMPRETEC should target high-performing entrepreneurs who appear able and willing to pay for quality services, even though it is recognized that sometimes there is natural pressure to broaden target groups for social reasons. UNCTAD still seems to believe that turning around and consolidating ailing firms could be considered a positive objective, although it is recognized that this might adversely affect moves towards sustainability. EMPRETEC in Argentina and Colombia have, in fact, decided to concentrate resources on selected promising high-tech businesses considered to have potential also for the economy despite the fact that there may be a lengthy period before success is achieved. EMPRETEC Argentina in particular, from the start of its operation (1988) has focused services on the most promising, innovative entrepreneurs.

Some EMPRETEC programmes have also had problems. In Nigeria and Venezuela, UNCTAD claims that government agencies have intervened too much to try to control the programme through selection of staff and beneficiaries, making it less successful in achieving its aims.

Chilean Case

In 1990, the Chilean government was dissatisfied with the extent to which policy instruments that had been set up for SME, e.g. the technical assistance funds (FAT) and credit insurance bonus coupons (CUBOS) were not reaching the target groups due to their lack of information on how to use these facilities. The Ministry of the Economy therefore outlined a concept of development projects (PROFOs) in which associations of SMEs from a given sector grouped together to network and develop their competitiveness. The government agreed to subsidize part of the financing costs over a three-year period. The major goals of this initiative were:

- to introduce new product designs of higher value added and quality, and to access new sources of technology
- to look for new national and international markets
- to upgrade the skills of both workers and managers
- to improve access to sources of financing, while cutting costs.

In 1998, a study was undertaken of 290 companies, from different production sectors, that had participated in the PROFOs programme. The interviewees stated that significant progress had been made in labour organization, marketing strategies and improving production management, all attributed to the influence of PROFOs. Also, through PROFO, quality control, automation and production planning were introduced in many of the SMEs. The training of managers and workers was improved and there was increased access to sources of support through co-operation with competitors, larger firms, universities, NGOs and public institutions.

In answer to whether the PROFOs raised the competitiveness of SMEs, the companies interviewed stated they had had a significant growth in employment and productivity of the order of 10–15 per cent (more significant in employment rather than productivity). Companies that had been operating longer created more jobs than the newer ones. The reverse was true in productivity growth; newer companies showed more growth in productivity, in some cases up to 30 per cent.

The PROFO programme has managed in some way to correct the imbalance in access to financing and skilled manpower between larger firms and SMEs. Getting a PROFO group working took time. One PROFO business owner said that it was only in the second year that they started to work together. The Chilean presenter thought that PROFO experience in Chile had been relatively successful in achieving benefits through collaborative efforts.

Cases in West Africa

Another example of integrated SME capacity-building was the case of two West African BDS in Burkina Faso and Senegal supported by French bilateral aid. The two organizations operated differently. In Burkina Faso the CAPEO Foundation, which also received financial aid from the Canadian Aid programme

(CIDA), tried to provide services directly through its own professional staff. It was originally launched in 1991 as a project of the French bilateral programme to last seven years. In 1998 it was planned that it should be transformed into the Enterprise Foundation, which would gradually take over the activities of CA-PEO. It should be recalled that this attempt at the creation of a BDS organization was in one of the least developed countries of the world where, in fact, there was at the time no real capacity or expertise in the field of consultancy for SME.

The target group for CAPEO was enterprises that had been in operation for at least a year, had some kind of internal organization, a turnover of the equivalent of between US$10 000 and US$360 000 with about 5–50 employees, and that would agree to work with CAPEO in a serious fashion and try to carry out the recommendations made. CAPEO's activities included both training and advisory services, but its main work was in preparing requests for finance to local institutions and to help the clients to approach potential financiers. At the beginning, CAPEO offered its services free of charge but after 1997 it started charging for its services.

The development of CAPEO has not been as originally planned. The third phase (from 1996) to establish a national foundation was, by agreement, postponed to 2001. CAPEO had an annual budget of US$136 000 in 1999 but this represents a cut of 25 per cent from the budgets of 1996 and 1997. This was so that a higher proportion of the actual costs should be covered from income and the administrative costs should be substantially reduced.

The other West African BDS organization was a private sector foundation in Senegal – FSP – which started later than CAPEO in early 1996. It did not offer direct support from its own staff, but rather helped to make expertise available to enterprises and business associations from a fund of over US$5M provided by an IDA credit from the World Bank. The FSP offered individual enterprises and groups of entrepreneurs access to local and foreign consultants. It also aimed to help business organizations to provide better support and information services to their members.

FSP selected and followed up the service providers. This involved accreditation of those eligible, and taking off the list those whose work was sub-standard. There are two distinct phases in the FSP programme: identification and registration of the service provider, which requires screening applicants and review of qualifications and experience, and then the contracting of a provider after selection by the client.

In all, there have been 530 requests to the FSP, with 278 of them approved for contracts. Eighty per cent of these were for enterprises, the remainder for associations. Requests for assistance in management accounted for 40 per cent of the total but technological and marketing also provided almost half. One of the disturbing features of FSP was that 44 per cent of its budget covered administrative costs; hence the efforts to reduce these costs.

Both CAPEO and FSP felt that, although wishing to follow a demand-driven approach, the rejection rate was too high. Many of the enterprises were not able to identify their real needs without help. CAPEO therefore introduced a form of 'pre-diagnostic' service to help formulate the type of assistance really needed.

The presenter of the paper thought that both CAPEO and FSP would remain dependent on external subsidies for some time to come. The French aid organization felt there might be a problem to find ways of linking subsidies closely to activities and to quality of service, so as not to subsidize fees for mediocre service providers charging higher fees than justified.

BDS through NGOs

The International Development Research Centre (IDRC) of Canada presented a paper on high-impact, cost-effective BDS for SME. The paper described 10 NGOs in different regions.[3] The NGOs and case studies involved are given in Table 1.1.

The participating agencies mentioned in Table 1.1 all target poor people [over 90 per cent of clients have an annual income of less than US$300 in the case of Sarvodaya (Sri Lanka)]. They try to involve more women in business and aim at social empowerment of the poor and deprived. The need for cost recovery and sustainability is more a constraint than an objective.

All the participating NGOs have been engaged with the small-scale sector for some years.

- EWW targets small-scale producers, primarily products related to agriculture.
- The majority of ITDG's markets are enterprises employing fewer than five people in seven sectors: food production, agri-processing, manufacturing, transport, mining, building materials and shelter, and energy.
- MEDA's direct investment and assistance is entrepreneurially oriented and has tended to be in agriculture products, particularly businesses that service the producers. It helps with planning and obtains finance from CIDA for its work.
- The enterprises assisted by Sarvodaya are self-employment activities, mostly in non-farm activities (due to the non-violent philosophy of the NGO, businesses involved in the killing of animals are excluded).
- TechnoServe works primarily with agricultural firms in the 5 to 100+ employee range in both productive and trading sectors.

The Intermediate Technology Development Group (ITDG) of the UK tries to use market mechanisms to deliver services. In the Zimbabwe light engineering workshops project, they offer a profitable tool-hire service which helps to draw in artisans for other BDS.

MEDA expects that, in the course of time, subsidies will be replaced by businesses paying for BDS.

Sarvodaya has a service network of over 2150 village organizations in Sri Lanka. The monthly meeting of these village bodies is an inexpensive method of Sarvodaya announcing and launching new support programmes as well as an occasion for monitoring progress of clients.

Enterprise Works Worldwide (EEW) has developed a comprehensive set of performance indicators, which helps it evaluate its major projects. Information is

Table 1.1 The Case Study Projects

Enterprise Works Worldwide (EWW)	Zimbabwe Oil Press Project Ltd., Zimbabwe Coffee Producers, El Salvador
Intermediate Technology Development Group (ITDG)	Light Engineering Workshops, Zimbabwe Food Processing, Bangladesh
Mennonite Economic Development Associates (MEDA) (a religious-based NGO)	Joint Venture Marketing Company, Bolivia Cocoa co-operatives, Haiti
Sarvodaya	Ornamental Fish Production, Sri Lanka Pineapple Growers, Sri Lanka
TechnoServe	Irrigated Agricultural Groups, El Salvador Multipurpose Co-operatives, Ghana

stored in a computerized database for easy retrieval. An annual report analyses progress for project and updates the organizational portfolio, as well as lessons learned.

IDRC has found that a key factor for success in all projects is the knowledge of projects staff of the sector and technology involved. EWW and ITDG use prior knowledge to transfer technology and to innovate and adapt. Sarvodaya uses government and academics to inform themselves of the specifics of such activities as fish rearing and to train the producers. MEDA relies on experienced business people to oversee field projects. IDRC has also concluded that a significant asset of the international NGOs is their international market links.

Business centres and advisory services

There were a number of presentations at the Conference of donor support to SME through business centres. These cases reviewed the experience of such centres in different countries in Latin America, Asia, Eastern Europe and Russia. Three other papers covered cases of consultancy services set up in Ghana, planned for Jamaica and implemented as part of an SME-supported project in Poland.

These papers showed the importance given by donor agencies to creating a suitable institutional form for the delivery of BDS. Not all the centres were developed with the same organizational form, nor did all try to deliver the same products. Some were principally concerned with enhancing the co-operation between SMEs in the same sector, as in the Swisscontact case in the Philippines where eight different centres were set up, four of which were operated by the local chambers of commerce and industry (CCI) for provincial cities, and four by sectoral associations in such fields as jewellery, handicrafts, automotive repair and engineering workshops. Those operated by the CCI mainly offered training and office services, with some help in organizing trade fairs and assisting in legal matters. The four operated by the sectoral associations were really centres grouping together similar firms to establish common retail outlets (jewellery), bulk purchasing services (handicrafts and automotive workshops), and a credit service for the procurement of materials (for engineering workshops). The outreach in these different centres varied from 10 or so in the case of the jewellery, to 200 for the CCI organized centre in Oro.

In Indonesia, the eight business centres on the heavily populated island of Java offered advisory and direct consultancy services for a smaller number of medium sized businesses. These eight centres had an outreach of only approximately 300 clients. In Indonesia, the centres offered services according to the client's demands, and the donor did not prescribe the type of services they could offer. Early on, some of the consultancy was of a strictly technical nature, as in the automotive and engineering sub-sectors, but soon it was discovered that the clients were not prepared to pay for this as they could obtain this type of knowledge at no charge from agents or suppliers. As a result, the business centres tended to provide more advice on management.

The examples in Indonesia and the Philippines raised the issue of ownership, and highlight the problems of acquiring more finance from sources other than donors. Government and public funding would raise the issue of control. After one or two years of operation in various forms, the donor contribution was planned to drop to about 25 per cent of costs, on the assumption that the income generated from the centre's activities would provide 75 per cent of total income.

In both cases in Eastern Europe, that of the three business centres described in Romania and the business support centres incorporated in the British-supported Polish enterprise project, donor support covered almost all operating expenses in the early stages. For the first three years after UNIDO set up the Romanian UN Centres in 1991 with funding from the United Nations Development Programme (UNDP), and some input from the governments of Romania and the Netherlands, the centre was fully subsidized. Most of the effort before 1994 was in hiring and training consultants, and the production and distribution of material on business management. Some limited advice was given to entrepreneurs starting new businesses.

By 1994, there were already some private local consultants and other donor-sponsored business advisory services operating in Bucharest. The donors therefore decided to change from direct counselling of enterprises to training consultants and helping to build up the capacity of private organizations to offer such services in provincial cities which were not being adequately served. Although these provincial centres have now been operating for over four years, none of them is likely to achieve self-sustainability in the near future. UNIDO believes that at least one of the centres might become self-supporting from fees if it was allowed to serve larger enterprises. In another city, a business association or the chamber of commerce might subsidize the centre on behalf of its membership and the business community. The third centre might increase revenue through diversification outside the delivery of BDS. UNIDO believes each centre will have to find the appropriate mix of fees and services and seek out subsidies where required. The diversification of fees proposed in the case of other business centres refer to special contracts to carry out studies for donors, governments or local authorities, or for offering help to NGOs, and might also include retail sales of documents, manuals, books, videos and/or office or computer services.

The presenters admitted that there was no way of knowing how the three Romanian centres had influenced the growth of private sector consulting firms. The possibilities of unfair competition was recognized but it was believed that this was not a serious problem. In Romania, in at least one of the centres – Galati – the significant subsidy from the chamber of commerce was positive recognition of the help provided to SME.

An important example of centres presented, was the case of the Enterprise Development Centres (EDC) created in various Latin American countries – Costa Rica, El Salvador, Argentina and Colombia – at the initiative of the Inter-American Development Bank (IADB). The role of the EDCs was to help SMEs – with five to 99 employees – identify their needs, to advise them in hiring BDS, to share the costs of consultants and to assess jointly the results. The EDC also aimed to develop a market for BDS consultants at the local and regional levels.

An executive executing agency was set up for each project within a private sector organization (chambers of industry, business associations or foundations working with SMEs). The executing agencies have a national co-ordination office to plan, co-ordinate and monitor EDC activities. The Argentine agency was structured as a foundation, while in Colombia, an established partner was used. In Costa Rica and El Salvador the local participating agencies are also branches of an existing organization. Each EDC has a small team of experienced professionals. Of the 10 EDCs that were set up, three were in major cities of Argentina (outside Buenos Aries) and of Colombia, and two were national centres in the smaller countries, Costa Rica and El Salvador. By mid-1998, half the companies had called on EDC services at least twice.

EDCs are usually accommodated in the premises of the host institutions, which may vary. In one case it was a university with a strong business school. IADB financed the technical staff of each EDC and a portion of the costs of hiring outside consultants to provide BDS to local firms. The firms receiving services paid a share of the costs, the proportion increasing with time.

According to IADB, the EDC project had achieved success by assisting 5800 different firms in the four countries – over 3300 in Costa Rica and El Salvador. Nearly two-thirds of the firms had fewer than 20 workers, with firms of 20 to 100 workers accounting for over 25 per cent.

By 1999 the projects in Costa Rica and El Salvador were nearing completion but it was decided to extend them. The projects in Argentina and Colombia were half-way through, but still depended heavily (68 per cent and 65 per cent respectively) on subsidies. In Costa Rica and El Salvador, after longer experience, benefit from subsidies ranged from 58 per cent for Costa Rica to 45 per cent for El Salvador. In Rafaela, Argentina, approximately 40 per cent were billed to the firms, whereas the best Colombian centres managed to bill only 30 per cent of the cost.

One presentation concerned the creation of business centres (BSCs) in Russia[4] in eight major provincial cities from St Petersburg to Vladivostok. The primary goal of these BSCs, set up by USAID's New Business Development Programme (NBDP) in 1993, was to offer direct help to Russian small business, to create business support organizations and to support the growth of small business. These BSCs not only directly helped SMEs using the staff of these centres, they also sought to establish links to work together with what are referred to as 'strategic partners', organizations and programmes that could also provide BSDS to SMEs. These 'strategic partners' included universities and technical colleges in the various cities, and training organizations in the fields of business administration and industrial management. The programme helped to create business information libraries, databases and Internet services.

However, in 1997, after 3½ years of the NBOP, USAID's assistance was ended and the eight centres were forced to continue their activities on a self-sustaining basis. Eighteen months after the withdrawal of USAID support, all the centres were still in existence. In moving to self-sustainability, the BSCs had to focus on specialist services for which there was demand within the region. While supported by USAID, the centres helped to create the support business associations which later helped potential entrepreneurs. As these were not products and services which could cover costs, the centres were forced to move to income-generating fields. Thus the move to sustainability reduced the spread of BSC services, focusing them on groups that were able to pay. Unfortunately, self-sustainability meant that the centres could not continue supporting:

- potential entrepreneurs – often women and young people
- micro-enterprises
- small enterprises in start-up
- SMEs that had serious financial problems and could not pay for services
- business associations and NGOs.

The experience of the Russian BSC programme led to some key conclusions.

- It was important to select cities where local government was receptive to assistance, where a critical mass of private businesses existed and there was potentially a demand for BDS.

- Cities should be selected where there were active institutions to support SME and business associations or development agencies that would be reliable partners.
- The centres should be run as businesses. Staff should be few and selected carefully.
- Key business sectors should be identified and BDS should be focused mainly on these sectors.
- The programme should be kept flexible, and change when the situation demands.

In the discussions that followed these presentations on the business centre approach, there were some participants who felt that this should not be the real focus in BDS development. It should be development of a market for private sector consultants and the demand for their services. The centre approach might be applicable in provincial centres where there were very few private service providers operating, and more specialized professionals were needed. The question was raised whether the BD centres, set up by donors, regarded themselves as 'facilitators' of a transitional and promotional nature, or more long-term direct service providers. Where the centres were both facilitators and direct suppliers of services, some thought they might create market distortions; they might offer unfair competition to private firms. Others thought that introducing a second tier institution, as the centres were, could be costly and might impede generation of more direct relationships between the firms and consultants working with them. Centres might be more useful, it was argued by some, as small units that made limited, more diagnostic, interventions and then acted as brokers for the hiring of consultants to provide more far-reaching services.

Some participants feared that some of these centres were judged by how much they received in fees from firms. There was little information on the quality of services provided, their cost-effectiveness, outreach or benefit for the receiving firms. Some discussants questioned the cases – as in Romania – where service providers in centres enlarged their client group to raise more income. There were also some doubts as to whether the diversification into other income-generating projects, apart from BDS, to reduce subsidies was desirable as it could, in the course of time, change the character of the centre. Others saw less of a problem in this, seeing it as the flexibility that every enterprise (and institution) needs to survive.

There was some discussion of matching schemes, which provided donor contributions approximately equal to that generated through fees or other income generating efforts. Such schemes were considered by some as expensive and tending to increase the duration and amount of subsidies. Others thought matching schemes could be designed to attain a gradual reduction of subsidized BDS.

Opinions differed on subsidies. There were those who thought that if the services for SME were of good quality and achieved positive results, there was no *long-term* need for subsidies. They recognized that, as far as micro-business clients are concerned, there is not, as yet, the type of service developed that is simple and cheap enough. For this sector, there was a stronger case for subsidies. Other participants believed that there was a need to decide whom it was more effective to subsidize – the client or the service provider.

Advisory Services

There were also presented two cases of advisory services. One was the Enterprise Support Services for Africa (ESSA), funded by the Canadian

International Development Agency (CIDA), started in February 1996 to work with the International Finance Corporation (IFC) to help SMEs in Ghana that had received financing from the IFC African Project Development facility (APDF). ESSA had the role of helping APDF recipients to manage their companies better and to resolve organizational problems, particularly related to production and marketing. The ESSA pilot scheme was to last three years (1996–1999), acting as a broker between the SMEs being helped and consulting companies. The delivery of services was to be by outside consultants and institutions.

The paper reviewed the first two years of ESSA's operation. Experience in implementation was different from what had been expected, and the client base was broader than envisaged. Not only did firms need support after they received financing, but also help in preparing plans to submit to the APDF. The demand for services was greater than had been foreseen and the ability of consulting firms to respond to the needs higher than expected. Finally, the early ESSA clients were really in need of resolving immediate problems rather than more basic improvement in operations and procedures. Several of the cases were expanding small enterprises.

ESSA was called upon to fulfil three different roles; first there was working with SMEs to provide, on a cost shared basis, consulting assistance to solve the firms' immediate problems. The second role required ESSA to monitor the work of the Ghanaian consultants to ensure they met the needs of the client. ESSA support was for firms owned by Ghanaians employing more than six people. Annual turnover should be within the established SME range – up to US$400 000 annual turnover for small enterprises and to US$1m for medium. The firm had to be willing and able to share the costs of the consultancy and provide evidence that it could benefit from the services offered and was ready to carry out the recommendations. Most of the clients fell into the 'small' category. While ESSA planned to deal with 30 firms by the end of March 1999, it actually had 42 clients by the end of 1998.

There was some direct competition in training in the delivery of consultancy services, mainly from EMPRETEC Ghana (EGF). Many participants thought that this competition might be healthy, but the paper seemed to view it as wasteful. Some of the clients of ESSA had previously worked with EMPRETEC. SMEs preferred ESSA's approach, it was claimed, because it set targets and monitored the consultants' progress in meeting them.

All clients of ESSA were required to pay an increasing proportion of the costs of the service. In the first two years this amounted to approximately C$9600 (US$6800), about one-third of the overhead and direct costs. The paper claimed that 45 per cent of firms had increased sales and 36 per cent had increased profitability by more than 10 per cent as a result of ESSA's intervention. CIDA sees ESSA as having a catalytic role since the consulting community has grown and the success of clients has impacted not only on their own firms but also on others within the sub-sector.

The second case presented was that of the development of BDS within the Polish–British Enterprise Project (PBEP).[5] The PBEP began operations in 1994 supported by the UK Department for International Development (DFID) working in Eastern Poland around the cities of Bialystok and Lublin. Non-profit foundations and local public-private sector partnerships were set up.

The target group assisted by the PBEP was off-farm enterprises with employment of between five and 100. Initially 80 per cent of the cost of consultancy for up to 30 person-days provided by an accredited consultant was offered, but this subsidy has been reduced. The high subsidy in the early days encouraged many people to apply and screening was needed to identify those able to make effective use of a consultant's help. Reduced subsidies have resulted in self-screening through a willingness/ability to pay. In Lublin, where the management is striving harder to make the consultancy self-sustaining, there is strong pressure to deliver services to any clients willing to pay the fees – which has led to contracts with larger companies. Between the second half of 1995 and the first half of 1998 the average client size grew from 92 to 261. The figures seem to show that the demand for consultancy followed the level of subsidy. In the first half of 1997, the staff in Bialystok were so alarmed by the drop in demand when the subsidy was reduced from 50 to 30 per cent that they raised it to 40 per cent in an effort to maintain the outreach. From a peak of 91 consultancies in a six-month period, these had fallen to 33 by late 1998.

The paper pointed to a number of features that adversely affected the demand for consultants. These were:

- mistrust of consultants, especially those supported by donors
- lack of development of business network among SMEs; less information passed on
- the requirement from lending institutions for business plans, which most SMEs do not use after the credit is obtained. Thus consultancy is used as a step to credit rather than a positive input.
- SME expectations that such services will be offered free or heavily subsidized.

The extent to which consultancy was subsidized is shown from the figure that in the first half of 1998 the *full direct* costs of each consultancy was US$2468, of which SMEs paid 70 per cent. However, when staff and overhead costs are included, SMEs paid only 40–45 per cent of the cost.

The fee level for consultants was set at the market rate of US$83 per day, paid in local currency (the dollar value may go down). Compared with other matching grant consultancy schemes, this rate is not high, which seems to show that fees were not inflated by subsidies. However, many are only part-time consultants, often working as academics. There is no evidence that BPEP distorted the market for SME consultancies in Bialystok and Lublin, although there has been distortion by other donor and government interventions.

The paper makes some comments on the extent to which this project has been successful in developing SME consultancy. It claims there is now:

- a more positive view of consultants, but more on an individual business basis
- a greater willingness to pay – some enterprises that have benefited from consultancy are now ready to pay the full price, but this is not general
- more supply-side resources. There are now 48 accredited consultants (including part-time subcontractors) – previously there were none.

The Polish case seemed to raise the question of a project in which the BDS provider was both a facilitator and a 'direct doer'. There also appeared to be a form of subsidy dependence and expectation.

BDS for micro-businesses

Another paper described ISTARN[6] (Informal Sector Training and Resource Network) in the Masvingo province of Zimbabwe, which supported the informal

11

business sector, funded by the German Aid programme. ISTARN's major areas of activity were: apprenticeship, small business advice, informal sector associations and marketing support.

The apprenticeship programme was involved in helping potential entrepreneurs into self-employment in carpentry, metalworking, dressmaking, electronic appliance repairs, hairdressing, and motor and refrigeration mechanics. Graduate trainees are given access to hire purchase of tools, repayable within a year.

The Small Business Advisors programme (SBA), a major component of IST-ARN, had two functions, first to work with client businesses to identify problems; the second function was to track business performance to establish whether a correlation exists between interventions by the project and business growth. The financial monitoring tool was a Business Information Form (busiform) developed to test the performance of a business over a period. The SBA service worked with a credit NGO, Zambuko, which opened an office in the district in 1997 to set up a programme with a fund for lending to its own clients. SBA makes charges when preparing a business plan, when providing formal training, and after preparing a successful loan application for a client.

ISTARN also facilitated the formation of Informal Sector Business Associations (ISAs) in the seven district centres of the Masvingo province. ISA purchased raw materials wholesale (primarily timber and steel) and sold them at competitive prices to small businesses. Other ISA activities have involved setting up a fund from trading profits for short-term lending to members and contributing to the tool hire purchase scheme.

A recent ISTARN initiative is a programme to promote intermediary marketing operations in specific sub-sectors to sell informal-sector products into wider markets. The purpose was to break out of the restricted market in which new informal businesses compete.

One paper of a different nature was prepared by the World Bank[7] on a proposal for an experimental network of business development centres in Jamaica to be known as MicroNet, Inc. It was intended as a discussion input to the conference on two major issues: that of aiming at outreach and financial viability through for-profit private sector provision of BDS to low-income micro-businesses, and how to make greater use of information technology. The Micro-Net concept grew out of a collaboration between the Jamaican government, the Jamaican Small Business Association, a BDS working group of Jamaican providers, and support from the Netherlands government.

To identify the needs of the micro-business sector, a sample of 433 entrepreneurs in eight locations across the island were surveyed by local consultants in July 1997. Ongoing businesses felt they needed help in marketing, but most thought that this was due to the competition rather than to their own lack of effort. Preference was for specialized training and short courses, and businessmen were prepared to pay for such training.

The proposed MicroNet, Inc. would help, in a financially sustainable manner, a large number of micro-businesses to penetrate new markets, by demonstrating new products. MicroNet would be designed to 'outreach' about 20 000 clients and offer a mix of three mutually supportive services – MicroKnowledge, to improve basic business skills; MicroMarket, ways to reach new markets; and MicroTech, new technology to help solve business problems.

The MicroKnowledge concept follows the techniques of the World Bank's Grassroots Management Training (GMT) which was operated successfully for

12

over six years in several African countries and in three states in India. GMT is an interactive, participatory methodology based on the assumption that the trainees have experience and basic technical skills to run their business but need help in improving their management and marketing. MicroNet would be financed through equity contributions of a joint venture of two groups – a Jamaican investment group of successful businesses (likely to come from the retail sector) and an international investor with previous experience in the provision of BDS.

The presentation gave results of an economic evaluation of the use of GMT carried out in 1997 in the states of Rajistan, Orissa and Bihar in India, where 80 per cent reported a significant impact on revenues and profits. Many changed their marketing pattern, kept better financial records and expanded their businesses. It was proposed that MicroNet would use as performance indicators: number and gender of clients, financial sustainability, and evaluation of clients' performance changes.

The MicroNet proposal created some interest among the participants but was seen more as an attempt to provide services directly from the branches of the organization rather than as a 'facilitator' to create a market for private consultants. It was thought that micro-businesses, the target group of the proposal, would be both unable and unwilling to pay fees to make the proposal sustainable and profitable, which would be needed to interest private investors. MicroNet might have to resort to cross-subsidization across firm size or product mix, or to rely on donor support or non-BDS income-generating activities.

Business linkages and incubators

SME cluster and network development

A *network* was defined as a group of firms that co-operate on a joint development project; *cluster* is a term used to indicate a sectoral and geographical concentration of enterprises that can give rise to external economies. The term *networking* refers to the overall action of establishing relationships through networks and cultures.

The paper presented by UNIDO argued that inter-firm co-operation in clusters is not always spontaneous. Networking relationships can speed the process of forming co-operative relationships within clusters and networks by spreading information and innovative approaches. There is quite a volume of literature now available from those who have studied and demonstrated the fostering of co-operative relations within SME clusters, drawn from countries such as Brazil, Mexico and India.

UNIDO's experience was in Central America. In Honduras, SME networks were created by a special institution (CERTEC) which acted as a networking promotion agency. In Nicaragua, UNIDO claims that networking achieved a significant influence on policy making at the national level. The development of networks also created economies of scale in the delivery of BDS. In Mexico there was a cluster project which promoted vertical integration through the direct involvement of large-scale manufacturers. In Jamaica, cluster-based development became the core of the national SME support agency through the creation of specialized sectoral service centres – for garments, furniture, etc.

The UNIDO paper sets out some lessons learned from the five years of experience in network and cluster projects. Network development services must show flexibility and aim at visible improvements to the advantage of the participating SMEs. Cost recovery should be introduced as soon as possible to avoid the beneficiaries becoming accustomed to subsidies. There is no single model that can be followed in implementing cluster and network promotion in all countries, so that the services developed can be in line with the needs of the local entrepreneurs.

Another subject discussed at the conference was that of business incubators, with the focus on the experience of the host country, Brazil. Incubators first appeared in the industrial countries in the early 1980s, and later in the 1990s in middle-income countries, such as China, Brazil, Turkey, South Korea, Taiwan and Indonesia, as well as now in Central and Eastern European countries in transition. Location in an incubator increased the chance of a small business's survival, according to the presenters of this paper.

Brazil, the host country of the conference, had 74 business incubators, mostly in the south and south-east, with 614 SMEs located on them, employing 2700 people (29 per cent women). The breakdown of the incubator tenants shows the tendencies towards higher technology. They included 33 per cent in computing software, 14 per cent in electronics and 9 per cent in bio-technology. The incubator programme in Brazil has already graduated 226 companies.

The two Brazilian business incubators reviewed in greater detail in the paper were Biominas (in Minas Gerais) and Parq Tec (in Sao Carlos, a medium sized city north of Brazil's major business centre, Sao Paulo). Biominas began operating in 1994 but Parq Tec has had a much longer experience, since 1984. Both these incubators are sponsored through partnerships with the authorities at the city, state and federal levels as well as with universities, research institutes and private businesses. Both were developed on local initiative but with significant national support. The Biominas Incubator works closely with the state government, the municipalities involved and with SEBRAE, the national SME support organization, helping also in developing business plans, sourcing technology, securing licences and permits from government agencies for products, as well as offering such everyday services as faxing, photocopying, telephone services, laboratory services and secure storage for materials and products.

The Parq Tec Incubator is also a separate legal entity, organized by Fundacao Parq Tec. Parq Tec offers use of common facilities – an electronic and computer laboratory, technical information centre and mechanical workshop. Parq Tec also provides technology and marketing services and helps organize trade fairs and distribution networks.

The paper maintains that the Parq Tec and Biominas incubators have been successful in starting new enterprises and developing linkages with universities and research centres. Both the incubators, as others in Brazil, rely on high levels of public subsidy. They face the challenge of developing new services and generating new income to supplement and ultimately replace public subsidies.

Volkov Business Incubator

An interesting case of a business incubator presented was that of the Volkov International Incubator in Russia, started in 1995 by the Alliance of American and Russian women, with particular emphasis on women-led business. Volkov has a population of 60 000 and is 130km north east of St Petersburg. This

14

incubator offers secure office and production space for rent; as well as business training, computer training, office services, business consultation, training for women in business, and help with access to credit. The incubator was funded over a three-year agreement by USAID, but now gets its income from fees.

Volkov was recognized as an extremely depressed municipality with enterprises, large and small, shutting down and not paying salaries. The proposal for an incubator was greeted with scepticism. The incubator now has 11 operating business tenants and four in the pipeline; three former tenants have graduated. The Volkov incubator has proved its value in fostering working relationships among tenants. The businesses are expected to grow and to move out of the incubator after about two years, while the main task of the incubator staff is to service and support tenant businesses. Against the general trend in Russia during this period, the number of registered small businesses in Volkov has increased from 540 to 1420 over three years, so that it appears the incubator has been a factor in encouraging entrepreneurship.

The Volkov incubator was started with a grant of US$900 000 over three years from USAID, of which US$400 000 was used to capitalize the credit and leasing programmes. Monthly operating expenses in 1998 were US$18 000–US$20 000, but after the economic crisis, this was reduced to US$7000 per month. At this reduced level the incubator will be 75 per cent financially self-sustainable based on income derived, 54 per cent from payments on leases, 12 per cent from rents, 8 per cent from training fees and 2 per cent in payment for office services.

Marketing services

One session at the Rio conference was devoted to services to help firms improve their marketing. Two papers were presented in this field, one which described an export marketing development organization for SME – AMKA in Tanzania – reviewing a project financed by DFID, the UK bilateral donor and the second, presented by the Microenterprise Unit of the IADB, describing cases from Latin America on the collective marketing of micro- and small enterprise projects.

AMKA, the Tanzanian NGO, was formed in 1994 to increase the value of industrial and agricultural output achieved through exports. The organization has very few staff – only three in 1998 – and its main source of income is the UK donor, DFID, which approved a four-year grant of US$557 000 in 1994 to help start the organization. In the first year, dependence on donor support was 94 per cent but this was reduced to 40 per cent by 1998. Part of this was replaced by other donors.

AMKA originated from an export development programme started by Traidcraft Exchange (TX), a UK-based 'fair trade' NGO. TX has played a significant role in building staff capacity, making contacts with other networks, and administrative development. Although AMKA started as dependent on TX, the two organizations now work as partners. Most of the UK donor funding was given to TX to help AMKA start its operations, recruit staff and generally introduce the required procedures to start operations. In the first four years of its operation, AMKA has acted as a facilitator between Tanzanian producers and overseas buyers. It provided export market information to producers and helped develop linkages with overseas buyers. It also helped the producers to participate in trade fairs and arranged quality standard audits for overseas buyers. By 1998, AMKA was working with 18 clients, but had provided services for as many as 23 throughout its operations. AMKA's target was to increase Tanzania's exports to a value of US$700 000. External evaluation, put the value of export sales generated through AMKA's services as in US$1.1m to 1.2m over four years, although the organization claims a higher figure.

A major issue highlighted by AMKA's experience is that, like every aid-funded intervention, helping in export marketing is a fusion of social and economic objectives. The 'fair trade' approach guides organizations to a particular type of client rather than to commercial buyers. Combining social and business objectives remains a problem for organizations like AMKA.

The IADB paper describes those cases where the donor set up marketing services in the form of common sales organizations. Since products, producers and sectors vary, it is not feasible to develop guidelines that are applicable for providing integrated market services, along sectoral lines, to fit all situations.

The most established of the three cases was the Promotora de Comercio Social (PCS) set up in Colombia in 1983 to provide marketing services to around 1000 micro-businesses with fewer than 10 employees. The PCS has build up a network of buyers – mostly department stores and supermarkets locally and nationally – in some cases involving subcontracting assignments from the local textile industry. PCS buys goods direct from the producers and resells them at a competitive price in the market with a fixed seller's margin. It also sub-contracts in cases where PCS participates in bidding, and competes for orders from local government and departmental stores larger than any single enterprise can supply. Additional services provided by PCS include: design and development of new products, packaging, improved product quality and quality sampling of merchandise, to the following sectors: food products, leather, handicrafts and miscellaneous craft and decorative items. PCS also makes an advance payment of up to 50 per cent of the order value to buy the materials. After 15 years of effort, it is reported that PCS's annual sales are of the order of US$3.4m equivalent, and it managed to make a profit of US$93 485 in 1997.

The second of these marketing organizations is PROARTE, a private, for-profit company in Nicaragua which serves as an intermediary between artisans and international buyers. Founded as an NGO in 1993, PROARTE became a private for-profit company in 1996. It first made contact with the Alternative Trade Organizations (ATO) (with which AMKA also worked) but, finding this a limited market in the long term, moved on to more commercial international buyers. PROARTE works with low-income artisans with fewer than five employees (30 per cent women). It sets its own standards, decides who will be clients and rejects products that don't meet its requirements. Although founded with grants and soft loans, PROARTE now operates without subsidies but does receive some limited assistance for specific purposes, e.g. to cover costs to take part in trade fairs. PROARTE takes a mark-up of approximately 50 per cent on all goods, although it may vary this margin depending on the items concerned.

The third case covers El Salvador where a co-operative, PROEXSAL (Sociedad Cooperativa de Productores y Exportadores del Salvador), works with another NGO that provides the technical assistance to small producers of agricultural products, mainly organic fruits and vegetables, which has a growing market in El Salvador. PROEXSAL now generates enough income to cover all costs, and earns a small net profit. As a co-operative, the clients are also the owners. PROEXSAL has grown rapidly in three years to annual sales of US$680 000.

The three institutions differ in their strategies. PCS tries to reach the largest number of low-income producers and provide them with increased local markets for low-priced products. PROARTE has tried to penetrate the international market with the aim of generating a profit, while providing handicraft producers with access to profitable markets. It pays more attention to level of profitability for each product. PROEXSAL has developed a strategy aimed at providing marketing services to a limited group of producers, leaving the more technical services to another NGO.

The two cases presented demonstrated fundamentally different approaches to providing BDS in the field of marketing. AMKA aimed, with a small staff, to work directly with individual firms as a 'facilitator' without engaging directly in sales itself. It is, however, reviewing its position and there are those who are advising it to set up a direct exporting agency itself. The cases described by IADB are all organizations that act as direct intermediaries between buyers, local or international, and producers. However, the IADB cases concern very low-income producers, mainly artisans who would be unable to handle direct exporting and need services to help market their products.

Training – voucher programmes

A session was devoted to BDS services (using innovative methods) in training. Two of the papers reviewed the use of a voucher mechanism to stimulate demand for training programmes. The first of these was in the World Bank's Micro and Small Enterprises Training and Technology project in Kenya approved in 1994. The project was later restructured, and implementation began in 1998.

The project targets two groups – those that employ 1–10 workers which are run by women or demonstrate potential for growth, and small firms employing 11–50 employees. The target group is in fact 30 per cent of all Micro and Small Enterprises (MSEs) in Kenya. Eligible micro-enterprises can purchase training in vouchers for employees or owner managers for 10–30 per cent of face value, varying with the type of course. Small enterprises, the larger category in the target group, can purchase vouchers for 30–50 per cent of cost. It is planned that 24 000 micro-enterprise participants and 2000 from small firms – that is 8 per cent of all firms in the target group – will benefit from the voucher programme over four years.

A project co-ordination office (PCO) within the government directs project activities and assesses the demand and the training facilities available. The pilot programme gave out 430 vouchers to test the programme. The PCO will manage a directory of qualified trainers and BDS providers and will print and market the vouchers to BDS providers, skilled workers, training institutions, business associations, entrepreneurs and to private voucher allocation agencies using NGOs and consulting firms, etc. The allocation agencies are paid 25 per cent of the value of the vouchers issued. The PCO ensures the training or service is carried out to standards and makes payments to these providers to redeem vouchers.

The Kenya Voucher Programme is run as a decentralized activity. The allocation agency is issued with a volume of voucher applications to be sold to microbusinesses for about US$2 each. The application provides data for project monitoring and also how to screen applicants. The allocation agency then goes through the directory of training providers with the entrepreneur and decides which of them would be appropriate for the firm.

Another presentation[8] on voucher programmes discussed the lessons learnt from an earlier programme in Paraguay, started in 1995. The Paraguay programme lasted two years and a further couple of months of 1998 with support from the IADB. There was strong growth in the programme, with seasonal peaks and troughs. During a preparatory period, participating institutions were recruited and the programme advertised. The second phase – the 'take-off' – was faster, lasting only half the first phase. During the second phase 29 264 vouchers were redeemed as compared to 19 287 in the first phase. There was an increasing number of non-voucher trainees during both phases of the programme. These were participants who were not micro-entrepreneurs and not eligible for a voucher, e.g. housewives and students. Significantly, some of the non-voucher participants were also micro-entrepreneurs who had exhausted their allocation of six vouchers but wanted more training.

In the Paraguay programme, there was an increased level of subsidy in phase II, probably due to the participant institutions becoming adept in deriving maximum voucher income. There was a proposal, originally, to reduce the vouchers' nominal value over time but this was never carried out, although due to inflation the value did decrease in real terms. It was fixed at the equivalent of US$20 but was equal to about US$15 at the end of the project.

Based on the considered success of the Paraguay programme, IADB is launching new initiatives on vouchers in Latin America and the Caribbean. Programmes have been approved for Ecuador, Argentina and Venezuela based on the experience of Paraguay, but in Venezuela training vouchers are being offered for further training to retrenched public sector workers. Voucher programmes are also in various stages of processing for El Salvador, Haiti, Guyana, Guatemala and Nicaragua.

The voucher programme in Paraguay offers greater information to potential purchasers of training. Training institutions compete with one another within the voucher schemes to innovate their products to increase demand. In Paraguay it was also learnt that there is a need to institute robust fraud and quality control systems together with extensive information dissemination. In the view of the presenters and of participants, there is still the problem of finding credible, impartial and reliable institutions to finance and administer voucher programmes.

Technology

ApproTEC in Kenya

One panel of the conference was devoted to the transfer of technology through NDS where a case study[9] dealt with the introduction of appropriate technologies through an NGO – ApproTEC – set up in Kenya in 1991. This NGO was involved in the promotion and development of a range of new technologies, a new technology for oil seed pressing, and the use of the 'Moneymaker' pedal irrigation pump.

ApproTEC's principal clients are SME engineering workshops with fewer than six employees, that are considered to have potential for development. These are only the first-line clients; the ultimate beneficiaries may be a much larger heterogeneous group – those who use the equipment produced. The oil-seed press is used not only by farmers to press their own seeds but also sometimes by retailers who want to control their own production. There are other users engaged in poultry and livestock who want a reliable source of seed cakes at hand.

ApproTEC does not aim at financial sustainability through charges to SMEs. It regards development of appropriate technologies for SME as a needed public investment. ApproTEC charges modest fees to the manufacturers, mostly for training in the new technology and for the jigs and fixtures required. No fee is charged for the idea or the costs incurred by ApproTEC in developing the technology. ApproTEC argues that the manufacturer's investment in the new technologies is actually much greater than the fees paid to ApproTEC since they have to buy machine tools or welding sets to produce the ApproTEC products, and there is no financial support for this. Over the years ApproTEC has received funding from USAID, the Netherlands and the EU, but the most significant donor has been DFID of the UK.

ApproTEC claims to have promoted 8000 new private sector jobs through the sale of 4100 pieces of equipment at the cost of US$340 per job. The cost per technology set sold is around $650 of which around $500 comes from donors. Over 700 oil seed presses have now been bought by entrepreneurs and groups, and over 70 per cent of these are believed to be in active use. ApproTEC's own impact studies show that each press has directly created 2.5 new jobs. The pedal pump has been more successful, with more than 2500 sold throughout Kenya. Pump owners have realized an increase in their income of between 200 and 400 per cent.

ApproTEC claims to have developed into the major provider of specialized technology-based opportunities in East Africa. It is demand led and regards its success as due to its strong business orientation in relation to both the producers and the users of the equipment it develops, promoting only equipment for which there is a market. It is ready to 'spin-off able entrepreneurial sub-units that have the potential to develop into new businesses.

The ApproTEC case generated a discussion on whether an approach that does not aim for BDS to become financially sustainable can be justified. ApproTEC argues that the market has failed and that without financial help on design, development and promotion, appropriate technologies will not be introduced. Claiming that there are wider public benefits (e.g. employment creation) to be derived from these technologies, it is a valid use of public subsidies through donor funds to invest in the development of these technologies.

The ApproTEC case also raises the question whether a BDS organization can play an entrepreneurial role in identifying and creating businesses. There have been many failures in such attempts by BDS, but it may be that, with a 'business-like' ethos, in some situations BDS organizations can do this successfully without displacing other businesses.

BDS experience in India

A paper detailed some experience in India in 'Business Development and Technology Improvement Services for Microenterprises'. The publicly owned Small Industries Development Bank of India (SIDBI) has for several years been helping the micro-enterprise sector through its Promotion & Development programme (P&D), with both financial and non-financial services. The P&D programme has grown steadily over the past seven years partly in collaboration with the Swiss Agency for Development and Cooperation (SDC).

The components of SIDBI's P&D include:

- a rural industry programme to help establish viable enterprises in rural areas
- entrepreneurship development programmes for enhancing entrepreneurial traits and providing information and guidance for setting up one's own business, conducted for rural entrepreneurs, women and disadvantaged groups

- a technology fund – a fund for individual initiatives towards technology transfer
- a marketing fund – intended to provide loan or grant support to MSE for market research, product improvement, advertising, participation in trade fairs, setting up showrooms and warehousing facilities
- a skill-cum-technology upgradation programme (STUP) – to strengthen managerial and technical competence, and self-assessment by entrepreneurs
- a cluster technology upgrading programme (CTUP) – for the identification of improved technology and the needs of clusters for industrial innovation.

The Rural Industries Programme (RIP), active for four years, now operates in 36 districts in 11 of India's 25 states. SIDBI had sponsored 750 EDPs to March 1998, with 50 per cent of them focused on rural youth and 25 per cent specifically on poor women. The Technology Fund has not been so successful. Created three years ago, fewer than 10 technology support activities have been developed and fund utilization has been only 25 per cent. The Marketing Fund, on the other hand, has been increasingly popular and by March 1998, 68 proposals had been approved. It has particularly helped rural enterprises to find urban markets and has helped home delivery marketing of spices, honey and jams to urban households.

The paper states that SIDBI paid out starting expenses of around US$2000 per district to start up each RIP, and there are figures that suggest the RIP has been a cost-effective programme. Figures show that the expenditure per unit established through the EDPs was US$137 but the average returns on investments in these smaller enterprises has been, it is claimed, over 200 per cent. The Marketing Fund has made total disbursements of over US$1m but there are no figures as to its cost-effectiveness. Under pressure from SIDBI, both the STUP and the CTUP have made efforts to recover costs from fees. In the STUP, sample data suggest that, on average, institutions have recovered from participants 35 per cent of the average US$1700 cost. Under the CTUP, SIDBI pays fees to technical consultants for reviewing the modernization needs of clusters of industries. Over the 20 clusters covered, SIDBI spent roughly US$380 000. These have included substantial programmes in the bicycle parts industry in Ludhiana and in shoe-making in the North-East which, it is reported, have resulted in considerable improvements. There have been increased sales and turnover many times SIDBI's initial investment.

The Indian example evoked interest among participants because of its strong sponsorship by a large public bank and its sectoral focus. The programme shows that success can be achieved by using existing appropriate service providers, whether in the private sector or as public institutions. There are moves to cost-effectiveness but progress is variable.

Business linkages

The Manicaland Project in Zimbabwe

The Manicaland Business Linkages Project (MBLP), described in a paper at the conference, is one of the first projects under the Confederation of Zimbabwean Industries (CZI) small business programme. MBLP is a bilateral business development and project to Zimbabwe, supported by NORAD – the Norwegian Agency for Development Co-operation. The sub-sectors identified for business linkages were the forestry/timber, horticulture, tourism and furniture manufacture.

The MBLP was built on the three building blocks of business linkages: information, capacity-building and capital. As for information, the buyers need to know the potential producers of goods and services and suppliers need to know who will be the buyers of their products and services. In the MBLP, buyers and suppliers are helped to identify current market demand and to form linkages. Most of the 139 linkages promoted were in forestry (67%) where, it is estimated, 1250 new jobs were created at US$150 each.

Capacity-building is generally needed to ensure that suppliers can meet their obligations. Buyers know best the specifications and the delivery of the products they require. Buyer mentoring – the buyers helping their suppliers – is at the heart of the MBLP. In general, capacity-building is not carried out by the MBLP itself; rather it facilitates access to training from specialist consultants or from institutions. If needed, 'buy-in' services will be used in training (for individuals or groups) or for specialist problem solving through technical or managerial assistance.

As to capital to buy equipment and build infrastructure, the MBLP, as in all business linkages, helps to identify real credit needs and to reduce credit through buyers cutting the supplier's need for working capital, either by supplying direct credit to the supplier, or by improving the supplier's access to credit from financial institutions through guarantees.

Identifying opportunities helps both buyers and suppliers locate mutually profitable linkages. MBLP offers three types of such identification:

- Buyer Open Houses: these give small groups of potential suppliers a chance to meet potential buyers;
- Supplier Capacity Audits: which assess the ability of an enterprise to supply specific goods or services.

Unfortunately the Zimbabwean economy has, in the recent past, gone into a severe decline. Suppliers' profits are being squeezed but so far there are no reports in MBLP of either suppliers or buyers abandoning linkages. The MBLP follows the principles that in linkages both the buyer and the seller must profit. The buyer must have a sustainable approach to developing supplier capacity. The MBLP strongly believes in using Manicaland and Zimbabwean resources wherever possible.

In the case of new linkages, the issue of power balance is important. When a large buyer makes purchases from a small supplier, the buyer has the power to exploit the situation. If a small supplier can sell to several different customers, there will be less dependence on a single buyer. Buyers who look to the long-term learn that it is not in their interest to exploit suppliers.

Subcontracting promotion

Within the framework of business linkages, a paper was presented by UNIDO on the promotion of lessons learnt from the promoting sub-contracting and partnership relationships of SMEs with larger enterprises and among themselves. The object of the UNIDO programme was to strengthen the capacity of SMEs in developing countries and economies in transition to meet the requirements of subcontracting. Subcontracting and Partnership Exchanges (SPXs) were set up in 30 different countries to act as centres for technical information and 'match-making' for industrial subcontracting agreements between main contractors, suppliers and subcontractors. The SPXs help in deveoping a roster of subcontractors, suppliers and main contractors. They also:

- store data for rapid retrieval on existing production capacities and capabilities
- identify subcontracting, supply and partnership enquiries and disseminate them to enterprises that potentially could fulfil these orders
- assist potential subcontractors and suppliers in organizing clusters and associations, and negotiating subcontracting agreements.

UNIDO also provided legal statutes and standard terms of reference for setting up SPXs to be operated as 'not for profit' private sector organizations.

As part of this programme, UNIDO has surveyed and developed standard instruments and methods for the further development of industrial subcontracting. It has been working on: policy issues and legislation, a guide to creation and operation of SPXs, computer programs for database management, and model contracts for subcontracting arrangements.

UNIDO also advises governments on how to create a favourable environment for promoting more industrial subcontracting. Examples of industrial legislation proposed include incentives to encourage large enterprises to decentralize production through subcontracting and outsourcing, measures to improve inter-enterprise credit schemes and terms of payment, tax regulations to ensure that SMEs that act as subcontractors or suppliers are not penalized, and customs regulations to facilitate international subcontracting. UNIDO also encourages governments to follow public procurement policies to encourage participation by SMEs, directly or through subcontracting.

Between 1984 and 1997, 54 SPXs were established with UNIDO help, of which 45 are still in operation with 15 588 registered companies. In Latin America, 32 SPXs have been created in 14 countries and a regional Latin American network of SPXs has been formed (ALABSUB – Association Latino Americana de Bolsas de Subcontractación). A similar regional network of SPXs in North Africa (Algeria, Egypt, Jordan, Tunisia, and Morocco) is being formed.

The SPXs have attained a degree of sustainability. There operational budget is generally financed from four components. These are:

- from state or public institutions, at least 10 per cent of the budget but not more than 50 per cent
- from professional associations, federations – at least 10 per cent of the budget
- affiliated enterprises themselves; in all cases these fees amount to at least 10 per cent
- fees raised from services to non-members as well as to members, such as:
  - participation in subcontracting fairs and business meetings
  - training seminars and conferences
  - market surveys – national and international
  - sectoral studies on investment requirements and incentives
  - technology and quality audits and assistance
  - legal assistance in preparing contracts, etc.

SPX does not receive commissions on contracts awarded. SPX costs are low, with a minimum staff, consisting of a manager, one or two engineers and one or two secretaries. SPXs usually have about three furnished offices, a meeting room and operate within a host institution. The equipment needed consists of two personal computers, a photocopying machine, two or three telephone and fax lines, and possibly a vehicle for visiting firms. SPXs are generally housed in chambers of commerce, federation of industries or business associations, but they may operate independently.

SPXs are mainly focused in the metalworking, mechanical, electrical and electronic industries, where most subcontracting takes place, and to a lesser extent in plastics, textiles, clothing, woodworking, ceramics and some others. Subcontracting also occurs in services such as repair and maintenance, accounting, computer services, packaging, transportation, etc. SPXs are sometimes considered transitional organizations that may die after a few years when most contacts have been established directly. However, with some flexibility, the experience is that SPXs can go on operating actively, making new contacts after 10 or 15 years. SPXs can play a vital role in promoting long-term industrial subcontracting. They can be major instruments for introducing the outsourcing of operations and components to specialized suppliers on a long-term basis rather than simply for coping with peak demands.

Matching grant schemes

The subject of matching grants was discussed at various sessions of the conference. The World Bank submitted a paper describing cases from two different countries – Chile and Mauritius – where this approach was used.

The current Chilean approach to support small enterprises covers a wide range of programmes in areas such as technology, export promotion, workers' training and management advice. The matching grant scheme in Chile was intended to move from supply- to demand-driven services, through the subsidization of private consulting services. Previous public sector implementation of BDS, despite some innovations, produced some of the usual defects of earlier supply-driven approaches, such as lack of adequate cost sharing, lack of client participation in selecting consultants and a lack of market orientation. The FAT and PROFO programmes (described in Chapter 13) covered a wide range of activities in areas such as financial management, marketing, quality control, design and production processes and systems.

Under FAT, a small enterprise submits a request for support for a specific consultant activity which is approved on a first come, first served basis. FAT provides only a low level of subsidy – an upper limit of US$2500 per project – intended to support the initial stage using private consultants. A PROFO project generally consists of five or more firms with a shared objective.

These programmes are open to a range of SSIs, but not to micro-enterprises. Eligibility requires minimum annual sales of US$80 000 and an upper limit of US$3.4m. Both these level of subsidy – for PROFO up to US$100 000 per project per annum – and the type of activities eligible, favour SMEs. Budgetary support for the two programmes was US$25.4m in 1998.

A major objective of the FAT and PROFO programmes was to create a network of capable private agencies, operating autonomously but with accountability. Because of the long distances within the country, a decentralized regional network was created. Agents were based around business organizations with a sectoral approach taken, to promote collaboration and joint sectoral activities rather than increasing competition. CORFO – the National Development Corporation – was actively involved in the initial phases of selecting promising applicants and working with them closely by requiring them to submit each project for approval. As confidence in the agent increased, reviews were carried out only after implementation, on a sample basis. Firms were required to pay their contribution to the agent prior to starting the project. The consultant would be paid after the work was done satisfactorily, approved by CORFO. A registry of approved consultants was prepared, maintained by CORFO at the regional level. In general, consultants that operated nationally were preferred rather than local or international applicants.

Evaluations of the FAT and PROFO programmes undertaken in 1997 by the University of Chile showed that participating firms reported broad gains in a variety of measures, with a reasonable portion of benefits attributed to programmes. Anecdotal evidence suggests some success in creating a private market for SME consultancy services.

In the second case, that of Mauritius, conditions were different. The focus was on the upgrading of technological capacity through a Technology Diffusion Scheme (TDS) developed in 1993. The TDS offered a range of services similar to the Chilean PROFO scheme, such as product quality, design, process technology and productivity improvement. The subsidy was 50 per cent so that half the fee had to be paid by the recipient firms. Most projects were small, with an average of US$10 000, but TDS was also able to support large firms up to a value of US$100 000 in subsidy per project. Nevertheless, smaller firms were more attracted to the scheme and over the life of the scheme the average grant size dropped from US$15 100 to US$9800.

The programme was funded by a World Bank loan of US$2.1m for the four-year period 1994–1998, during which the programme supported 225 projects in 153 firms. Services to a value of US$5.1m (including the firms' contributions) were provided under the TDS. The World Bank financed US$450 000 in operation costs, which represented 8.8 per cent of the cost of services provided.

Like the Chilean Scheme, the TDS was operated by a private agent under contract, selected through competitive international bidding. A foreign provider was preferred as the temporary nature of the intervention did not justify the creation of a local institution. The TDS agent maintained a register of 204 consultants based on technical assessment, with 52 per cent actually providing services under the scheme. Most of the selection of consultants was carried out by the participating firm.

The TDS interventions saw an increase in sales for participating firms averaging 49 per cent, with exports reported growing by 53 per cent. Increased productivity and new product development also resulted from TDS's efforts.

The two programmes in Chile and Mauritius share the basic approach of demand-driven private sector implementation with the aim of creating a sustained market for consultant service provision. The programmes showed the private sector that BDS could offer significant benefits and be cost effective. In Chile, the building of a network of agents for long-term provision of services has a potential for building local capacity, and the system would probably benefit in the future from more competition. In Mauritius, although the TDS was executed by an international consulting firm hired under competitive bidding, local business development agencies did participate as service providers and so there was some capacity building. The participation of larger firms in the Mauritius programme had a demonstration effect on the small firms, and may result in business linkages. There is still a need to oversee the consultants' participation in the programme to ensure quality of services. There is also a need to provide as much reliable information as possible in the register of consultants to enable firms to make proper selections.

Entrepreneurship development programmes

Entrepreneurship development programmes (EDP) were dealt with in a special panel where two cases were presented – that of CEFE, [German Technical Corporation – GTZ] and SEON,[10] a special programme carried out in the Netherlands to encourage immigrants to set up small businesses.

CEFE offers a comprehensive set of training instruments to stimulate positive interventions in the development of small enterprises by using modern training technologies and action learning methods. The international CEFE network started 10 years ago and now operates in 60 countries around the world through 200 institutions. More than 2000 people have participated in the programme (referred to as 'CEFistas'). The CEFE network, it is claimed, is based on the motivation, energy and creativity of the groups of CEFistas.

CEFE uses techniques based on the 'achievement motivation' approach pioneered by McLeland in USA, 30 years ago.

To ascertain the changes wrought among those who had participated in the CEFE programmes, in November 1998 a questionnaire was distributed to a sample of 150, selected globally at random. Seventy of them replied giving a picture as to how the participation in the programme had affected them professionally and personally. Nearly a third replied that they had experienced an improvement in their entrepreneurial skills, 30 per cent replied that they had increased their technical knowledge, and 40 per cent professed to have developed new competencies.[11] The questionnaire asked the impact CEFE had had on personal development and over 35 per cent replied that they had observed an improvement in their behaviour and attitudes, 76 per cent replied that they now knew themselves better and 80 per cent that they had a better understanding of their environment. In answer to the question if their personal incomes had improved following the CEFE training, 80 per cent said that they had, and in the case of half of these, by more than 40 per cent.

An independent evaluation was also commissioned in 1994 to assess the impact CEFE had on the different target groups. The evaluation team found that 82 per cent of former CEFE participants claimed that through what they had learned in CEFE they were able to increase their managerial skills. In 86 per cent of the cases, the groups trained in further CEFE programmes were able to develop their businesses further, through greater competence as entrepreneurs. It was claimed that each participant created, on average, 4.5 jobs as a result of the training.

Stimulated by the enthusiasm and increased competence of the staff members who had taken part in CEFE training, organizations reported improved operation of their institutions. The paper gave details of two special cases – Fundacion Kitti in Argentina and Fundasol in Uruguay. The first developments in Kitti were initiated through contacts with Fundasol, which had changed into an entrepreneurial organization, spreading business development training not only throughout Uruguay but also across the border into Argentina. Kitti never received any German funding; it managed to generate adequate fees from its training activities and at the same time extended its area of operation throughout the country.

A further case from Sri Lanka, one of the first countries to undertake a CEFE programme, described how the counterpart organization (SEEDS) – a part of the NGO Sarvodaya – realized that free entrepreneurship training of low cost and inadequate quality by non-committed trainers was not really effective.

Higher quality professional training, where participants paid fees to trainers, achieved much better results.

The second presentation involving UNEDP was of rather a different nature. It concerned the programme of SEON (Social Economic Entrepreneurship in the Netherlands) and was focused on migrants who needed to be absorbed into the economy. The aim of SEON was to identify those among the migrants who had the trades considered necessary for success in establishing businesses and then to put them through a development programme to help them start small enterprises.

The SEON programme was based on concepts and experience developed in the 1980s in creating refugee entrepreneurs in Kenya through a project executed by ILO and UNCHR (UN High Commission for Refugees). Later on, the programme in Kenya became SPAREK (Special Programme for Assistance to Refugee Entrepreneurs in Kenya) and a separate NGO. Both SPAREK and SEON were also designed on the McCleland approach, with innovation introduced in India.

The SEON programme differed from other EDPs in that at an early stage a screening was made of those who were considered to be potential for success, and that more linkages were forged between the EDP programme and management training, financing and advisory services.

The SEON paper was presented as an example of the transfer of experience from South to North, i.e. from Kenya to the Netherlands. It was carried out by a Netherlands consulting organization under contract with the Netherlands government. The consultants have worked closely with the Triodos Bank, a Netherlands Financial Institution which is actively involved in programmes financing small businesses.

Regional BDS programmes

FIT Programme of ILO

A paper presented by the ILO outlines the experiences in providing BDS though private sector channels, responding to market demand. The FIT[12] project, started in 1993, aimed to identify services for which small-scale entrepreneurs were willing to pay the full costs.

One of the problems recognized early on was that entrepreneurs could not be expected to pay for services that they had not seen and of which they had no past experience. Unencumbered by previous experiences, FIT listened carefully to what the entrepreneurs had to say, to discover what they considered to be their constraints and problems, what type of BDS they needed and for which they might be willing to pay. Services identified through this dialogue were then marketed on a pilot basis; initially partly subsidized, with clients giving feedback on how they viewed the service. Modifications were then introduced as quickly as possible, based on the feedback, to try to make them fit more closely to what the entrepreneurs wanted. Significantly, the services that emerged were:

- services which entrepreneurs were already providing to each other informally
- services already provided within the private sector but which had been largely ignored by development agencies
- services already provided by the private sector in industrialized countries but not yet in the developing world.

The entrepreneurs considered they could benefit from increased contact with each other, particularly with those who had been more successful. FIT therefore started to organize visits to other businesses, so developing a type of 'business tourism'. There have now been over 1400 trips in six countries in East and West Africa, from which useful experience has been gained. Entrepreneurs pay the full price for such trips providing that the costs are kept down and the marketing is right. Willingness to pay is, of course, not the only criterion for arranging such visits; they also had to have a substantial development impact. As a result of these visits, entrepreneurs identified new production processes, safer working practices, new product designs, new sources of spare parts and improved relations with customers and employees.

Apart from 'business tourism', FIT has experimented with a range of forums in which entrepreneurs can communicate more effectively with customers and traders. Meetings were set up between metalworkers and farmers for whom the former made tools and equipment. The entrepreneurs learned how to design and develop new improved products to suit their customers. This process has been formalized as a service called 'user-led innovation'.

In Uganda, FIT identified 160 independent trainers and 89 small-scale private training institutions offering services to small businesses. In Zimbabwe, 90 small training businesses have been identified by FIT. These little-known training companies offer courses in business management, accounting, exporting, office management, and sometimes vocational skills too. The vocational skills in Zimbabwe seem to have been focused on dressmaking and tailoring, whereas in Uganda and Tanzania a much wider range was offered.

A study of BDS provision in the UK revealed that many of the services were publicly funded and were designed with different objectives in view. There is, the paper noted, a greater emphasis on financial sustainability in developing countries. However, there were some BDS provided in the UK on a commercial basis which included magazines aimed at growing small businesses, which generated revenue through the sale of advertising to larger companies, organization of regional multi-sectoral exhibitions for businesses and support services provided as part of franchise packages. FIT tried a pilot introduction of a publication aimed at the small enterprise market. Recognizing that commercial information was difficult for SMEs to obtain in developing countries, FIT is planning to launch advertising journals in four countries for distribution to local business communities, where advertisements will be sold to larger as well as to SMEs. The SMEs are a potential market for larger companies.

Before introducing new BDS on a commercial basis, a search is made by FIT to see if anybody is offering a similar service. FIT would then consider going into partnership with a local entrepreneur to offer the service. In this respect, FIT has moved away from being a project office and more towards investing in BDS which it is hoped can become commercially viable. The local partner for a new service would have to provide at least 25 per cent of the start-up capital either in cash or in kind, and should bring expertise and contacts. Ideally, the partner should also be a small enterprise. All BDS need to be innovative for identifying new services that can be offered to small enterprises on a commercial basis.

IADB presented a paper describing a regional strategy for business growth using non-financial services or BDSs as demonstrated in the case of Nueva Viscaya,[13] a sparsely populated region in Northern Mexico within the states of Chihuahua and Durango. The regional approach was based on a close relationship between a group of leading entrepreneurs and the local university in the capital, Parral. A key group of local businessmen helped to create a School of International Economics in the University to focus on regional economic needs.

The Economics School worked with a core of entrepreneurs to review the region's assets and comparative advantages to work out a strategy for future growth. The next step was the creation of a business development centre for research in economic and technological development within the region, with local businessmen. This centre, CIDEyT, was a low-budget operation with a strong involvement of the business community. CIDEyT launched the first phase of the regional strategy by providing business services and support for 'start-ups' and expansion of local firms.

The goal of the strategy was to support 600 small firms, drawn from diverse sectors and locations, through technical assistance and training. The aim was to increase production and sales by about 10 per cent in 80 per cent of the firms helped and to create 3000 new jobs in five years in the region, with salaries above the minimum wage.

The actual results were well above the projected goals. In less than one year of the three-year project, the new job creation was 600 jobs. This compares favourably with the five-year goal of 3000 new jobs. The project has served more than 900 firms, 300 more than originally projected for the project's life of three years.

The progress achieved in Nueva Viscaya since the creation of CIDEyT in 1993, and particularly in the last year (1997/98), is sufficiently significant to confirm the success of this model of regional development using non-financial services.

The case demonstrates the innovative use of university resources, including students. As part of their studies, students at the local university undertook market studies and diagnoses of firms' needs, as well as help in the introduction of computer software and new marketing approaches. It claimed CIDEyT helped to build an enterprise culture in the region of Nueva Viscaya through this project.

Use of information technology to deliver BDS

Two papers were delivered at the conference, one sponsored by the Soros Foundation and presented by Faculty Members of St Louis University in the USA entitled 'The Potentials and Pitfalls of using the Internet to Deliver BDS to SMEs'[14] and the second on I.T. development for micro and small enterprises (MSE) in the Philippines.

The first presentation referred to this whole new field of development as the promotion of 'distance consulting' and pointed out three major pitfalls. First, there was need for an elaborate telecommunication and consulting infrastructure which did not yet exist in much of the world. Second, even if the infrastructure did exist, at the early stages only a handful of entrepreneurs would make use of such help and, finally, even among the latter small group, there was the problem of cultural differences and lack of shared knowledge and experience that limited possible assistance. Still, the presenter was optimistic and considered that distance consulting had great promise and that the pitfalls should be regarded as problems to be resolved.

Like all BDS consulting organizations, distance consulting would have to stand up to the same performance measures as other BDS, such as: number of clients and proportion of target population, number of types of services provided, client satisfaction, new firms and jobs created and sales and profit improvements in client firms. The paper goes on to present four examples, two from the USA, one from Finland and one from Canada. All four used the Internet, in two cases exclusively and the other two in conjunction with other forms of delivery.

The first example, for the USA, concerned a major accounting firm that created a market for distance consulting from its existing SME customers, with the service heavily concentrated in the technology and manufacturing sector. Started in 1996, by end 1998 the programme had 14 000 subscribers. The second US example was the programme of the Senior Core of Retired Executives (SCORE), started in 1997 through the Internet, to widen the SCORE services offered. The network involves 800 of SCORE's 12 400 affiliated consultants. The third example, from Finland, was that of the University of Oulus LearnNet, a university outreach programme focusing on hi-tech firms in Finland. The programme operates with a grant from the EU. The fourth programme, that of the University of Victoria in Canada, was a converted computer-administered system aiming at three outcomes: improving the preparation of new entrepreneurs, better business planning and, hopefully, reducing business failures.

It is clear that at present, the group of SME owners that were willing to use BDS Internet services was only a small portion of the total SME sector. The presenters of the paper indicated that studies seemed to show that the first likely clients were those involved in high technology, or technology-driven firms. Clients might include in the first instance:

- businesses in the computer industry
- manufacturing sub-contractor firms linked to electronic interchange with main contractors
- media and advertising firms
- financial insurance firms.

In conclusion, the paper was highly positive in recommending that BDS organizations start using the Internet to deliver services to SMEs. Use of the Internet for SME consulting is still in its infancy, but all indications point to a promising outcome of future development in this field.

The second paper dealt with information technology and its use for BDS in the Philippines,[15] examining the experience of that country in the provision of basic and higher value-added information and communication technology based business services to MSEs. It gives examples from a private sector provider of public calling offices, and a non-profit BDS provider – the Laguna SME Service Centre.

The key findings of the study of ICT-based BDS to MSEs are:

- MSEs in the Philippines will continue to demand basic IT services through common facilities. Private providers can operate successfully if they find the right mix to satisfy MSE demand for these services.
- ILT services can improve the efficiency of business operations, even at the MSE level.
- The private sector can be more successful in meeting the needs for IT services from SMEs. There is a danger that competition might result in a lower coverage of low-income areas. There is need to experiment with lower-cost business models.
- Internet-based information services fit well with other BDS.
- Donor support is needed to experiment in market-oriented, Internet-based information services for MSEs.

The paper ends by giving an account of the activities and the degree of success of the Bayantel Public Call Offices Company – the sole private provider of a full range of voice and data services in the Philippines from around 150 branches and 250 franchise Public Calling Offices nationwide.

Viability and performance indicators

The final two papers of the conference dealt with the financial viability of BDS, one presented by a representative of the IADB and one by a consultant of USAID, proposing a performance measurement framework for BDS.

The IADB paper drew on an earlier survey conducted by the author of 182 BDS providers operating in 10 countries in Latin America, presenting the view, not widely held, that BDS offered in conjunction with credit usually faced low demand due to such services being out of line with the entrepreneur's real needs, and reaching only credit clients. Evidence, according to the paper, showed that potential BDS clients may not be the same as the micro-credit market. A figure quoted is that less than 30 per cent in one study in Ecuador were actually clients that demanded both credit and BDS together from the same institution.

The paper defined 'sustainability' as referring to a service provider or institution which is able to cover the costs of the provision of the services through fees or payments made by clients for the services they received. It is pointed out that both institutions and private consultants offering BDS may provide services, some of which are profitable and some of which are not. There may be cross-subsidization from one service to another and from one client group to another, particularly in institutions and consulting firms.

BDS providers may cover costs on the basis of cross-subsidization of smaller by larger clients, and from services for which clients are ready to pay, to those for which they are less willing to do so. They may also obtain income through an unrelated income-generating activity, referred in this paper as the 'car wash' or 'bake sale' approach, in which a BDS provider operates a profit-making activity which has no connection to its main mission.

The paper presents a matrix which attempts to show estimations of cost recovery for different BDS serving micro-enterprises. Services such as accounting and legal advice, technology access (use of machines) or marketing, have the potential for completely covering costs. The paper quotes examples where this has been the case. However, it then presents a list of other activities, such as training, technical advice and information, where the level of cost recovery is somewhere between 12 and 20 per cent, but may go as high as 50 per cent. The paper stresses the importance of costing each activity, to separate those for which there is full cost recovery from those where there is not. The paper concludes that the more that BDS can innovate and specialize, the more the BDS provider could reach the upper levels of cost recovery. It is argued that there is not such a strong correlation between scale of operations and service viability. Analysis shows that each service break-even volume of operations will vary according to factors such as the local market, the delivery mechanism, the sub-sector, the client, and so forth. There should be a clear difference between donor-supported BDS to compensate for market imperfections, and private sector services which are offered at prices which cover costs. The paper argues in favour of maximizing cost recovery at whatever level is attainable. Even when clients are poor, if a service allows them to increase their incomes they should be willing to share this increase with the service provider who has helped them to make this increase.

The final paper was devoted to proposals for a BDS performance measurement framework, which proposed a set of indicators for collecting and reporting information on the performance of BDS programmes, primarily focused on micro-enterprises. A summary matrix of the framework is included in the paper, divided according to the goals, which are set out as: scale of operations, outreach, impact, cost effectiveness, and sustainability. The measurement indicators are then given in columns as related to four groups of players that donors typically would analyse. These are: customers, service providers, service facilitators and market place. The 'customer' is defined as the beneficiary of the service, usually an enterprise, while the 'service provider' interacts directly with the customers who supply the service. The latter may be private businesses, government agencies or NGOs. The service 'facilitator' is defined as the designer and developer of the service and the direct purveyor of the funds to do so. This is usually an NGO or government agency, although the original fund source may be elsewhere. It is pointed out that the 'facilitator' may also be the 'provider', but there are many cases where the two functions are separated. The 'market' refers to the economy at large, including all the businesses that might be affected by the BDS through replicating what the service has demonstrated.

Each of the different goals is analysed in the paper in greater detail. *Scale* is given as the number of clients receiving the BDS and how many enterprises and institutions have been enabled to deliver the services. How has the number of clients increased over time, and is a competitive market developing?

The indicator for *outreach* would measure the extent to which the services are reaching the target group, possibly broken into special groups, such as women, the poor, ethnic minorities, rural areas, etc. As regards *impact*, the indicator would give the extent to which the BDS has changed the behaviour or business practices of clients. How many are improving their businesses and increasing outputs through changed practices? How many are satisfied and returning to the service and how many are improving their businesses as regards outputs? This indicator is primarily concerned with the impact on the businesses receiving the service rather than the wider impact on the institutions providing or 'facilitating' the BDS, or on the community as a whole.

As to *cost effectiveness*, the indicators would question whether the programme is the best use of the funds available? How much does it cost to help an entrepreneur to access BDS? In the case of cost effectiveness, the paper sets out a hypothetical cost effectiveness report detailing the type of programme costs as against benefits achieved.

The indicator for *sustainability* refers to the situation regarding a client entrepreneur, his or her investment in the BDS and the extent to which providers giving the service recover the costs involved and are independent of subsidies given by BDS facilitators. The example gives actual figures as to the sustainability and cost recovery of the service given by the Kenya NGO, ApproTEC, in introducing the oil press to various customers.

This paper aroused a great deal of interest among the participants, and it was agreed that a number of donors would do further work together in developing the measurement framework for BDS performance.

Notes

1 EMPRETEC is a combination of EMPRESAS (enterprises) and TECNULOGIAS (technologies) first used to describe the programme in Argentina in 1988 when it was started. (Note: Titles and authors are given only for papers *not* published in full)
2 EMPRETEC Programme in Selected Latin American Countries: An assessment – UNCTAD.

3 In all, 10 case studies were selected.

4 *Business Development in Russia: New Business Development Programme* by I. Astrakhan, World Bank, C. Stinger, Deloitte Touche Tohmatsu, Yanboukhtina, Business Support Centre Foundation.

5 *Polish–British Enterprise Project: Developing a Business Consultancy Programme*, C. Sealy. A Gibson, DFID – UK.

6 *ISTARN – An Approach to Informal Sector Business Support in Zimbabwe*; A Carlton and D. Hancock – GTZ.

7 *Jamaica MicroNet Incorporated: Increasing Business Success in Low-Income Communities*, J. Hanna, T. Wilde [The World Bank].

8 *Voucher Training Model: What Next, After Paraguay* – L. Goldmark – IADB.

9 *ApproTEC, Kenya: Developing Technology-Based Business Opportunities*, M. Havers – DFID – UK.

10 *The SEON Case*; Klaas Molenaar FACET BV – Netherlands Ministry of Foreign Affairs.

11 The total percentage of replies came to over 150, since each respondent could name more than one aspect of the professional impact on themselves.

12 FIT stands for 'Farm Implements and Tools', the name of a small programme started by ILO in East Africa in the 1980s to bring micro-businesses and small workshops together with farmers to improve and extend production of implements for the agricultural community. The programme has blossomed into a much larger range of activities but the convenient acronym is still being used.

13 *A Regional Strategy for Business Growth through Non-Financial Services: The Case of Nueva Viscaya, Mexico*, J. Mazza, M. Parga [IADB].

14 *Distance Consulting: Potentials and Pitfalls in Using the Internet to Deliver Business Development Services to SMEs*, J. Katz and M. Murray, Saint Louis University – Soros.

15 *How to be Demand-Led: Lessons for BDS Providers from Information & Communication Services in the Philippines*; A O Miehibradt – USAID.

2. The emerging strategy for building Business Development Service markets

WILLIAM F. STEEL, JIM TANBURN and KRIS HALLBERG

A PARADIGM SHIFT is emerging in the approach of international donor and development agencies to promoting small enterprise development[1] through the business development service (BDS) that support them. The emerging strategy focuses on developing markets for BDS that are appropriate to and demanded by small enterprises, rather than on the direct provision of BDS by governments and donors. The lessons of recent experience show that facilitating the provision of services by private providers and stimulating the demand for these services by small enterprise clients is an effective way to raise the coverage, quality, and sustainability of these services and increase their impact on small enterprise performance.

The shift toward market provision of BDS reflects a move toward a 'systems approach' analogous to the micro-finance revolution. As with micro-finance, it leads to emphasis on being businesslike and demand-led at the institutional level. However, whereas the current emphasis in micro-finance is on building the operational capacity of micro-finance institutions, the emphasis in developing BDS markets is more on forging strategic partnerships with potential private BDS suppliers and helping them develop suitable products. The new approach attempts to facilitate transactions between small enterprise 'clients' (as opposed to 'beneficiaries') and BDS providers seeking to develop profitable market niches.

These lessons have emerged from the presentations and discussions at the March 1999 conference on 'Building a Modern and Effective Business Development Services Industry for Small Enterprises' in Rio de Janeiro, Brazil, as well as the September 1998 conference on 'Business Development Service: How Sustainable Can They Really Be?' in Harare, Zimbabwe.[2] This paper summarizes the conclusions from these conferences regarding strategic approach. It is intended to provide a context for the core principles of implementation at the meso- and micro-levels[3] and for revision of the Donor Committee Guidelines for Donor-Funded Interventions.[4]

Criteria for evaluating experience

Developing small enterprises is regarded as a means of promoting both economic growth and poverty alleviation objectives. First, relatively high labour intensity and flexibility in adapting to changing markets give small enterprises the potential to leverage limited capital into high rates of output and employment growth. Second, as the means through which a large proportion of the population earns a livelihood in developing economies with small formal employment sectors, small enterprises offer important potential to offset poverty, especially if their productivity and market access can be increased.

For these reasons, governments and donor agencies have long sought to support the development of small enterprises through financial assistance and complementary business development services to raise the capacity of enterprises to use investment funds productively. Despite the substantial resources poured into small enterprise development since the 1970s, evidence of sustained impact and widely accepted methodologies remains scarce. Donors are increasingly concerned to demonstrate the effectiveness of investment in small enterprise development.

These objectives and concerns led the Donor Committee to define four principal criteria for evaluating the effectiveness of programmes to assist the small enterprise sector: sustainability, outreach, impact, and cost effectiveness.

- *Sustainability* refers mainly to financial sustainability, i.e. the ability of the service provider, or of a specific product, to cover the full costs of service provision with revenues generated from clients and other non-subsidy revenues. 'Sustainability' has also been applied at both institutional and firm levels: i.e. the continued operation of the service provider (regardless of funding source) and the profitability or survival of the small enterprise client (also covered under 'impact').
- *Outreach* (or coverage) refers to the number or proportion of clients (individuals, enterprises, or organizations) served in the target market or client population that the programme is designed to serve. Defining target market segments is particularly important to minimize potential trade-offs between outreach and other criteria. For example, trying to reach large numbers of relatively poor clients may undermine cost-effectiveness unless suitable instruments are chosen, while impact in terms of high growth rates may imply targeting relatively larger enterprises with maximum potential for expansion.[5]
- *Impact* refers to the effects of the programme in achieving its objectives, usually defined as an improvement in performance at three levels: the individual enterprises receiving services; the social impact of the programme at the household and community levels; or, more broadly, the market, sector, or economy.
- *Cost effectiveness* (or efficiency) is the provision of services (of a given quality) at the lowest possible cost. Cost effectiveness is especially important in assessing services that have important social impact or spread effects but are unlikely to achieve full financial self-sustainability and hence may involve continued subsidies. At the institutional level, management efficiency is important in achieving sustainability.

These criteria are interrelated, and their relative importance may vary according to the market segment, subsector, type of service, and specific objectives involved. Views may differ on how to apply and measure them (see Section III below). Nevertheless, discussion of the experience of the case studies presented at the conferences with respect to these criteria elicited broad consensus on strategies that are most likely to achieve favourable results.

Promoting market development

The most important conclusion of the conferences was a consensus among donor agencies on the importance of a paradigm shift in small enterprise development. The new strategy emphasizes the *development of markets for BDS* by building both the demand on the part of small enterprises and the supply of services oriented towards their needs, as well as the information and delivery mechanisms to make BDS markets function effectively.

The old approach assumed that the market for BDS is virtually non-existent in most developing countries, that the demand for services by small enterprises is low because of their inability to pay, and that such services cannot be provided profitably. Hence it was concluded that services must be provided directly by government agencies and donor programmes and that they must be heavily subsidized. The nature, quality, and price of services were determined by the perceptions of governments and donors as to small enterprise needs and ability to pay, rather than by the demands and willingness to pay for services as expressed by small enterprises themselves.

Unfortunately, public provision of services has distorted BDS markets. When services are highly subsidized, existing and potential private providers may find it difficult to compete against them, so that the private provision of services is crowded out. The financial scale and types of instruments used in donor-funded programmes often reflect international consulting rates and the constraints of donor agencies, rather than the conditions of local markets and the products most useful to local small enterprises.[6] To the extent it has been measured and evaluated (infrequently in practice), the impact of government programmes on small enterprise performance has been quite limited.

Understanding existing markets

The starting point for BDS market development must be an understanding of what already exists, in order to build upon products and methods that have proven effective in the local context. This should include an assessment of the characteristics, needs, and willingness-to-pay of different types of small enterprises; what services are currently provided and by whom; and the nature of market failures that constrain market development.[7] Informal, indigenous markets (for example, apprenticeships) may exist and offer insights into appropriate methodologies and products. Knowing the degree of competition in local BDS markets, the extent of subsidization of publicly-funded services, and the availability of information on service providers and service impact, will help governments and donors design interventions that will develop, rather than distort, BDS markets.

Developing products

While common wisdom may suggest that micro-enterprises and low-income clients are generally unaware of the value of BDS and are unlikely to bear much of the costs, this may be because low-cost services suited to their needs have not been developed. The success of many micro-finance institutions demonstrates that the poor will demand and pay for BDS products which are designed and marketed well. Hence an important challenge in developing BDS markets, especially to serve the lower-end mass market, is to develop low-cost products suited to low-income micro-enterprises. If profitable BDS products are available, competition among providers can hasten their spread to the mass market.

Developing profitable products suitable for micro-enterprises and low-income clients is also important because of the strategy's emphasis on financial self-sustainability. The drive for sustainability creates the incentive for BDS providers to drift toward the upper end of the market – medium-scale, growth-oriented enterprises – since products for that market segment are currently better developed and more profitable. While experience is limited, there was a feeling among many conference participants that, with right design and delivery mechanisms, suitable low-cost products can profitably meet the needs of even the smallest enterprises. They are indeed a 'mass market' that can be attractive to private service providers.

Developing institutions and delivery mechanisms

To provide services in a cost-effective and financially self-sustainable manner, BDS providers need to be business-like and demand-led. Experience shows that private sector providers tend to be more business-like and demand-led than public institutions, whose orientation toward 'head counts' of numbers served or funds disbursed and lack of client orientation have often resulted in high cost and low effectiveness. This has led to an emphasis on building the capacity of private BDS providers and on developing partnerships with the private sector. However, forging partnerships with private institutions can pose difficulties for donors and governments, who may lack the capacity to identify, work with and monitor a wide range of decentralized organizations. Hence it is recognized that this strategy may temporarily involve 'facilitating organizations' as agents to assist in building the capacity of the direct BDS providers.[8] These evolving roles are presented in Figure 2.1.

Given the diversity of small enterprise clients and different local contexts, no single type of delivery model fits all. Different types of institutions – for-profit firms, industry associations, NGOs, and private voluntary organizations) and different levels of delivery (direct service providers, BDS intermediaries or 'brokers') may be needed.

While assistance to build the capacity of BDS providers is an important part of developing the supply side, institution-building alone may not yield the types of products that could enhance both competition and sustainability in the market as a whole. Hence it is important to focus on developing suitable products, including through incentives given to BDS suppliers to improve their performance in reaching under-served market niches.

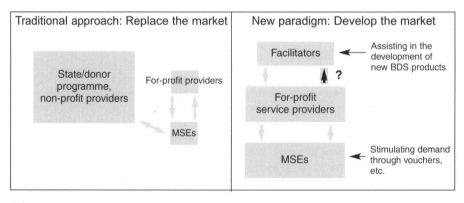

Figure 2.1

The critical role of information

Market information that is needed for transactions to occur can be considered a public good, and the government may be able to play a role in gathering and disseminating market data or in facilitating access of small producers (especially potential exporters) to tools such as the Internet. In spite of its 'public good'

36

nature, case studies reveal that small enterprises are willing to pay for information that provides direct benefits in market access and improved product quality. Indeed, transactional information is one of the more profitable areas of BDS for small enterprises (see Section IV below).

Inadequate information can also be a cause of market failure in BDS markets. When BDS markets are underdeveloped, firms have little basis for assessing the value of these services, and suppliers cannot evaluate whether likely revenues would cover costs. Overcoming this information gap is one justification for voucher and matching grant programmes, which encourage small entrepreneurs to utilize BDS by lowering the cost to the enterprise without reducing the returns to the suppliers.[9] The subsidies inherent in these programmes may be justified by their demonstration effect, as participants will make other firms aware of the value of these services and more willing to pay for them.

The role of government

The role of government in this approach is to establish a suitable context for market transactions, to provide underpinning infrastructure and education, and avoid crowding out private providers (or forestalling their emergence) through direct provision of competing services.[10] Thus, governments can help by ensuring that the legal and judicial system supports low-cost contract enforcement; creating a socio-cultural context that values entrepreneurship and profit-seeking; facilitating the flow of market information through data collection and a good communications system; expanding literacy and numeracy to raise the productivity of training of entrepreneurs and workers; making transport, electricity and water widely available at reasonable cost (small enterprises are less able than larger ones to provide these themselves); and making sure that the policy 'playing field' is level in terms of ease of registration, taxes and investment incentives for small as well as large enterprises. Even without direct service delivery, the public agenda is large, and governments need a strategic approach to prioritize their interventions according to the means available.

Measuring performance

Experience shows that BDS providers are more likely to succeed if they closely monitor their performance, as a way of gaining control over costs, ensuring that the target market segment is being reached, and that clients are satisfied with the mix and quality of services offered.[11] Programme managers can use this information to feed back into the design of market strategy, service products, and delivery mechanisms. This is the core of the performance-based approach advocated in the Donor Committee strategy.

When BDS programmes are supported financially by governments or donors, making funding contingent upon the achievement of performance objectives can both help to improve the management of BDS institutions and ensure accountability in the use of funds. This implies a contractual relationship between governments/donors and BDS institutions that defines and rewards results in terms of institutional development and client impact. Performance contracts should include clear exit strategies in case of underperformance, as well as entry criteria to receive initial (or continued) funding.

When subsidies are provided, it is especially important to evaluate the impact of services on the performance of the target group of small enterprises. Where such impact can be demonstrated, the cost-effectiveness of providers in delivering these services becomes an important input into decisions on the level and duration of subsidies. Information on impact and cost effectiveness will help donors and governments to identify the right mix of incentives to encourage product development and financial self-sustainability. For non-subsidized programmes, measurement of impact beyond that needed for programme management is less relevant.

The new emphasis on the development of BDS markets implies that a whole new category of performance indicators is relevant. These indicators would measure the breadth and depth of the market, probably for specific BDS products, both before and after external interventions. Increasing the range of indicators to include assessment of market development will probably require significant additional resources. It will be important to set priorities for performance measurement, so that monitoring costs remain in proportion to those of the intervention itself.

Successful implementation of a performance-based approach – by both BDS institutions and funding providers – requires indicators that provide the desired information and that can be gathered systematically at reasonable cost. While a consensus has emerged on the categories of results that should be measured, there is still no consensus on exactly which indicators to measure, nor how they should be measured. Much remains to be done to build consensus and derive specific benchmarks. The paper by Mary McVay (Chapter 24) makes a start in this direction, and forms the basis for current efforts by a Donor Committee Task Force to agree on a set of standard indicators.

Achieving sustainability

An important focus of the Donor Committee's efforts to build consensus on best practices in supporting BDS for small enterprises has been on sustainability; indeed, this was the principal theme of the conference held in Zimbabwe. We recognize that not all services must or can achieve full cost recovery. In particular, for those services that have 'public good' characteristics (such as certain types of information and training), there may be a justification for subsidies even in the long run.

The Harare and Rio events provided a number of case studies that suggest which types of services and which types of clients currently achieve a good level of cost recovery (see Figure 2.2). Note that, in the absence of standard performance indicators, the information is not strictly comparable, so the data presented are only illustrative. For example, some case studies reported the degree of

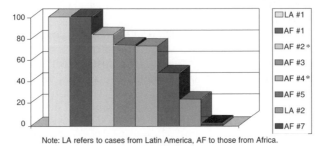

Note: LA refers to cases from Latin America, AF to those from Africa.

Figure 2.2   *Cost recovery in training (%)*

cost recovery relative to direct costs only (shown on the graphs with a *), while others reported it relative to total costs.

Data from training projects suggest that this service can indeed be offered sustainably, but that some organizations have apparently chosen to subsidize it to a high degree. In general, the impact which these subsidies have had on existing for-profit training providers has not been considered in any depth, triggering increased consideration for the BDS market as a whole.

Similarly, data from marketing programmes show that several organizations have achieved, or are about to achieve, full financial sustainability (see Figure 2.3). Indeed, this activity can be so profitable that some have questioned whether donor agencies should be directly involved in it at all. Again, this is the sort of debate that has triggered consideration of stimulating BDS markets (assisting a wide range of entrepreneurial traders to provide marketing services more effectively) rather than directly providing the service through one organization.

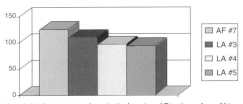

Note: LA refers to cases from Latin America, AF to those from Africa

Figure 2.3   *Cost recovery in marketing (%)*

Notes

1 The term 'small enterprise' is used to refer generally to the lower end of the range of firms in terms of size and capabilities, including micro-enterprises and medium-sized firms as well as small enterprises, however these may be defined in individual country contexts. In developing and targeting specific services, it may be useful to break out these more detailed market segments.

2 These conferences were co-sponsored by the Committee of Donor Agencies for Small Enterprise Development. The Brazil conference was also sponsored by the Inter-American Development Bank, along with a complementary conference focusing on experience in Latin America and the Caribbean. The Zimbabwe conference, focusing on African experience, was also sponsored by the British Department for International Development and the International Labour Office. The Harare Conference proceedings are contained in a working paper entitled 'Business Development Services: How Sustainable Can They Really Be?' by Jim Tanburn.

3 See Alan Gibson, 'Framework for BDS for SMEs', keynote presentation.

4 The Donor Committee paper on 'Business Development Services for SMEs: Preliminary Guidelines for Donor-Funded Interventions,' as well as papers from the Rio and Harare conferences, are available on the following Website: *http://www.ilo.org/public/ english/65entrep/isep/bds/donor/index.htm*

5 Note, however, that the performance measurement framework proposed by McVay/ USAID during the Rio Conference uses the term 'scale' to refer to numbers reached, and 'outreach' to refer to the degree to which services achieve social objectives (poverty alleviation, etc.)

6 In East Africa, for example, donor-funded local staff earn about US$1500 per month, while local BDS providers make about US$150 per month.

7 An example of efforts to assess local BDS markets is contained in Chapter 16 on Jamaica Micronet.

8 One example of a facilitating organization is the FIT programme, which makes new training products available to private-sector trainers in Uganda and Zimbabwe; it also develops innovative BDS products for 'business tourism', which it makes available to travel agents. Similarly, ApproTEC develops agro-processing equipment suitable for micro-enterprises; this equipment is then manufactured and sold by Kenyan metal-workers on a for-profit basis. While both organizations charge the BDS providers for their facilitation support, both require on-going subsidies if they are to continue to develop new BDS products.

9 See the chapters on voucher programmes (Goldmark, 23, Steel/Riley, 12) and matching grants (Crisafulli, 13).

10 See the same paper, on the issue of 'subsidiarity'.

11 See the core principles 2, 5, and 7 in Gibson, Chapter 8.

PART II   ENTREPRENEURSHIP DEVELOPMENT PROGRAMMES

3. The case of CEFE – a new look at entrepreneurship

RAINER KOLSHORN and UWE WEIHERT

ALL ALONG THE ups and downs of fashion in technical co-operation, *training* has without any doubt maintained its popularity and leading role within the now highly diversified range of existing tools for business development promotion. And although decades ago innovative teaching methods had already begun to revolutionize pedagogy, the resistance towards a more outreaching and sustainable introduction of dynamic and modern learning methodologies in adult education has been considerable in general, and particularly in the field of business development training.

The case study of CEFE, which is a comprehensive set of training instruments designed to stimulate positive interventions in the small enterprise development process with the use of modern training technologies based on the cornerstones of experiential and action learning methods, shows that, if certain principles laid out later were to be followed, sustainability and outreach could become in-built elements of a broad development strategy in training.

However, why should we bother at all about sustainability and outreach of training if for so many years business development training has been delivered in endless packages to improve the management know-how of small business owners? Isn't enough enough?

The world is facing a process of economic globalization which almost no country can avoid. While, on the one hand, cheap products from industrial mass production are flooding markets in developing countries, forcing traditional small producers out of the market, more and more products of the 'Third World' compete with local production in industrialized countries. While the growth rate of economic output is still increasing, the disparity of material wealth is accelerating. Our changing environment has created the need to add new elements to human skills. Training has to build up these new enterprising competencies needed by its clientele.

Business development training is not a self-fulfilling event, it has to cope with the huge extent of the problem. It is not sufficient to scrape only the surface and train a few entrepreneurs and managers. Business development training also has to go far beyond mere economic issues; it has a very important function for business development, but also a societal role to play. Training thus has also to be delivered by other vehicles which allow mass training approaches. And business development training has to give an equal chance to employees and employers for small businesses to grow and be successful in the globalized world of tomorrow.

But how can we ensure that business development training covers them all?

The case of CEFE has, over time, generated interesting insights and clues about some principles and mechanisms that can support sustainable and self-standing development in training. The principal lesson we have learnt is that the

41

design of a sustainable mass delivery system of business development training should argue about whether the principle of inside-out is being respected.

What do we mean by that? What are the most important mechanisms and results of the CEFE strategy to overcome several of the major 'home-made' obstacles which frequently limit significant spreading and lasting transfer of newly designed training methodologies towards local partners?

Taking into account both the very intensive overall training of people looking into all aspects of their business life, and also the various shorter courses which cover only certain technical or personal aspects in business, the 200 institutions and 2000 'CEFistas' of the International CEFE Network in around 60 countries are trying to improve the economic key competencies of roughly 100 000 people annually. This number is still low compared to the problems involved, but is steadily growing without any additional (and quite meagre) funding of activities through GTZ or CEFE International (which is a supra-regional programme funded by the German government).

The CEFE Network is mainly based on the motivation, energy, creativity and enthusiasm which is inherent inside the network – the CEFistas. They themselves care for the spreading of the methodology because it's the market which decides what the network institutions and the CEFistas can offer. It's in the self-interest of the CEFistas and their organizations that their market is growing, thus producing sustainability and outreach. In a world of change and very limited financial resources, donor-driven approaches do not survive. They are not appropriate to 'make it grow'; rather, they should adopt a strategy to create favourable conditions to 'let it grow'.

The individual change: the impact of CEFE training on CEFistas

In November 1998 we sent out a questionnaire to more than 140 CEFistas selected at random on a world-wide level. Seventy of them replied giving a detailed picture of their motivation to support the spreading of CEFE in their respective countries. In brief, the result was that it was mainly the impact that the methodology had produced on themselves which made them so supportive. Around 200 different impact criteria were mentioned by them.

If one carefully studies the nature of the diverse responses, it becomes clear that the specific training methodology applied obviously touches both the minds and the hearts of the people. For the respondents it was not only important that they increased their technical knowledge about what to teach their target group; improving their own enterprise skills or acquiring new competencies was considered by them to have had significantly more impact on their own life. Nearly 87 per cent found that they did increase their personal competencies through the CEFE training; in particular, their enterprise skills improved, they developed new competencies and a higher degree of curiosity and creativity. Sixty-three per cent of them said that they also increased their technical competencies with a better understanding of their target groups, which included technical skills, conceptual capabilities and more entrepreneurial awareness.

However, their conclusion was that the teaching of only technical matters doesn't provide the ability to apply what one has learnt in one's job. Only the development of their enterprise competencies (planning, risk management, problem-solving, creativity, effectiveness, striving for quality, etc.) together with the increase in technical subjects, made them better trainers and gave them more confidence and motivation in their work.

What about their personal growth independent of their workplace, but rather in their private life?

Respondents argued that their CEFE training improved some key life competencies which can be categorized under the headings of 'I know myself better' (76%) and 'I can better deal with my environment' (80%), which gave them an additional push or motivation to practise their newly acquired competencies in all aspects of their life. From the viewpoint of CEFE International, this aspect results from three basic training ingredients:

- 'experiential learning', which allows trainees to experience and 'live' new and still unknown real-life situations, or confront situations already known in the class-room and see them in a new way through the results they achieved with their action
- 'action learning', which means you are working on your own life case during the training and thus are able to transfer your newly acquired competencies directly to your own life
- 'learning to be more enterprising', which is far more than being a better businessman and includes seeing and doing things from a different, more competent perspective and which covers your whole personality.

Approaches and methodologies that are able to integrate qualities which turn the multipliers into beneficiaries by enabling them to profit extensively from the tools while using them, do create considerable energy for sustainability and outreach from within the multiplier: The principle of inside-out!

The business change: the impact of CEFE training on the target groups

Professional motivation, however, is also directly linked to your satisfaction in what you are doing.

In 1994, CEFE International was scrutinized by an internationally renowned team of independent experts in an evaluation of the impact CEFE has on its different target groups. The team was commissioned by the Federal Ministry of Economic Co-operation (BMZ) – the funding ministry of CEFE International. The team used a methodological mix of instruments to find out about CEFE's relevance for the different target groups (for details see the WebPages of CEFE International *http://www.gtz.de/cefe/*).

This team came to the conclusion that the CEFE approach to training can in general be evaluated as totally positive regarding the educational aspects, and positive with some minor limitations regarding the development aspects (at that time some questions were raised about outreach and sustainability). A few of the major findings should be highlighted.

- Participants found CEFE to be useful or very useful:
  - at 95% for their present job
  - at 93% for their personal development
  - at 91% for the development of their entrepreneurial competencies
  - at 86% for the development of their business
  - at 82% for the increase of their managerial know-how.
- 80% of the participants claimed that their personal income increased by a minimum of 30% after the CEFE course.
- Participants created an average of 4.5 new jobs after the CEFE course.

Obviously, CEFE is not only meant to create more competence, personal satisfaction and more income for the trainers (the CEFistas) but also for their target groups for whom the system has been designed. You, being a better trainer, can train others to become more enterprising, it's you who can initiate this process: The principle of inside-out functions again because now your clients create benefits for themselves and for others from inside-out.

Both parties, the CEFistas as well as their clients, grow personally and professionally, are subsequently more successful, and develop a desire to share what they have experienced: sustainability and outreach are strengthened. Being a better and 'convinced' trainer by experiencing the impact of the training yourself, gives you and your message more credibility and adds to the effectiveness of the technique.

The institutional change: the impact of CEFE at the meso level

The principle of inside-out becomes even more visible once we look at the developments in many countries at the institutional level. While all organizations, including those presented at the conference, have had to react to the tendencies created by global change during the last decade, this reaction seems to have been more pronounced for institutions using CEFE.

Driven by the motivation, enthusiasm and new competencies of their staff, as well as of their clients, these institutions were often facing a push from inside in order to become a learning organization. A slow but steady 'contamination' of the organizations took place through the increased competencies of their staff. It doesn't take the organizations long to recognize that training others in enterprise competencies is forcing you as an organization to become more enterprising, especially when automatic funding from donors becomes scarce.

Let us look at some of the CEFE network institutions and the way in which they have reacted to the fact that the money they got from the German government was insufficient to fund the programme.

The case of Fundasol, Uruguay: sustainability and outreach through product development

Initially Fundasol came into contact with the CEFE approach when a bilateral project was started in 1988. Fundasol thus became the first partner institution of CEFE International in Latin America, and it was still not yet clear if the whole methodological CEFE approach would function there given the totally different socio-economic and cultural environment compared to where CEFE was originally developed[1].

Historically, the first CEFE activities of Fundasol started in 1989 with a business starter course and a training of trainers, which were designed more or less the same way as that known and practised in Asia.

However, with Uruguay being such a small market for new ventures, it soon became obvious that there was not enough interest on the part of potential clients for these types of courses, which needed a very intensive four-weeks/160 hours attendance of participants and were later charged at a fee of US$150 per participant. However, the initial doubts about CEFE's cultural or socio-economic acceptance proved to be unfounded.

After a thorough analysis of the market in 1990, it was decided to move in three directions; first, to modularize the existing business starter course into four subsequent one-week modules, which could more easily be attended and paid for by the potential clients; second, to use the CEFE methodology in the design of shorter courses (20 hours) on specific subjects for existing entrepreneurs, which initially concentrated on subjects such as financial management, financial analysis, entrepreneurial competence, productivity management and growth management (each module was 'sold' at US$50 per participant); and third, to pioneer the CEFE approach in other countries in Latin America through the training of trainers of neighbouring counties, which was also identified as an additional source of income.

All these three strategies contributed to Fundasol's earnings, especially the second strategy, which generated enough interest and income in the upcoming market for training to encourage Fundasol to diversify further the existing training product range in the light of a predictable phasing-out of the bilateral project. Project money and expertise was still used to develop training packages (20 hours) for existing entrepreneurs on entrepreneurial management and creativity, marketing (1991) and personnel management (1993), and to design information packs on marketing, sales and formalization (1991), business start-up and registration procedures (1992).

It was interesting to see that these new courses were also designed in the light of the upcoming strong, albeit subsidized, training competitor Empretec, which partly operates with a comparable training technology, but which didn't charge the clients at that time and was not 'allowed' to move into product diversification. Obviously, this competition stimulated Fundasol's creativity to use to the full extent the flexibility of the CEFE method to design more courses for target groups where Empretec couldn't compete, or where Fundasol had a competitive advantage, or which were not catered for at all.

In the course of time new target groups were explored. Modules for rural entrepreneurs (20–50 hours) were developed for horticulture, dairies, apiculture (1994), cattle-breeding, cattle-trade and for associative enterprises (1996); further modules for the existing clients (48 hours) concentrated on total quality management (1995), macro business prospects (1996), and post-training follow-up (1996). Also, new developments came to upgrade and consolidate the competencies and skills of the CEFE trainers in these various fields. Finally, a board-game was introduced with the brokerage of CEFE International to upgrade the economic competencies of farmers (1997).

It may be recalled that the bilateral project had ended long ago and that since then all new developments were created by Fundasol itself, all development costs were borne by its own funds.

This case shows that the original institution has dramatically changed from a donor fund-spending NGO into a dynamic entrepreneurial organization operating successfully in the market of business development training. The way the principle of inside-out worked at the institutional level was that the user of the tool (CEFE) became a beneficiary; a training approach thought of as a tool became an integral part of the institutional structure.

The case of Fundación Kittl, Bariloche, Argentina: sustainability and outreach through market penetration and expansion

Kittl came into contact with CEFE in 1994 through Fundasol, which used its excellent contacts in Argentina to market CEFE beyond the Uruguayan borders. Kittl and Fundasol received no German funding for their joint activities; furthermore, within Kittl's own CEFE activities they have never received German finance.

After initial training and organizational advice given by Fundasol, Kittl started its first two pilot CEFE courses with 58 participants in July 1995 in the city of

Bariloche, experimenting from the very beginning not only with existing entrepreneurs but also in introducing CEFE into the educational sector at secondary level. They were paid for this by the municipal authorities and a private secondary school.

In 1996, the total number of people trained by Kittl rose to 242 trainees, who were mostly covered through a programme of the National Ministry of Social Development. However, one more experiment was conducted by training employees of a company which paid for this experiment.

In 1997, the total number of trainees rose to 440 participants living in various towns of the region of Patagonia, paid for by the various municipal authorities; and in 1998 rose again to a total of 966 trainees, who were financed by several different sources, such as the municipal authorities, the Ministry, the private secondary school and by two associations of micro-entrepreneurs.

This expansion was achieved by spreading both geographically and also sector-wise. In 1998 Kittl operated at an average distance of 800km from its own office in Bariloche, training a wide range of different target groups (entrepreneurs in agro-based industries, civil servants, youth, employees, association members). One necessary precondition for this expansion towards different target groups was the flexibility of the CEFE approach to develop tailor-made training products based on a target group analysis, and a subsequent combination of general methodological training principles and a toolbox of facilitation techniques and simulation exercises.

The future strategy of Kittl encompasses the following activities:

- building up local expertise through the training of more trainers
- professionalization of the existing trainers through working in changing interdisciplinary trainer teams with the objective that everybody can substitute everybody
- market analysis to further explore new opportunities to be exploited with yet to be developed products
- permanent upgrading of human resources.

What were the reasons for this rapid expansion of activities in the past, all initiated by Kittl itself and financed by various national, regional or local sources?

In those years 'before CEFE', Kittl was able to generate training expertise in management and in technical training of labourers, but didn't target entrepreneurs at all. Because of the insufficient local and regional demand in these fields, it identified small entrepreneurs as being a major source of income for them; however, it was lacking a suitable training technology which would offer various characteristics deemed to be necessary as prerequisites. These were identified as:

- professional attractiveness for the existing freelance trainers
- opportunity to maximize the interdisciplinary background of these trainers
- non-academic training, as the existing university-style teaching wasn't appreciated at all by entrepreneurs
- flexibility for adaptation
- potential for the design of new products for new target groups.

When they encountered CEFE they found that the methodology met their requirements.

After carefully studying the market of entrepreneurship training and observing the type of training which was offered, Kittl from the very beginning developed its training products under the implicit assumption that they, being newcomers, could penetrate the market successfully only on the basis of satisfied clients; that even one bad experience would lead to the failure of the whole strategy; that, however, the satisfaction of clients would create more clients.

A second strategic choice was taken when Kittl decided *not* to start its initial CEFE activities with the training of entrepreneurs but instead to concentrate on the training of 'multipliers', assigned by the various local townships to promote small businesses in their communities. These 'multipliers' were civil servants who had already been trained but who were still lacking professionalism in their work. The reason for this decision was that in Patagonia huge distances exist between the various municipalities and that covering the whole of Patagonia would necessitate local promoters in each place, with Kittl not having this capacity and also not wanting to build this up. Over a period of one year these people were trained with small modules on different topics. They are now the base on which Kittl is building its 'greenhouse of the CEFE methodology' and they were the ones who made Kittl's work with entrepreneurs possible. They organized the first batch of entrepreneur-trainees and they cared for more opportunities in this region of vast distances.

Finally, with the growth of experience with their target groups and careful observation of the movements in the market, a third strategic decision was taken in 1997 to liaise with the training centre of the ILO in Turin in order to establish a distance-learning system which could bridge the prevailing distances in Patagonia.

After three years of experience with CEFE, Kittl has identified the following learning points:

- Take an entrepreneurial attitude yourself: what I tell others to do I should also do.
- Most important in training is what success the participant can achieve for himself.
- Define a human resource policy for your institution.
- Develop an internal permanent innovation attitude.
- As a model and methodology, CEFE has distinct advantages compared with others; most important, however, are the level of development and professionalism, the grade of flexibility, and the fact that CEFE doesn't separate feeling from thinking in the courses.
- Work with the method, don't try to reinvent the wheel.
- Investigate the market carefully to develop appropriate strategies and a plan of action; a permanent SWOT-analysis is mandatory.
- Your clients are never the ones you think they could be.
- The impact of training is much greater if it is embedded in local promotion policies.
- Experiment with what already exists.
- It is very difficult to stay in the market for business development training without some external funding.

The case of Sri Lanka: sustainability and outreach by introducing and spreading a training methodology through the creation of an institutional network

One of the first countries in which CEFE worked was Sri Lanka. Already in 1989 two pilot courses were run on a test basis, with a very positive outcome and high acceptance by the target clientele. As one of the results, the Sri Lanka Business Development Centre (SLBDC), a not-for-profit foundation with public and private sector representation on the board, requested a long-term bilateral project which, despite some reluctance on the part of the German and Sri Lankan governments, finally took off in 1995.

From the very beginning of the project it was clear that SLBDCs position in the market of non-financial assistance to small business development' had suffered because of policy changes and a general shortage of funds. In order not to weaken the early phase of introduction of CEFE into the country, and because of the interest of its management, the Industrial Services Bureau (ISB), a parastatal organization, supported the build-up of CEFE capacity. This was also encouraged by the positive experience of the case of South Africa, where CEFE had been introduced through a network of NGOs.

In 1997, when it became obvious that the project strategy to expand the range of partners had proved to be successful (in 1998 ISB had the strongest human resource capacity in CEFE), a decision was taken to widen the range of partners, with the side-effect that more geographical areas could be covered.

These new partners were the Sarvodaya Economic Enterprises Development Services (SEEDS), a private company linked to the well-known Sarvodaya NGO; a consultancy firm named Business Consultancy Services (BCS Pvt. Ltd.); the Sewalanka Foundation (NGO); the Southern Development Authority (SDA, GO with mandate to develop the Southern Region); the North Eastern Provincial Council (NEPC, Provincial Government); Jaffna University; and the Provincial Enterprise Promotion Centre (PEPC) in the Central Province.

The mixture of partner organizations is diverse by nature; some are heavily involved as implementers, others as funding sources, most (but not all) trying to spearhead the cause of CEFE, particularly in and for rural areas. Politically, CEFE (among others) is supported by the Ministry of Plan Implementation and Parliamentary Affairs, Regional Development Division (RDD), which took a real interest only when the network of organizations was growing and becoming politically important. These days the Ministry renders a lot of general support.

What were the most important impulses which led to the present involvement of a network of multiple CEFE partners?

Most important was the pressure exerted by the Sri Lankan and the German governments to give more relevance to CEFE training in rural areas. The experience of the first phase had demonstrated that any expansion of CEFE activities in terms of the organizational base, regional coverage, and number of people trained, could be achieved only through the inclusion of more partners.

Why were all the new Partner Organizations (PO) interested to join?

The reasons were manifold. Some POs learnt about CEFE in so-called Appreciation Workshops (APWs) and decided that this was what they wanted or needed; other POs found CEFE a useful instrument in the frame of their mandate (e.g. provincial enterprise promotion, promotion of members of Sarvodaya in the context of village societies); again, others understood the CEFE potential for their own income generation; they market themselves and are 'selling' the approach to other donor agencies such as UNHCR, UNDP and the EU or to other BMZ-funded projects, and some are even selling CEFE to other ministries and NGOs.

One very important factor was that a couple of trained CEFistas had moved to another organization (i.e. SEEDS) and wanted to introduce CEFE into their new institutions, the principle of inside-out.

Today the dynamic development within the POs has brought its own benefit to the network; it is getting many requests from more organizations that want to join. The strategy on accepting new partners has been designed on the basis of tapping new markets and new regions with a sizeable potential and a limited competition with the existing partners, or at least no threat to their CEFE business. Today, target groups for CEFE training range from micro- to medium-sized entrepreneurs, potential and existing, in Sinhala and Tamil areas and languages. This includes in (ex-)war areas refugees, displaced and resettled people, and also vocational trainees. The network also strives to include the capital, Colombo, and the sectors of higher and management education.

Whoever wants to join, however, has to accept the following self-given mission and long-term vision of the network:

- CEFE should become the leading quality entrepreneurship training product in Sri Lanka.
- For this to be achieved, the network needs a core of highly committed trainers.
- For this to be achieved, the network has established and maintains quality consciousness, which is a rare phenomenon in training in Sri Lanka.
- For this to be achieved, a core of organizations should carry on with CEFE after project end, which implies that they can market the training.
- For this to be achieved, the reputation of entrepreneurship training has to change from bad (low-cost, low-quality training which is given free to the wrong people by non-committed trainers without much result-orientation) to better (high quality, professional trainers, right participants self-selected through participation fees, and proven results).

With this mission and vision the project can today concentrate on supporting the growing network in marketing, promotion and publicity, and in the development of human resources (trainers) and new training products.

The network change: liberalizing the system

The principle of inside-out finally had its effect on GTZ's or CEFE International's position and policy regarding which role it should play as initiator of the whole CEFE case. It took some years of experience before we made the turning point which so many others are still not willing to do. This is our strategy of today:

Decentralization and liberalization. The major challenges in donor-driven development efforts consist in actually reaching – directly or indirectly – those who are in need (target group attainment), in 'making the difference' (outreach), and making the difference in a lasting and further development-stimulating manner (sustainability). CEFE International's present response to the challenges is born out of a long (and sometimes painful) learning process, which in time led to the application of two principles in the transfer of training technology: decentralization and liberalization.

Institutional structures as foundations. Decentralization has first to do with the understanding that only institutional local structures (and not so much independent persons) are adequate recipients to integrate and promote new training methodologies, as only they can in the long run assure the application, adaptation and further development of more effective educational methods and techniques according to local needs and context conditions. These local structures have to be, or to become, as self-reliant as possible, in order to continue offering training products after the supporting donor agencies have pulled out.

Accepting and enhancing the principle of change. Liberalization, on the other hand, implies that the transferred product or service is not understood as the final stage of wisdom, which has to be safeguarded in its contents and form under all circumstances. There is, and there must be, scope for change. And if change is to be, it makes more sense to create favourable conditions to make it happen and spur its expression through vision and principle-oriented guidance. The concept of liberalization is therefore not identical with an attitude of *laissez-faire*.

Perceiving the real scope of the product. The application of both principles implies that the product 'transfer of training methodologies' goes beyond the mere delivery of training for trainer workshops. There is a *before* and an *after* to this particular transfer intervention that have to be considered. A strategy for the insertion of the methodology into the promotional environment has to be defined just as well as follow-up and backstopping measures to guarantee not only an adequate application of the methodology but a strengthened partner, able to keep on walking the road of modern business development training independently.

Main strategy elements. Structures and change – two apparently antagonistic but vital concepts to contribute to outreach and sustainability – had to be brought together in a progressive and fruitful tension. GTZ/CEFE International's strategy to achieve this challenge has been based upon the following key elements:

- creating and enhancing supportive local institutional structures
- generating an international CEFE network
- introducing and promoting instruments to stimulate the exchange of information, knowledge, innovation and experience
- contributing to human resource development of key actors involved in business development training.

'Rooting' through long-term projects. The long-term project approach as used by GTZ represents an ideal stepping-stone to introduce, transfer and accompany the training technology within the local institutional environment of SME-Promotion, or, of course, in other areas such as vocational training or education. These long-term projects can be called ideal in the sense that their highly participatory approach, their financial autonomy and flexibility, as well as their time dimension, make it possible to realize in co-responsibility with the partners the necessary complementary measures (for instance organizational development) within a time horizon that allows technologies to mature and settle down within the local idiosyncrasy. Over the years, many SME projects all over the world have thus been the point of departure to set off national and regional CEFE movements, often leading to a thorough change in the existing business training culture in the country. Depending on the set-up and nature of the project, CEFE International as a specialized unit within GTZ is usually involved in the conceptual lay-out of the interventions as well as in the realization and follow-up of the activities. In the case of lacking regular GTZ-projects with SME orientation, CEFE International often fostered and realized a variety of promotional and training events responding to local demands of national organizations and institutions in order to stimulate the spread of the methodology.

Weaving the net. In time, and through the process of monitored skill acquisition, experience and further upgrading within the methodology, more and more people and institutions reached levels of qualification that made them valuable resource agents. By actively using this newly grown local know-how in the further spreading of the technology beyond regional and national frontiers, an international network of CEFE practitioners was gradually built up. CEFE International's original intermediary function – connecting and channelling resources within and even over the continents – has in the meantime in some regions become less and less necessary. Direct lines of communication and interaction have replaced its task as a bridging tool.

Lessons learnt. 'The best way to be prepared for change is to base the preparation on change.'

- Give your approach a face and you create identification.
- Make it a tool which delivers insights that spur continuous personal growth and you create long-term support, and the wish to share and to spread the 'news'.
- Make business training an adventure that goes beyond business training and you create a more profound and thorough impact through synergic spill-overs into neighbouring fields of life.
- Build its methodology on principles rather than on content and knowledge, and you create a tool with the ability toward self-renovation, further development and change.
- Give it the freedom to change according to circumstances and you create adequateness and acceptance.
- Be a facilitator, not a controller, of the process and focus your support on strengthening the above fundamentals, and sustainability and outreach will be the built-in results of the process.

Trust the principle of inside-out.

Note

1 CEFE was originally developed in a bilateral integrated urban development project in Bhaktapur, Nepal under the aspect of promoting business starters.

4.   The Empretec Ghana Foundation

ALAN GIBSON

The Empretec Ghana Foundation has emerged as a strong organization, with a motivated staff, delivering a broad range of training and consultancy services to growth-orientated SMEs. This chapter describes its strengths, which owe much to the vision of its leadership, and include a business-like culture and a commitment to moving towards financial sustainability. Empretec's staff and services have been developed with the help of 'mentors', funded at considerable cost by donor agencies. The chapter questions whether this level of intervention creates organizations that can achieve sustainability.

EMPRETEC IS AN INTERNATIONAL entrepreneurship and capacity-building programme currently operating in 10 countries in Africa and Latin America. Begun in 1988 and co-ordinated globally by UNCTAD, it is a broad programme united by several core features, including a focus on entrepreneurship training workshops and high growth potential SMEs. However, the Empretec country programmes are almost entirely autonomous in relation to strategy, operations and structure.

The Empretec programme in Ghana began in 1990. Its mission, established in 1994, is: 'To build high-quality, growth-oriented, internationally competitive entrepreneurs through training, business advice and access to technology and finance'. The programme has progressed through three clear stages in its development:

(1) *Start-up and survival.* From 1990 to 1994, its activities were based primarily around entrepreneurship workshops and, to a lesser extent, management seminars, with a limited number of consultancy and advisory services. Empretec then had three professional staff, all on secondment from other organizations.
(2) *Growth.* From 1994 to 1997, Empretec changed from a development project into an independent foundation, the Empretec Ghana Foundation (Empretec); staff numbers increased to over 60; budget levels rose by three- or fourfold as more donor-funded projects were awarded to it; the product portfolio broadened to place more emphasis on consultancy and credit facilitation as well as credit services directly; and, most important, sustainability was given greater strategic priority.
(3) *Consolidation.* Empretec is currently concentrating on becoming more efficient and effective in developing and delivering products.

This case study examines Empretec to see whether lessons and principles of good practice in BDS, can be learned from this case to be applied elsewhere, and whether useful benchmark performance indicators have been used by Empretec to monitor progress.

The organization – Empretec's great strength

From an early stage in its life, the institutional development of Empretec has been given a high level of importance by Empretec management; i.e. while the importance of the products delivered and the impact of these on clients was recognized, these were always seen within the context of the organization.

Empretec has 66 staff, of whom 50 are engaged directly or indirectly in BDS. From the outset, staff development has been encouraged and training programmes are arranged for all staff. In late 1997 and the beginning of 1998, two senior staff, including the previous chief executive officer, resigned but overall staff turnover is low. During the recent period of growth, staff numbers increased substantially and the quality of these incoming staff – their insight, innovation and commitment – is striking. All professional staff have university degrees, diplomas or an equivalent professional qualification.

Empretec's working culture has been developed consciously by its management. It is:

- 'corporate': for example, with dress standards laid down for all staff
- diligent: staff work long hours and, given the power shortages, have to be prepared to be flexible
- business-oriented: both in the language used by staff and in their approach to work: for example, developing a transactional relationship with clients and assessing the costs and revenues from different products
- based on a shared vision: the direction of the organization and its values are strongly held by staff; there is a perceptible sense of ownership among all staff.

Empretec's appeal to potential employees stems from a professional environment, personal and developmental challenge and financial gain (salaries are competitive with organizations such as banks).

Another advantage to employees derives from Empretec's status as an independent foundation. 'Classic' development projects have a beginning and an end, and they often do not offer an environment in which people, products and systems can be expected to develop in the long term. Becoming an independent foundation also allows Empretec more flexibility in funding: rather than being funded rigidly against budget lines, Empretec now receives a negotiated management fee for its services from donors for delivering particular projects.

Until recently, Empretec had been led by a strong chief executive officer (CEO) who had built a strong management team around him. His approach to management – inclusive, creating an appropriate working culture, and with a strong business orientation – helped to define the organization. At the heart of this approach is the view that Empretec had to be close to its clients in order to work successfully with them. Empretec's corporate culture is not that of a micro-enterprise – it is too formal and structured for that – but it has some similarities with that of the SMEs who constitute its key client group.

Most important in terms of leadership and Empretec's evolution, considerable funding has supported the CEO's vision, rather than ideas adopted from the donors. Specifically, the UK consultancy company (Rural Investment Overseas) which has managed DFID's inputs into Empretec has been able to develop an intensive 'mentoring' type of working relationship with them which provides new ideas, advice and training but which has not removed basic ownership from Empretec itself. This is a difficult balance to achieve, but one which is crucial if technical assistance resources are to be used successfully.

Financial capacity

Empretec has working relationships with a number of donor agencies. In its initial phase of development, UNDP was its key donor partner and clearly very influential in developing its product base. Since 1994, however, DFID has been the largest funder. How this process has been managed is one of its distinctive characteristics – through a consultancy company. However, it is important to acknowledge that Empretec has also been the beneficiary of a significant amount of investment by donors.

Most donor support is consumed in the delivery of products and in running the organization, but considerable resources have been devoted specifically to investment in equipment, human development and new products. In the period 1994–97, US$200 000 was spent on staff training alone and US$160 000 on capital equipment. In the current period, 1997–2000, at least US$200 000 will be spent on specific product development or broader institutional development (for example, improved information systems). In addition, the mentoring role of the external consultant is a significant expense (approximately US$100 000 per annum). These figures emphasize that although the path through which institutional development support has been offered is important, the scale of resources committed to them is also significant (i.e. it is not just *how*, but *how much!*). At a rough estimate, at least US$1500–2000 per employee per annum has been invested in Empretec by DFID alone on institutional and product development. It is premature to assess the worth of this investment; however, its scale is noteworthy.

Making sustainability a priority

Only after Empretec was born as an organization did sustainability move seriously on to its agenda. From the outset, Empretec has sought to operationalize sustainability and confront its implications in relation to, among other aspects:

- the product mix: focusing on products where SME clients will pay
- organizational culture: developing in a tight and business-like way
- the structure: developing appropriate legal and operational structures
- the client base: focusing on 'winners' in the formal sector, where SMEs' needs can be identified and they are prepared to pay an appropriate price for services to address them.

Empretec's ultimate aim is to make client businesses more sustainable. However, in practical terms, the drive for sustainability is manifested primarily in Empretec's ability to operate with reduced dependence on external donor funds. For Empretec, this is a practical, measurable 'proxy' indicator of client sustainability and a key indicator of Empretec's performance. Table 4.1 appears to indicate renewed progress by Empretec towards achieving its goal of 40 per cent cost coverage by the year 2000, after overhead costs more than doubled in the period of expansion in 1995–96.

Table 4.1 Empretec's financing

	Overhead costs (US$)	Internally generated funds (US$)	%
1995	281 000	137 000	49
1996	547 000	154 000	28
1997	487 000	180 000	37

The 'downside' of the extensive institutional development process and expansion that Empretec has undertaken (and which has brought many already-mentioned benefits) is an overhead base which is difficult to support through revenue-earning activity. The current financial and staff time recording systems do not allow a precise analysis here. However, it appears that:

- around half the salary cost is incurred by people with no direct revenue-generating role (in a commercial consultancy this is likely to be no more than 20 per cent)
- revenue-generating staff spend a relatively small proportion of their time actually delivering fee-earning products (compared to 70–80 per cent in a commercial consultancy)
- expenditure classified under 'administration' accounts for over 60 per cent of costs.

Out of the total amount of staff resource available, every fee-earning day is dwarfed by every non-fee earning day. This situation presents several challenges: getting more people to think about delivering products (for example, in the IT division); developing internal systems so that the real resource usage picture is evident; separating out those costs that can be attributed directly to donor requirements (for example, impact assessment) rather than Empretec needs; and, overall, reversing the existing imbalance between productive and unproductive time.

One possible reason for Empretec's relatively high cost base is that the institutional development process has sought to serve two clients (SMEs and donors) who have different institutional expectations: entrepreneurial provider of services compared to competent manager of projects. Certainly, the current era of reducing external support will expose Empretec to the harsher pressures of SME market conditions.

The most significant business management trend in the 1980s and 1990s has been the drive for more clarity and focus. Businesses have sought to concentrate on their *core competence* or to restructure to allow different parts of the same organization to develop distinctive areas of expertise. Thus far, Empretec has developed as a multi-product entity with an integrated structure. While some degree of specialization does take place, even the credit service (operated separately from BDS) still has the same terms and conditions for employees. The *potential* benefits of a 'split and focus' approach are well known. It may provide the opportunity for greater management responsibility and control; for more transparent performance assessment; and for more specific marketing and pricing approaches. Within Empretec's current product range, there are several possibilities for such decentralization; indeed, initial discussions have begun for both credit and training products.

Empretec's staff resource to date has developed within a relatively secure context. During a period of growth, when staff numbers have risen considerably, there have been many opportunities for staff development within Empretec as a whole. In the current, maturing phase, when the emphasis is more on efficiency improvements, there are different challenges for staff. Increasingly, staff rewards will be linked to performance resulting in greater exposure to market uncertainties and, in a very practical sense, placing them closer to the realities of their client's situation.

Empretec's business services – revenues and costs

The services Empretec offers to SMEs are summarized in Table 4.2. These products are aimed at improving business efficiency, facilitating access to finance and improving business linkages. SMEs become Empretec clients either after participation in the 10-day flagship entrepreneurship programme, or after discussions with the client services manager and an initial diagnostic health check. In both cases, the entry process should lead, first, to the SME client becoming more acquainted with Empretec and, second, to Empretec becoming more informed of the SME's BDS needs.

Comparison of revenues against costs for different products is limited by the absence of in-house systems for measuring direct costs on non-training products. However, from the range of products that Empretec offers to its clients (excluding credit sourcing), it is clear that training is the only one in which revenues from clients are greater than direct costs. Indeed, training accounts for over half of internally generated income. Table 4.3 shows the approximate relationship between revenues and costs for different training products in 1997.

Within the training field, the most profitable type of product for Empretec is one where the direct clients are not SMEs *per se* but rather other organizations working with SMEs, such as banks. Training services marketed directly at SMEs (i.e. where there is no external third party) struggle to break even in Empretec.

Table 4.2 Product data summary sheet in 1997

| Product | Product delivery | | Client outreach | | Price to client |
	Target	Actual	Target	Actual	(US$)
TRAINING					
Entrepreneurship workshops (10 days)	1	2	24	52	$250
Short programmes/seminars		27		400	Avg. of $50
Bankers' programme		7		161	Avg. of $280
Customized training programmes		2			$30
CONSULTANCY/ EXTENSION					
British Executive Service Overseas (matching SMEs with volunteer advisers)	20	19	20	19	$100 (processing) $250–500/month
Technology and enterprise dev. Fund (matching SMEs with specialized consultants)	50	52	50	52	50 per cent of consultant's fee
Business development planning fund		28		28	10 per cent of consultant's fee
Facilitating linkages through support for travel	6	4	6	4	
Diagnostic health checks	120 (both)	60 (both)	120 (both)	60 (both)	$125 – old clients $100 – new clients
CREDIT FACILITATION					
Loan monitoring service					1 per cent of loan amount
Clients accounting and book-keeping service	50	22	50	22	$75 per quarter; $300 – whole year

Table 4.3 Revenues versus costs for different Empretec training products in 1997

Training product	Percentage of direct costs covered by revenues
Management workshops	98
Business awareness seminars	74
Entrepreneurship workshops	88
'Negotiation for linkages' workshop	107
In-plant training	200 +
Contract workshops	200 +
Special projects	154

Empretec's approach to pricing is changing. In its initial phase of development, pricing was not given a high priority. Now, as the sustainability imperative takes hold, appropriate pricing is being given greater attention. In general, training products are expected not only to cover costs but to generate a contribution to overheads of at least 30 per cent. In one-to-one products, Empretec is seeking to raise its prices, although it is still some way below full direct cost coverage. In some other product areas, such as the subsidized consultancy contracts, prices are effectively fixed by the arrangements with donors. For micro-enterprise clients and where Empretec has unique products, Empretec's approach is driven more by what the market will bear than a costs calculation.

Product marketing is an acknowledged current area of weakness within Empretec. Training products are marketed through, for example, a brochure with the year's main programmes and through newspaper advertising. However, it is clear that Empretec clients often hear of Empretec only by word of mouth.

The most distinctive aspect of Empretec's approach to marketing is the role of the Empretec Forum. In all countries in which Empretec operates, an organization of SME clients is established. This is intended to play a number of roles: representing members, helping to create a new business class, enhancing networks and inter-firm learning and encouraging joint ventures. The Empretec Forum in Ghana is located within Empretec and through it receives donor funds. Forum meetings every month in each of its three main centres are key opportunities for Empretec staff to sell products, to receive feedback and to build greater client loyalty.

Learning from experience

In relation to its products, Empretec is a leading market player in BDS in Ghana, pursuing an increasingly assertive approach to pricing and which – supported by donor funds – has shown considerable innovation in product development. Moreover, a close relationship between Empretec and its clients provides the basis for effective product development. For training products, especially where the immediate clients are not SMEs, Empretec has succeeded in achieving healthy margins. Some key lessons emerge from Empretec's experience.

SME clients will pay full direct costs for appropriate training products. Empretec's experience is that training programmes aimed at high-growth-potential SMEs can be priced to cover direct delivery costs and generate a significant contribution to overhead costs. Empretec has shown that there can be a genuine demand for short, focused training programmes for SMEs. There is demand for generic cross-sectoral programmes, such as negotiation skills, quality customer care. However, there seems to be greater potential in more specialized, sector-specific programmes where there is a wider area of common interest between the participants; i.e. sector can offer a more useful focus for training than business size.

Making credit a part of a broader package. Accepted best practice in microfinance and BDS encourages separation of non-financial and financial services for SMEs. Empretec's success in creating a healthy loan portfolio – achieved by rigorously separating it from other activities – does not change the wider experience of finance/non-finance mixing (one that is characterized by failure) but does show that it can be done. More significant than the credit service itself, however, is the impact of credit on Empretec's overall offer to clients. Certainly, in Ghana's current tight financial conditions, Empretec staff have no doubts that the lure of credit has helped Empretec to attract clients. While it would be imprudent to interpret this as an argument for BDS to be offered alongside finance, it does show the importance of successful BDS being presented in a way that is meaningful to SMEs and the value of linkages with credit providers.

Learning from overseas. Empretec's experience suggests that there is scope for transferring specific product ideas, provided that these are adapted to the local institutional environment. Current developments in Empretec – particularly the development of sectoral training programmes – draw heavily on experiences from other countries.

Choosing the right mix of products

Having committed itself to pursuing a business-like mode of operations, Empretec is now seeking to follow this rationale to its conclusion. Tight financial analysis of each product's performance demonstrates its worth to customers; Empretec's decision-making on products will increasingly be guided by this to pursue one product as against another. Of course, products that emerge weakest from this analysis might not be dropped. There may be good reasons to continue with products such as counselling and diagnostic health checks; they, for example, may lead clients to other services, provide portfolio balance or useful client feedback. However, it does mean that the reasons for delivering products with low cost coverage will be transparent.

Using financial analysis in decision-making, however, exposes a real tension in Empretec. In a market place where there are many non-SME players, such as donors, banks, and larger businesses, it is clear that a demand-led, revenue-enhancing approach takes Empretec away from supplying services directly to SMEs without the financial involvement of a third party. This is partly attributable to the changes created by donors, but also to the inevitable attraction of products aimed at larger, sectoral clients.

Monitoring costs and revenues also reveals that SME clients will usually not pay the full costs of 'one-to-one' BDS products. While Empretec does charge for all its main one-to-one products, the maximum direct cost coverage achieved is 50 per cent, and is usually significantly less than this. Underpinning the logic of subsidized consultancy schemes is the expectation (or hope) that the matchmaking role performed by an intermediary such as Empretec will make both parties appreciate the benefits of working together and encourage the development of a 'natural' market. There are few signs that this is really happening with Empretec's clients; and customers are still unprepared to pay the full costs. Scaling-up this type of product, therefore, can be done only by increasing financial support for product delivery.

Acknowledging this situation, Empretec is currently seeking to develop a new approach to SME business consultancy and has established a new agency for this purpose, Ghana Executive Service Overseas (GESO). Modelling itself on BESO, this would essentially allow retired managers the opportunity to use their experience and skills for specific assignments with SMEs. For companies, this would be a chance to tap into a relatively low-cost source of expertise. For the SME sector, it might permit a more sustainable market in consultancy services to be created. It is likely that the cost of GESO advisers would be no more than 20–30 per cent of the prevailing market rate. GESO is at an early phase of development and it is too early yet to make any authoritative assessment of it.

The clients

As with many of its other internal systems, Empretec is investing heavily in a new client information system which should include data on client profile, services accessed and impact. However, currently data on clients are not compiled comprehensively; the information below is therefore slightly impressionistic.

Empretec's intended focus is on high-growth potential SME 'winners', with a total asset base in the range US$40 000–US$400 000 and which are registered companies. Given this target group, it is not surprising that Empretec clients for BDS are predominately male (in Empretec's credit service, however, 53 per cent of clients are women), generally from the wealthier sections of Ghanaian society, and often well-educated. Although not homogeneous, this is certainly a relatively articulate and economically strong group. Poor people benefit only indirectly from the programme. Clients represent a variety of sectors in services and manufacturing. Surveys have shown that average employment in client companies is approximately 20–30, but ranging from below five to more than 100.

Empretec has over 650 SMEs on its database: the cumulative total of SMEs that have used services since its inception. Of these, around 150 at any one time are core, active clients; i.e. SMEs that regularly use Empretec services and participate in the Forum. Given the breadth of products delivered by Empretec, aggregate figures on cost per client are of limited relevance, but if it is assumed that Empretec had around 300 to 500 individual clients in 1997, external costs per client were probably around US$500–1000 (including all donor costs: overheads plus capital).

Impact on clients

A number of separate surveys have confirmed that clients are growing.

- *Employment*. A survey of 59 companies in 1997 showed that over a three-year period clients' employment grew by approximately 12 per cent per annum. An earlier 1995 survey showed a similar scale of growth. With an average size of 18–19 employees, this is equivalent to around 2–3 additional jobs per annum (though given doubts about the reliability of the data, caution should be shown in extrapolating these figures to the wider body of Empretec clients).
- *Sales*. A real increase of 25 per cent per annum for sales.

The aggregate picture that emerges from Empretec's and external reviewers' analyses of impact is that there has been a marked general improvement in

60

performance among clients. Most clients do feel that they have benefited from the programme. Empretec acknowledges, however, that there are questions over the extent to which these changes can be attributed to its input. Certainly, these businesses have performed well above average compared with the national trend, but they are a deliberately targeted, exclusive group; i.e. one would expect them to perform better than average.

There are many questions on clients emerging from Empretec's current work to which no categorical answers can be given. For example, is the client profile shifting up-scale as Empretec product prices are increased? Are clients being retained? Is there actually a small number of clients who are generating a disproportionate amount of income? How can client information be used more effectively in product marketing and product development?

Empretec's current investment programme to develop a user-driven computer-based system should provide timely relevant analyses to Empretec managers, which will help in improving the quality of work and in reducing costs.

However, donor agencies investing in Empretec's work clearly have to take account of wider impact concerns than Empretec itself, whose main focus is client fees and client feedback. Although the 'impact issue' has been live in Empretec for several years, as Empretec acknowledges, it has not been addressed satisfactorily. Impact assessment exercises have been undertaken but their quality and usefulness have been limited. The big questions associated with impact – what to measure, how to collect data, what scale of resources to devote to the task – are now being confronted.

Conclusions and implications

Empretec is a dynamic organization which has undergone considerable development since its birth in 1990. It has progressed from a small start-up project to a major independent foundation with a broad portfolio of products aimed at SMEs. Assessing the overall performance of Empretec is hampered by an absence of 'hard' data on client impact. Nonetheless, from the preceding analysis is it clear that Empretec's experience has been characterized by a number of significant achievements. While there are many positive aspects of Empretec's performance, three core accomplishments can be cited:

- *The development of a strong institutional capacity*, which is manifested, for example, in the high level of competencies among staff; the improving systems; the tangible sense of ownership and commitment within the organization; and, overall, an extremely positive and business-like working culture.
- *The development of growing financial autonomy:* one key dimension of institutional capacity is reducing Empretec's dependence of on external donor funding. Direct donor funding now accounts for less than two-thirds of overhead costs.
- *The development of financially sustainable products:* Empretec increasingly seeks not only to cover direct costs but to generate a contribution to overheads through its training products. Appropriately designed training products for growth-oriented SMEs should at least cover all their direct costs from charges.

A number of lessons emerge from Empretec's experience which are of wider relevance to BDS organizations. These generally reaffirm key principles from the Donor Committee Guidelines (1998).

- *Building on strong leadership and vision:* Empretec has developed a strong sense of its own identity and the path ahead, built around a vibrant leader and management team. External assistance has supported rather than imposed a forward direction.
- *A business-like working culture:* the values of Empretec, shared widely in the organization, is that it should approach its mission in a business-like manner. Most important, Empretec's relationship with its clients is transactional, based around payment for services.
- *Productive technical assistance:* with a strong organizational base, technical assistance from external consultants has not threatened Empretec management's ownership; rather it has allowed Empretec to improve its organization and products.
- *Operationalizing sustainability:* sustainability is manifested primarily in clear financial targets but also guides Empretec in relation to product development and structure; it is more than an abstract notion.
- *Realistic market pricing:* SMEs with growth potential at the upper-end of the SME spectrum, will pay a full cost for suitable training products and Empretec's pricing policy aims at modest profit margins. For one-to-one products, it is clear that SMEs will usually not pay the full cost.
- *A commitment to measurement:* while the wider monitoring and evaluation system is still under development, measurement of performance with respect to financial information is at the heart of operations.
- *Making the organization a priority:* assisted by considerable and long-term external support, institutional development – not just products – has always been a key aspect of Empretec development.

Wider issues

Can BDS organizations be developed without creating an unsustainable cost base? While Empretec has developed generally in a business-like way, its cost structure is not that of a for-profit business. Essentially, too many resources are currently not fee-earning. The relatively expensive organizational capacity-development process may thus take Empretec away from the SMEs whom they aspire to being close to and undermine the possibility of achieving improved financial sustainability. Among the possible reasons for this situation are that Empretec is obliged to have additional capacity to serve both donors and its SME clients. It may also be that donor assistance guides Empretec towards copying BDS agencies from industrialized countries: competent but perhaps out-of-place in the market conditions of a low-income developing economy.

Can demand-led BDS organizations maintain an SME focus? An organization such as Empretec, driven by the need to enhance revenues to cover a comparatively high overhead base, will obviously seek to work with clients with the most purchasing power where potentially higher margins can be achieved. In a market situation such as that of Ghana and more widely in Africa, where other donor-supported agencies are active, and opportunities may also exist in sector-focused programmes, there are strong pressures on BDS organizations to reduce the proportion of their portfolio that is delivered to SMEs directly.

How can more 'natural' market conditions be created for BDS? Unlike micro-finance, where there is growing agreement that best practice requires minimal delivery subsidy, in BDS many products are subsidized heavily, a practice common in industrialized nations. This is especially the case for one-to-one products (such as counselling and consultancy) where direct cost recovery rates are low and the prospects of them emerging as sustainable products for delivery seem low. The degree to which current mismatches in supply and demand are reduced or strengthened by subsidies is a moot point. However, the over-arching challenge for donor agencies is to intervene to create conditions where SME demands guide BDS organizations.

Reference

Committee of Donor Agencies for Small Enterprise Development (1998); *Business Development Services for SMEs: Preliminary guidelines for donor-funded interventions.*

5. Development projects: a partnership experience in Chile

J.M. BENAVENTE

Background and design

Early policy design

BY LATE 1990 THE Chilean Ministry of the Economy had already noted some European initiatives and realized that individual action could hardly respond to the export development needs of SMEs. Some outside catalyst was required to potentiate such initiatives, opening the door to benefits far superior to the sum total of individual benefits accrued, if any. For example, the outcome of trade missions abroad might be quite different if they were organized by a pool of businessmen rather than undertaken separately.

A second driver was the realization that new across-the-board policy instruments set for small enterprises – e.g. the Technical Assistance Funds (FAT) and Credit Insurance Bonus Coupons (CUBOS) – were not reaching those target groups due to lack of both information and experience among businessmen on how to operate with those facilities.[1] They were used to the government's traditional and helpful role to give them a hand but were scarcely familiar with the kind of 'third tier policies' under which financial matters were channeled through the banking system.

As a result, the Ministry of the Economy originally outlined the concept of 'Development Projects' (PROFOs) as an association of small and medium-size businesses from a given industry and location, pooled together to develop their international competitiveness. The state would subsidize part of the financing cost of those projects over a three-year period, considered as a minimum for business owners to learn the basics about the benefits of working jointly through an association. In time, the subsidy would be phased out and the businessmen could then take over independent management of the own organization. The partnership would be both among business owners and between them and government agencies (or a private entity accredited by the government) which in turn would channel the funds disbursed by the government and provide the basic procedural guidelines for collective action.

The more specific goals of this initiative can be broken down into those designed to boost the development of individual participating companies, to foster collective action by the pool of businesses, and to improve their relations with the environment, both the market *per se* and local institutions.

Some specific company-oriented targets are:

- In the area of management, to enhance professional skills either by bringing in professional staff or introducing modern accounting and information techniques and medium-term strategic planning. The latter is crucial to help business owners determine their key objectives and targets as players in the production arena. In other words, the idea is to find the optimum niche in the productive chain.
- Concerning productive and technological processes, the goal is to introduce new product designs of higher value added and quality, to improve the

internal organization of shop floors, and to access new sources of technology and financing for technological innovation.

- On the marketing side, the basic objectives include looking for new local and international markets, and here organizing visits to other countries is a *sine qua non* strategy; access to new input vendors and to new subcontracting relations either among PROFO members or elsewhere.
- In the area of human resources, the emphasis is on training both workers and executives and seeking new ways in which workers can play a more participative role.
- In financing, the purpose is to improve access to funding sources and while cutting financial costs, which could mean more.

Consolidation of each group of businesses further assumes setting certain goals such as strengthening mutual trust bonds, co-operative and complementary actions, for example to develop joint production arrangements or to hire technicians and consultants perhaps not affordable by each company individually. Other kinds of co-operative actions are exchange of information and joint negotiation with major buyers. It is also extremely important to develop contacts and ties with other central and local government agencies, with teaching institutions – particularly universities and technical institutes – as well as with other public and private corporations to pursue new joint programmes. This involvement with the outside environment is of the utmost importance. The basic philosophy behind this policy is to achieve productive change, not just in participating businesses but also among the local public and private institutional framework of which they are part. Competitiveness is not only a matter of internal company change. It also assumes development of effective institutions in a variety of spheres, e.g. education, technology, finance, legal, and infrastructure, among others. These institutions also contribute to the stronger social and productive fabric that makes a truly competitive system.

Finally, it is hoped that as the PROFOs develop they will also help to develop the market, enhancing the demand appeal of SMEs *vis-à-vis* their consumers, suppliers, consultants and financing agents. Lack of a powerful enough demand often stems the development of a supply of services and consultants, which in fact perpetuates the vicious circle of small business slackness. As they boost their own demand for collective action locally, they stimulate the growth of supply.

Evaluation findings

This section presents a summary of some key findings highlighted by the formal evaluation of the PROFOs programme in Chile. A methodological description and details of the study not discussed here are found in Universidad de Chile (1997) and Benavente (1998).

The universe studied involved 290 companies from several productive sectors ranging all the way from tourism to the engineering industry. The field survey took approximately three months. The total sample included a control group of similar companies that had not benefited from the programme; this was done to provide statistical control by way of differentials in the variables that might skew results.

Intermediate impact and underlying determining factors

There are two levels to approach assessment of the programme's impact in response to actions taken by a company. The first consists of statistical tables describing the type of innovation made and the importance assigned by each company to PROFO, i.e. by means of a frequency distribution and mean intensity table as well as their related frequency diagrams. Second, through a behavior model that will be explained later in this chapter.

In terms of business management, the interviewees stated that the most significant progress was made in labour organization, in implementing marketing strategies, and in focusing on production. In all cases, the importance attributed to PROFO was statistically significant. However, a comparison with the control groups indicates that the significant differences between both groups of companies lie in: company organization, strategic planning (significant to 90 per cent), and implementation of marketing strategies (significant at a 99 per cent degree of confidence). In other words, there are at least three actions focusing on business organization where the PROFO companies did better than the control group, and according to the answers this would be directly correlated with participation in the programme.

On the matter of process innovations, the most relevant have been the introduction of quality control, automation and production planning. In all cases, the importance attributed to PROFO was statistically significant. However, a comparison with the control group shows no significant differences in the answers. According to the findings, the PROFO companies have brought innovation to their processes, but to an extent statistically indistinguishable from those outside the programme. The same can be said regarding product innovation.

The benefits in the area of human resource management centre on the training of managers, workers and clerical personnel. In all three the PROFO variable was statistically significant, and in managerial staff and worker training the assumption that PROFOs performed better than the control group was not refuted.

Another area where the PROFO appears to have produced significant differences relative to control groups was the improved ability of companies interviewed to access the National Industrial Extension System. In fact, on issues such as 'better access to support facilities,' 'technical co-operation with competitors, universities, NGOs and public institutions,' and improved 'ability to access public funding sourcees', the importance attributable to the programme was statistically significant.

Along with the impact analysis, questions were asked about the key obstacles currently faced by the companies interviewed that hinder a better performance. This was construed to mean unaddressed issues that an eventually redesigned programme should take into account.

According to the answers given, and ranked strictly by order of priority, the 'lack of financing' stands out as the most important item for nearly half the companies interviewed. It is followed by 'a lack of skilled production workers' and 'overdependence on just a few clients,' tied in second place. This shows that although the programme did indeed advance some solutions to market flaws, these still persist, primarily with regard to a shortage of skilled labour as well as in financing, and a poorly diversified customer base.

Finally, the fourth-ranking barrier is 'economic policy'. This reflect a certain concern shown by companies operating in the textile, apparel and related industries about their 'inability to compete with their Southeast Asia counterparts, with exchange appreciation and tariff reduction.'[2] The instrument has fallen short of expectations with regard to these issues.

Concerning the concrete and direct benefits perceived by each company as delivered by the programme, some are 'intangible', such as information on markets, technologies and business opportunities. Under concrete benefits, the number one listed was the higher profits due to sales increase. To achieve this goal, the businessmen said they resorted more to tools conducive to generating information (fairs and visits, improved knowledge of support institutions) than to strictly technological skills.

Two key disadvantages stand out among others mentioned, both for their relevance and order of magnitude: too short a period of actual support and no facility to finance investments in plant and equipment. The role of the manager of the group is highlighted – the third-ranking difficulty mentioned was the inability to find skilled managers. Given the importance of this job, responders were asked to name some qualities required in an 'ideal' manager's profile. The most frequent replies were: managerial skills, initiative and communication skills. On the other hand, 'knowledge of the business' ranked higher than 'experience in production and professional skills', which indicates that companies would rather have 'sales-oriented' than 'technically-oriented' managers.

Finally, on the ideal make-up of the group of companies, the businessmen suggested that engaging suppliers, some of them with expertise in exports, and a subsequent development of the group into a true partnership, would be desirable. In contrast with this view, they felt that the presence of companies of widely different sizes and discrepant goals would be detrimental.

Explanation of the findings

While a company may have attributed its decision to undertake a given action to PROFO, actually a number of factors may have affected the effects reported. Some of these concern the class and extent of services received under the PROFO, others have to do with each company's unique features. In the attempt to answer this question a statistical model was designed to estimate the probability that a given business would adopt a specific action in response to the services received under the programme facilities.[3,4] The findings refer the 17 most important actions stated by companies as resulting from the programme.

First, the replies coming from the different sectors are heterogeneous with regard to some of these actions. For example, the inclusion of textile and apparel manufacturers increases the probability that the programme will have a major impact on actions leading to a 'reorganization of labour' via a definition of job stations and specific roles in the company, and also raises the likelihood that the programme was most relevant in the item training of managerial staff in modern management practices. On the other hand, timber processing and furniture companies increased the probability that the programme is important to improve business relations among the PROFO companies; this was the finding also for companies in the metal foundry sector.

Results suggest that the difficulty in finding skilled managers for the group, though not affecting all actions undertaken, certainly has a heavy impact on some of them. So the higher turnover of managers under the PROFO reduces the probability of the programme having a positive impact in job reorganization, product enhancement, worker training, improving the ability to negotiate with customers, and boosting business relations with other companies in the PROFO. It also lowers the probability that the programme will have a positive impact by increasing technical co-operation with public institutions and private consultants. All of the above underscores the fact that having a steady leadership in the group is a relevant variable, and if the matter is not addressed it may offset any positive impact the programme may have.

The know-how of specific agents running the programme also generates differential effects on certain actions. Thus, the private agent, ASEXMA, was shown to be more expert and/or more effective in helping the programme achieve a stronger impact in promoting modern 'marketing strategies', in improving business relations among PROFO companies, and in boosting technical co-operation among the companies in PROFO. On the other hand, the public intermediary agent, SERCOTEC, appears to be most effective in promoting the adoption of on-the-job safety standards and the training of workers and administrative staff. In short, the private agent had a greater impact on joint and collaborative work among the companies than did the public agent. On the other actions there are no significant differences between the private and the public agents.

On the other hand, concerning plant size, the findings suggest that the greatest impact of the programme is not necessarily felt by the bigger companies. The variable experience generally shows negative coefficients, indicating a certain tendency for the programme to weigh more heavily in action decisions made by younger businesses.

A last paragraph on the variable 'duration': it has been statistically significant in nearly all actions undertaken by the companies. It follows that the longer a company stays in the PROFO, the higher the probability that the programme will have a positive impact on the actions it takes.[5]

Impact on policy goals

To answer the key question of whether the PROFOs have contributed to the competitiveness of SMEs to a sufficient degree so as to trim down structural heterogeneity, the core issue in this evaluation was to show evidence that the above achievements would not have occurred in the absence of the programme. The most accurate way of demonstrating the net impact of the programme is by using a control group for comparison. Thus, the performance of companies that actively participated in PROFOs was compared to the averages of their respective industries. The chief advantage of focusing on relative changes is that one can offset any unique industry-specific or regional bias.

Results show that, on average, the companies interviewed have experienced a statistically significant growth in employment, in real wages paid, and in productivity in absolute terms (respectively, 13%, 10.3% and 8.3%). However, relative to their own industries, the statistically significant growth was accomplished only in employment (11.6%), with no significant results either in productivity or salary growth.[6]

Nevertheless, the above findings may be strongly skewed by different underlying data, such as intermediary agent, sector, plant size and expertise.[7]

In order to pinpoint the effect of each such variable and advance some additional assumptions, a statistical model was developed and will be described in greater detail below.[8]

Factors underlying the differences in job creation

Broadly speaking, findings indicate first of all that there are sizable differences in effects by sector: the rubber and steel sectors create fewer jobs than industry as a whole, while the heavy machinery sector generates more jobs than its respective industry.

On the other hand, the time spent by a company in PROFO seems to be relevant; for each additional year in the programme, the differential annual growth rate of employment increases by six percentage points. The variable heterogeneity is important; so the less similar the businesses are between the group, the greater the job generation. This supports the assumption that big companies are needed to stimulate smaller ones, but negates the idea that having similar businesses is a *sine qua non* for co-operative association.

For the other variables, the plus sign next to production experience just shows that older companies have created more jobs than the newer ones; the variable manager, the turn, suggests that problems were experienced in job generation by PROFOs companies that had a high manager turnover. Strong rivalry between PROFO companies seems to be a positive impact variable as far as employment is concerned; while companies with several plants and PROFOs with too many participating companies show negative coefficients in terms of employment. Finally, the variable sales reveals that job creation was negatively correlated to size.

Factors underlying the differences in salary growth

Results again suggest different responses per sector; however, the degree of diversity here is smaller than in the case of employment rate.

Another explanatory variable is experience, which is shown to have a positive correlation to the relative growth of salaries, though its absolute coefficient is quite low. The variables 'duration' and 'manager' are significant only to an 80 per cent level of confidence, but they reveal that PROFOs where manager turnover rates have been high show relative salary growth rates 12 percentage points lower than those that have the same manager throughout. The variable duration, on the other hand, indicates that for each additional year in the programme salaries grow by an additional 5 per cent relatively speaking.

The variable heterogeneity indicates that the more heterogeneous the group, i.e. if the variation coefficient of company size grows by one unit, the growth rate of salaries increases by 33 per cent, and this result is significant for all levels of confidence. The variables 'plants' and 'sales' suggest that companies with a single plant and smaller businesses have achieved the highest relative wage growth rates. Finally, the variable 'competition' or 'rivalry' indicates that the lower this factor the higher the growth, while the variable number suggests that the more companies involved the worse will be the performance of the programme. However, the statistical significance of the two latter variables is low.

Factors underlying the differences in productivity growth

This is the variable where one finds the widest diversity of sectoral responses, with significant variations between the rubber sector at one extreme and the wine industry on the other.

The variable experience indicates that the newer companies have benefited the most, showing positive relative growth rates in productivity. The variable agent suggests that PROFOs managed by ASEXMA have a 31 per cent higher relative growth rate in productivity than those managed by SERCOTEC. The variable heterogeneity shows a positive relative growth rate, supporting the idea that variance in company size within a PROFO is an advantage.

This section is a summary of the cost–benefit analysis performed on the programme. The cost–benefit analysis consisted in accounting for both programme-generated income due to increased sales reported by the participating companies and costs such as manpower, raw materials, programme administration costs, as well as the investments made by public agents and the businessmen alike.

To compute the benefits, account was taken of the fact that the PROFOs in general have performed better than their respective industries only in terms of relative growth of employment, while the effect was nil concerning productivity. Obviously, the upward effect on employment should have resulted in a relative growth of sales. If that is so, the main benefit from this programme lies in the higher sales it has generated, which in turn materializes into a rise of the same magnitude in 'consumer surpluses'. The key assumption of this analysis is that the companies studied are price 'takers' and therefore face a perfectly elastic demand curve.[9]

The findings indicate that the mean annual growth rate of sales is 11 per cent (the same as employment growth). This shows that the growth of these companies has been greater than that of their industries but also that the source of this growth was due rather to the cumulative effect of several factors than to improvements in productivity.[10]

As a whole, the 15 PROFOs analysed report an additional income (higher consumer surplus) of over US$10 000 000 a year. The drivers of this increase are scattered and behave in a strongly heterogeneous way, although in general the ASEXMA PROFOs account for 60 per cent of the gross income and the remaining 40 per cent were brought in by SERCOTEC. This should be no surprise, however, because while the sales growth rates of both groups is similar, the 'average size' of the ASEXMA PROFOs is greater than that of SERCOTEC companies, showing that the private agent specialized in bigger companies.

The sectoral income breakdown indicates a heavy concentration in two sectors: machinery (60%) and wines (29%), with mean per company annual income increases of a little over US$100 000 in both cases. The timber PROFOs have made only a marginal contribution (9%, with per company income increases of US$20 000), while the contribution of textiles is nil.

The production and sales growth of PROFOs companies relative to their respective industries surely involves resources that must be accurately assessed in terms of their opportunity cost. Thus, two such resources seem to be relevant – manpower and semiprocessed inputs.

To better evaluate additional manpower costs, the annual 'additional' employment generated by the PROFOs companies was computed, and this figure was valued at current labour market prices.

On the other hand, to avoid underestimating the programme costs, one should bear in mind that a growth in sales also implies more intensive use of raw materials and inputs. Furthermore, the costs evaluated must include those associated with the programme's administration and operation.

To compute the profitability ratio, the corporate surplus (income) and direct costs (operating costs) were first discounted at an annual 10 per cent rate at the start of the programme, assuming for 'duration of the project' the full three years of operation of each PROFO.

For each dollar invested by a company in the programme, 2.4 additional dollars were generated. The profitable PROFOs appear to be Wines 1, Wines 2,

Software, Cindex, Unemas, Timber and Furniture, Unifama and Machine Engineering. However, a key element in these results has been the remarkable sales increase of PROFO 'Wines 1', which accounts for 40 per cent of the surplus. On the other hand, if one removes it from the estimation, the benefit–cost ratio would fall to 1.4 but the programme would still be profitable.[11]

It is also useful to explore the magnitude of the fiscal effort in terms of funds committed by the government to finance the programme. As a counterpart, treasury will also boost its revenues thanks to the programme and the resulting collection of value-added taxes and taxes on earnings.

Given the above, just considering the fiscal costs and the higher revenues arising from the VAT collected on additional sales, from the fiscal standpoint the programme generated a 3.2 cost–benefit profitability ratio (from the 15 PROFOs analysed alone). In other words, for each peso the government put into the programme, it would ultimately collect three pesos due to a rise in income. In short, the programme does not seem to entail a heavy burden to treasury (a little over US$600 000 per year), which is more than offset by the increased tax collection.

Summary and conclusions

Evaluation of the development programmes (PROFOs) shows that this instrument can have a positive impact on participating companies. In response to the assistance granted, some such companies have carried out substantial changes in some production and corporate practices, and this has reflected in productivity and wage improvements.

Results point to the conclusion that their main achievements have focused primarily on three areas:

- improved corporate organization and management (adoption of planning practices, better specification of roles and functions, focus on production to accomplish economies of scale, and adoption of modern marketing strategies)
- improved human resource development (more access to managerial and worker training)
- improved access to the National Extension System (mainly technological institutions, advisers, consultants, and even development funds like the Technological Fund, Fontec, and the Technical Assistance Funds, FAT).

However, the scope of programme's benefits is more modest in terms of fostering significant improvements and stimulating development and enhancement of manufacturing processes and/or products (except for changes in layout or in automation).

In other areas affected by the programme it was found that companies benefit most if they take a more intensive part in it. From this standpoint, a reduction of the entry money withholding and an extension of the programme duration by at least one year might increase the number of companies recording a favourable impact. However, merely extending the term is not enough – intensity is also important. So it would be advisable to bring down the management turnover rates because it is detrimental both to the potential benefits and to economic and policy outcome of the programme. Alternatively, the learning rate should be speeded up via a more transparent managerial role on the part of the intermediary agent and/or managers.

The type of intermediary agent also makes a difference, and it is clear that a private agent built around talents from corporate associations in general turns out better economic returns and increases the likelihood of expanding the potential for technical and business co-operation among participating companies.

The programme has shown that it is selective *ex post* given the sectoral differences in relation to the kind of actions performed by the distinct sectors and the results observed in productivity. In this regard, the heavy machinery PROFOs have been more receptive considering the number of actions implemented under the programme and a better productivity record. This sector is also proof that productivity growth does not necessarily go hand in hand with job cuts. Smaller and newer companies have also evidenced greater receptiveness and stronger benefits.

As to how the group should be structured, there are two important aspects to be considered. First, the need to have some measure of heterogeneity among the companies (perhaps one or two bigger companies – and especially exporters – to act as role models for the others), and second, companies with their own markets and little overlapping.

The programme has nevertheless worked well enough to correct such market pitfalls as access to financing for investment and innovation on an equal footing with large corporations, and access to skilled manpower. All companies pointed to these factors as their main obstacles. The need to supplement the programme with other equity investment and innovation financing facilities might be looked into. On the other hand, there is a need to assess the basic skills of the working force. Many training efforts fail because of 'the workers' inability to retain the information imparted' and for lack of a clear incentive programme to motivate workers for on-the-job training. Many of the businessmen stated that 'the workers do not want to learn', but the fact is that corporate management makes no commitment to raise wages, and at the same time requires training to be done after working hours.

An important finding is that consolidating the programme in-house depends heavily on the capabilities of the intermediary agent and the manager. Most of the managers interviewed were more oriented to management than to production and, among other things, it was noted that consulting services performed under the programme were strongly skewed toward the former.

Theory suggests that it is harder to build co-operation between companies around 'hard' technologies than around the so-called 'soft' technologies. For the latter to work, the group must have non-competing and technologically similar businesses, but even then the labour division issue and the 'free rider' problem will come up. It might be better in technological environments to direct the facility to individual plant level, not requiring any kind of partnership effort.

Finally, it should not be forgotten that the demands of group work considerably increase co-ordination costs and the time needed to reach consensus. To quote a PROFO business owner, 'we are asked to work as a group, but during the first year we got to know each other and overcame our mutual distrust; in the second year we started to work together, and finally in the third year the programme is over.'

Last, but not least, the cost–benefit analysis suggests that the programme is 'socially profitable' an does not involve massive government budget spending, which is more than offset by the increased revenues thanks to the taxes generated by the companies involved.

The experience with PROFOs in Chile has been relatively successful. It has created an institutional framework to tape the benefits of collaborative efforts. It is particularly useful in situations where production scales and expertise are not enough to reach the minimum threshold for the companies involved to achieve sustainable development.

The Chilean experience suggests that not all partnerships have been successful. Success has hinged on factors such as the design of the facility, and substantially on the unique features of each association formed.

These development projects are a great step forward in Chilean industrial policy by adding market considerations to the allocation of public funds. The role played by the intermediary agents in the whole process is crucial and constitutes a pioneering experience for South American countries.

Other experiences with intermediary agents, such as the FAT, suggest that such institutions have narrowed the information gap between know-how providers and demanders, helping to focus government support and to promote the dissemination of facilities to assist SMEs. This in turn has allowed third-tier institutions to concentrate on their supervisory role as well as in setting up an institutional framework to help those trapped by their size and isolation.

References and further reading

Benavente, José Miguel 'La Experiencia de los PROFOs en Chile'. Informe Corporación de Fomento (CORFO). Octubre 1998.

Davis, Steven, John Haltiwanger, and Scott Schuh. 'Small Business and Job Creation: Dissecting the Myth and Reassessing the Facts', *Working Paper 4492* National Bureau of Economic Research, October 1993.

Flamm, Kenneth. 'The Changing Pattern of Industrial Robot Use', in Richard M. Cyert and David Cl. Mowery (eds.) *The Impact of Technological Change on Employment and Economic Growth.* Cambridge, MA: Ballinger Publishing Co., 1988.

Fuentes, Rodrigo. 'Openness and Economic Efficiency: Evidence from the Chilean Manufacturing Industry'. *Estudios de Economia*, Vol. 22, No. 2 (1995).

Harrison, Bennett. 'Industrial Districts: Old Wine in New Bottles' *Regional Studies*, Vol. 25 (5) 1991.

Houthakker, H.S. and Lester D. Taylor. *Consumer Demand in the United States: Analysis and Profections.* Cambridge, MA: Harvard University Press, 1970.

Kelley, Maryellen R. and Harvey Brooks. *The State of Computerised Automation in U.S. Manufacturing.* Cambridge, MA: Centre for Business and Government, Harvard University, 1988.

Krugman, Paul. *Geography and Trade.* Cambridge, MA: Cambridge University Press, 1991.

Lazonick, William, *Business Organisation and the Myth of the Market Economy.* Cambridge, MA: Cambridge University Press, 1991.

Mansfield, Edwin. 'Technological Change in Robotics: Japan and the United States', *Managerial and Decision Economics*, Spring 1989.

Miller, Edward M. 'Size of Firm and Size of Plant', *Southern Economic Journal*, April 1978.

Montero, Cecilia. Metodología de Evaluación de Programas de Fomento (PROFO), mimeo, CIEPLAN, 1995.

Nootebaum, Bart. 'Firm Size Effects on Transaction Costs', *Small Business Economics*, May 1993.

Oldsman, Eric (1993). Do Manufacturing Extension Programs Matter?, in *Evaluating Industrial Modernisation. Methods and Results in the Evaluation of Industrial Modernisation Programs.* Edited by Shapira, Philip and Youtie, Jan. Georgia Institute of Technology, January 1994.

Scherer, F.M. 'Industrial Structure, Scale Economies, and Worker Alienation,' *Essays on Industrial Organisation in Honor of Joe S. Bain.* Cambridge, MA: Ballinger Publishing Co., 1976.

Schmidt, Christoph M. and Klaus F. Zimmermann. 'Work Characteristics, Firm Size and Wagers', *The Review of Economics and Statistics* 73 (4), November 1991.

Shapira, Philip, Jan Youtie and J. David Roessner. *Evaluating Industrial Modernisation Programs: Issues, Practices and Strategies.* Georgia Institute of Technology, January 1994.

Rephann, Terrance and Philip Shapira. 'Survey of Technology Use in West Virginia Manufacturing', *Report to the West Virginia University Industrial Extension Service*, December 1, 1993.

Universidad de Chile. Departamento de Economía. Informe Final. Impacto del Instrumento PROFO en la Pequeña y Mediana Empresa. Abril, 1997.

Notes

1. This also was the conclusion of studies by University of Chile (1997) and SERCOTEC (Technical Corporation Service) the main organisation supporting small enterprises.
2. As indicated by the interviews made.
3. In fact, the model intends to explain the probability that a given company undertake an action that the responder attributes to the programme. A company may take an action but not attribute it to the services offered by the PROFOs.
4. Model and variable specifications are in Universidad de Chile (1997) and Benavente (1998).
5. An exercise was run to determine how long it would take for the probability that a company take any of the pre-defined actions to increase by 50 per cent. The concept of 'mean dose' was used (see Universidad de Chile 1997).
6. See Table 5.2 in the Appendix.
7. A detailed breakdown by criterion employed is found in Universidad de Chile (1997) between Tables 19 and 31.
8. Again, see Universidad de Chile (1997) and Benavente (1998) for a detailed analysis of the methodology adopted.
9. This implies that as the sales of these companies increase, they will be able to place their production 'at the same prices' and without crowding out the competition. For this reason the benefits of 'fund disbursements' were not considered. Another key assumption is the lack of distortions in the markets where the PROFOs companies operate, which will allow them to work with private prices. To compute income increase due to programme-driven sales, the author had to overcome the problem that, with rare exceptions, there was never full quantitative information for the totality of companies in each PROFO. Therefore, only those PROFOs with a certain number of significant answers were included (over 50 per cent quantitative answers per PROFO); non-responding companies were assigned the 'average' of the responding companies' answers.
10. See Table 5.3 in the Appendix.
11. It must be borne in mind that certain factors may induce either an overestimation and underestimation of profitability. Among the former are disconsideration of the indirect programme costs (for example, the percentage of administrative resources devoted by CORFO to programme monitoring, additional investments, etc). The latter include consideration of 'static' benefits only; this means assuming that the PROFOs companies perform better than industry overall only during their three years in the programme, with no consideration for the learning dynamics. For this reason, these findings must be interpreted as merely 'indicative' of positive profitability.
12. Four digit differential to the industry.

Appendix

Table 5.1 presents the results according to the frequency of affirmative answers to each question (paired successful outcomes for purposes of the related inferences). The second column shows the percentage of a given affirmative result over the total number of answers to a given question; the third column presents the percentage of companies that attributed the success of the previous question substantially to the PROFO; the last column displays the answer of the control group companies. Finally, the asterisks in column one mean that there is a statistically significant difference between the actions of PROFO companies and the control group. (Significance at 1% ***, at 5% ** and at 10% *).

Table 5.1 Actions taken by the companies

	Actions taken by PROFO companies	Importance attributed to PROFO	Actions taken by control group companies
Business management			
(adopted or changed)			
The organization*	64%	25%	43%
Strategic planning*	64%	32%	43%
Marketing strategies***	69%	41%	36%
Defined roles for job stations	79%	30%	79%
Focused on production	77%	22%	93%
Process innovation			
Computer automation*	33%	16%	18%
Quality control	47%	22%	43%
Layout*	39%	13%	21%
Job safety standards	45%	17%	71%
Information collection	34%	34%	23%
Production innovation			
Improved existing products	62%	25%	69%
Management of human resources			
Worker training***	38%	28%	8%
Management training***	62%	48%	15%
Increased worker participation in production and quality improvement	40%	15%	67%
Outside relations			
Scope of Business			
Improve skills in customer negotiations	63%	30%	50%
Increased national coverage*	45%	21%	23%
Improved trade relations with other businessmen of the same PROFO	65%	53%	–
Improved ability to access public support facilities***	56%	41%	8%
Outside relations			
Technological Scope			
Public Institutions***	32%	23%	0%
Customers	47%	12%	31%
Suppliers	30%	5%	38%
Businessmen in the PROFO***	41%	27%	0%
Universities***	17%	9%	0%
NGOs***	14%	8%	0%
Outside relations			
Financial Affairs			
Project development skills	47%	26%	50%
Ability to access institutional funding***	50%	32%	17%

Table 5.2 presents the overall results for the total sample of companies with quantitative data. The three first columns display raw data, i.e. not considering industrial sector, while the last three show relative changes *vis-à-vis* the industry. The penultimate row highlights the statistical significance of those changes.

Table 5.2   **PROFOs – basic statistics (mean annual growth rates)**

	Employment	Manpower productivity	Salaries	Employment differential	Salary differential	Productivity differential
Mean	0.131	0.083	0.103	0.116	0.023	0.017
Standard deviation	0.259	0.428	0.212	0.167	0.230	0.467
Confidence	95%	95%	95%	95%	60%	28%
Observations	102	102	75	102	75	102

Table 5.3   **Annual income increments produced by the programme**

PROFO name	Agent	Annual growth in sales[12]	Annual income (1994 US$)	%
Metalec1	Sercotec	0.34	1 211 484	11.2
Metalfuturo	Sercotec	0.16	301 467	2.8
La Ligua	Sercotec	0.01	15 009	0.1
Aemet	Sercotec	0.23	553 042	5.1
Unemas	Sercotec	0.06	159 850	1.5
Textiles VIII	ASEXMA	−0.02	−110 204	−1.0
Heavy machinery	Sercotec	0.17	1 589 502	14.8
Timer & Furniture	Sercotec	0.13	469 606	4.3
Arts & Crafts	Sercotec	−0.05	−5467	−0.0
Unifama	Sercotec	0.15	348 166	3.2
Wines 1	ASEXMA	0.14	2 074 830	19.2
Wines 2	ASEXMA	0.05	1 127 962	10.4
Software	ASEXMA	0.33	2 784 225	25.8
Cindex	ASEXMA	0.03	367 114	3.4
Rubber Mix	Sercotec	−0.03	−85 208	−0.8
Total		0.11	10 801 381	100.0

6. High-impact, Cost-effective Business Development Services Through NGOs

KENNETH E. LOUCKS

Introduction

THE PURPOSE OF THIS project is to carry out an analysis of approaches to the design and delivery of various business development services (BDS) as related to outcomes of cost effectiveness, sustainability and impact. The research objective is to generate principles of good practice that can guide future activity in the design, implementation and evaluation of BDS activities. It is intended that the results will inform the development community:[1]

- about the experience of five NGOs in the provision of business development services (BDS)[2] in selected projects
- about the advantages and difficulties associated with alternative types of business development services and methods for delivering the services
- on lessons learned on the design of new business development services
- on experience relevant to the debate over minimalist credit vs. business development services.

The research objective is to generate principles of good practice that can guide future activity in the design, implementation and evaluation of BDS activities. As the purpose involves a retrospective review of complex operational links in diverse projects and settings, the case study was chosen as the most appropriate methodology.

Previous work

Recent evidence suggests that minimalist credit – which has come to be the primary instrument of small producer support in Third World development – tends to have little impact in terms of enhancing agricultural and manufacturing capacity and productivity. Small enterprises generally need improved access to markets and to a range of productive resources in addition to finance in order to break out of the saturated, low-value markets in which they are often trapped.

These case studies on BDS are undertaken in a context of previous work on the characteristics of good projects and performance indicators. There is a solid body of advice on policy for NGOs, based on lessons learned, but not a great deal is available on operational or field-level benchmarks regarding the actual design and delivery of BDS.

McVay derived a series of principles of project design from research of BDS practitioner field activity. Most of these are reinforced in Gibson's policy guidelines for donor interventions:

- services should be demand driven, not supply driven
- an accurate need assessment is an important first step; this usually requires involvement of potential clients
- a focus on particular sectors or services helps develop services that are more relevant than services designed for a general audience

- institutions should specialize in providing a few key services, and create link-ages with other institutions that can provide complementary services
- service delivery should be business-like; fees for services is an important part of this
- programmes need to reach scale, which is often achieved through 'leveraged' interventions (one-off interventions that affect large numbers of entrepreneurs, such as policy changes, introducing new technology, etc.)
- programmes need to develop sustainable service delivery mechanisms, usually through NGOs or the private sector.

The Inter-American Development Bank and others have called for research in the field to establish a catalogue of business development services, for further analysis of 'the relationship between the demand and supply of BDS services, and defining reasonable expectations for the sustainability of BDS programmes'. They are also working on the development of an analytical framework for BDS performance. A review of this literature points to some consensus on several key issues.

- The broad performance indicators that will be most useful in defining the effectiveness of development work focused on the delivery of business development services are impact, cost effectiveness, scale and cost recovery/financial sustainability.
- A research agenda needs to be carried out that will establish some standard-ization of BDS outputs and benchmarks for performance in the areas of scale, impact and cost effectiveness.[3]
- More case study research is needed, and analysis of case study research should lead to development of a series of best practices to be applied by practitioners at the field level.

Other issues arising from previous work include:

- does the provision of BDS have the potential to cover costs and to become sustainable?
- the inherent tension between the development assistance role of BDS and the aspiration to become commercially viable. Which contexts lend themselves to the predominance of one approach over the other, and what mix of the two approaches can still manage cost-effectiveness?
- premises for service planning and implementation
- finally, although recognizing the need for the establishment of benchmark criteria for 'best practice', maybe not enough has been said of the folly of supposing that a universal or standardized approach is a feasible or even a desirable objective. The context specificity of the different approaches and experiences can be distilled for principles, but can there ever be measurement tools that can yield equally comparable results across the variety of sectors and locations of these services? There needs to be debate and discussion in this forum and in the wider literature on the very premiss behind the search for 'best practice' and a close look at the more realistic goal of investigating and delineating *good* practice in its myriad forms and contexts.

The case study research design

As the purpose of the research involves a retrospective review of complex oper-ational links in diverse projects and settings, the case study was chosen as the most appropriate methodology. The three services that have been targeted for study are:

- business planning and managerial assistance
- technology development and adaptation
- market assessment and development of market linkages.

The cases

Each of the NGOs provided an institutional profile and a brief description of 82 projects proposed for inclusion in the study. The considerations for screening the proposed projects down to a set of 10 for case studies included the following:

- geographic location
- sub-sector representation
- rural/urban setting
- gender representation
- effectiveness performance – cost, impact, sustainability
- breadth and depth of available project documentation.

Table 6.1   The Case Study Projects

Enterprise Works Worldwide	Zimbabwe Oil Press Project Ltd., Zimbabwe Coffee Producers, El Salvador
Intermediate Technology Development Group	Light Engineering Workshops, Zimbabwe Food Processing, Bangladesh
Mennonite Economic Development Associates	Joint Venture Marketing Company, Bolivia Cocoa co-operatives, Haiti
Sarvodaya	Ornamental Fish Production, Sri Lanka Pineapple Growers, Sri Lanka
TechnoServe	Irrigated Agricultural Groups, El Salvador Multipurpose Co-operatives, Ghana

The various cases include a mix of BDS services and take place in different production sectors, macro-policy environments, and socioeconomic contexts. The projects also vary in the amount of funding, geographic location, and size. Some of the projects being studied also provide credit or equity capital to allow producers to take advantage of productivity enhancements, and the role of this access in the quality and impact of BDS is also being considered in the ongoing studies. While the focus on the three business development services will remain, the relationship to other services offered could not be ignored, and in particular the relationship of BDS and access to, or the provision of, credit will be an element in some of the cases.

To date, four of the 10 case studies have been initiated and first drafts have been prepared. The entire sample of 10 case studies will be subjected to a second level of analysis by the NGO representatives of the project steering committee, who also represent different specialties and experience backgrounds.[4]

Guide to case study preparation

In general the case studies are to describe and analyse the services, the client interface, and the strategy and operations of the local delivery organization.[5]

The case study researchers will describe:

- the business development service activity
- who was involved in this activity (for example stakeholders, service providers, affiliated organizations) and the level and nature of their involvement in design and delivery
- how it was done, including any innovative aspects of the design and delivery process, tools, techniques, workbooks, checklists, etc.
- the management of the organization and the project: planning, organization, supervision, monitoring and evaluation
- the performance of the project on measurements of cost effectiveness, impact, and sustainability.

The analysis will:

- identify causal relationships (both positive and negative) that can be established between elements of the design and delivery of the business development services and the performance outcomes
- make an assessment of lessons learned from the case study and recommendations on aspects of design and delivery within the context of the project
- derive an overview of BDS principles and practices that might be worthy of emulation.

Descriptions of services and performance indicators

Services

- *Marketing* includes services related to the design/selection, pricing, sale and distribution of products, advertising or promotional activities, and acquiring access to raw materials, inputs, and equipment. Acquiring access or developing distribution linkages to foreign markets and/or suppliers (exporting or importing) is considered a marketing activity.
- *Technology transfer* refers specifically to helping entrepreneurs access and use new inputs, equipment, or production processes, which can increase their efficiency, scale, and returns. Production includes the actual production of agricultural, manufactured, or artisan goods, as well as the rendering of services that involve production, such as bicycle or automobile repair, food preparation, tailoring, shoemaking, etc.
- *Management* refers to the tasks of directing the business, which include financial planning, and record keeping, hiring, training, and firing employees, and long- and short-term business planning.

Performance indicators

- *Impact* refers to positive and negative effects on the economic and social well-being of individuals, households and communities. Impact encompasses the magnitude of the effects as well as the scale (number of people affected). In projects where this is relevant it may also include effects on public health or environmental quality and natural resource base.
- *Cost effectiveness* is a measure of the efficiency of service delivery that compares the project outputs (achievements in terms of activities or the resulting impacts) and the costs. It may vary considerably (positively or negatively) with the funding and geographic scale of the activities.

80

- *Sustainability* has several aspects – the ability to maintain BDS services or levels of impact after the project funding has concluded. The sustainability of service delivery examines the extent to which BDS activities can be continued. This can be achieved in diverse ways such as obtaining full cost recovery from clients for further NGO activities; tapping a continuing source of related income; institutional strengthening of NGOs, or working through co-operatives and other producer or trade associations. The sustainability of impact involves enabling clients to continue their activities without the need of additional project assistance or spinning off of BDS activities into self-sustaining enterprises.

Table 6.2 lists a number of indicators that can be used to assess performance on these criteria. In deriving the list of indicators the project steering committee (one representative of each participating NGO) recognized that some may not apply to all projects and others may need to be modified in certain cases. But they are specific enough to focus on the three key issues of impact, cost effectiveness and sustainability while recognizing that benefits may be derived by the delivery organization and the larger society as well as the clients who are direct recipients of the BDS. The effectiveness of the BDS will be assessed through available project data and may be supplemented by a limited amount of field research. At the level of the individual case study this methodology will permit the identification of cause and effect relationships between effectiveness outcomes and DBS design elements. A secondary analysis of all 10 cases will permit a number of comparative questions to be addressed.

The participating agencies

This project is a collaborative effort between four international and one national SME support organization.[6] The five NGOs whose projects are being reviewed in the ongoing project discussed in this chapter are in the business of generating incomes and economic growth for small producers. The overall goal of their BDS activities is to build more competitive enterprises through innovative and value-adding productivity and marketing improvements.

Enterprise Works Worldwide (formerly Appropriate Technology International) has programmes in Africa, Asia and Latin America. Services provided include: sub-sector analysis and business planning; technology adaptation and commercialization; improved access to raw materials; product and service development; market assessment and marketing activities; business and technical assistance and training; common service facilities; and institutional capacity building.

The *Intermediate Technology Development Group* (ITDG) has programmes of support to small producers in Africa, Asia and Latin America. Most of the projects supported and implemented by Intermediate Technology are intended to demonstrate or prove a technological innovation or an alternative approach to improving the performance of small-scale producers. They therefore have a large element of research or experimentation in them, and they have been undertaken as much with a view to learning lessons as to delivering support services.

Mennonite Enterprise Development Assistance (MEDA) is an association of Christians in business and the professions, committed to applying biblical teachings in the marketplace. MEDA aims to work with the poorest of the

Table 6.2 Examples of indicators used by participating NGOs in BDS project monitoring for evaluation

	Cost effectiveness*	Impact‡	Sustainability
Local delivery organization	Absolute costs and trends per: ● client ● business start ● course offered ● consultant hour Costs relative to client fees, and affordability Gross/net profit – margins surplus Case load per professional staff Management staff ratios Overhead to salary ratios	● Demographic profile of clients reached ● No. of clients served ● Total clients as percentage of target group ● Quantity of BDS services/projects delivered ● No. of professional staff hired and trained ● New delivery partnerships ● New BDS 'products' ● MIS in place and used for planning and cost control – trends	Growth in: ● no. of clients ● unsolicited non-nominated clients ● fee revenue ● endowments, grants ● profitability/surplus ● local training, research personnel ● new delivery partnerships ● regular meetings of key stakeholders ●planning for new and improved services Reductions in: ● costs per client ● subsidy (sustaining grant)
Client	Increases in: ● operating margins ● value added ● assets ● local sourcing Decreases in: input costs/quantities	Revenues (cost savings) from: ● new technology adopted ● management practices implemented ● new product lines ● new distribution channels New sources of financing accessed	Trends in: ● debt/equity ratio ● net income ● new product revenues ● gross revenues ● percentage of household income from the business
Society/economy of project locale	Low domestic subsidy to: ● delivery organization ● clients Relative cost per: ● job created ● business created	Increase in (net) domestic ● goods production ● service supply ● jobs – achieve target group objectives – breakout full time, part time, paid, unpaid, male, female ● investment ● new programme competitors emerge	● Foreign exchange earned/saved ● Reduction in foreign workers/ownership ● Increases in target group participation numbers/rate ● Increases in tax revenues ● Increases in domestic value added ● Replication by government ● Expansion to other parts of the country

*The components of costs should be identified. In particular whether the costs are on a cash flow or accrual basis, whether local delivery organization costs include relevant overheads of the local, national and international affiliates, whether sustaining grants and or subsidies from any sources are included and their amounts in any case.
‡Qualitative information can be cited where non-quantitative objectives such as for gender equity, environmental sustainability and indigenous capacity, are explicit goals of the project.

economically active, and targets women. It works in Latin America, the Caribbean, Africa and Asia where it develops pilot projects and programmes that establish viable businesses through the provision of credit, business training and interventions addressing production and marketing barriers.

TechnoServe works in Africa, Latin America and Poland, with programmes to create and strengthen micro-, small and medium-scale businesses. Services include sub-sector analysis, agri-business planning, private sector market linkages, institutional capacity building, and commercialization of smallholder agriculture. TechnoServe uses six core indicators to measure the impact of its projects: community investment, outreach, jobs, income, sustainability, and cost effectiveness.

Sarvodaya Economic Enterprise Development Services (SEEDS) is the economic development division of Sarvodaya Shramadana Movement, a voluntary NGO which implements two broad 'empowerment programmes'. One deals with spiritual, moral, cultural and political empowerment, and the other covers social, economic and technological empowerment. The economic empowerment programme is implemented through three specialist units: the Rural Enterprises Programme (REP), the Management Training Institute (MTI), and the Rural Economic Development Services (REDS) – the focus of the case studies.

The initial cases

Zimbabwe Light Engineering Workshops

Using a sub-sector approach, Intermediate Technology has worked with small-scale manufacturers on the development, production, and maintenance of the 'tools of production' (capital goods) for a wide range of small-scale productive activities. This has included work with rural blacksmiths, welding shops and small machine shops. The project has introduced grinding mills, ice making machines and other products to be marketed to people who will use them to generate business income. A recent service innovation, the subject of this case study, was the creation of a cost-recovering tool-hire service as a focus – and a magnet to draw in active artisans – for other BDS such as product and skills development. This commercial enterprise is achieving a significant scale of impact through its focus on strategically placed engineering workshops.

Zimbabwe Oil Press Project Ltd.. The project is designed by Enterprise Works Worldwide to: help small-scale oilseed growers and other micro-entrepreneurs capture the value added through local processing of oilseeds by the use of ram presses; increase rural consumers' access to low-cost edible oil; and produce seedcake for animal feed. The Zimbabwe Oil Press Project Ltd. (ZOPP) was created in 1996 as a commercial entity that serves as a broker between press manufacturers and distributors, acts as a wholesaler of presses and is currently seeking to establish a mass manufacturing facility that would export low-cost presses to other African countries. Each press sold is the basis of a small local business that presses oil for local producers.

Ornamental Fish Production Promotion. The Rural Enterprise Development Section (REDS) of Sarvodaya identified the production of ornamental fish as an opportunity appropriate for low-income people and undertook to promote the industry through its network of community organizations. The objective of the ornamental fish production project was to provide a higher margin alternative to traditional agriculture by introducing an environmentally friendly, economically viable product to supplement farm incomes or replace the traditional crop farming. For this project the services of REDS included identification of the opportunity, preparation of a prototype feasibility study, recruitment of potential farmers, organization of technical training 'fish clinics', networking of producers with wholesalers, follow-up extension services and organization of producers into information sharing clusters. From the outset the project was treated as a one-time, marginal cost activity with only a nominal sum charged to the trainees.

ASOMEX (Export and Marketing Services Company). MEDA spearheaded the cultivation of a new crop of edible beans in Bolivia among smallholder, colonizer farmers (settlers). The beams allowed farmers nearly to double their incomes. MEDA led in opening the first export markets for Bolivian beans to Brazil and this was followed by the formation of a national association of bean producers (ASOPROF). ASOPROF and MEDA invested in a commercial marketing company called ASOMEX with a mandate to process export orders for ASOPROF and to seek markets for other products. ASOMEX offers competitive marketing and export services of three types: Export processing services (documentation; logistics, transportation and financial arrangements with the buyer) for ASOPROF; brokering, through buying from producers and selling for export; commission services, market research and contact development to bring buyers and sellers together.

Some interim findings and conclusions

Mission and markets

The participating NGOs tend to target the people at the poverty end of the income spectrum with a mission that is not based solely on economic values. All strive to achieve equitable involvement of women. For those whose purpose is social empowerment, the need for cost recovery and sustainable enterprises is more a constraint than an objective.

- 'Over 90 per cent of clients are poorest of the poor, annual income less than US$3000' (Sarvodaya).
- MEDA aims to work with the poorest of the economically active, and targets women.
- 'ITDG enables poor people in the South to develop and use skills and technologies which give them more control over their lives and which contribute to the sustainable development of their communities.'
- TechnoServe focuses 'on the productive poor – those willing to make financial and sweat equity investments in commercial activities'.
- Enterprise Works Worldwide's mission is 'to alleviate poverty through business development programmes that enable small-scale producers of agricultural and other commodities to build more competitive enterprises'.

An issue, given that target groups are of modest means, is the degree to which cost recovery and the standard for recovery is deemed appropriate. The range in the sample is from those who seek a contribution to direct costs (Sarvodaya and ITDG) through those who seek recovery of direct costs and a contribution to overheads (TechnoServe and Enterprise Works Worldwide) to those who seek recovery of direct costs, overheads and a profitable enterprise.

Target sectors

Although quite diverse, all participating NGOs are engaged primarily with the small-scale sector.

- Enterprise Works Worldwide emphasizes small-scale producers, primarily but not exclusively, of agricultural products.
- The majority of ITDG's market is enterprises employing fewer than five people in seven sectors: food production, agri-processing, manufacturing, transport, mining, building materials and shelter, and energy.
- The enterprises assisted by Sarvodaya are self-employment activities, with most being in non-farm activities (due to the non-violent philosophy of the NGO, those businesses involved in the killing of animals are excluded).
- TechnoServe works primarily with agricultural firms in the five to 100+ employee range in both productive and trading sectors as well as with linkage and service providers.
- MEDA's direct investment and technical assistance approach is entrepreneurially oriented to opportunities, but practice has tended to be in agriculture products, particularly businesses that service the producers.

An issue with such a diverse group of industries is the accumulation of expertise in the distinct competencies required for the success of each sub-sector while remaining cost effective relative to the scale of the beneficiary. The cases studied include instances where the ability of project managers to design and implement business services was handicapped by inadequate knowledge or experience of the target sector.

Monitoring and managing effectiveness

In recent years participating agencies show evidence of increasing work to design and implement performance measures as evaluation tools and as part of the management information system for planning and control.[7] They range from a highly commercial and financial set of measures suited to MEDA's direct investment in joint venture businesses to Sarvodaya's approach to monitoring the progress of village societies through five stages of 'graduation'. TechnoServe has 10 years of experience with a proprietary system of measuring and analysing cost effectiveness and the overall impact of their business development activities. The principal use of the effectiveness measures is still for accountability purposes to stakeholders, particularly donors and other funders. However, there is evidence of the information being used for managerial decision-making and strategic planning purposes.

- MEDA's country managers produce monthly and quarterly financial reports, including full financial data on each partner. In addition, mid-year and annual reports and analyses of impact and performance to date are carried out. This information is used to make go/no go investment decisions about the progression of undertakings through the project, the programme, and the business stages of MEDA's approach to the establishment of sustainable businesses.
- Enterprise Works Worldwide uses data collected on a comprehensive set of indicators for strategic planning purposes as well as project management decisions, particularly in costing and pricing of services for improved cost recovery. Projects identified as cost effective are being rapidly replicated in additional locations, thus increasing outreach impact. Sustainability is being built by emphasizing cost recovery and scaling up successful activities into for-profit operations in which Enterprise Works Worldwide retains an equity position. Enterprise Works Worldwide utilizes a similar approach with its

partner organizations to improve their impact and cost recovery so that the BDS offered by them remains sustainable. Enterprise Works Worldwide is rapidly expanding its outreach and impact by increasing its focus on a limited number of programme areas for specialization.

The business of business development services

MEDA's approach to international development work is the establishment of sustainable businesses through a three-stage process of phased investment. A concept paper based on 'reasonable' levels of research launches the project stage. This stage is time-limited and financed by MEDA's core budget, a pool of member contributions and financing through CIDA's NGO Division. The programme stage is the development of a plan of operations, which includes a management plan and a proposal for securing the financing needed. At this stage, subsidies should decline as the project shows its ability to recover costs, and if they do not the programme is terminated. During the business stage the ability to manage operations and govern the company should be clear and profit should be evident. The need for a subsidy is replaced by the businesses repaying their loans, paying for BDS and returning a profit to MEDA.

- ITDG creatively uses market mechanisms for the delivery of project services and dissemination of the benefits that they generate. For instance, in the Zimbabwe Light Engineering Workshops project they demonstrate the use of a profitable tool-hire service as a focus and a magnet to draw in active artisans for other BDS such as product and skills development.
- Sarvodaya extends its outreach and services through a network of over 2150 village organizations. Sarvodaya provided technical assistance for the creation and development of these organizations, but they are now independent institutions owned and managed by the villagers. The monthly meetings of these village organizations offer an inexpensive means for Sarvodaya's BDS divisions to announce and launch new programmes as well as a venue for monitoring the progress of clients. Sarvodaya is able to test the market quickly and scale up successful pilot projects.
- Enterprise Works Worldwide has developed a comprehensive set of performance indicators to supplement its process of conducting mid-term and final evaluations of all major projects. Key project characteristics and impact information are compiled in a computerized database for easy retrieval and analysis. An annual report is prepared, analysing the information by project, geographic region, substantive programme area, and the organizational portfolio. It also synthesizes the principal programmatic lessons learned. The system tracks programme inputs and activities as well as impact project budgets and expenditures, donor and project partner involvement, expected dates and completion dates for baseline data studies and evaluations and known replications elsewhere. Enterprise Works Worldwide makes extensive use of the information in strategic and operational planning as well as reporting to stakeholders.

The transition to a commercial entity[8]

The Enterprise Works Worldwide (ZOPP), ITDG Light Engineering and MEDA/ASOMEX cases address the issue of development projects transitioning to separate, self-sustaining businesses. REDS did not have total cost recovery as a goal but has reached a point where the cost of supporting the programme is reduced to levels acceptable to Sarvodaya. None of the projects has attained self-sufficiency as yet, but the ITDG and Enterprise Works Worldwide projects at least cover direct costs and make a contribution to overheads. ASOMEX is marginally profitable. The gestation period for these self-sustaining business development services enterprises has been long and not without missteps.

Project identification

The impetus for the projects was different in each case. The Light Engineering Workshop Project emerged as a result of a study commissioned by IT Zimbabwe in 1991. This was followed by a research project to gain further understanding of the sector. The ZOPP project was initiated as a pilot activity in Zimbabwe by an NGO familiar with the previous work done by Enterprise Works Worldwide in Tanzania. This later evolved into a larger joint effort of WUSC Enterprise Works Worldwide and other development organizations. Staff that attended a government briefing session identified the Sarvodaya project. Upon hearing of unfilled demand for ornamental fish, staff undertook a study of the industry and generated prototype feasibility studies to determine viability for their clients. In all cases the planning attempts to be market driven involved more of a sector study than a market needs assessment.[9] This approach was accompanied by misjudgments on product/service features, underpricing, and some aborted product/service lines.

Supervising staff and projects

A key success factor for all of the projects is knowledge of the industry and the technology involved on the part of project staff. Enterprise Works Worldwide and ITDG utilized prior knowledge and technology development to transfer technology from outside and then innovated and adapted in Zimbabwe. Sarvodaya utilized government, university and private sector experts to inform themselves of the specifics of fish rearing and the industry structure and to train the producers. MEDA relies on its resources of experienced business people to oversee field projects through a management information system. however several projects experienced inefficiencies in the early stages with both voluntary and forced turnover of key personnel. Clearly the more diverse the projects and sectors an NGO engages in, the less industry-specific knowledge the management will have as a basis to select project personnel, to assess the viability of staff plans or to initiate remedial action when problems are encountered.

Market development and NGO value added

The development of markets for their clientele is a central element in all of the projects. For Sarvodaya this was primarily a matter of using the contact network of their own organization and the government ministries to provide an introductory service for producers, buyers, and suppliers. ZOPP and the Light Engineering Workshop Project have utilized the international networks of their NGOs to seek out international markets. MEDA has used the contacts of their sponsoring business members to establish both supplier and buyer relationships. A principal asset of the international NGOs is their market links outside the project countries which enables them to source and qualify contacts inexpensively.

Business development services as an industry

The cases afford some observations on the conference theme of Building a Modern and Effective Development Services Industry. Previous literature has suggested that 'services should be demand driven, not supply driven'. However, in the case of Enterprise Works Worldwide and ITDG the need had been established by their experience in other countries. Their situation is similar to other international firms taking a product or service to a new market. An analogy with fast-food franchises is not far-fetched. The franchiser format is taken to many countries with only minor adaptations for local tastes. In fact NGOs could use a supply-driven approach in some cases. The ZOPP project and the ornamental fish project found themselves advising their clients on how to set up and manage their business to make use of the product/service that was being provided. This is akin to preparing a franchise manual, and the clients would have benefited from the NGOs taking on more of the franchiser activities. More generally, when international NGOs take established products and services in fragmented industries to new markets, they would benefit from the strategic orientation to the cloning, chaining and franchising strategies used by international firms in the private sector.

The bottom line

The performance data and the analysis are not yet in a usable form and hence the aim to link good practice with performance on the indicators awaits final submission of the case study reports. But a tentative conclusion is that because these projects at best cover their direct costs, their ability to reinvest in maintaining and advancing their knowledge and technology base is compromised. On the other hand, none seems at risk of losing its support base. All projects can point to significant benefits derived by their clients, and favourable cost–benefit ratios. Specific usable findings await completion of the case studies, but at this point we are assured that the case studies are of projects that merit examination and will lead to operational guidance for programme design and delivery.

Notes

1. It is not the purpose of this study to evaluate organisations or compare development conditions in the different countries. The measure of success for this study will be the influence it has on the consideration or conduct of business development services projects in a range of sectors.
2. BDS is the term currently being applied by practitioners and donors to non-financial assistance to small and micro-enterprises.
3. There is much inconsistency in the use of the terms 'best practices' and 'benchmarking' in the development field. Benchmarking refers to the process of establishing standards of outputs relative to inputs by continuously measuring a firm against the industry leader. It is thus a measure of productivity or efficiency. Best practice, on the other hand, identifies methods or work processes whose output best meet customer requirements. It is thus a measure of effectiveness.
4. As case studies are the appropriate methodology when studying complex relationships that change over time, many of the questions and much of the learning is dependent on an analysis and inductive interpretation that will take place only when the individual cases are all completed.
5. The researchers receive terms of reference that, in addition to a project overview, provide representative guiding questions on what is to be described and the analyses to

be undertaken. They receive as well a set of descriptions of the subset of business development services, examples of project monitoring indicators to be used to determine project effectiveness on cost, impact and sustainability, and a personal briefing.

6. The research is being supported by Canada's International Development Research Center (IDRC). Since its inception in 1970, IDRC has designed and implemented a wide range of research projects focused on aspects of small-scale enterprise. Research that can enhance the productivity of SMEs remains a current priority with IDRC.

7. The work of the NGOs is the source of many of the indicators in Table 6.2.

8. The Sarvodaya project is primarily concerned with cost effectiveness and a reasonable (unspecified) recovery rate on their direct costs.

9. The distinction here is between a market feasibility study and a consumer orientation. One determines whether or not services will be in sufficient demand as to command fees that will at least recover the full costs of providing them. A consumer orientation emphasizes the goal of satisfying customers, using interdisciplinary research to gain an understanding of what satisfaction is, how to measure it, change it, and orient managers to their customers.

Bibliography

Jonathan Dawson with Andy Jeans: *Looking Beyond Credit: Business development services and the promotion of innovation among small producers.* Intermediate Technology Publications, 1998.

Mary McVay: 'Business Development Services for Micro-enterprises: A situation assessment. *CARE*, October, 1996.

Alan Gibson: *Business Development Services for SMEs: Preliminary guidelines for donor-funded interventions.* International Labour Office, October, 1997.

Lara Goldmark: *Business Development Services: A framework for analysis.* Inter-American Development Bank, 1996.

Clifton Barton: *Microenterprise Business Development Services: Defining institutional options and indicators of performance*, USAID, Microenterprise Best Practice (MBP) Project, September 1997.

Robert C. Camp: *Benchmarking: The search for industry best practices that lead to superior performance.* Milwaukee, WI, 1989.

Michael D. Johnson: *Customer Orientation and Market Action.* Prentice Hall Canada, 1998.

7. Comparing two West African BDS experiences

MICHEL BOTZUNG

THERE HAVE BEEN profound changes over the last ten years in the provision of support to small and medium-sized enterprises in French-speaking West Africa. This chapter aims to shed some light on current discussions in this area through an analysis of two West African experiences: the Private Sector Foundation (Fondation pour le Secteur Privé), in Senegal and the CAPEO Foundation [Ouagadougou Micro-enterprise Support Cell], in Burkina Faso. These two experiences illustrate how, in different national contexts, non-financial services for small and medium-sized enterprises in Africa have developed.

The two experiences share the same overall objective, namely to increase the know-how and business potential of existing SMEs by providing access to appropriate advisory, support and training services. However, beyond this common objective, the two approaches have significant differences.

The FSP (Fondation du Secteur Privé) is in essence a body designed to facilitate access to services by meeting part of their cost. In short, the foundation is in contact with the operators (business consultancies, research consultancies and consultants) working with its existing or potential clientele. CAPEO, on the other hand, provides services directly through its own agents. They are longer established, having developed their services over the years.

The experiences of CAPEO and FSP cast light on the basic problems faced in non-financial services today. They provide some up-to-date experiences in terms of: payment aspects of such services; their sustainability; the relevance of the services to the wishes and demands of clients; and the alternative approaches of sub-contracting to other agents/agencies or direct service provision. Finally, they offer some interesting points of comparison between their different operational contexts (Senegal and Burkina Faso) and their work approaches (sub-contracting and direct provision, respectively).

We shall develop our analysis on the basis of a first section describing the two approaches. The second section will attempt to draw out possible conclusions from these experiences. Finally, we shall examine conclusions in the light of future trends.

The approaches of CAPEO and the Fondation du Secteur Prive

CAPEO: a business services institution

With bilateral funding from Canada (through CIDA), the Desjardins International Development body launched, developed and still supports the CAPEO experience in providing advisory services to small enterprises in Burkina Faso. Having become operational in the autumn of 1991, the experience now has a sufficient track record to draw out some lessons.

Origin and background: supporting micro-enterprise development

An initial phase (1988–90) of surveys and studies of the informal urban sector in Burkina Faso led to the definition of a support programme called 'Ouagadougou

Microenterprise Support Cell' (CAPEO). It became operational in November 1991 and it was intended to operate for seven years (1991–98) as a project under bilateral development co-operation before a Fondation Entreprendre [Enterprise Foundation] would be set up and gradually take over the activities of CAPEO.

Selection criteria for target enterprises

The project aimed at increasing employment creation in the private sector, to mitigate the effects of structural adjustment. The most appropriate segments for this goal were those selected from across the broad sweep of micro-enterprise.

On the basis of various criteria (including the viability of the sector, its potential in processing raw materials and in labour-intensive employment creation, adding value, etc.) specific sectors were selected (wood- and metalworking, food processing, craft industries, building materials, mechanics, etc.). In 1996, additional criteria were developed, more with regard to the nature and performance of the entrepreneur, so as to select a clientele that could maximise its use of access to services:

- The enterprise should have been operating for at least one year.
- It should have a modicum of internal organization.
- It should have a turnover of between FCFA 5 millions and 200 million (between US$9000 and US$360 000).
- It should have between five and 50 employees.
- It must agree work with CAPEO in a spirit of confidence and transparency.

These criteria allow a better picture to be built up of the entrepreneurs in question, and their business strategies. In practice, applying these criteria led very quickly to existing enterprises being favoured. In part, this was because the criteria served to discourage the many unrealistic project proposals that could be made, and to give priority to clients with demonstrable qualities of seriousness, determination and perseverance.

A mixed package of advisory, training and facilitation services

The package of services on offer was entirely non-financial, with three key approaches.

Advisory support services. Advisory support services are the principal activity of CAPEO and they comprise mainly support to production, advise in accounting and management, advice on sales and marketing, organization and administration. These services are provided by business counsellors, which helps a keen knowledge of the local environment to be developed, and common training needs for several enterprises to be identified.

Training modules. This activity comprises classroom training sessions for entrepreneurs. For the last six years, CAPEO has undertaken an annual training programme on about ten topics. The topics and contents of training courses are developed on the basis of the needs of entrepreneurs expressed during advisory support activities or during evaluation sessions.

Facilitating entrepreneurs' access to finance. The main work here is in the preparation of requests for finance for submission to local finance and project institutions. To this end, CAPEO prepares the project bearers to present, argue for and defend their project. The second step is to help project bearers to identify and approach potential financiers. For this purpose, CAPEO has drawn up collaborative agreements with several local financial institutions; this facilitates access to credit for their client enterprises.

During CAPEO's initial period, all of these services were provided free of charge. However, CAPEO decided to start billing for all its services[1] in 1997, after consulting clients on their degree of satisfaction with services ('if we pay, then it's because we are really interested'), linked to the general wish to achieve financial break-even.

The CAPEO operating cycle

CAPEO's activities are based on being demand driven: it makes its services available, and responds to the demands of potential clients. There is no pre-set cycle of services (the entrepreneur comes to CAPEO with a specific problem to be resolved.) A package of services is delivered according to the following operating cycle:

STEP 1 – *Completion of the enterprise form:* the entrepreneur comes to CAPEO to request information about the support on offer from CAPEO. After a brief interview, a one-page so-called enterprise form is completed on which the entrepreneur can express her or his needs, and on the basis of which a business counsellor is assigned to the case.

STEP 2 – *Assessment of the enterprise form:* the enterprise form is read, and discussed according to CAPEO criteria. This meeting decides if the enterprise will be assisted or not, and which business counsellor is assigned the case. A business counsellor may be asked to visit the site of the enterprise to get additional information for a final decision by CAPEO if the information on the enterprise form is incomplete or illegible, or if additional information is required better to assess the request.

STEP 3 – *Pre-diagnostic:* once the case has been accepted for receiving CAPEO's services, the business counsellor undertakes a pre-diagnostic check of the enterprise. During this meeting, the conditions for CAPEO support are clearly explained to the entrepreneur (a spirit of frank collaboration, high degree of transparency, confidentiality and discretion, sharing costs of responsibilities – 'we do not put ourselves in charge'). This pre-diagnostic check lasts a day at most, and allows the business counsellor to get to know the enterprise better, to identify areas of support and, above all, to discuss with the entrepreneur the needs that she or he had completed on the enterprise form. Where necessary, a more detailed and specialized business diagnosis can be undertaken later.

STEP 4 – *Report back* (pre-diagnostic or diagnosis) *and proposal of services to entrepreneur:* a document is drawn up summarizing the diagnostic, outlining proposed areas collaboration, specifying the type of expertise required, the conditions for collaboration (sharing of costs and responsibilities) and proposing a work schedule.

STEP 5 – *Collaborative agreement:* this contract details the work to be undertaken, expected results, costs, work schedule, clauses on breach of contract and settlement of dispute. This contract provides the basis for collaboration between the enterprise and CAPEO.

STEP 6 – *Participation in annual training programme:* this programme is open, on an *à la carte* basis, to the head of the enterprise and its employees according to need. There is no obligation to participate in the training programme (the price is very attractive compared with the training on offer by private training providers.)

CAPEO as an institution

CAPEO has been through three successive phases of institutional development. The first phase (November 1991 to September 1994) was of experimentation, consolidation of methodologies, staff training and demonstration of services to the clientele.

A second phase (October 1994 – September 1996) put more emphasis on the consolidation of gains, and strengthening the autonomy of the cell at two levels:

- financial and organizational, with in-service training, recruitment of a national director, streamlining of norms and procedures, and financial analysis of income and expenditure
- transition from a project structure to an institution with more continuity.

The principal goal of the third phase (October 1996 – September 2001), is to establish a Burkinabé institution which will take over the activities of CAPEO. The goal is to reach a level of 40 per cent recovery of operating costs by the year 2000. At present, CAPEO has a national director, four business counsellors, an accountant, a cashier, a librarian, a secretary-receptionist, two watchmen and two drivers. A technical assistant provides back-up.

The annual budget (operations, interviews, small acquisitions) of CAPEO[2] is about FCFA 75 million (approximately US$136 000) in 1999. The budget is shrinking in size (from FCFA 100 million in 1996 and 1997, and FCFA 85 million in 1998) so as to ensure that costs are being minimized and that the rate of cost recovery from services delivered is rising.

The Fondation du Secteur Privé (Senegal), a mechanism to facilitate access to services

FSP has been facilitating access to small and medium-sized enterprises in Senegal to advisory and training services, through a co-funding facility, since early 1996.

Origins

The Fondation du Secteur Privé aims at significantly increasing the range of expertise available to enterprises, employers' organizations and professional associations. It has a support fund of FCFA 3 billion (approximately US$5 450 000) using a loan from the IDA. Its specific objectives are:

- to provide individual entrepreneurs and groups of entrepreneurs with access to local and foreign expertise. It uses partial grants to provide sub-projects of support and advice in various areas (management, marketing and training). The goal is to develop the capacities of private companies by improving the quality of services on offer, and access to these services.
- to contribute to the reorganization of employers' organizations and professional associations so as to be able to provide their members with the best available support and information services.

- to finance, or participate financially in, studies on issues of business strategy and management.

A range of services for enterprises and professional organizations

The Foundation aims to serve two groups: small and medium-sized enterprises, and employers' organizations. There are two underlying principles: services are provided in response to a specific demand by a potential client, and on the basis of cost-sharing between the Foundation and the client.

FSP procedures

The agreement between the Government of Senegal and the FSP contains a number of guiding principles which should govern the institution's operation (independence, impartiality, efficiency and confidentiality). These principles, which are sacrosanct for all parties, are described in a procedures manual which covers all operational steps, from the identification of a request for assistance through to the evaluation of the results of the assistance provided through the Foundation.

The procedures of the FSP deal in part with the selection and follow-up of service providers. They cover the steps of accrediting service providers, and of imposing sanctions, whether positive or negative (being removed from the list of service providers) after provision of services. The procedures also cover the relationship between the Foundation and its clients.

Procedures vis-à-vis *service providers.* There are two distinct phases here.

The first phase covers the *process of identification and registration* of the service provider. Here the Foundation builds up its database. Just as there is a relationship between the Foundation and the client, the process of accreditation of the service provider (research consultancy firm, business consultancy company or private consultant) is based on the latter's written request. The principle of 'demand driven' thus also applies to the service providers.

The second phase of *contracting the service provider*, is started on the initiative of the Foundation. When a funding agreement has been reached with a beneficiary, the Foundation starts the procedure of selection of a service provider, which will culminate in the awarding of a contract. Appointments are made on the basis of a call for tenders. Normally, a restricted call for tenders is preferred. When the contract is awarded to a service provider, the latter will be subject to:

- follow-up and monitoring of the state of progress of work at hand
- regular checks on the state of progress of work at hand
- an evaluation of the service provider at the end of the contracted work.

Procedures in relation to clients. The co-funding facility of the Foundation is generally open to any enterprise (regardless of size or sector) that can:

- present proof of the legal status of the enterprise (or group of enterprises)
- present an eligible request for support (see list of services below)
- present a request for funding no higher than the ceiling (FCFA 20 million, approximately US$36 000);
- commit itself to providing its share of the cost of the service.

Those enterprises that meet these minimal conditions can submit a request for assistance to the Foundation in the form of a dossier of a request for funding. The procedure then follows this path:

- request for funding
- registration of request for funding (secretariat of technical division, technical director, head of project)
- evaluation of project (head of project)
- project selection (technical commission, held at least every two weeks)
- notification of acceptance or rejection of request
- when a project is accepted, the terms of reference of the call for tenders are drawn up (technical division, the entrepreneur and eventually an independent expert).

Some quantitative[3] results of FSP interventions

In all, of the 530 requests registered by the Foundation since its establishment, 278 requests submitted by 225 beneficiaries (of which 80 per cent are enterprises) have been approved.

The distribution of projects financed is shown in Table 7.1, using the five priority areas of the Foundation.

Table 7.1   Distribution of projects

Objectives	Number	Percent
Improvement of management capacities	110	40
Improvement of technical and technological know-how	40	14
Lowering costs of production	18	6
Facilitation access to credit	27	10
Improved market penetration	83	30
Total	278	100

Areas	Number	Percent
Assistance in management	105	38
Training	85	31
Studies	29	10
Commercial promotion	49	18
Partnership development	10	3
Total	278	100

The objective with regard to increasing management capacities has benefited from the largest share of resources (more than 40 per cent of the Foundation's commitments). The most heavily financed activities are the establishment of accounting and management systems, and training.

Here the major focus has been on assisting businesses to familiarize themselves with an accounting system recently introduced in the sub-region, which is common to all the countries of the West African Economic and Monetary Union. Along the same lines, the second most heavily funded set of operational objectives is the strengthening of technical and technological know-how. In all, the strengthening of technical and management capacities accounts for more than 60 per cent of funding.

Table 7.2   Trends in overall demand, and acceptance rates

	1st half 97	2nd half 97	1st half 98	Total since 1996
Requests received	124	183	96	530
Requests accepted	57	110	69	278
Rate of acceptance	46%	60%	72%	52%

On average, the Foundation has rejected one in every two requests since the start of its work. The rejection rate has fallen considerably, from 54% in the first half of 1997 to 28% in the first half of 1998. This is due to a greater involvement of experts from the Foundation in the identification and formulation of requests.

The operating costs of FSP

The costs of management and accumulated commitments of the Foundation were, at 30 June 1998, FCFA 924 million (approximately US$1.68 million). The breakdown is thus:

• equipment and investments (1.3% of total)
• operations (44.2%)
• co-funding (54.4%).

The Fondation du Secteur Privé has never had the intention of becoming a permanent institution. Its original project document foresaw the closure of the body in 2001. This therefore raises the issue of how to ensure the continuity of the facilitation of enterprise implementation.

Following the above presentation of the supply and demand for the services of CAPEO and the FSP, we shall now proceed to a comparison, which will permit certain comments to be made, and some lessons to be drawn.

Comments and lessons

We shall focus on three major problem areas in support services to small and medium-sized enterprises. First, there is the issue of matching services on offer as a response to the demand of potential clients or users. What lessons can the two experiences teach us in terms of defining a demand-driven approach? In particular, what can they teach us regarding the formulation of needs by the entrepreneurs themselves and the impact that this choice has had on the institution and its procedures?

The second point is more concerned with client approval of services. Nowadays, the entrepreneurs and their representative associations are more involved in the assessment than in the definition of services. Their opinions are sought after more systematically than before in terms of assessing the appropriateness and quality of services on offer. What lessons are there for us to be drawn from an analysis of the two experiences?

The third point is the classic one of payment for these services. Both cases cut themselves free from the errors of the past as far as support services were concerned. Are they better balanced now financially? Can they – indeed, should they – look forward to a degree of permanence? This issue leads us to examine the role and place of subsidies.

The demand-driven approach: client makes request, then gets access to support services

The demand-driven approach is a well-known, and now widely accepted principle. A demand-driven service is based on giving access to services in response to a request by a potential client. The advantages are obvious, and numerous.

We see here, first of all, a break with the past in terms of the strategy of services on offer which was practised on a very wide scale until the mid-1990s. That consisted of offering entrepreneurs a complete range of services, often inter-linked, in order to strengthen their known-how. Its underlying tenet was 'we know better than the entrepreneur what s/he needs or will find useful or profitable'.

The provision of a demand-driven service rests on the principle of free choice. Each entrepreneur is free to request services, or not. This free choice means that the requester will express a real need, and will not, as in the past, walk a convoluted and compulsory path through all sorts of services while s/he wanted something else (such as access to credit). Last, but not least, a strategy which responds to an expressed need means that it can be easier to get the service paid for (at least in part). It can mean increased efficiency in the services on offer: instead of being on offer to a set of passive beneficiaries, many of whom will not necessarily use the know-how and advice received, they will be available to motivated entrepreneurs, who know what they want, and are thus *a priori* more prepared to profit from the services.

Both CAPEO and FSP follow the same principle: services are never compulsory, but respond to a request. What comments and lessons can the practices of FSP and CAPEO give us here?

Matching supply and demand is not simple: the decisive role of the go-between

There is much intermediation to be undertaken here. It is based primarily on the dissemination of information: potential clients have to know that services exist, and they have to see how these services may respond to their needs. This information work is easier for CAPEO, which has the benefit of age (having been operational for eight years), and of the 'manageable' size of its operating area. The task of the FSP is complicated by the wide range of support activities, and the diversity of SMEs, in Senegal. It is noteworthy that the FSP has recently appointed a consultant to market its services to medium-scale enterprises.

Even more than the provision of information in order to increase the numbers of relevant requests, there is much work to be done in the area of expressing needs. The work of both CAPEO and the FSP has amply shown that one cannot wait passively for needs to express themselves. The reality is that, with the exception perhaps of medium enterprises, few potential clients are capable of precisely expressing their need. Furthermore, an entrepreneur's analysis of his possible problems can be subjective and inexact.

The benefit of experience and hindsight in this area has led both organizations to pay attention to a phase of pre-diagnostic which serves to 'validate' the request. In the case of the FSP, this is a new idea. It is born from a wish to restrict the causes of rejection of requests (54% of requests in the first half of 1997 were rejected), but equally from a desire to ease the work of the service providers, who have hitherto often been faced with difficult start-up situations in the enterprises they work with. In fact, the consultant often has to decipher the request and its rationale, with regard to the objective situation of the business, before being able to provide the expected advisory services.

It is the accumulation of all these reasons that has pushed the FSP to introduce the pre-diagnostic procedure on a systematic basis. This means that the Foundation will appoint a consultant[4] on the basis of a contract of mutual consent to undertake a brief assessment of the enterprise. The study must include a set of recommendations on the strengths and weaknesses of the enterprise. On the basis of these, an operational plan will be proposed to the enterprise. Experience has shown that for most of the micro-enterprises that requested support from the Foundation, the conclusions of the pre-diagnostic procedure led to changes to the initial request. This procedure had already been integrated by CAPEO in its procedures (see Step 3: *the pre-diagnostic*).

A serious pre-diagnostic has to be part of any demand-driven approach dealing with micro and small enterprises. it is a phase which has a cost, and it implies more involvement of the experts of the institutions concerned in identifying and formulating needs for assistance.

An implicit selection of clients

The statistics available do not provide adequate data for giving precise profiles of the clients of the two institutions. Nonetheless, what information is available tends to suggest that the degree of appropriateness to the smallest enterprises is not particularly high. There are several reasons for this.

The place occupied by very small enterprises among the clientele of the institutions is due in part to the need to provide proof of the formal legal existence of the enterprise (as in the procedure of the FSP) and in part to the need for the enterprise to co-finance the cost of the service. Furthermore, the difficulty in clearly expressing a need in relation to the real problems of the enterprise (and not necessarily as they are seen by the entrepreneur!) does not facilitate access for very small enterprises to services of which they are often not aware. Finally, the last obstacle – but by no means the smallest one – lies in the level of service offered. The experience of the FSP would seem to show that the overwhelming majority of consultants and research consultancies are not familiar with the strategies and methods of operation used by very small enterprises in managing their businesses; the result is a lack of cultural understanding, and difficulty in putting forward usable advice.

This problem can be avoided to some extent when services are provided directly by business counsellors (as in the case of CAPEO), since the closeness of the counsellors and the length of their association with the entrepreneurs leads to better mutual acquaintance.

The provision of business development services would seem to be most appropriate when dealing with enterprises that have reached a certain size. In the case of very small enterprises, more intermediation is needed. This includes a preliminary assessment of the potential value of the services to the enterprises, and 'training' – or orientation – of the consultants in the ways of this particular target group. What is needed, ultimately, in the case of the smallest enterprises is a proactive strategy (on the part of the foundation) of reaching out to this group, and showing a clear willingness to respond to requests.

Client approval of services

A corollary to the provision of services in response to requests, the approval of the service by the client or the user, has now been accepted by a number of institutions providing support services. The client has to give, in one way or another, her or his opinion of the quality and the appropriateness of the service *vis-à-vis* needs. How do the FSP and CAPEO deal with this?

For its part, CAPEO assesses the level of satisfaction of participants in training sessions, using classical evaluation tools (sheets, etc.) It also makes use of individual interviews to involve entrepreneurs in shaping services. However, ultimately CAPEO remains dependent on repeat requests (indicating a faithful clientele) and genuine financial participation (payment by the entrepreneur) in service provision as a means of measuring the degree of satisfaction among entrepreneurs.

The FSP has gone further in this regard and, as well as specific assessments of client satisfaction, it has set up measures that require the entrepreneur to give a 'green light' at each stage of the service provision process.

Thus, an enterprise receiving assistance from the Foundation participates at each stage of the request, in particular in the selection of the service provider and in drawing up the terms of reference for the work to be assigned to the provider. The entrepreneur also gives his or her own assessment of the service provider and each stage of the service process requires his approval.

The key stage in relations between the Foundation and the service provider is at the time of the provisional report. Here, the Foundation carries out a technical evaluation of the consultant's work with regard to the terms of reference for the service provider. The client is involved in this work, and is bound to give his or her opinion on how the consultant had responded to needs. When the beneficiary is satisfied and the staff of the Foundation have technically approved the work done, the document is accepted and the consultant is given the go-ahead to start producing the final report. In the case of the beneficiary being dissatisfied, the Foundation assesses the reasons given, and evaluates whether or not they are compatible with the needs that were expressed by the entrepreneur and which helped to shape the terms of reference. The consultant is then requested to focus more on the needs of the beneficiary, by making more use of the methodology originally proposed in the winning tender. The consultant then has to present a second provisional report, which will be evaluated in the same way. When the second provisional report is received, the Foundation assesses the ability of the service provider to meet the needs of the beneficiary. In the event of dissatisfaction, the beneficiary can request that the service provider is removed from the case; a new procedure is then started to select a new provider.[5]

This close involvement of clients in the approval of services sometimes gives rise to some small problems in the form of delayed payment of service providers. The consultants claim that many enterprises would seem to be inclined to delay the completion of service provision in order to delay making the final payment.

Client approval of the services is an essential element of matching them to client needs. Further, client satisfaction and approval also provide a basic element of justification and approval of any subsidies made to the support institutions.

Payment for services

The question of payment for services provided has rightly become a fundamental point in the assessment of these advisory services. The accent now is upon the permanent nature and sustainability of services, in a break with previous practices which were characterized by the 'project approach' which was temporary, coming from outside and totally subsidized. The permanence of an institution depends on its having a) an appropriate legal status, b) properly developed know-how and capable, motivated and loyal human resources and c) financial viability.

We shall restrict our analysis here to the third element, namely the issue of payment for services. This issue touches on a number of questions:

- Does payment by clients cover the operating costs, maintenance costs and small investments of the institutions?
- Do the institutions have additional sustainable resources which can guarantee the permanence of the service?

Both the FSP and CAPEO have adopted and introduced the principle of insisting on co-financing of services by clients. They have each drawn up detailed pricing schedules which depend on the kind and cost of service provided, and sometimes on the type of client.

At CAPEO this policy of payment for services has been implemented only recently (less than two years ago) and it should mean that the costs of the institution are increasingly covered. It should be noted that, typically, the introduction of paying for services has led to some client desertion.

At the FSP, different procedures are used. The Foundation takes the cost of service provision (which is easier to do in the case of external service providers) and charges a modular rate based on the cost of the service, with the share to be paid by the client increasing with the cost (see Tables 7.3 and 7.5). The rating systems of both institutions illustrate the same system, namely that the client pays a share of the cost of the service, with the dual objectives of facilitating access to services and contributing in part to cost recovery for the organization. They both apply the principle of financial participation by the entrepreneur, based on the size of business and the cost of the service.

Table 7.3 Classification and rates of advisory support services of CAPEO[6]

Type of enterprise	Turnover	Cost borne by CAPEO	Cost borne by enterprise
Income-generating activities Any small enterprise	FCFA 0 to 5 million FCFA 5 to 25 million	70%	30%
Very small enterprise Small enterprise	FCFA 25 to 50 million FCFA 50 to 100 million	50%	50%
Medium-sized enterprise Large-scale enterprise	FCFA 100 to 200 million More than FCFA 200 million	30%	70%

Table 7.4 Rates for other CAPEO services

Types of service	Group I	Group II	Group III
Preparation of funding proposal	FCFA 10 000 to 25 000	FCFA 50 000 to 75 000	FCFA 150 000 to 200 000
Training sessions 3-day sessions 4-day sessions	FCFA 15 000 FCFA 20 000	FCFA 30 000 FCFA 40 000	FCFA 45 000 FCFA 60 000

Table 7.5   Sharing the costs of FSP services

Total cost of services	Cost borne by entrepreneur	Cost borne by Foundation
< FCFA 1.25 million	25%	75%
Between FCFA 1.25 million and 10 million	50%	50%
Above FCFA 10 million	70%	30%

The FSP is currently considering how to improve the level of use of the co-financing budget line. In addition to possibly imposing a ceiling on drawing rights (a maximum of FCFA 20 million in total withdrawals per enterprise) and placing more emphasis on large-scale enterprises as clientele, one possibility could be to increase the level of the Foundation's share to 65 per cent (in fact, this reduces the requirements made of entrepreneurs and means that more money can be disbursed quickly!)

The question of whether or not the payment made by clients covers the costs of the institution is not of any interest to FSP. In fact, in this case the share of the entrepreneur is not paid to the Foundation but to the service provider. For FSP, the question is rather how to change the balance between co-financing activities and operating costs. As of 30 June 1998, the FSP had expenditure of approximately FCFA 925 million, of which 1.3 per cent was invested, 44.2 per cent was used for operating costs, and 54.4 per cent for co-financing activities. This means that the operating costs[7] were relatively high compared to activities.

The question of cost recovery is, however, relevant to CAPEO.

Although precise figures are not available, the difficulty of achieving cost recovery can be seen in the requirements made by the donor agency for meeting certain cost recovery rates in the first years of Phase III (Autumn 1996 – Autumn 2001). The targeted rates of recovery were set at 20 per cent for 1998, rising to a level of 40 per cent in 2001. The goal here, clearly, is not to achieve total cost recovery, but a level of cost recovery that is 'reasonable'. In the long run, if it is to be permanent, the institution will have to find additional resources to top-up payments by clients.

In effect, while using different methods, both institutions remain dependent on external resources for guaranteeing their services on a permanent basis. On this point, any tangible change in the position of either CAPEO or the FSP is rather feeble. Their approaches still require external subsidisation in part.

If subsidies are going to continue to be part of the picture, the question arises of how to limit their negative effects. Structural systematic subsidization could negate all efforts being made to achieve financial break-even, to create alternative methods of funding, to minimize operating costs and, perhaps above, to delink subsidies from productivity.

There are well-known and accepted forms of subsidization which gradually reduce subsidies, or allocated them only to particular budget lines. The case of the FSP underlines the importance of arriving at a formula that will expand to cover subsidies to service providers.

What the FSP actually does is pay for part of the costs of services provided, without reducing the pressure of the client on the service provider. Where it could have given subsidies to the service provider, it has chosen to subsidize the client partially to give him access to the service.

There are several advantages to this principle of partial subsidization of the client rather than the institution providing services. Instead of favouring one particular institution or service provider, it introduces a basic element of competition, by allowing the entrepreneur to select from among several consultants, research consultancies or institutions. The approach also means that there is a basic degree of client approval of the quality and appropriateness of the service provided. Finally, the subsidy is linked to the actual provision of a service. It makes possible service provision, and does not guarantee the existence of an institution if the level of service provision is (too) weak.

Some concluding remarks

A comparison of the approaches of CAPEO and the FSP illustrates rather well the current problems in the area of developing modern and efficient support services for small and medium-sized enterprises. Furthermore, each organization is also faced with issues specific to its own case.

The issue of permanence does not have the same implications for each institution. For CAPEO, it is obviously *the* key issue. The intended establishment of a Fondation Entreprendre (Enterprise Foundation) in 1998 was designed to deal with the question of legal status for the institution. However, CAPEO has still to find a way to improve the rate of cost recovery from charges made for services provided, and to increase the loyalty of staff. For the FSP, the issues have more to do with the future of the mechanism: should it be continued, or should it be stopped? The question cannot be answered without dealing with the imperative need to improve FSP's efficiency by attaining a better ratio between co-financing commitments and operating costs.

Both experiences are a good reflection of the current state of the art in the provision of advice and support to small and medium-sized enterprises. Thus, at the time of the establishment of CAPEO in 1991, know-how in Burkina Faso in advisory support services still had to be developed. At that time, it was not possible to envisage a mechanism that would facilitate access to existing resources. Today, on the other hand, it is reasonably possible to imagine that the existence of CAPEO, and its training of several generations of staff, has led to the emergence of a real capacity and expertise in this field. The situation was very different in Senegal in 1996, when there were already numerous research consultancies and consultants, with a high degree of competition. It would have been difficult to consider adding another service provider to the existing constellation, as if the expertise did not exist.

However, this analysis of CAPEO and the FSP has not provided many elements for dealing with two important problems, which will require research and experimentation in the future.

On the one hand, both bodies remain heavily dependent on external subsidies. This issue must be tackled seriously, both in terms of finding ways to link subsidization more closely to activities, and of setting up more sustainable funding mechanisms for these services (a support fund of the kind used in the professional training community, and parity funding, are approaches which come to mind.)

On the other hand, access by the smallest enterprises to support services continues to be difficult. Here several elements converge, including the ability of this target group actually to contribute a share of the cost, the need to demonstrate beforehand the value and impact of the service, but also the difficulties of consultants and counsellors in properly understanding the operations and strategies of these micro-entrepreneurs. Just how these entrepreneurs can access support services is an area worthy of further experimentation.

Notes

1. This point will be revisited in the second section of this paper, in the part dealing with payment of support services.
2. We do not have an income and expenditure account of the institution.
3. The figures have been derived from FSP reports and studies.
4. This consultant will be excluded from providing possible services in this contract.
5. This situation has arisen in two cases since the Foundation became operational. One research consultancy company was excluded from the Foundation's database.
6. US$1 is equivalent to approximately FCFA 550.
7. This figure could perhaps be seen as a reflection of a certain administrative cumbersomeness, since it has not changed very much as co-financing commitments have changed. However, we hypothesize that it includes in part the cost of intermediation between the requester and the service provider.

8. Swisscontact: business centre approach in Indonesia and the Philippines

ALAN GIBSON and ROBERT HITCHINS

SWISSCONTACT (SC) is a Swiss-based NGO working in 18 countries in Asia, Africa, Latin America and Central and Eastern Europe. It designs and implements programmes in three priority fields: vocational education, urban ecology and small enterprise development. The last of these has assumed greater importance in recent years, as SC has come to regard small enterprises as central both to wider economic development and to efforts to improve vocational skills and the environment.

SC's analysis of business development services (BDS) has emerged from this greater commitment to small enterprise development. It originated in its programmes in Peru and Ecuador and from a BDS environment characterized by:

- an adequate offer of BDS and weak demand for BDS from SMEs, supported by non-sustainable subsidies from government or donors
- a poorly functioning BDS market
- prevailing support for BDS from government and donors which did not address this the supply-demand inconsistency.

Supported by the Swiss Agency for Development and Co-operation (SDC), SC's response has been to develop the business centre approach. Specifically, by intervening at the meso level, it tries to create sustainable, functioning BDS markets.

Based on experience in Latin America in the mid-1990s, SC first began its business centre approach in Indonesia and the Philippines in 1996–97. The programme in Indonesia is focused on Java, and by mid-1998 covered eight business centres (at various stages of development); in the Philippines, eight business centres are spread throughout five regions. Table 8.1 offers a brief outline of each of these.

This case study examines the business centre experience of SC in Indonesia and the Philippines. It describes the approach in detail, especially in Indonesia, where the experience of three business centres are explored in some depth, but the primary focus is on the issues emerging from the business centre experience, which are of wider interest. Its main objective is to identify key lessons and principles of good practice in BDS and, where possible, benchmark performance indicators.

Services

There are two levels of service[1]:

- most important, services offered by SC to business centres through their intervention
- services offered by business centres to their SME clients.

Table 8.1 Main business centres supported by SC in Indonesia and the Philippines

Name of business centre	Organization type operating business centre	Main services	Outreach (approx.)
The Phillipines			
Jewellery	Small-scale jewellery producers' association	Retail outlet for members aimed at offering them higher prices	8–10
Palatan	Women's handicraft and woven products group	Retail outlet and bulk buying service for key inputs	33
IMAB-MPCI	Association of automotive workshop owners, with small to medium-sized businesses	Bulk buying service for main inputs and common service facilities with two machines	24
Fenema	Association of small metalworking and engineering workshops	Material credit service plus retail outlet	45
Oro	Chamber of commerce and industry	Training, marketing fairs and 'brokering'	200
Baguio SME	Chamber of commerce and industry	Training and office services	30
Timpuyog	Chamber of commerce and industry	Training and office services	25
Laguna	Chamber of commerce and industry	Business registration and training	50
Indonesia			
WPU Bandung	Formerly Swisscontact project office	Technical, management and administrative assistance, access to credit	
Centrama	Formed from a large NGO supporting SME development	Management and administrative assistance, access and credit	
Karmacon	Formed from a private management consulting and accounting firm	Management and administrative assistance, access to credit	
WPU Malang	Formerly Swisscontact project office	Technical, management and administrative assistance, access to credit	Approximately 300 clients for project as a whole
KOPISMA	Association for automative component parts producing SMEs	Raw material purchase for members, marketing assistance	
Sentra (Y3PI)	Individual	Training service to tourism hospitality organizations	
Spektra	Former NGO	Brokering/market intermediation	
Produksi Bersih Benefita (PBB)	Former Swisscontact staff member specializing in ecologically-sound production processes in workshops	Consultancy for cleaner production and services	

SC support for the business centres is based on financial and technical support. The precise nature of this support varies between the Philippines and Indonesia, and has evolved through time. The key characteristics are:

- *A contract-based relationship:* in Indonesia this is a detailed document, based on a business proposal by the business centre; in the Philippines this is a brief memorandum of understanding with an agreed annual work plan.
- *Finance-based incentives:* are the heart of the intervention. Criteria for incentives vary: in the Philippines, gross profit for specific products is used; in Indonesia, incentives have been offered at an institutional (rather than product) level, although this is now changing. In all cases, incentives are non-repayable.
- *Other financial support:* SC's offer may also involve support for initial investment and pre-operational costs, usually on a shared basis, again non-repayable grants.
- *Time-bound:* financial support is limited to a particular time period: 1–3 years in Indonesia; 3–5 years in the Philippines, but with exit provisions if 'the deal' is not working.
- *Financial limits:* are evolving and are complicated by the types of financial support offered. In the Philippines, the financial range is US$4–15 000 per annum; in Indonesia, the range extends from US$16 000 to US$50 000 annually.
- *Non-financial technical support:* this may take the form of skills training, new product ideas or 'one-to-one' counselling support. Recent training in Indonesia includes business plan preparation, gender analysis, CEFE and in-house training for consultants. Payment is usually not required for these services.

Table 8.2 summarizes the main characteristics of SC's offer to business centres in Indonesia and the Philippines. SC's experience is recent,[2] and there is continuous learning. Indeed, especially in Indonesia, SC's learning objective is leading it to examine private sector models of business investment, such as venture capital companies. Among the key drivers of change are the following:

- *Ownership and commitment:* giving less and demanding more from business centre partners as an indication of their commitment. This has implications for the proportion of costs/investments covered and method (more emphasis on incentives) of support. In particular, the ownership of those running business centres (see Box 8.1) is to be strengthened through a direct financial stake in the organization.
- *Partner selection:* Swisscontact's offer and that of its partner business centres are related; partner selection and service offer need to be considered together. For example, selecting and developing business centres based on present capacity may mean reduced technical support.
- *Time-scale:* there is a dilemma here between ensuring that a relationship is of sufficient duration to make a difference, but that it is not so long that a dependency takes over.
- *'Unnatural' funding flows:* financial support for business centres is often 'front-end loaded' when initial investment and operational cost support is given. This can create a heavy overhead burden – earlier and larger than would be normal in a commercial situation. One idea being considered here to mitigate this problem is to deliver supply on a leasing basis.

Table 8.2   Core characteristics of the Swisscontact offer to business centres

| | Indonesia | | | The Philippines | |
	I	II	III	I	II
Phase	I	II	III	I	II
Basis for financial support	Actual income	Targeted against actual income	Contribution margin	Gross profit	New scheme (not yet finalized)
Time period	2–3 years; 7% quarterly increase in self-financing until 70% achieved	1–2 years	1–2 years	3-year agreements but commitment to five years' support	Reducing time scales
Incentive-base	Self-financing ratio – revenue against expenditure, which has to increase by 7% per quarter. Payments made against performance	Actual self-financing ratio against target. Payments agreed in advance and disbursed if target achieved	Self-financing ratio is based on the contribution of gross profit to overhead	Gross profit on individual products – up to 100% offered	Similar to earlier system
Investment	Two business centres (WPUs) were part of original project. Transfer of project assets to new entities	Matching investment between Swisscontact and operator up to US$50 000 each	Equipment supplied on a lease basis. Transferred to business centre based on performance	Matching investment (50:50 basis)	Similar to earlier system
Pre-operational support	Not relevant – pre-operational WPUs were Swisscontact	As part of investment	Working capital paid as cash advance	Up to 100% for first 6 months; reducing by 25% in 6-monthly steps	Possibly reduced timescale
Technical support	Skills and product-specific training; one-to-one advice	Skills and product-specific training; one-to-one advice	Major emphasis: regular visits, study tours and joint planning	Similar support within transactional framework	
Total amount (approx. financial support only)	US$17–23 000 per annum	US$33–50 000 per annum	Not yet clear	US$4–15 000 per annum (average of US$12 000)	Possibly increasing average size

108

Box 8.1   Key players in business centre ownership

Ownership is a critical issue in the business centre approach, not only in the legal sense but – just as important – in the sense of who *runs*, and is *committed* to it. There are three main 'players' with some claim to ownership.

Operator: SC enters into a contract with a second party – the operator – to form a business centre. Each party provides equal investment and a degree of on-going support. Operators are generally a larger organization, such as a consulting firm or NGO, with experience in the field. The operator is either the 100% owner or, in Indonesia, sometimes the co-owner with the business centre management.

Business centre management: the management is responsible for running the centre. They are seen as a distinctive entity in Indonesia, less formally in the Philippines. Generally they do not make significant financial investments in the business centre, although in one scheme SC investment in the business centre is transferred to the management as a shareholding.

Swisscontact: as a foreign NGO, SC cannot to have a shareholding in the business centres, despite their significant investment; SC's contribution is considered. However the contractual relationship between SC and the operator gives SC a strong interest in the business centres' development.

- *Improving technical support:* generally outside the transactional rationale which underpins the financial arrangement; i.e. offered without anything in return. Without a clear transactional basis to the technical support relationship, confusion can arise over its real purpose (capacity-building against accountability). Ideas for change here include allocating business centres a specified period of time for technical assistance and SC taking equity in business centres, thus giving their advice – as co-owners.
- *Tightening the relationship:* critical to the approach is the role of SC; it has to be business-like both in relation to its capacity and its orientation. This can be difficult because, although it is seeking to be *like* a business, it is *not*, of course, a business! In particular, the firmness to rightly enforce agreements, especially in a time of crisis, has not always been evident. Yet the logic of the approach compels it to be firm and practical.

Business centre services to SMEs

The business centre approach is neither service or sector specific[3]. SC does not seek to prescribe the type of services that business centres offer; the primary focus is on the development of institutions to offer services for which there is a demand.

As a result, business centres offer a broad range of services. In Indonesia, these are mainly management training and consulting (see Table 8.3). Originally, business centres offered technical services in specific sectors. One of the first business centres, WPU Bandung, offered technical consultancy services in the automotive and machine component sub-sector. However, SMEs could access this knowledge at no charge from agents, buyers, suppliers or trade associations. Generally, business centres are targeting management and administrative skills and systems, problems which become more acute as SMEs develop.

Table 8.3   Sources of revenue in Indonesian business centres (%)[4]

	WPU Bandung	Centrama	Karmacon
Technical training	6		
Management training	3	91	8
Consulting/access to credit	28		92
Other business activities	21	5	
Non-SME income	42	4	

In the Philippines, business centres fall in two categories: *business* and *trade* centres. The former deliver services similar to those in Indonesia – business services and training – but with a particular emphasis on market services (such as trade exhibitions). Trade business centres are engaged in retail, supply and hire services in particular sectors (such as jewellery, woven products and automotive workshops), often in competition with other commercial organizations.

The Asian financial crisis in 1997–98 severely affected business centres in Indonesia, resulting in focused efforts on generating revenue for survival. Under this pressure, business centres have innovated. One business centre saw a market opportunity for assisting SMEs with restructuring and staff reduction programmes (see Box 8.2). Business centres have become involved with larger public organizations that subsidize SME development services. Motivated by the need to survive, business centres may develop services and market relationships not directly with SMEs but rather with an intermediary institution. This question is examined later.

Box 8.2   Selling via larger institutions in Indonesia

Centrama has moved away from the product portfolio envisaged in its original business plan. As yet it has not established a fixed new range of products and services; it is still in a 'survival-only' stage. However one of its conscious strategies has been to develop relationships with large institutions, particularly a major university in Surabaya, Institut Teknologi Sepuluh Nopember Surabaya (ITS). The rationale behind this new selling policy is that by providing a packet of workshop, training, and consultancy to ITS, Centrama will:

- overcome the difficulties it has experienced in selling services direct to SMEs due to reduced 'purchasing power'; ITS pays the full cost of services to Centrama but passes on less than 50 per cent of these costs to participants
- minimize the risk of preparing training material and promoting courses – the onus to 'fill' the training course lies with the institution
- reduce the cost of delivering training for the business centre, as ITS underwrites the cost of training facilities, refreshments and so on.

In the Philippines, SC has supported the development of management training materials by a specialist institution, while in Indonesia SC support has allowed business centres access to programmes such as CEFE. Business centres themselves – not SE – generally take the lead role in product development.[5]

The client base

SC and its principal donor, SDC, are concerned with the situation of SMEs and the people that are affected by them (employees, households, consumers, etc.). From a development perspective, business centres are a means to an end and so SC does need to have an understanding of the kind of changes caused by its intervention.

Size and sector

SC's target group of enterprises with whom business centres should work is defined in both Indonesia and the Philippines. In the former, it is businesses with a turnover of US$50 000–US$2m and 5–100 employees; in the Philippines it is businesses with assets of US$5000–US$2m and 5–50 employees. In practice, these limits are not followed rigidly. Some business centres do work with start-up and micro-businesses – especially the trade business centres in the Philippines and those business centres in both countries that have contracts with government or university institutions to deliver services to start-ups. However, the general client base is well above the micro level. Such businesses have a greater willingness to pay for services; capacity to make use of services; and a need for services. There is no overall sector orientation in the client base. Clients of business centres include, for example, SMEs engaged in computer software, automotive repair and maintenance, jewellery manufacture, woven handicraft production, small-scale finance, timber, catering and component assembly.

Gender

Gender equity is a principle of SC. In the Philippines, every business centre agreement has a small gender component financed fully by SC. In practice, the majority of SME clients of business centres are not owned by women. Indeed, since business centres deal mainly with existing businesses, mostly owned by men, there is a preponderance of men-owned SMEs in their client group. The gender commitment remains a challenge for SC.

Poverty

Most SME clients of business centres are clearly beyond the poverty limit, although their employees may be within it. However, SC argues that this kind of intervention does lead to poverty reduction since the strengthening of the SME sector is important for speedy economic development and employment creation.

Outreach

Detailed figures for numbers of SME clients are not collected systematically by business centres. Moreover, great caution should be attached to outreach figures since the nature of contact may be very different depending on the service. For example, Oro Business centre in the Philippines undertakes short training programmes and organizes trade fairs with significant number of SMEs. Karmacon business centre in Indonesia offers intensive consultancy services for a small number of medium-sized businesses. In the Philippines, client outreach figures per business centre range from more than 200 to less than 10. Best estimates for the Philippines are that around 400 SMEs are or have been clients of eight business centres; in Indonesia, from eight business centres, the equivalent figure is around 300 SMEs, although with more intensive services.

The market

The all-pervasive government influence

In training, counselling and consulting there is a skewed pricing structure in which most services are offered with subsidies, free or – in the most extreme case in Indonesia – with incentive payments for attendance! There are a variety of government initiatives to support SME development; state-owned enterprises have to form linkages with SMEs and contribute 1–5 per cent of profits to SME development, and the large-scale private sector is encouraged to follow a similar practice. Official support has led to an unhealthy culture of corruption and largesse in the BDS market.

In the Philippines, there is a longer history of enterprise development support. The focal points of government schemes are first, the Department of Trade and Industry (DTI) and, second, Small and Medium Enterprise Development (SMED) Councils in every province, which play a 'facilitating and co-ordinating role in SME development'. There is an array of schemes available (potentially) to SMEs, many of questionable efficacy. Amid this confusion of activity, there is a gradual withdrawal of direct provision by government and an intention to encourage private BDS providers. To add to the picture, as in Indonesia, donor agencies acting with or without government are active.

All of the above activity distorts the market for BDS. Certainly for some business centres, such as WPU Bandung, the availability of free or cheap services is perceived as a serious competitive threat. For others (Karmacon), the preponderance of free activity offers an opportunity to market themselves as professional providers of high quality, relevant services at an appropriate price (in contrast to amateur, low quality, irrelevant subsidized providers). For others (especially in the Philippines) government-supported schemes provide an opportunity for revenue at lower risk than in dealing with SMEs direct. The original rationale for business centres, in terms of 'free' sustainable markets, underestimated the extent to which newly-developed business centres would still have to work within a highly imperfect market.

Commercial competition

In the Philippines, trade business centres, operated by small membership associations, are offering services that are in direct competition with the private sector. The jewellery association has set up a retail operation, Palatan weavers have a retail unit and a bulk buying service, and the IMAB-MPCI operate a common machine service facility. In these cases, the competitive offer from business centres is often based on their closeness to their clients (members), low margins and highly favourable terms (generous credit). For most business centres, while private sector competition may exist, it is secondary to the influence of the government and/or donors. Some business centres in Indonesia are moving into activities that are directly competitive with commercial companies.

Market interventions by donors usually distort in some way! Abstract discussions of what is and is not a valid intervention to remedy market (or state) deficiencies can become confused. Nonetheless, the underlying approach of business centres is to try to commercialize business development services for SMEs which otherwise would be delivered ineffectively, supported by unsustainable subsidies; it is concerned with developing a working market in services for SMEs. Given this, it raises the question why business centres are being supported in markets which are, to a degree, functioning.[6]

Financial viability

The guiding rationale of the business-centre approach is that an institution will be developed which offers services that SMEs demand. Financial information is at the heart of the business centre approach, providing a window on:

- business centres' performance in relation to these service and institutional objectives; and
- a 'proxy' indicator of the impact they are having on their clients.

In Indonesia, each business centre is required to submit standardized monthly financial statements; similarly in the Philippines, monthly statements are required, supplemented by quarterly audits and more detailed bi-annual reports by an independent accountant. However, since the nature of the financial relationship is different in each country, the reporting information is also different. In Indonesia, there is no requirement that direct costs of service provision are reported, nor does SC impose any system of internal controls. It is the aggregate picture that is of interest; business centres, it is assumed, make rational choices regarding the optimal allocation of inputs and the pricing of products to achieve financial targets. In the Philippines, more detailed information is required because of the nature of the financial agreement.

Services

In the Philippines, financial incentives are offered against records of gross profit for key services; it is therefore important that prices at least cover direct costs. Gross profit margins vary between business centres and products; marketing trade fairs at the Oro business centre have a margin of 300–400 per cent; the common service facility offered by IMAB-MPCI makes less than 20 per cent. Salary costs, which account for more than half of all costs, are all treated as overheads. In most cases fees are not sufficient to cover overheads.

In Indonesia, while all business centres have developed business plans that provide information about the input and delivery costs of most products, they do not maintain product-specific cost centres. Business centres often seem to have a 'rule of thumb' for the break-even price of their products. All business centres are committed to charging fees for services and at the very least try to charge direct cost-covering prices. In the Philippines, it is less clear that pricing takes account of the overhead cost burden but, as self-financing become more imperative, this should happen.

Institution

The core, bottom-line indicator of business centre performance is financial sustainability[7]. Business centre performance by this criterion is summarized in Table 8.4. It is clear that around half the business centres are in considerable financial difficulty while the other half are showing signs of progressing closer to sustainability. Centrama in Indonesia has suffered from the effects of the

Table 8.4 Financial sustainability performance of business centres[8]

	Business centre	% financial sustainabilty*
Indonesia	WPU Bandung	45
	Centrama	35
	Karmacon	125
Philippines	Jewellary	15
	Palatan	150
	Fenema	35
	IMAB-MPCI	80
	Baguio SME	20
	Timpuyog	10
	Oro	60
	Laguna	45

*(most recent approx. figures)

prevailing financial crisis and has failed to achieve targets for several months (35% self-financing against a target of 70%–80%). In the Philippines, in Timpuyog, Jewellery and Baguio SME there is very little activity; in IMAB-MPCI and Fenema real revenue collection from members is far behind the reported value – and there are serious case flow problems.

The two most successful business centres according to these figures are Palatan and Karmacon – organizations at polar extremes in the business centre spectrum. The former stems from a semi-voluntary (and therefore with low overheads) women's group of weavers and handicraft producers supported to set up their own retail unit and bulk buying operation; it is the bulk buying operation – made possible by SC-provided capital – that is the key to their success. Karmacon, in contrast, springs from a large consultancy group, supported to provide services to a smaller set of clients than they previously addressed but who, nonetheless, have considerable purchasing power.

Funding mechanism

The SC business centre programme in Indonesia is supported entirely by SDC and was established in October 1996. The initial phase finished in December 1998. The business centre component is part of a broader based project comprising components for enterprise development, professional and vocational training and environment protection. The budget for the business centre component is US$530 000 out of the project total of US1.71m; approximately 30 per cent of total project budget. Including its share of management costs, the business centre programme accounts for approximately US$590 000 over three years.

The programme in the Philippines is supported principally by SDC, with a smaller proportion coming from other sources. Its initial phase of funding also finished at the end of 1998. The proportion of the budget allocated to business centres has grown since 1996; in 1998 it accounted for around 45 per cent of the budget and including its share of management costs; this was equivalent to approximately US$280 000.

Institutional analysis

The business centre approach is not only concerned with the development of financially sustainable BDS providers and their broader institutional development; but with the development of the skills, knowledge, systems and linkages to strengthen such centres for the long term. To some extent, business centres' record on financial sustainability (Table 8.4) is an indication of their degree of institutional development, and in the long term it could be argued that all institutional development factors are subsumed within this indicator. For business centres, four aspects of institutional development are relevant: ownership, capacity, systems and linkages[9].

Ownership

Just as with SMEs themselves, the issue of ownership – legal and personal – is central to the performance of business centres. It is this quality of ownership and commitment that confers on SMEs (and business centres) their distinctive entrepreneurial character. Strong personal ownership is not, in itself, sufficient for success, but is a pre-condition.

In this light, it is self-evident that the most successful business centres – such as Oro – are run by people with a strong sense of ownership. Several other issues affect the degree to which ownership is strongly present in a business centre:

- *Operator and business centre management:* in both countries there is a split between those who legally own the business centre (the operator) and those who run it (the management).
- *SC support:* SC support can sometimes be perceived as 'unwelcome interference' and even undermine people's personal sense of business centre ownership. In both Indonesia and the Philippines there are examples of SC's advice being interpreted as outside their genuine scope of responsibility (Box 8.3).
- *Selection processes:* in general, business centres in Indonesia exhibit a much stronger sense of ownership than those in the Philippines. One factor is the selection process – through a detailed tendering procedure – which demands that they devote considerable resources of time and money (a fee is charged for tender submission) to the development of a plan to which they are committed. Business centres previously did not go through this demanding process.
- *Working with large organizations:* in both countries, business centres are sometimes part of larger organizations, such as chambers of commerce or consultancy businesses. In these situations, it is important that the business centre is able to establish its own identity rather than be submerged within the bigger organization.
- *Working with associations:* business centres in the Philippines which have emerged from membership associations face competing ownership pressures. On the one hand, members (clients) want good services on the most favourable terms; on the other, business centre managements want to charge prices that will enable them to reach financial sustainability in the long term. Usually, the short-term perspective wins to the detriment of the centre.

Capacity

Capacity includes not only the skills and knowledge of business centres but also the extent to which they are sufficiently business-focused.

In Indonesia, all business centres exhibit relatively high levels of technical capacity and commitment to human resource development. All business centres had staff with higher educational backgrounds. Staff training was budgeted for in all cases; either in-house, through SC or from external sources. Staff numbers are usually 5–6 permanent staff, 2–3 of whom are fee-generating. The level of small business experience is relatively limited, although some staff have worked in the private sector, e.g. banking. Business centres both develop and deliver services directly, or sub-contract where appropriate.

In the Philippines, the situation is more mixed. Most trade business centres deliver services directly, but their approach to pricing and marketing reveals weakness and lack of experience. Business centres offering training and consulting often have a limited administrative capacity and little ability to deliver services directly. Staff numbers are usually smaller than in Indonesia, with 2–4 staff and often some voluntary input. As in Indonesia, resources from SC are allocated specifically to human resource development. Much of SC's one-to-one technical assistance is aimed at developing people.

116

Three preliminary points emerge from the above:

- Business centres are more successful when they have a specific product which they know how to deliver, and know that SMEs want. Weak business centres, especially in the Philippines, usually don't have this. The most recent thinking in SC Indonesia emphasizes the importance of working with individuals as the core around which the centres may be developed.
- While sub-contracting is a valid means of delivering services, business centres which have no capacity to deliver directly may be perceived (and act) as just facilitating 'shells'.
- Business centres are more likely to be successful if they have a capacity to deliver services and a strong business instinct from the outset on which they can build. Business centres that are new to business are less likely to be successful.

Systems

Being relatively 'young' organizations with low levels of staff and activity, management systems in business centres are not fully developed. In many respects this reflects the experience of most small enterprises where systems develop from experience and to meet a tangible need, not through a rigid external reporting mechanism. Three types of system can be mentioned.

Measurement of inputs and cost. While SC's approach is based around very tight monitoring and analysis of financial performance, similarly rigorous systems of cost control and measurement have not yet been introduced within business centres. In the Philippines, where business centres are smaller and the incentive system is based around detailed analysis of income and expenditure figures, this is less problematic. However, in Indonesia, where the recording and measurement of inputs for product development and delivery was analysed in some depth in the business plans, detailed product-based measurement is not undertaken. To a considerable degree, this reflects SC's focus on self-financing targets for aggregate income, rather than for profitability, and also their view that internal systems are essentially the concern of the business centre.

Measurement of impact. Business centres are businesses; the underpinning indicator of performance is therefore financial. Measuring impact – changes which take place in SME clients – imposes a burden on business centres. Client information and data *can be* an important resource for businesses, in developing networks, selling services and assessing demand and market trends. However, most business centres either do not perceive benefits from this information or do not have the capacity to collect and use it; there is a sense that this kind of information is really the concern of the donor.

Remuneration and rewards. A few business centres have developed, or are planning to develop, performance-related components in their reward systems but it is certainly too early to assess their impact on overall business centre performance, either as personal performance (fee generated), as specific activity bonus (delivering a given service), or institutional performance (profit-related bonus or a dividend for shareholders).

117

Linkages

Business centres in Indonesia tend to have relatively developed networks, reflecting the fact that they have often been active in their area of interest for some time. These networks include venture capital companies, universities, state-owned firms and co-operatives, chambers of commerce and the NGO sector. In the Philippines, business centres operated by chambers of commerce usually also have strong supply-side networks; indeed, they are often represented on SMED councils and other SME development forums. Trade business centres, although less well connected, are still often aware of the opportunities from government schemes. In neither country are linkages significant constraints on business centre development.

The cost of the institutional development process

It is still relatively early in the development of business centres to make categorical statements on the cost of their development. In all the business centres supported by SC in Indonesia and the Philippines, financial and/or technical assistance is still being given; business centre development is not completed. The analysis is still fluid; it is premature to assert that $x of inputs gives a 'developed' self-financing centre. Nor is it easy to give average per annum figures; support is front-end loaded; business centres are different; and support may cease if targets are not met. With these caveats, the following can be said about the cost of business centre institutional development:

- Direct per annum costs of financial support to the donor (SC) vary between approximately US$12 000 in the Philippines and US$35 000 in Indonesia (in Peru, the comparable figure is US$20 000).
- Significant differences in the proposed duration of support mean that the total amount per business centre also varies. In the Philippines over three years it is likely to be US$20 000–25 000; in Indonesia (and Peru) approximately US$60 000.
- SC does not break down the value of its technical support to business centres. This is likely to be around 25–50 per cent of total financial support. Nor is there any attempt to apportion related overheads to specific business centres. Figures from the Philippines suggest that the ratio of financial support to technical support and overheads is approximately 1:1.5. In Indonesia and Peru it is probably closer to 1:1 since larger amounts are given per business centre.
- The total cost of reaching SMEs (the business centre clients) to SC is around US$600–700 per SME. However, as with all the above figures, their apparently relatively high expense can be misleading. The rationale for the business centre approach is that by investing (money and time) in a short period, long-term sustainability is achieved. Should this happen, per annum cost figures are spread over a longer period and should therefore be much lower.

Impact

There has been no detailed impact assessment on SME clients of business centres. Anecdotally, there are many examples of positive client feedback. Clearly, the onus for generating data lies with SC, and if business centres are to be involved this would have to be incorporated into contractual agreements with them and they might have to be paid to do so.

Current approaches do not seek to measure a baseline of business centre development at the start of their relationship with SC. There is a tacit assumption that business centre development can be attributed to SC inputs and is truly *additional*.

Achievements of business centres approach

The development of an innovative approach to donor support of BDS provision

Perhaps the most noteworthy achievement of the SMEP intervention is its commitment to learning and innovation that has openly set out to address the core global problems of sustainability and effectiveness in BDS.

The development of market-based, business-like BDS providers

Business centres may represent a potentially effective type of BDS provider, more business-like than traditional development partners, as for example in:

- relatively high levels of financial sustainability (some centres)
- motivation to generate revenue
- products that SMEs are prepared to pay for
- a strong sense of identity as a commercial entity.

Issues

Given the innovative nature of SC's approach it is not surprising that there are a number of important issues that remain substantially unresolved.

How much should we measure to maintain the business-development rationale?

Inherent in the business centre approach is a belief that the worlds of business and development – so often regarded as opposites – are closely related. Business skills and disciplines and the development of functioning BDS markets are building blocks on which development objectives can be pursued. One of the challenges posed by this alliance of business and development is in measurement. There are two key issues here:

- Avoiding distortion: the imposition of onerous administrative and monitoring systems can distort an organization's cost base and revenue-earning capacity. A key lesson from micro-finance is that systems of measurement need to be appropriate (in terms of technology, scale and cost) to the level of an organization's capacity and activity. This lesson is equally relevant to BDS.
- While it may be inappropriate to expect business centres to assess impact, SC has to be concerned with wider impact and outreach. Donor agencies represent a variety of stakeholders, such as governments and taxpayers, and cannot simply be concerned with the 'bottom line'. Getting the right balance may involve commissioning external organizations to monitor, or paying centres to undertake this service.

How to build business-like BDS organizations through donor support

Under this heading numerous issues arise, including:

- How can technical support for product and skills development be included as part of the overall relationship?

- How can a stronger sense of ownership develop in those who are running business centres?
- How to avoid the creation of 'bloated' cost structures which usually bear the hallmark of donors rather than business?

Creating a conducive environment for BDS market development

In this context, business centres seeking to maximize revenue will – logically – move towards institutions that offer the most revenue-earning potential. There are major risks here: any form of transactional relationship may be weakened, overall effectiveness reduced, and dependence on uncertain sources of funds (government budgets) increased. In the longer term, as with micro-finance, the business centre approach is most likely to be successful when governments and donors collaborate on developing a more detailed picture of BDS. Attempts to create sustainable BDS markets may easily be undermined by ill-considered interventions.

Working with the private sector

A direct corollary of working with new types of partner is facing the challenge of engaging with established private sector enterprises (such as consulting firms and accountants). The approach is analogous to the experience of micro-finance in attempting to focus commercial companies towards SMEs (downscaling), as opposed to developing services from the bottom upwards via NGOs (upgrading).

Donors need to be clear that:

- there will be *additional* impact from their intervention – for example, a new client group or new services
- support will not simply *displace* investment for activities that the private sector was already undertaking or planning to undertake.

Bibliography

Committee of Donor Agencies for Small Enterprise Development (1998); *Business Development Services for SMEs: Preliminary Guidelines for Donor-Funded Interventions.*

Durham University Business School, Small Business Centre (1990); *Managing Small Business Growth: A Guide for Trainers.*

Edgcomb, E., Cawley, J., (eds), (1993); *An institutional guide for enterprise development organisations*, The Small Enterprise Education and Promotion Network (SEEP).

Gibb, A.A. (1988); 'Enterprise culture: its meaning and implications for education and training', ILO.

Notes

1. While it is not usual for intervening agencies to refer to what they do as 'services', 'products' or an 'offer', these are appropriate terms here (and are used interchangeably); SC itself needs to play a business-like role for the business centre approach to be successful and has to perceive of its work in these terms.
2. Although in both countries Swisscontact arrived at the business centre approach through its experience of other types of intervention.
3. With the exception of trade business centres in the Philippines, although there are questions here over the potentially distorting effect on markets.

4. Represents payments for services directly from SMEs, indirectly via intermediary organizations, and also non-SME related services, including those undertaken for SC.
5. In Peru, SC is pursuing a more systematic approach to product development and is seeking to establish 'second tier' support institutions in the BDS 'industry' that provides services to business centres. A key role in Peru is franchizing training methodologies from abroad.
6. Indeed, the SC experience in Peru warns specifically against supporting services of this kind.
7. The definition of this indicator varies slightly; in the Philippines it is gross profit against overheads; in Indonesia it has been income against total expenditure, but is now similar to the Philippines.
8. Calculated using the most recent figures for the Philippines (mainly first quarter 1998 data) and the average figure in the first five months of 1998 for Indonesia; Indonesian figures are given for only three business centres.
9. There are other 'frameworks' for institutional assessment – for example the growth framework of Durham University Business School and the SEEP institutional development framework; the headings used here borrow from these and other sources.

9. Enterprise Development Centres in Latin America

ANTONIO GARCIA TABUENCA and JUAN JOSÉ LLISTERRI

The EDC project

Introduction and object of the initiative

THE ENTERPRISE DEVELOPMENT CENTRES (EDC), of recent creation in several Latin American countries, are an initiative of the Inter-American Development Bank (IADB) and are targeted on two main objectives: the invigoration of the business development service market from the demand side, and the creation of a sustainable institutional framework. They have been created with the intent to support the transformation and modernization of the production structures in small and medium-sized enterprises existing in the region. Resources from the Multilateral Investment Fund (MIF), a fund under the IADB management, have been used.

The role of EDCs is to aid small and medium-size enterprises (SMEs) – 5 to 99 employees – in the identification of their managerial and technical challenges; to counsel them when hiring business development services (BDS) in the market, to share the cost of consultants, and finally, to proceed to a joint assessment of results generated from the use of these services. Therefore, EDC projects attempt to enhance the local BDS market, at the local and regional levels, by promoting new demand from participating firms.

Additional goals are: to promote collective actions for SME groups, to better target local BDS supply, to strengthen private sector organizations via their participation in the management of the centres, and, lastly, to contribute, with contents from the local level, to regional or national small enterprise policy design and evaluation.

The expected result of the national projects (in the 3–4 year projected time-frame) is the consolidation of a network of 10 private, self-financed enterprise development centres to effectively boost the demand for technical assistance by the SMEs.

The goal of this paper is to describe those profiles common to all the above-mentioned EDCs and assess their performance.[1] Following the required task of data standardization, which has been annotated with qualitative remarks by the stakeholders, this chapter offers a temporary outlook and a comparative analysis of results deemed most significant: the scope of the projects in terms of number of beneficiary firms, size of targeted firms, type of BDS intermediated by the centres, degree of client satisfaction, collective demand for services by groups of firms, revenues generated and sustainability of the EDCs, impact of the projects on the supply of BDS, and the learning processes of participating institutions. The analysis offers a better understanding of the IADB/MIF Pilot Projects and leads to draw relevant lessons for further actions to develop the BDS market and benefit SME development.

EDC structure

The executing agency in each project is a private sector organization (chambers of industry, corporate associations and other foundations or entities working to promote both industry and regional development and SMEs). See Table 9.1.

Table 9.1 Enterprise Development Centres (EDC) in Lating America

Country	Project name	National Executive Agency	Time frame	No. of local ent.	EDC
Costa Rica	Competitiveness for Small Enterprise (PROGRESE)	Costa Rican Chamber of Industry (CICR)	1995/98 Ext.: 2000	6[2]	7 CEEMs[1]
El Salvador	Support to Productive Development and Competitiveness (SIAPE)	National Private Sector Association (ANEP)	1995/98 Ext.: 2000	7[3]	7 CEEMs[1]
Argentina	Network of Enterprise Development Centers	Argentine Industrial Union of (UIA)	1996/99	12 (3 Foundations)[4]	– Rafaela – Mar del Plata – San Rafael
Colombia	National Program for Enterprise Development Centers	Confecámaras	1996/99 Prev: 2000	14 (5 Regional Executive Units)[5]	– Bogota – Medellín – Cali – Barranquilla – Bucaramanga

[1]CEEMs: Corporate extension centres, using premises and staff from executive organizations.
[2]Technological Management Center Foundation, Costa Rican Coalition for Development Initiatives, Bolivar Program, Chamber of Costa Rican Experters, Costa Rican Union of Private Sector Chambers and Associations.
[3]ASI, COEXPORT, FUSADES, Santa Ana Chamber of Commerce and Industry, CCI of San Salvador, CCI of San Miguel.
[4]*Rafaela:* Castellanos Dept. Commercial and Industrial Center, Foreign Trade Chamber, Chamber of Metallurgical Industries, Foundation for Regional Development, Center for Industry, Commerce and Farming, Las Colonias Dept., San Francisco Association of Metallurgical Industries; *Mar del Plata:* Commercial, Industrial and Production Union; *San Rafael:* San Rafael Chamber of Industry, Commerce and Agriculture and Cattle Breeding.
[5]*Santa Fe de Bogotá:* Chamber of Commerce of Bogotá, ACOPI; *Medellín:* University EAFIT, ACOPI, Chamber of Commerce Medellín; *Calli:* Chamber of Commerce Cali, ACOPI, Universidad del Valle; *Barranquilla:* Chamber of Commerce Baranquilla, ACOPI, CORPES/Costa Atlántica; *Bucaramanga:* Chamber of Commerce Bucaramanga, Universidad Autónoma, ACOPI.

Each National Executing Agency has a national co-ordination office or unit whose stated mission is to draft annual plans, co-ordinate and monitor EDC activities, regulate managerial procedures, and encourage, through networked activities, the joint use of instruments, methods and expertise.

Argentina and Colombia have regional executive agencies. The Argentine agency is legally structured as a foundation, while in Colombia executive roles have been commissioned to a partner entity. Local participating agencies from Costa Rica and El Salvador have an in-house branch office or enterprise extension centre (CEEM) to provide all project services. The institutional and strategic management of each EDC is handled by a steering committee.

Each EDC has a small team of expert professionals who act as internal consultants for the centre. This team is led by a manager selected in a thorough process by the steering committee. This manager co-ordinates promotional activities established in an annual management plan drawn up according to corporate criteria. The staff further includes two or three professionals (usually engineers or economists), a managing officer and, on occasion, a deputy manager. Some centres have also included an 'in-house program co-ordinator', a staff member assigned to a specific task. All technical staff – including the manager – working for the EDC are paid according to a professional services agreement negotiated on an annual basis and in accordance to the rate of target completion. Therefore, there are no labour ties. As a rule, compensation criteria are dictated by market practices. In some instances a results-based incentive compensation scheme was attempted but results have so far been inconclusive. However, the administrative staff do have contractual and labour ties with the local leader institution.

Offices are usually located at the premises of those host institutions (one case being a university with a strong business and corporate services school calling) playing the regional leading role. In some cases, these facilities, for the most part modest in terms of space and infrastructure, are so closely imbedded in the premises that differentiating them from the host institution would be quite difficult were it not for the sign identifying the EDC project. Other hosts, however, provide locations with increased autonomy, that are easier to identify, affording, in turn, the degree of management independence required for the project.

EDC operation normally follows this scheme: each EDC, acting in accordance with its marketing strategy, promotes its own services as a service intermediator – normally via door-to-door visits – for SMEs and offers a preliminary diagnosis of the firm's needs. When an SME asks the EDC for a service, independently of whether EDC staff originally identified it or not, the centre calls on several expert consultants for bids that are later, and with its due breakdown, submitted to the firm for its consideration. The company is then in the position to select the best fit consultant. A service contract binding all three parties – the company, the EDC and the consultant – is drawn up. At the completion of the hired services, the firm will pay the EDC the costs agreed to in the contract, less the amount – the MIF grant – brought in by the EDC; the EDC will pay the consultant the fee provided for in the contract.

Services (training, information and, occasionally, direct technical assistance) may also be rendered directly by the centres through their own technical staff or through the local co-executing agencies which hire full-time agents to prolong the project. This latter format is more readily applicable in Costa Rica and El Salvador.

The price or fees charged to the firms only partially cover service costs; the MIF grant writes off the amounts fixed. However, the share of the cost paid by the firms increases with time in such a way that by the project's end, the hiring firm must be paying the total amounts due for the services provided. This gradual increase in the share paid by the firms should produce, in the end, economically feasible and sustainable projects. BDS rates have been established in line with market prices of like services available and depending on the firms' ability to pay. For services not available in a given market, the reference utilized was its implementation cost.

Financing centre projects

Contributions from the IADB/MIF are destined primarily to finance the technical staff in each EDC and a portion of the costs derived from hiring outside consultants to provide services to local firms. The local partner's contributions are earmarked to finance the infrastructure of the EDC (offices, equipment, etc.) as well as to compensate administrative staff. Finally, and as shown in Table 9.2, a third component of the financing arrangement for the project in Argentina and Colombia comes from the income earned by each centre after billing beneficiary companies. In El Salvador and Costa Rica practically all income is 'saved' to a sustainability fund.

There are two types of projects in terms of their cost and financing: the first, adopted by the two small Central American countries, needs the IADB/MIF to put in 75 per cent of the total cost while local partners are accountable for the

Table 9.2 Financing of EDC projects and contributions (in US$)

Country	Total project cost	IADB/MIF		Local ent.		EDC income service sales		Reserve fund (sustainability)
		Contribuition	%	Contribution	%	Contribution	%	% of income
Costa Rica	3 340 000	2 491 000	74.6	701 000	21.0	148 000	4.4	913 000 100.0
El Salvador	2 758 000	2 070 000	75.0	688 000	25.0	(1)		1 195 200 100.0
Argentina	15 254 660	8 475 000	55.6	2 908 100	19.1	3 871 560	25.3	931 890 20.0
Colombia	10 314 547	5 966 641	57.9	1 227 906	11.9	3 120 000	30.2	936 000 30.0

(1) All EDC income received from the companies is allocated to the *Sustainability* Fund.

remaining 25 per cent. The uncertainty of generating income from the sale of services in smaller countries advises against having project completion dependent on the income generated. The second approach, adopted in the relatively larger countries, calls for IADB/MIF financing of close to 55 per cent and the remaining 45 per cent must be supplied by the local entities and through income generated by the EDC itself.

The concept of EDC sustainability is based on the assumption that for each project, once the MIF contribution is no longer supplied (at the end of the third or fourth), the centre will be charging market rates and may even secure a discount from BDS providers, given its role as an intermediator and confidence generator with entrepreneurs. This discount offered by providers, or the mediation fee charged to the firms, would cover the EDC overhead costs.

Each EDC will retain a percentage of the income generated through the selling of their services to set up a reserve or sustainability fund (Table 9.2). This arrangement aims to promote a discipline and manner of thinking contributory to programme continuity and sustainability. The use of these reserve funds would extend the impact of the IADB/MIF contribution beyond the expected project duration, provided the EDCs have managed to save a portion of their earnings.

Results

The analysis of provisional results of EDC projects focuses on four core issues: the scope of service coverage from the demand side; the cost of providing new services, the income generated and the degree of self-financing; the apparent impact on SME service suppliers; and the learning curve for the institutional consolidation of EDCs.

Reach of EDC services on target companies

The first indicator used is the number of companies assisted by the centres; in second place is the size of these firms; next is a review of features included in EDC intermediated services; and in last position is a report on the degree of satisfaction of EDC user firms.

Scope of enterprise coverage. Table 9.3 displays a biannual breakdown that shows not only the growing number of companies assisted by an EDC for the first time, but also the importance the initiative has had in the general performance of those SMEs lying within the arm's length of each centre. Data currently available include companies receiving a broad scope of services, individual companies, and groups of firms.

Table 9.3 Company coverage by the EDCs: *new companies* receiving assistance (through December 31, 1998)[1]

Country	Sem I 1995	Sem II 1995	Sem I 1996	Sem II 1996	Sem I 1997	Sem II 1997	Sem I 1998	Sem II 1998	Total Number	%s/TG
Costa Rica	0	0	70	230	433	480	614	387	2214	45.9
El Salvador	28	246	160	261	142	87	66	137	1127	11.6
Argentina	–	–	–	–	201	394	413	482	1490	29.5
– EDC Rafaela	–	–	–	–	125	182	292	303	902	35.5
– EDC Mar del P.	–	–	–	–	25	141	31	134	331	26.3
– San Rafael	–	–	–	–	51	71	90	45	257	20.6
Colombia	–	–	–	–	19	104	203	655	981	6.7
– EDC Bogotá	–	–	–	–	–	14	42	141	197	3
– EDC Medellín	–	–	–	–	8	18	40	126	192	7
– EDC Cali	–	–	–	–	–	19	36	86	141	5.5
– EDC Barranquilla	–	–	–	–	11	26	69	270	376	3.5
– EDC Bucaraman.	–	–	–	–	–	27	16	32	75	4.2
Total	28	246	230	491	795	1065	1296	1661	5812	17

[1]Note that in Costa Rica and El Salvador the projects would be, at this date, almost completed, however they have been prolonged up to the year 2000. Argentina and Colombia are halfway into the projects (Table 9.1).
[2]*SME* Target Group (TG): manufacturing formal enterprises with between 5 and 99 employees and belonging to the area of influence of an EDC or set of EDCs. Data extracted from official statistics and from project reports.

The following general conclusions and considerations can be drawn:

- The EDC project has achieved substantial success by promoting over 5800 different firms to become true seekers in the enterprise services markets of the four countries involved. Over 3300 of them came from two small countries (Costa Rica and El Salvador). EDCs in the four participating countries have provided services to over 17 per cent of accounted formal SMEs, which is a meaningful percentage once one considers the span of the SME universe in the target group.
- The number of companies served by EDCs is, on the whole, growing; hence it is a reflection of the increased positive impact of the project. Factors with an influence on the progress of enterprise coverage are:
  ○ the point of departure for each particular centre. Take-off for centres well integrated in their business communities (Rafaela, Argentina) included a very large number of clients due to their acquired expertise.
  ○ independent marketing strategies for each EDC. While some centres adopted a broad coverage approach, others chose to focus intensively on a reduced number of companies and pay better attention to them, especially in the early stages when the centre was still new.
  ○ the conceivable exhaustion of the target market. In El Salvador, for example, the number of companies assisted per semester declined in 1997. Saturation of the target company niche, cutbacks in outside funding as the project nears completion or – more likely – the need to focus on companies that can actually pay might be the fundamental reasons ruling this pattern of behaviour.

Company size. Table 9.4 classifies firms into three different size determined groups: firms with fewer than 20 employees; firms with 21 to 99 employees, and firms with over 99 employees (this last group is 'off target', their larger size makes them ineligible for subsidy).

126

Table 9.4 Size of firms assisted by the EDC (through June 30, 1998)

Country	1–20 employees		21–99 employees		>99 employees		Total
	number	%s/tot	number	%s/tot	number	%s/tot	
Costa Rica	939	51.4	665	36.4	(1) 223	12.2	1827
El Salvador	748	75.6	220	22.2	22	2.2	990
Argentina	831	82.4	137	13.6	(2) 40	4.0	1008
Colombia	119	36.5	177	54.3	30	9.2	326
Total	2637	63.5	1199	28.9	315	7.6	4151

(1) During the first semester of 1998, the EDC in Costa Rica saw a considerable increase in services supplied to firms exceeding 99 employees (135 units; i.e. 60 per cent of the 223 total).
(2) Of the 40 companies with over 100 employees, 37 are working with the Rafaela EDC.

These data, additional quantitative information available from the EDC, and direct observation lead to the following considerations.

- As expected, the smaller ventures prevail, firms with fewer than 20 workers account for nearly two-thirds of the total; firms with 20–100 workers represent a percentage greater than 25 per cent of the total. This indicator may gauge the type and design of future programmes carried out by the centres. The lower rank of the first segment requires that services be more basic and that they be suitable for more extensive marketing of EDC services. Conversely, mid-sized companies (approximately 100 workers) embarked on a modernization effort require more intensive, sophisticated and value-added programmes and services. The comparative data show that, for the most part, it is mid-sized firms that extract the most benefit from innovation and they, too, create a favourable atmosphere for positive outside influences.
- From the information available for each country on the development of average client company size, one can state that the centres are being forced, by the natural process of the projects, to meet billing and sustainability targets and, therefore, shift the focus of their marketing effort towards companies of larger relative size.
- Working beyond the scope of what is considered eligible (>99 workers) are enterprises from Costa Rica, Colombia – whose 'target market' stretches to 199 employees – and the Rafaela EDC (Argentina): in all, one out of every 13 companies assisted has more than 100 employees. That 'off-target' firms be rendered services is a situation prompted by: the proactive approach of some centres (given the strategic regional significance of certain firms); an attempt to effectively market the EDC's technical capabilities; and by a certain degree of pressure put out by the more solvent demand segment – at no subsidy. This situation, in turn, allows for a cross-subsidy to be offered to smaller companies. Among the services available for off-target firms are: customized management training programmes (Costa Rica and Argentina); creation of firm groups for quality certification; drafting of strategic company plans (Colombia); arrangements related to the subcontracting of groups of firms by large regional sector driver companies (Argentina, Costa Rica).
- In more than one instance, a larger corporation – whose top managers are linked to industry associations that are partners in the project – has hired services from the EDC to enhance its standing and business objectives.

Types of services offered directly by EDC or through its intermediation. Each project establishes what services the EDC will offer to national or local companies. However, in all cases, the services arrangement matured away from each centre's original marketing and services supply plans in response to the qualitative input put across by the firms involved. Adaptation was also called for in order to allow the centre to react promptly to changing supply and demand structures. The most prevalent arrangement of these services have been drawn from a survey of the total range offered by the 10 EDCs. According to the survey and according to business and demand figures (since the two variables are often linked), the three most successful types of services supplied are:

First, *Training in business management skills* (a wide variety of subjects concerning the production and business cycle) via continuous improvement techniques. Second, *Technical assistance through consultancy tools*, a service lead by programmes focused on the spawning and running of systems destined to certify *industrial quality* (in Colombia assistance targeted primarily on diagnostic 'corporate competitive assessment' projects and on 'improvement specific' projects). Third, *Marketing and export support services* (usually foreign trade promotion programmes).

However, centre managers also foster programmes that are of significant importance to them in their attempt to reach higher value-added rankings. Included, among others, are: the encouragement of networks (El Salvador); a subcontracting exchange and electronic commerce opportunities (Costa Rica); strategic planning and management – under the national training program – (Colombia); programmes to enhance company management – business workshops, organization and development of top managers – (Argentina/Rafaela); sector-specific programmes (Argentina: Mar del Plata, San Rafael and Rafaela).

Gauging user satisfaction. Table 9.5 analyses services to new EDC clients and the rate at which these new clients have repeatedly demanded the same service. We understand that a high repetition rate may imply that the service is highly esteemed by the clients, especially if we consider the fact that they pay for it. The

Table 9.5   Repetition rate versus total number of assistance services to companies (new + repetitions) by semester

Country	Sem I 1995	Sem II 1995	Sem I 1996	Sem II 1996	Sem I 1997	Sem II 1997	Sem I 1998	Total	RR (1)
Costa Rica	0	0	70	238	455	568	698	2029	1.1
El Salvador	26	292	306	799	296	233	194	2146	2.2
Argentina	–	–	–	–	216	594	628	1438	1.4
– Rafaela EDC	–	–	–	–	123	358	448	929	1.6
– Mar del P. EDC	–	–	–	–	25	141	31	197	1.0
– San Rafael	–	–	–	–	68	95	149	312	1.5
Colombia	–	–	–	–	28	151	231	410	1.3
– Bogotá EDC	–	–	–	–	–	17	46	63	1.1
– Medellín EDC	–	–	–	–	8	21	52	81	1.2
– Cali EDC	–	–	–	–	–	28	45	73	1.3
– Barranquilla EDC	–	–	–	–	20	38	56	114	1.1
– Bucaraman. EDC	–	–	–	–	–	47	32	79	1.8
Total	26	292	376	1037	995	1546	1751	6023	1.5

(1) RR: Repitition rate of companies requesting more than one service from the EDC, equivalent to the ratio between the total number of assistance services and the same for the new companies on the Table 9.3. Computed only for the total number of assistance services provided by each EDC.

repetition rate shows to what degree firms (and the centre) are willing to receive (and offer) new services of increased value-added.

The set of data available point to the following conclusions.

- By mid-1998 services had been rendered on over 6000 occasions. The repetition rate is 1.5; a figure meaning that, on the average, half the companies calling on EDC services were assisted twice; this seems to reflect reasonable customer satisfaction.
- El Salvador and the Rafaela/Argentina EDC are above average. The projects of Colombia (still too new to produce client loyalty) and Costa Rica (seeking new clients of higher purchasing power) have a lower rate of repeated assistance to the same companies. These results would lead one to believe that, on the whole, the EDC performance is extensive rather than intensive; that is, probably due to time constraints in the struggle to meet their targets, the centres have chosen an 'all-out attack' on the widespread SME market, especially during the first two years of project development. Every centre manager and technical staff member can 'sell' their product better in the short run – and early more credibility for it – if they show figures meaning unbroken growth. The first figures available for an enterprise promotion entity are those relative to the total number of companies assisted.

Costs of, and income obtained from, services provided

Operating costs of the services. Table 9.6 displays a review of the costs of those services rendered by hiring outside consultants, it further shows a breakdown of the proportion subsidized by the IADB/MIF and the proportion put across directly by the companies to the centres in order to cover total operating costs. From the standpoint of amounts billed by the EDCs, the latter entry is their actual income, a key element if they wish to meet project goals and future sustainability.

Table 9.6 Cost of services: IADB/MIF financing and EDC income (US$ as at June 1998)

Country	No. of semesters (1)	Outside consultant costs	IADB/MIF financing		EDC income from the companies	
			Amount	% of total	Amount	% of total
Costa Rica	5/9	912 140	529 577	58.1	382 563	41.9
El Salvador	7/11	391 580	178 085	45.5	213 495	54.5
Argentina	3/8	844 566	552 361	65.4	292 205	34.6
– Rafaela EDC	3/8	501 897	304 127	60.6	197 770	39.4
– Mar del Plata EDC	3/8	187 821	130 907	69.7	56 914	30.3
– San Rafael EDC	3/8	154 848	117 327	75.8	37 521	24.2
Colombia (2)	3/8	705 838	428 514	68.4	223 324	31.6
– Bogotá EDC	2/8	137 816	90 345	65.6	47 471	34.4
– Medellín EDC	3/8	187 678	125 555	66.9	62 123	33.1
– Cali EDC	2/8	77 544	57 204	73.8	20 340	26.2
– Barranquilla EDC	3/8	218 273	147 712	67.7	70 561	32.3
– Bucaramange EDC	2/8	84 527	61 698	73.0	22 829	27.0

(1) Semesters of real EDC activity over the total scheduled, including extensions authorized by the IADB.
(2) In Colombia the cost of outside consultants includes part of the funds brought in by the centres themselves from direct consulting services linked to some of their own services (Preliminary projections and Comprehensive competitiveness studies). Subsidized contributions here means both what is directly financed through IADB/MIF funds and the portion offered indirectly by the EDC.

Table 9.6 suggests that:

- The projects in Colombia and Argentina, although practically halfway through completion, still depend heavily (68 per cent in one case and 65 per cent the other) on subsidies in order to render their services to the companies. The logical assumption is that this rate will gradually decline as the project progresses until it is, at last, cancelled. In Costa Rica and El Salvador, two initiatives that enjoy extensions, the average subsidies to date range from a high of 58 per cent for Costa Rica to a lower 45 per cent for El Salvador.
- El Salvador stands out as the centre that received the most income from its companies in relative terms, followed by the EDC in Costa Rica. Among the Argentine centres, Rafaela leads in billing – approximately 40 per cent – while San Rafael falls just short of 25 per cent of the total. Of the Colombian centres, Bogotá, Medellín and Barranquilla managed to bill companies for more than 30 per cent of the total cost of their services.
- Until June 1998, aid from the MIF has meant approximately half the cost of outside services, even in Costa Rica and El Salvador, where they are at the final stages of the project. It is worth noting how these two countries have maintained the same subsidy rate despite their stepped-up efforts during the last two terms to earn more revenues. In other words, there seems to be a limit or specific obstruction preventing the centres, at least for the duration of the projects, from tapping the existing and developed market so as to earn enough to become sustainable intermediator entities.
- These same variables (subsidy and income paid by the companies) should be specifically analysed for the different types of services and different size companies. The EDCs often discuss what should be the top-most admissible subsidized amount per project and per company because raising this mark allows for greater income from companies of higher investment and compensation capabilities. Conversely, smaller companies, or those from markedly backward areas, seem to find more difficulty in paying their share of the cost of services and need a higher subsidy.
- The success of an EDC hinges on its institutional consolidation, on the management and skill of its technical staff, but also, and in a significant manner, on the financial support they can get over a period longer than the programmed three/four year span.
- The institutional development of a centre goes hand-in-hand with the degree of social involvement or entrepreneurial culture of the region where it is located. This attribute cannot be generated spontaneously but rather results from complex social, political, economic and financial relations that need time to mature. In this sense, a more developed market for BDS would allow a reduction (or even complete removal) of the subsidies sooner than in weaker markets.

Fix costs and the EDC sustainability fund. Another way of looking at the sustainability of a centre is through either the ratio between its operative result or profits[2] and the EDC's fixed costs, or the ratio between income from the billing of firms and fixed costs. This latter approach is developed later. Table 9.7 was created from data available to the authors relative to the centre's fixed costs, reflects the behaviour of this variable for each EDC, and gives an idea of the cost of the structure that could eventually be financed by revenues generated by the intermediation of BDS:

130

- Of projects developed by the larger countries, Argentina, so far, nearly reaches a full fix cost covering of 80 per cent (the Rafaela EDC stands out with 113 per cent of self-generated funds, and contributing considerably to raise the Argentine average). The Colombian project, has had a strong forward push in 1998 (the Medellín EDC on the high end).
- Of the smaller countries, Costa Rica reaches 33 per cent while El Salvador is at 26 per cent. It is apparent that, as it nears the end of the project, the centre improves its self-financing performance, be it because of a stricter selection of a reduced number of clients (El Salvador), or the attraction of larger clients (Costa Rica), or an increase in fees, or for embarking on new and more profitable activities.
- The greater the share of the cost of outside consultants covered by income from client companies the higher the likelihood of sustainability, provided that fixed costs are held within reasonable limits *vis-à-vis* the size of the market. This likelihood is also greater as the project closes in on its completion date. Likewise, it seems that larger markets (most often in larger countries) are more favourable to greater sustainability.

Table 9.7   % of fixed expenses covered by income of the EDC in by December 31, 1998[1]

Country	1995	1996	1997	1998	Total
Costa Rica	–	5.1	42.3	51.9	30.0
El Salvador	9.9	19.0	19.0	42.8	26.0
Argentina	–	–	35.4	79.5	62.8
– Rafaela EDC	–	–	61.6	113.1	100.3
– Mar del Plata EDC	–	–	24.1	26.4	25.0
– San Rafael EDC	–	–	15.4	47	28.2
Colombia	–	–	7.1	68.1	42.5
– Bogotá EDC	–	–	2.8	43.8	33.8
– Medellín EDC	–	–	3.6	174.3	81.0
– Cali EDC	–	–	6.4	32.5	21.1
– Barranquilla EDC	–	–	13.6	64.9	41.7
– Bucaramanga EDC	–	–	10.4	65.4	33.1

(1) This table shows income received from billing consultancy services provided to companies. EDCs often have additional sources of income in the services they provide directly through their own consultants.

Table 9.8 displays the results and forecasts for the sustainability (or reserve) fund set up in each EDC as required in the original project. This fund is fed by a percentage of the income generated by the centres and is a very good instrument to measure the operational status and/or health of each EDC. In Costa Rica, three-quarters of forecast amounts have been surpassed. The other countries are still far from the target (in El Salvador, centre management is optimistic, based on the billing outlook of the past few months). Rafaela, Argentina, has reached approximately 45 per cent of its forecast numbers. As projects come close to an end the importance of the sustainability fund emerges as a matter of survival of the whole project. In the case of El Salvador, the creation of a foundation as a joint effort with GTZ and FUNDES local affiliates is being considered as a way of guaranteeing the sustainability of the EDC.

131

Table 9.8   Reserve or fund (by December 31, 1998)

Country	No. of semesters (1)	Forecast in the project (US$)	Actual figures	
			Amount (2) (US$)	% of total
Costa Rica	6 s/ 9	913 658	(3) 693 653	75.9
El Salvador	7 s/ 11	1 195 200	298 490	25.0
Argentine	3 s/ 8	681 850	158 519	23.2
– Rafaela EDC	3 s/ 8	255 970	(4) 115 373	45.1
– Mar del Plata EDC	3 s/ 8	212 940	19 301	9.1
– San Rafael EDC	3 s/ 8	212 940	23 845	11.2
Colombia (5)	3 s/ 8	936 000	169 441	18.1

(1) Semesters of actual EDC operation over the total scheduled, including extensions authorized by the IADB.
(2) EDC figures for total income (income from both outside hiring and internal services0.
(3) Computed according to the accrual accounting practice (issue of invoice upon service execution).
(4) The fund is not yet established in Colombia. Thus, its figures were computed globally by applying the 30 per cent set by the project to the income figure (the share covered by the companies).

Supply of consultant services

Setting up a BDS market is the major mission of the EDC project. The fundamental aspect to consider is that to articulate between supply and demand is precisely the same as market intermediation, as the EDCs add value to the services rendered through them by external consultants. EDC have rosters of registered consultants and occasionally issue 'certificates' to local professionals; professors and businessmen working as SME consultants. No evidence exists to confirm that the use of these rosters has either a positive or negative consequence, with perhaps the single exception that in some countries the number of domestic consultants has grown substantially, replacing the international consultants originally hired by the centres. Experience has shown that the process of selecting a consultant may originate from initiatives from either of the three parties involved: the consultant party itself may offer its services and at subsidized rates (and if there is no effective competition, fees might be artificially raised); the seeking firm by presenting a previously identified service provider; or, on most occasions, EDC staff, who will submit a list of prospective consultants, leaving the final decision to the firm alone.

On the other hand, there are limitations to the development of local consultants, especially due to a lack of expertise and an, as yet, unproven quality. In addition, the firms often prefer the reputation and confidentiality offered by consultants located in large cities. It is therefore arguable whether the EDCs should support the supply side when there is almost no BDS market at all. Several EDCs have been very active in creating programmes to train consultants.

The number of consultants who have joined the project varies in the different countries and centres. As at June 1998, 101 consultants had completed 304 services in Costa Rica. In El Salvador the EDC has intermediated the services of 72 different consultants. The absolute figures for these two countries can be positively assessed, particularly given the fact that both have made significant efforts, more actively in the last 18 months, to create, boost and consolidate a previously meager local consulting market which remained unable to take off since demand was not large enough to foster an increased supply. Further information is required in order to be able to correlate between new consultants providing services to SMEs and the profile of client companies, type of service they render, profile of the new consultants and, more significantly, their level of expertise and professional quality.

Institutionalization of the project and the learning curve

The EDC project aims to create or enlarge a BDS market system which would necessarily involve local partners from the private sector. The idea, therefore, was to set up an institutional market intermediation framework with support from non-governmental organizations with the calling and, preferably, technical skills and experience to stimulate BDS demand.

All four countries involve in the initiative produced different agreements to govern partner involvement in the projects; the main efforts, however, were targeted on summoning industry associations deeply rooted in national or regional SMEs. For the most part, based on available project data, the results appear to be encouraging; however, obstacles have been many. All in, the experience lets us draw the following general conclusions:

- In nearly all instances the start-up took much longer than expected (six to 18 months). The fact that institutional exchanges fared better may be due to two main factors: first, an existing structure of partnerships (and of business management); and second, a culture of institutional co-operation (and of conflict resolution). Furthermore, the process of learning to perform a new task also required the selection and training of a team; the preparation of a first business plan reflecting regional market priorities; early action involving corporate identification and marketing; adoptive accounting and monitoring complex procedures required by the IADB, and learning from progressive evaluations. Indeed, every agent involved in the project has had to do some learning: institutions, managers/staff, consultants, companies and certainly the IADB/MIF.
- If a service facilitating institution aims to be effective, it must be able to generate trust. All parties involved in these pilot programmes must firmly believe in the project's worth and develop a relationship based on mutual trust in order to be able to convey a feeling of trust to a market consisting of companies needing the services, and the consultants to supply them. The early lack of trust has been one of the causes of the delays in attaining results. This is true both at the local/regional level and at the national level.
- The involvement of varied institutions enhances the institutional support to EDCs. In fact, the participation of universities, foundations, trade associations and local government agencies helps to alleviate rivalries. The MIF projects have excluded government from any involvement in the projects. However, experience has confirmed the importance of relying on support from local government, as well as working in harmony with the policies and programmes of the public sector at a national level.
- The management of EDCs must be independent from their sponsoring institutions in order to avoid transferring any existing discord between supporting institutions and to stimulate the pursuit of sustainability for their projects. When the EDCs were established as foundations, this allowed them to develop the institutional potential of each regional centre.
- There is a risk of institutional differences having a negative impact on the EDCs. The four countries studied offer examples taken from three different

sources: first, some participating institutions would like to regard the EDC as an extension of their own activities or programmes to help their members, and thus the project's purpose may be weakened. Next, some partner organizations might feel uneasy with the EDC project, because control of programmes formerly managed to such organizations are transferred to the EDC. Lastly, political institutions that have co-operated in the early stages of the project, because of their participation in previous comparable public initiatives, may feel the project owes them something, and hence give rise to institutional disputes.

Conclusions and recommendations

Although two of the projects are still far from complete, a review of results in all four projects studied here leads to the general conclusion that they are effectively meeting their objectives: to promote BDS market by increasing the demand for such services, and to create an increasingly better prepared institutional framework to promote the hiring of services, and with increasing financial sustainability.

Some of the most relevant lessons from this experience are:

- *Slow start-up and collection of results.* Unless projects have evolved from long past experience and are driven by highly dynamic institutions, the introduction of new functions to boost the market required a slow start-up and cautious procedures. It was not uncommon to have to wait for 12 to 24 months before the expected results become apparent. The process of the local entities taking over managerial responsibility; the recruitment, training and organizing of professional staff; defining a strategy for each EDC in its own market, and further developing it into a viable business plan; and establishing administrative and monitoring procedures (including IADB/MIF supervision) are the main reasons for the general slow start of the projects. A good project design, tailored to local needs and circumstances, and incorporating appropriate working resources, might hasten the launch of new projects.
- *The projects may have a significant impact on the target SME group*, not only due to the absolute number of companies assisted, but also because of the degree of influence that the assisted companies have on the whole body of eligible ventures. The marketing strategy of each EDC should set goals congruent with its medium- and long-term financial targets. Either a larger fund allotment, or income from billing for services rendered to the larger firms, are necessary in order to subsidize more companies, usually of smaller size, through extension of services. Given the limited availability of 'soft' funds, the scope and coverage of this type of action is necessarily limited. More detailed study of this kind of experience is needed to assess the trade-off between service extension and lack of sustainability.
- The issue of the *most appropriate type of service* to be mediated by the EDCs is closely bound to the concept of sustainability. Again, each EDC project must decide whether to operate through an extensive approach, reach a larger number of firms, and offer relatively basic services; or to focus on the provision of higher value-added services, and operate with added intensity on a better targeted, smaller, portion of the market. On the other hand, the stronger or weaker emphasis placed on the different services (strategic consulting, training, foreign trade, technology, quality assurance, etc) matches the needs in each location and the locally available competencies.

- *The sustainability (self-financing) of the EDC seems to have a limit* if the project goals include dissemination and extension activities, the cost of which cannot be entirely absorbed by the firms, especially the smaller ones. Continuity of EDC activity after the withdrawal of IADB/MIF financing will be supported through the sustainability funds, fed by the income generated during the life of the project. However, this continuity in the long term seems possible only if: EDC can secure new non-reimbursable financing from other donors or the government; or if they can strike a proper balance between remunerated and highly profitable activities and the other operations requiring a certain degree of subsidy. This second alternative is harder to accomplish successfully in those countries with smaller SME BDS markets. It would be advisable for centres to offer customized services to larger firms from which to reap benefits such as greater billing elasticity, a means to group smaller firms together to create one new, larger, unit, and increased regional standing and trust. Likewise, programmes involving collective use of BDS generate economies of scale for the cost of service, thus promoting co-operation among the companies, and improving their ability to pay.
- EDCs have an *impact on the supply of services to SMEs* simply because they generate a commercially attractive demand. In addition, as they promote these services, they play a role in quality control by publishing results in their reports to the customers. EDCs confer greater transparency to the consulting market by keeping a roster of the consultants who meet certain basic criteria. However, it seems inadvisable for EDCs to certify beforehand the quality of services rendered by these consultants. The EDC's role as intermediary should bar them from providing those services themselves, in direct competition with the local market's consultants. However, EDCs may develop into specialist consultants, particularly on primary supply deployment activities or when there are no private vendors for a specific type of service.
- The *institutional framework of the EDCs* is twofold. The first includes local and national non-governmental support institutions. In this case, contributions made by universities, foundations and business associations help to build relations of trust among all the parties involved, which can be further strengthened through the support of local government agencies. The other aspect is the organization of the EDC itself. It is crucial to ensure a professional, independent attitude prevails, with no interference in any dispute arising among the participating institutions that might eventually jeopardize the existence of the EDC. For this reason, and because it allows for a more professional management, it is recommended that the EDC be instituted as autonomous legal entities.

Conclusions

The experience accumulated from the first four EDC projects of the IADB/MIF is a valuable benchmark for other similar operations in Latin America and other regions, particularly because it offers a working model for service 'intermediation'. This preliminary analysis of results sheds some light on a number of issues for discussion. However, further studies must be carried out in order to analyse these experiences at a more advanced stage and to have a more in-depth evaluation of some areas that have yet to be studied. Meanwhile, the entrepreneurial institutional framework generated by EDC projects can offer performance standards relative to the promotion and modernization of firms, which can be duplicated and improved on by other private or public groups, especially given the lack of previous experience and the frailty of the promotional tools available for SMEs in Latin America.

Notes

1. Data from three sources were used to draft this paper: 1) data supplied by the commissioned administrators, collected through a project-specific survey (standardized data array, sustainability fund, and a survey on qualitative factors), updated in part as of December 1998; 2) progress assessment reports or tutorial reports and other forms of monitoring performed by independent consultants, and IADB reports; and 3) reference material and working documents by co-operation agencies, and from the Donor Committee on Small Enterprise Development.
2. This operative result (r) is obtained from: $r = v - (h + x + e)$, where 'v' stands for operating volume (= income + variables MIF contributions), 'h' is consultant fees, 'x' the expenses relative to the services provided by the EDC, and 'e' stands for structural or operating expenses (fixed).

10. The operation of three Romanian business centres

RICHARD M. KENNEDY, PHILIPPE SCHOLTES and CASPER SONESSON

The context

Introduction

THIS CASE STUDY DESCRIBES the operations of three business centres that operate in three different cities and regions of Romania. These centres were established in between mid-1994 and early 1995 to provide information and referral services, training, and counseling to small and medium enterprises (SMEs). They were established as private, non-profit organizations by the United Nations Industrial Development Organization (UNIDO) with modest initial subsidies for startup costs, but with a mandate to be self-sustaining thereafter. Through a combination of fees for services, earned income, and local subsidies, they have managed to not only survive but to grow substantially in the four years since.

This case study examines how the centres have managed to survive and prosper, and looks especially at the following issues:

- how sustainability is achieved
- the effects of sponsor involvement on the centres' operations
- changes in centres' objectives and activities resulting from the sustainability requirement and sponsor involvement
- crowding-out of the private sector.

Background

In 1991, UNIDO established a business centre in Bucharest to provide direct services to entrepreneurs. This was during the early stages of the country's transformation to a market economy. Few private enterprises existed and almost no information or support services were available to entrepreneurs or people interested in starting a business.

UNIDO, with funding from the United Nations Development Programme (UNDP), the Government of Romania, and the Government of the Netherlands, hired and trained nine Romanians as business counsellors. Operating from an office in central Bucharest, the counsellors produced books and materials related to business registration and operation, organized and conducted business information seminars and management training workshops, provided loan packaging and business planning assistance, and provided direct advice and counselling to clients on starting and operating a business. Not all these services were provided from the beginning, since the counsellors began with little business knowledge and no experience; as they received training and gained experience working with businesses, the variety of services increased.

After three years of operation, the ROM-UN Centre had 12 counsellors who had provided direct counselling to 1600 clients, in all sectors but with a predominance of industrial enterprises, and had organized 70 seminars and workshops. They had helped almost 800 clients with business planning, including 110 completed loan applications, of which 45 loans were approved for over US$12 million.

By 1994, however, it was apparent that the original rationale for having a subsidized centre was no longer as strong, since a number of private firms (as well as other donor-sponsored business advisory service providers) were then operating in the Bucharest market. UNIDO and UNDP made the decision to re-orient the project activities away from enterprise-level services toward building the capacity of other organizations to provide business advisory services in markets that were not being adequately served by the private sector or other organizations. That is, the UNIDO counsellors helped local groups establish business centres in judets (counties) outside of the Bucharest area.

Initially, UNIDO planned to establish 10 such centres, though eventually 16 were set up. The process began with round table discussions with local groups in various judets to gauge the need for a centre and the interest of local sponsors in having such a centre. UNIDO agreed to do the initial set-up of each centre, including preparing the legal documents, recruiting, selecting, and training staff, and providing the initial equipment required. Local groups, whether composed of government, private sector institutions, or local businesses, were then responsible for the leadership and support of the centre after an initial start-up and monitoring phase. A critical element in the decision to establish a centre was the commitment on the part of local sponsors to make the centre sustainable, whether through a combination of fees, other earned income, or subsidies by local sponsors.

Although all 16 centres are still in existence, they have had varying degrees of success. The three centres included in this case study were among the first 10 centres to be established, and are the largest of the 16. These centres are located in the cities of Brasov, Buzau, and Galati, and although all have legal names, they will in this case study be referred to as Brasov Centre, Buzau Centre, and Galati Centre. All three are independent non-profit organizations, established by founding sponsors who still exercise governance of the operations. The centres provide business-related services to enterprises and potential entrepreneurs in their areas.

The service

All three centres were created to provide the following services to SMEs:

- *information and referral:* providing walk-in or telephone clients with brief answers to basic questions on starting a business, or explaining where to go to register their business, to get forms or instructions, or more detailed information
- *general business counseling:* providing advice or assistance in dealing with specific issues or problems of a client, in areas such as marketing, market research, finance, production, taxes and governmental regulations, personnel, and equipment sourcing
- *loan packaging:* providing assistance in preparing business plans or loan applications in order to apply for financing from banks, governmental programmes, or other financing sources
- *training:* organizing and conducting workshops and seminars on subjects related to starting or operating a business.

However, by mid-1998, although all three continued to provide these original services to SMEs, the mix of services had changed substantially.

Brasov Centre

Brasov has continued to emphasize its SME activities, and has expanded its offerings to include specialized services in marketing research, marketing information, and human resource development. However, the largest increase in activity has come from implementing related programmes on behalf of donors or other partners. For example, an import/export consultancy programme has been established within Brasov Centre, with co-financing from the EU Phare programme. Brasov Centre has also organized and operated training programmes paid for by private companies (marketing), the Soros Foundation (entrepreneurship), VOCA (agriculture), UNDP (microcredit), and the World Bank (business training for unemployed people). By 1998, the majority of the centres' services were provided under these sponsored programmes, though the bulk of the activities of the centre were still related to their original mandate of providing services to SMEs or potential entrepreneurs.

Buzau Centre

Like the Brasov Centre, the Buzau Centre has continued and upgraded its SME work, but it has expanded into other areas as well. In 1996, it won an EU Phare tender to provide entrepreneurship training and counseling for unemployed persons, and administer a revolving loan guarantee fund. This led to the centre transforming itself into a local development agency, and undertaking sponsored projects not related to business, for the Romanian government (work safety staff training), the World Bank (social assistance; job creation), and several Phare projects (communication and negotiation skills training; building capacity of NGOs; training for local development). So, while it continues to provide services to SMEs, a substantial portion of its work is now in social or civic projects that may benefit, but are not directly related to, SME promotion.

Galati Centre

The Galati Centre has expanded its offerings for businesses substantially since its inception, though these services have not necessarily been for SMEs. It has introduced new services in the area of marketing research, quality management (including ISO 9000 services), and asset appraisal. The Galati Centre has also become a regional development centre, and diversified into activities financed by others. It implements an EU project management contract (Integrated Centre for Clothing and Embroidery) and is partner with the chamber of commerce in another EU project (to train staff to promote business partnerships in the EU), and operates a UNDP programme (microcredit). It has also participated in non-business projects for the EU (support to families with small children; support centre for the elderly). Despite its evolution into a regional development agency, however, the bulk of its work is still with SMEs.

Client base

Initially, the centres' clients were only SMEs, or people interested in starting a small business. In 1994 and 1995, 100 per cent of the clients of all three centres fell into this category. However, as the Brasov and Galati Centres expanded their line of business services, larger enterprises became customers. In the case of Brasov Centre, 15 per cent of the BDS clients in 1998 have been large enterprises, which are customers of the newer services developed by the centre, including customized selling and management training programmes, marketing research, feasibility studies, and human resource (employment) services. For the Galati Centre, large enterprises have accounted for around 10 per cent of the clientele since 1996, when it introduced services in market surveys, which have been used particularly by larger clients, and later assets appraisals, quality management and assurance, and services related to EU integration. The Buzau Centre, which expanded more into non-enterprise services, has not provided any services to large enterprises (though they have recently signed a contract to begin providing services to one large client).

Although only Galata has a significant proportion of large enterprises among its clientele, it is the only centre that has also increased the percentage of its clientele in the small category. Medium-sized enterprises have decreased. Brasov Centre, on the other hand, has shown a decrease from 55 per cent in 1995 to 30 per cent in 1998 in the number of 'small' enterprises, and for Buzau the proportion of small clients has also decreased, from 65 per cent in 1994 to 46 per cent in 1998.

The clientele of the three centres were initially almost entirely privately-owned businesses, but Galati Centre has attracted a significant percentage of state-owned businesses since 1996, especially for asset appraisal and other services needed for the process of privatization. In 1996 and 1997, 24 per cent of its clients were state-owned enterprises, and in 1998, 16 per cent were state-owned enterprises; 80–95 per cent of these state-owned enterprise clients were in about to be privatized. As Romania is still in the midst of its privatization programme, asset appraisals for state-owned enterprises has developed into a high-demand service, and one that generates considerable revenue for Galati Centre. Neither Brasov nor Buzau has developed a significant clientele among state firms.

Of course, all the above refers to end-user clients, i.e., enterprises or entrepreneurs receiving services developed by the centres. A significant part of all three centres' clients in recent years include donors, government agencies, NGOs, and private and public sector institutions that, while they do not receive services directly, are in effect paying for services that the centres deliver to others, some of which are businesses or potential entrepreneurs.

Market

The markets for the centres' BDS services are primarily local, although some expansion into other geographical markets has been undertaken or is planned. Generally, all three centres provide a mix of general business services, which includes counseling, feasibility studies, business planning, loan applications, along with special services unique to a centre, such as marketing surveys, asset appraisals, human resource services, and special training or management programmes. Their potential clients are, therefore, enterprises and potential entrepreneurs in the area, which generally corresponds to the 'judet', or county, territory. In Brasov, there are approximately 640 000 residents, and 27 500 registered companies, up from only 19 000 in 1995. In Buzau, the population was about 510 000 people in 1997, with the number of companies increasing from 8700 in 1994 to 12 500 in 1998. In Galati, the population is about 640 000, with the number of companies increasing from 12 000 in 1994 to 17 500 in 1998.

Despite being reasonable-sized counties, with an apparently fast-growing number of enterprises, neither the market for BDS services nor the supply of

BDS service providers seems very large. It is difficult to say definitively since no thorough analysis has been undertaken, but there are some indications that this is the case.

- None of the three centres has any indication that there is demand for its services going unmet, despite their being the main providers of these types of services in their area. This suggests that, despite the rapid rise in number of companies, the number of enterprises recognizing the need for counseling services, and having the funds to pay for them, is still relatively small.
- As part of this case study, an attempt was made to identify potential competitors to the centres. Often, those named by the centre managers, sponsors, clients, or other competitors were not private sector firms but other NGOs or non-profit institutions. While there are certainly many firms providing audit and tax-related services (which are required by law and therefore generate a steady demand) there are few BDS providers in the private sector dealing specifically with SMEs, or else their visibility is low.
- A few private sector competitors were identified and interviewed, and few expressed any concern over the competition by the centres. In most cases, they saw themselves as having a different, specialized niche, while the centres were seen as providing a comprehensive range of services, primarily for smaller enterprises that were unlikely to be their clients in any event.
- The fact that the founding sponsors of all three centres include chambers of commerce or business associations is an indication that the private sector perceived a need for such services in a market not being adequately served by existing firms or institutions.

In Bucharest, there is a thriving market for BDS services, and a rapidly increasing number of service providers. In the outlying judets, such as Brasov, Buzau, and Galati, however, the demand for services, and the supply of providers, seems to be much more modest. Initially, all three of these centres were established with start-up subsidies from UNIDO and the Government of Romania, and some still receive support from local governments, so there needs to be concern given to the effects of the centres on the growth of the private sector BDS providers. At this point, however, there is no indication that the centres are having a significant crowding out effect on the private sector.

Financial viability

The original mandate given by UNIDO and UNDP to the three organizations was to provide services to SMEs and potential entrepreneurs, and to become financially sustainable without additional UN support. It was left to the local sponsors of each centre to determine how sustainability was to be achieved, whether through fees for services to SMEs, other earned income, or subsidies. After almost four years of operation, all three centres have shown substantial growth, as measured by their annual employment and revenue totals. Employment has increased from two employees in 1995 to 11 in 1998 in Brasov, from four in 1994 to 16 in 1998 in Buzau, and from five in 1994 to 31 in 1998 in Galati. Total (adjusted) revenue of the three centres has grown from a combined US$77 000 in 1995 to US$305 000 in 1997, and 1998 totals will exceed US$400 000 by a large margin. In addition, the centres have more than covered their costs, as shown by the increase in net worth of the centres over time.

141

Viability of the organizations depends on many factors, but certainly a centre's financial position at any given time is the best indicator of viability. A review of the year-end balance sheets summary for the three centres (shown in Table 10.1), indicates that the organizations have all succeeded in increasing both total assets and their capital accounts over the period. Increased assets would indicate increased capacity of the organization, and increased capital account indicates greater financial strength.

The review of the past few years' history, plus the current financial condition, suggest that the centres have not only survived but have done well enough to position themselves for continued growth. A review of the revenue summaries of the three centres (presented below) shows that this apparent sustainability has come through three different strategies.

Table 10.1 Year-end balance sheet summaries (except to 30 September 1998) in US$

	1994	1995	1996	1997	1998
Brasov					
Total assets	x	2327	12 961	12 275	23 173
Total liabilities	x	1138	3770	4790	14 435
Net worth	x	1189	9191	7845	8738
Total liabilities & net worth	x	2327	12 961	12 635	23 173
Buzau					
Total assets	1535	4450	22 066	23 758	38 796
Total liabilities	1331	2700	4373	15 964	23 213
Net worth	204	1750	17 693	7794	15 583
Total liabilities & net worth	1535	4450	22 066	23 758	38 796
Galati					
Total assets	x	2065	5857	28 171	53 506
Total liabilities	x	2065	5857	23 897	49 232
Net worth	x	0	0	4274	4274
Total liabilities & net worth	x	2065	5857	28 171	53 506

Table 10.2 Revenue summaries, in US$ (annual, except to 30 September 1998)

Revenue	Information	Training	Loans	Consulting	Non-SME	Other	Total
Brasov Centre							
1994							
1995	140	2490	5871	3331	0	796	12 628
1996	0	8600	16 194	3686	8947	6784	44 211
1997	0	3655	9993	829	830	26 248	41 555
1998	0	5099	5769	12 518	45 134	67 380	135 900
Buzau Centre							
1994	0	0	12 959	0	0		12 959
1995	0	0	18 132	8194	0		26 326
1996	0	2618	13 537	7171	2792	34 468	60 586
1997	0	10 553	2114	1182	0	166 134	179 983
1998	0	0	4500	5878	0	140 149	150 527
Galati Centre							
1994							
1995	0	0	13 196	100	3750	20 140	37 186
1996	0	0	23 050	1717	6802	113 641	145 210
1997	0	0	7955	0	15 722	60 059	83 736
1998	0	0	8895	654	3812	96 817	110 178

From 1994 to 1996, the Brasov and Buzau centres did quite well financially as a result of the loan packaging activities. Loan packaging was a profitable business activity because there were a number of subsidized credit schemes for small businesses operating in Romania. Because entrepreneurs were receiving loans, or had real possibilities of receiving loans, they were willing to pay for the costs associated with applying, and the centres benefited from this. In addition, many of the clients who came in for loan applications returned for other general counseling services.

By 1996, interest rates had risen substantially and the subsidized credit schemes were either eliminated or significantly reduced. This resulted in a gradual decline in fees for finance-related services, and provided the impetus for both Brasov and Buzau to increase the range of their services and to look at other sources of income. Brasov, in particular, increased its offerings in general counseling and training programmes, while both Buzau and Brasov increased their non-enterprise services. Brasov's fee revenue increased from US$12 000 in 1995 to almost US$70 000 in the first nine months of 1998, and most of its 'other' revenue are contracts related to specialized consulting services. Buzau, by winning tenders to provide project management and other services, saw dramatic increases in non-enterprise revenue, from 0 in 1994 and 1995, to US$135 000 in 1997.

Brasov and Buzau Centres, therefore, had an initial strategy that was quite similar – to cover costs by providing business services to SMEs, especially in loan packaging. When this strategy stalled, they took somewhat different paths. Brasov Centre increased the range of its business-related services and therefore its fee revenue, whether paid by clients or by others, while Buzau Centre branched out into various non-business-related income-generating projects. Both saw substantial increases in revenue and centre size as a result.

Galati Centre has taken a completely different strategy for sustainability. Although founded and still governed by four sponsors, Galati Centre has intertwined itself with the Galati chamber of commerce. Initially, the Galati Chamber of Commerce provided subsidies in cash and in kind to the Galati Centre, so that it could offer free or subsidized services to local businesses. In 1995, for example, fees were only US$17 000 which was less than the US$20 000 of cash and in-kind subsidies provided by the founders, primarily the chamber of commerce. As the expertise of the staff grew, the Galati Centre was able to provide services to other groups that the Galati chamber of commerce served, including large enterprises. It was also able to do substantial work for donors and chamber partners, which led to increased income for Galati Centre. In 1996, fees increased to US$32 000 but subsidies and earned income generated US$113 641.

Viability for Galati Centre, therefore, was founded initially on the subsidies of the chamber of commerce, and although it remains closely associated with the chamber, the sustainability of the Galati Centre at its current level at least, is closely related both to subsidies and its ability to continue earning fees for managing projects with donors and partners of the chamber of commerce.

Subsidies

There were large subsidies involved in the startup of the network of judet business centres. UNIDO national staff spent several months visiting judets to discuss the need for a business centre, identified judets with groups that were both interested and willing to sponsor a business centre, and then helped to organize the centre. This included providing legal assistance for the preparation of the founding documents, recruiting and selecting staff, and providing the staff with training and materials. After startup, UNIDO staff provided supervision of the operation of the business centre, for two days a week, for the first four to six months of operation. Following this, UNIDO provided support on an occasional basis, at the request of centres, particularly for training staff. For example, at the end of 1997, UNIDO organized a training of trainers course for all interested centres to update the training skills of the judet centres' staffs.

There was also a cash subsidy provided to each of the centres prior to startup. UNIDO or (for some centres, such as Brasov Centre) the Romanian government provided a package of equipment that included computers, printers, copying machines, faxes and modems, telephone systems, and one vehicle. The subsidy totaled about US$13 000 for each centre.

Other than the startup and subsequent training subsidies provided by UNIDO and the Romanian government, direct subsidies by sponsors or donors have been a small part of the support of Brasov and Buzau centres. The major subsidy at Brasov and Buzau centres has been the provision of a Peace Corps volunteer, for varying lengths of time; in terms of other cash or equipment subsidies, however, Brasov has received less than US$10 000 to date, primarily from private companies and Peace Corps for logistical support, and Buzau has received even less. In Galati, however, subsidies have been the primary means of support. In Galati, the chamber of commerce has provided both in-kind and cash subsidies for the centre. The Galati Centre is housed free of charge in the chamber of commerce offices, and the chamber provides large cash subsidies as well. The Galati chamber of commerce has provided more than US$250 000 in subsidies since 1994, and the Galati Council has provided both cash and in-kind contributions as well, totaling about US$80 000. Non-monetary subsidies, in the form of association with sponsors and founders, were also mentioned by many interviewees; this gave centres easier access to decision makers and increased credibility with clients.

One important consideration is that all three centres now rely heavily on income earned, directly or indirectly, from outside projects or programmes for their financial support, and it is often difficult to determine whether these are, in effect subsidies or not. In this case study, it was assumed that funds given to an organization to support its usual work with SMEs was a subsidy, but that income obtained from work won by tender, or which supported a specific programme designed by another organization, would not be considered to be a subsidy. The value of these external contracts is not only in the financial support, which results in profits and assets that remain with the centres after the project ends, but also in the training and upgrading of skills that the centre staff received. Most of the recent training of centre staff has come, at no additional expense to the centre, as a result of the external projects that they have won, usually through a competitive process, and implemented.

Fees

All three centres have, from the very beginning, charged clients fees for services. In the case of Brasov and Buzau, the fees have been an important part of their total revenue, but with Galati, direct fees to clients have been a small part of their revenue.

The fees are not set strictly on an hourly basis, but are generally on a per-service or per-activity basis, for all three centres. For this study, estimates were made as to the fees that were generated in each centre per hour of consultant's or professional's time. As shown in Table 10.3, nothing is charged for basic information and referral, though only minimal time is spent per client for these services. Loan packaging and counseling are generally the lowest paid services, though in the case of Brasov they have increased to about US$10 per hour. Training services, on the other hand, are the most profitable, because several clients can be served, and charged, at once, and because custom training programmes are developed for larger clients, who can afford to pay higher fees.

Table 10.3

Services			Fees (US$/hour)		
	1994	1995	1996	1997	1998
Brasov Centre					
Information/referral					
Training		7	40	40	30
Loan/packaging		4	10	10	10
Consulting/counseling		4	10	10	10
Non-enterprise services			8	8	10
Buzua Centre					
Information/referral					
Training			10	20	25
Loan/packaging		4	4	5	5
Consulting/counseling	4	3	3	4	5
Non-enterprise services			10	20	25
Galati Centre					
Information/referral					
Training					
Loan/packaging	4	4	5	5	5
Consulting/counseling		4	5	3	5
Non-enterprise services	4	4	5	30	30

One component of the pricing strategy of all three centres is to differentiate between clients in the level of fees charged. All three have a policy of charging less to smaller clients, and covering those costs from revenue from larger firms or from contracts. In the case of the Galati Centre, chamber of commerce members are entitled to free services, while fees for contracts and non-enterprise services are quite high.

Product Development

Initially, the three centres had common services, which were approaches to loan packaging and business planning, counseling, and training that were provided as part of the initial training and staff development programme at startup. For example, there were standard modules, with printed materials, for workshops on business startup, basic bookkeeping, and marketing. In some cases, diversification was done as part of the regular BDS programmes of the centre, especially in Brasov and Galati. Most product development, however, has occurred in the context of the contracts and external programmes that the centres have implemented. As a result, the product development costs have been minimal, being mostly absorbed by the organizations awarding the contracts.

Funding Strategies

From the point of view of the original donors, UNIDO, UNDP, and the Government of Romania, the strategy was to establish centres that would not require continued subsidies from international donors. There was no expectation that the centres would be completely self-supporting from fees and earned income, but there was an expectation that the centres would be sustainable using local resources. That is, to the extent that subsidies would be needed, they should be provided at the local level, by those who presumably would benefit from them. To that extent, the strategy has been successful, since the centres have not only survived but managed to expand the size of their operations.

A second, and related, component of the funding strategy was to front-load the subsidy, rather than providing regular support over a longer period. The reason for this was to emphasize the local responsibility for the project, by not paying regular operating expenses; from the day the doors of the centre opened, local sponsors were responsible for its governance – including meeting payroll, if necessary.

From the point of view of the Founding Sponsors, the centres have also been successful. Their strategies were generally to support the centres so that economic development in the area would occur. In most cases, these sponsors have provided important support, through cash and in-kind subsidies, but also through governance of the centres.

Of course, the strategy of front-loading the donor subsidies, and shifting all operational and governance responsibility to the local level has led to moves away from the original SME objective. While all three continue to provide SME services, and certainly to think of themselves as business service providers for SMEs, the need for sustainability and the influence of local sponsors has led to diversification into services that are sometimes far from the original SME concept. Galati provides services to large enterprises, including state-owned ones, and is very involved in issues like EU integration, while Buzau has branched out into project management, even of social assistance projects. Brasov has remained closest to the original business centre concept, but has also developed larger clients and undertakes an increasing number of activities on behalf of donors, NGOs and other organizations interested in buying project management expertise.

Institutional analysis

The mission of all three centres has been to provide BDS services to small and medium-sized enterprises, and potential entrepreneurs. At the original donors' wish, this mission is imbedded in the by-laws of all three organizations. And, as noted above, all three centres remain committed to this mission, even if the need for sustainability, and the desire of some founding sponsors for broader economic activities, lead them into other areas.

The governance of the institutions is based on the fact that they are incorporated under the Foundations and Associations Law in Romania, which makes them private, non-profit organizations. Such foundations are exempt from some taxes related to specific services; if, at the end of the year, their revenue exceeds expenses, they are subject to taxes on the difference.

All three centres are governed by boards that are composed of representatives of the founding sponsors – one representative per sponsor. In Galati Centre, there are four founding sponsors (Galati Chamber of Commerce, Galati Prefecture, Galati County Council, and Dunarea de Jos University) and representatives of these four make up the board of directors. In Buzau, the same is true as the board consists of representatives of the Chamber of Commerce, the Buzau Prefecture, the Buzau Country Council, Buzau City Hall, and one private company. Brasov, however, has a different approach, in that only five private businessmen, all members of the founding Association of Entrepreneurs, make up the board of the Foundation.

The day-to-day operations are run by a centre manager, and it is notable that each centre has one strong executive who is, to a large extent, responsible for the centre's success. In the case of Brasov and Buzau centres, one manager has been there from the beginning and has played the dominant role in the growth and diversification of the centre. In the case of Galati Centre, there have been several managers, but the head of the Galati chamber of commerce has exercised primary control over the Centre's operations, and has been responsible for the funding and operational strategy the centre has followed.

The staffing of the three centres, over time, is shown in Table 10.4.

Table 10.4   Staff levels

Staff	1994	1995	1996	1997	1998
Brasov					
Total, of which:		2	6	8	11
Manager		1	1	1	1
Finance counsellor			1	1	1
Marketing				1	2
Other consultants			2	3	5
Secretarial		1	2	2	2
Buzau					
Total, of which:	4	6	10	14	16
Manager	1	1	1	1	1
Finance counsellor	3	2	3	3	3
Marketing	–	1	1	1	1
Other consultants		2	4	8	10
Secretarial			1	1	1
Galati					
Total, of which:	5	19	24	28	31
Manager	1	1	1	1	1
Finance counsellor	1	4	5	6	6
Marketing	–	1	2	2	2
Other consultants	2	12	14	17	20
Secretarial	1	1	2	2	2

It is apparent that the staffing has been kept at a minimum in terms of overhead costs. For the first two years, Buzau Centre employed no secretarial staff, and none of the three employs more than two secretarial staff at any one time. Professional staff have grown quite rapidly in the last two years, in response to the increased work from contracts and new services.

Finally, it should be noted that none of the centres operate in a vacuum. A network of centres has been created, to provide mutual support to each other. These are primarily the 16 centres created by UNIDO, with UNDP, Romanian and Dutch government funding, but also some centres that were established by other donors. A central liaison and co-ordinating organization (which uses the acronym FAIR) was established to market the services of the network centres, and to organize training and information activities on behalf of the network. At present, the centres (which are themselves the founders of FAIR) feel that they receive little benefit from the organization. In the future, however, it is possible that FAIR will play a central role in ensuring that the centres undertake joint activities to increase their capabilities and to strengthen their financial position.

Impact

All three centres measure their performance on the basis of enterprise-level or client-level services. None has any indicators that attempt to measure any effects on the wider economic or social environment of the areas in which they operate. This is the case even though all have expanded beyond BDS to undertake local or regional development activities. A summary of their results is shown in Table 10.5.

Table 10.5

	1994	1995	1996	1997	1998
Brasov Center					
No. of clients		158	290	370	360
No. of jobs		117	190	110	125
No. of trainees		20	125	75	105
No. of loans		22	15	10	12
Value of loans (US$)		1 113 732	5 646 114	3 919 020	26 982 139
Buzau Center					
No. of clients	143	331	513	1119	859
No. of jobs	36	242	465	94	35
No. of trainees	20	16	204	723	614
No. of loans	14	52	82	25	26
Value of loans (US$)	428 125	3 328 617	4 310 000	464 895	170 176
Galati Center					
No. of clients	65	75	102	120	124
No. of jobs	10	115	250	283	114
No. of trainees					
No. of loans	13	19	22	30	25
Value of loans (US$)	505 770	1 778 539	5 754 496	3 475 696	48 641 060

Despite the lack of information on the wider economic effects, the fact that the original sponsors are almost universally pleased with the performance of the centres, and that they continue to support them with extensive time and resources is an indication that they believe the centres are having an impact on the groups that they support. In the case of the prefectures and other government bodies, they are generally interested in wider regional or local development, while the associations and chambers of commerce are also interested in support for their members.

Summary

The opening of 16 business centres in outlying judets of Romania in 1994 and 1995 was intended to provide needed services that would be supported by local groups interested in development of the SME sector. Three of these centres were in Brasov, Buzau, and Galati, and four years later, they are still in business, and expanding, despite little additional support from the original donors, but with extensive support at the local level, from a combination of government agencies and private sector institutions.

- Although all are doing well, there is no indication that any of them could have achieved a self-supporting status solely from selling business development services to the original target group – SMEs.
- They have achieved sustainability in different ways. Brasov's experience seems to suggest that a centre may become self-supporting from fees if the market is expanded to larger enterprises. Galati shows that the services of a business-like centre can be important enough to businesses that an association of businesses (in this case, the chamber of commerce) will find it in its interest to subsidize the operations on behalf of its membership, and the general business community. Buzau Centre's experience indicates that sustainability is also possible by increasing revenue through diversification outside the general area of business services. What is needed, apparently, is for each centre to find the appropriate mix of fees for BDS, earned income from other sources, and subsidies that will support it financially.
- For all three, identifying sources of revenue besides fees from enterprises was important, and probably accounts for most of the growth of the three organizations. Whether in SME or business-related areas, or not, identifying and winning contracts or projects from donors, government, NGOs, and other institutions has been important. In Buzau, this was critical because the subsidies provided to the centre were very small. In Brasov and Galati, the earned income was not as critical, since they could probably have survived serving larger clients or (in Galati's case) receiving subsidies, but certainly both centres would have been much smaller without the external income.
- The work done on behalf of the donors and non-SME clients has also been instrumental in building the size and capability of the centres' staff and in developing new services, both of which provide increased capacity for the future. In many cases, these capabilities are related to SME services, though in others – particularly in Buzau – the services are in social or regional development activities, not in SME services. This was done at no cost to the centres, since these development costs were part, or a by-product, of their contracts or projects.
- The business-like orientation of the centres was important to ensure that costs were kept low enough in the early years so that the centres were supportable with low fees and small subsidies. It is likely that this business-like approach has also made them attractive partners for the donors, NGOs and other organizations that need work done in particular fields. Centres that are trying to improve the efficiency and productivity of SMEs bring that attitude and style to their own work.
- All of the centres have retained their original mission of support to SMEs, despite having expanded into other areas and clients. To some extent, this is a result of the original agreement with UNIDO in which this requirement was made a part of the by-laws of the centres, but it also reflects a commitment on the part of the sponsors to economic development in their areas. However, given the recent growth in income from project and contract work, it will be interesting to see how the mission changes in the next few years.

- It is not clear to what extent the three centres have adversely affected the growth of private sector consulting and advisory firms in their areas. Certainly, the possibility of unfair competition exists, especially as the centres earn outside income that can be used to subsidize some business services. As yet, there are no strong indications that the centres are having much effect on competition, perhaps because there have not been many potential competitors in the market.
- Perhaps what is most promising about the three centres is that their sustainability is based on support by those who are in a position to judge the value of the services they provide. Only in the case of the Galati Centre are large subsidies now provided, and presumably the chamber of commerce feels that SMEs in general, and its membership in particular, benefit enough to justify the subsidies provided.

11. Enterprise support services for Africa project

MARY M. LYNCH and KWAME YOUNG-GYAMPO

Background and history

THE INTERNATIONAL FINANCE CORPORATION (IFC) through the African Project Development Facility (APDF) is implementing the pilot phase of the Enterprise Support Services for African Project (ESSA) in Ghana. ESSA Ghana is being funded jointly by the Canadian International Development Agency (CIDA) and the IFC and provides support services to small and medium-sized enterprises (SMEs). Started in February 1996, the goal of the pilot was to 'determine the sustainability of ESSA as a vehicle for assisting small and medium sized firms'. The approach being tested by ESSA Ghana was to establish methods for brokering a relationship between SMEs and consultants that could provide specialized services to the SMEs. The intention was that these initiatives should have two results: to enhance the profitability of the SMEs; and to reinforce the capacity of local consulting firms to provide on-going services to private firms.

The original concept for ESSA was developed based on the experience throughout Africa with APDF. Programmes like APDF were in place to assist SMEs in receiving financing to undertake expansions or enter new markets. Limited assistance was available, however, to help the firms in improving their operations and maximizing their potential after the financing was in place. Even with new infusions of capital, firms were often not achieving their potential in terms of sales, employment, or growth. Two studies were undertaken in Ghana to determine the causes. These analyses identified two problem areas: few firms had adequate management information systems (MIS) in place that allowed them to manage their companies properly; and organizational and operational problems were seen particularly in production and marketing. Many of the firms had grown quickly but could not manage the rapid growth of the company from a few employees into small or medium-scale operations. SMEs needed outside assistance to improve their competitiveness. This type of assistance was not being provided by other groups at the time.

Based on these assessments, ESSA Ghana was set up on a pilot basis to test mechanisms for delivering support to SMEs. The pilot was to last three years (1996–1999) during which time it would be decided whether the concept had applicability to other parts of Africa. ESSA was to act primarily as a broker between participating SMEs and consulting companies. The ESSA staff would develop terms of reference for consulting assignments in MIS and operational issues, and assist in locating the appropriate consulting resources. Contracts would be entered into with the consultants and ESSA would monitor the work done. The actual delivery of services to the firms was to be undertaken by outside consultants and training institutes. The success of the pilot after only two years triggered the replication process in other areas of Africa, starting in April 1998. This chapter focuses specifically on ESSA Ghana, which is the model for replication.

ESSA services

The services provided by ESSA evolved during the pilot phase. Four important changes were made to the original concept to fit the needs at the firm level more closely. First, the potential client base was, in fact, broader than originally envisaged. The primary client base has not been firms that have received financing and need support to implement their expansion. In fact, ESSA services are being tapped both post-financing and pre-financing. Second, the role of ESSA shifted from being simply a broker of specialized consulting services to a more complex system of support for SMEs.

During the assessments of firm-level needs it became clear that interventions were needed in a number of areas within each firm, not simply one. To reflect these needs, ESSA began to build a series of consulting modules that would be undertaken over a longer period.

Third, it had originally been expected that the ability of Ghanaian consulting firms to service the needs of clients would be hampered by a lack of technical skills or expertise. In fact, this proved not to be the case. The difficulty was the appropriateness of the consultants' approach in dealing with private sector clients. A shift by the consultants was required towards a more participatory model that supported firms in their implementation of new ideas. Fourth, the initial design saw a strong focus on MIS and improving technical operations such as production procedures. While the initial ESSA clients needed this assistance, they were also in need of more immediate help with basic organizational and management structures. The process of graduating micro or small enterprises to larger firms meant that they had expanded the size of the operation. They had not, however, changed the way the company was structured and managed, or how decisions were made. The result was an inefficient organizational structure that constrained further development and caused increasing problems within the company.

ESSA developed three interrelated services. The primary service involves ESSA working with SMEs to provide, on a cost shared basis, critical consulting assistance to overcome the firms' immediate problems. ESSA staff undertake a detailed needs assessment with the companies. The staff then develop modules of specialized support which address MIS, technical, and/or management needs. These are implemented over a period of time, often with different consultants. The consulting services provided are highly specialized and have ranged from assistance with reorganizing operations to technical training in high technology communications packages. The result is a high level of involvement throughout the process by ESSA as an adviser at the firm level.

The second service involves ESSA working with Ghanaian consulting firms and individual consultants not only to broker their services to the companies but also to ensure that the process meets the needs of the SME client. Most of the SMEs were accustomed to a consulting approach that was relatively hands-off. Consultants were hired, provided with terms of reference, and then worked independently to provide 'expert advice' on various issues. ESSA encourages an approach that begins with a thorough assessment of the issues to be addressed and an outline of the work to be adopted. The private sector client are encouraged to be actively involved in the definition of the consultancy as well as throughout the consulting assignment. The consultants respond to the needs of the clients and provide specialized solutions to specific problems.

The final service provided by ESSA involves working with a training institution, the Ghana Institute of Management and Public Administration (GIMPA), as well as private training providers, to develop group courses which the SME clients can access on a fee basis. The courses include topics such as strategic planning, productivity and marketing, and are intended to complement the consulting work at the firm level. Clients are encouraged to send staff to these courses to supplement the firm-specific training that is provided under the consulting assignments.

Client base and outreach

The initial criteria for firms to qualify for ESSA support focused clearly on fast-growing SMEs:

- SME domiciled in Ghana employing more than six people
- annual turnover falls within the range considered SME as established by APDF/IFC (small enterprises – up to US$400 000 in annual turnover and medium enterprises – from US$400 000 to US$1 million)
- sufficient evidence that the company is financially able to implement the recommendations of the consultants and ESSA
- sufficient evidence that the company intends to, and is capable of, implementing the recommendations
- the company is willing and able to share the costs of the consultancy
- there is sufficient evidence that the business can improve its operations and benefit from the type of services offered by the project
- management agrees to work with the project and ESSA consultants to complete the activities agreed upon.

These criteria aimed at identifying firms that not only needed assistance but also had the right attitude towards change and the ability to implement recommendations. A point system was also developed to prioritize the clients after the initial screening. Points were allocated for the following factors: extent of cost-sharing agreed to; net employment generation; women's participation in the company in terms of ownership, management or employment; job creation multiplier effects; potential improvements in productivity, profitability and sales from ESSA intervention; successful completion of a credit programme such as APDF; willingness and capacity to implement recommendations; impact on the environment; potential for promotion of regional trade; and degree of support of Government of Ghana policy priorities.

Originally, ESSA was supposed to have dealt with 30 firms by the end of March 1999, by which time ESSA already had a client roster of 42 firms. The majority fall into the small category with sales less than US$400 000. Large companies obtaining ESSA support are included since they have a relatively high number of indirect beneficiaries or spinoff benefits and are seen to be important clients from a developmental perspective. For example, a number of agro-processing companies have few full-time staff but a high volume of sales derived from a large number of small, private, often individual growers. All of the large companies are expected to pay a higher proportion of the cost of the consultancy than that which is charged to smaller clients.

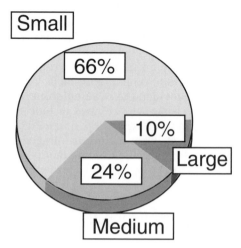

Figure 11.1 *ESSA clients by size*

The sectors represented by the clients are diverse. The firms represent a cross-section, from agriculture and agro-processing to high technology, with approximately one-third of the firms each in agriculture/agro-processing, manufacturing, and services. The service sector companies are in areas such as savings and loans, telecommunications, or software development.

All of the firms except one are limited liability companies. Sixty per cent of firms deal only with the local market. Five per cent are exclusively export oriented. The remaining companies deal with both export and local markets. Most of the firms are also relatively young. Forty-five per cent were started in 1990 or later. Only 10 per cent of the firms were started prior to 1980. While a majority of the firms are owned by men, 29 per cent are owned jointly by men and women, and another 7 per cent exclusively by women. The representation of women in client firms at decision-making levels has been higher than originally expected. Forty-seven per cent of the firms have women on their board of directors, 25 per cent have women as senior managers (such as general manager), and 50 per cent have women in some management roles. The firms participating in ESSA represent over 2000 direct employees. Only 8 per cent of these employees are women, however. This figure is low since many of the women in the largest companies work on a contractual basis and are not included in the employment figures.

Market

In the initial stages of development, ESSA Ghana made a conscious decision not to advertise its services widely, but instead to rely on referrals, word of mouth, and proactive searching for specific types of clients. The decision was based on two factors. First, ESAA was supposed to work with only 30 firms over a three-year period which meant that the clients had to be carefully selected. Second, ESSA wanted to make extensive assessments of the firms' capacity and readiness to change before approving them. This approach has allowed ESSA to develop a strong base of clients that are committed to changing their organizations. Those firms that contacted ESSA in search of more 'donor grants' were quickly identified and rejected. Those that have proceeded conform well to the selection criteria described above.

Extensive interviewing within Ghana has indicated that the demand in Ghana is substantial for these types of services. As the economy continues to open up, the number of small and medium-sized firms is increasing, with many of them becoming some of the most dynamic enterprises within Ghana. Industry groups such as the Private Enterprise Foundation, which is the umbrella body for private sector organizations in Ghana, see these firms as being the future for the private sector, replacing the old guard companies that are still tied to government subsidies and controls. The emerging companies are producing more sophisticated products, higher export quality, and increasingly diverse product lines. Their needs for support are also becoming more sophisticated.

ESSA does face some direct competition in terms of the delivery of similar services to SMEs by other agencies within Ghana in two areas: business consultancy, and training. The competition in the consulting area is primarily from Empresario Technologies Ghana (EMPRETEC). When it began in 1990 as a UN project, EMPRETEC initially focused on training and assisting firms in business planning. Since that time, it has developed into EMPRETEC Ghana Foundation, a private foundation, and has expanded its services to a wider range of consultancy areas, provision of credit, promotion of subcontracting relationships, and technology transfers.

At approximately the same time as the ESSA project was starting, EMPRETEC received funding from the World Bank to facilitate SME access to specialized consulting advice. The EMPRETEC focus was to be on companies with sales less than US$500 000 per year. It is in this area where the direct competition between the two groups could potentially develop.

Discussions were held within Ghana with a wide range of SMEs and consulting companies to establish whether ESSA and EMPRETEC were, in fact, in competition. On a theoretical level, a number of groups thought there was potential competition. On a practical level, however, few thought that the groups were in competition, given the diverse methods used for assisting firms. Two primary differences were identified. First, almost all of the consulting companies used by ESSA to date have worked with EMPRETEC. These companies indicated that the approach taken by the two groups was completely different. ESSA's contract makes it clear that the 'client' is the SME and their needs are the primary focus. ESAA also demands a participatory approach be developed between the consultant and the client firm and that milestones or outputs be contained in the consulting contract. Both the consultants and the client firms must meet their targets for participation. This was seen by the consultants as being unique – few had previously had performance-based contracts.

Another difference was also expressed by the SMEs interviewed. There was a consensus that ESSA services tended to be more specialized, more tailored to a firm's needs, and longer term. The level of service delivery, the integrated packages of assistance, and the flexibility in terms of timescale were seen as being unique characteristics of ESSA services that were not being offered in Ghana. Only one example of direct competition for a client between ESSA and EMPRETEC has been seen to date. Otherwise, the two groups have maintained separate client lists.

In terms of the group training courses sponsored by ESSA, these have faced competition in the past. Training targeted at firms is currently being provided in Ghana by a wide range of groups, including training institutes, private sector companies, and training suppliers. Initially, ESSA worked exclusively with GIMPA to develop and implement courses. ESSA's primary reason for sponsoring the courses was to ensure that the course content was specifically tailored to its SME clients' needs. Most of the SMEs taking the training indicated that they would not have considered using other private sector suppliers – primarily due to the cost and uncertainty regarding the appropriateness to their situation. ESSA has now expanded its training network and is working with a range of private suppliers to develop training courses which are specifically geared to SMEs and are at an affordable price. This will allow a development of the market, and more options for SMEs in the longer term.

Financial viability of services

Assessing the financial performance of ESSA is difficult at this point for a number of reasons. First, since ESSA is a pilot project, many of the costs over the first half of the project have been start-up and design related. This means that the actual client delivery costs need to be separated from start-up costs, better to assess ongoing financial performance. Second, ESSA has been servicing clients for only two years. Therefore, the experience to date is based on a limited number of contracts with clients. These may or may not be representative in the long term. Third, ESSA staff were initially reluctant to allocate their time and costs to various activities to allow a better comparison of the results achieved with the input costs. While this practice has been changed recently, information is not available at this point that allows a more accurate allocation of overhead or other costs to various client activities.

Despite these limitations, some comments can be made on the current financial performance of ESSA. The delivery costs of ESSA to clients can be broken into two categories. The first category is ESSA's ongoing costs of operation. With the shift in February 1998 to totally Ghanaian management, the overhead costs have stabilized at a level that will probably reflect future patterns. Based on the budget estimates for 1998/99, total overhead costs (for the entire operation) will be approximately C$260 000 per year. Assuming 25 active clients handled per year, the overhead costs per client would be approximately C$10 400 for 1998/99.

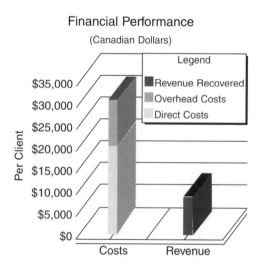

Figure 11.2 *Financial performance*

156

The second category of expenses is the direct cost of the consultants and training courses. These are the actual expenses paid to these groups to provide direct services to the SMEs. The average total direct cost per client for consultants to date has been approximately C$20 725.

Since the start of ESSA, a cost sharing scheme has been in place. All clients are required to share a portion of the direct costs of the services provided through ESSA. This has amounted to C$9600 or approximately one-third of the total overhead and direct costs. This proportion has been increasingly steadily over the two years of operation.

In developing ESSA Ghana, the issue of financial sustainability has dealt exclusively with the proportion of the direct costs of the consultancies that can be covered by the client firms – not the overall costs of delivery. In the original project document, a target of 45 per cent of the costs of direct services paid by the firms was set for 1999. This target has been met. Approximately 47 per cent of the total direct costs of the consultancies are being covered by the client firms.

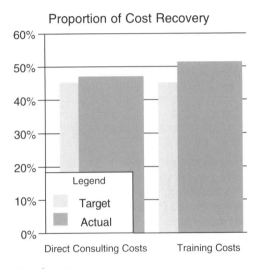

Figure 11.3 *Proportion of cost recovery*

The proportion of cost sharing has increased more rapidly than expected based on ESSA's businesslike approach to delivering services. ESSA undertakes individual assessments of the company's ability to implement recommendations, ensures that a clearly and explicitly developed proposal and workplan are available before establishing the contracts and cost sharing arrangements, and targets higher levels of cost recovery from larger firms, which are more able to pay. While many of the firms complained about the percentage being paid, they all saw the value in the services and were willing to pay for them. This willingness to pay was based on the fact that the company knew exactly what it was 'purchasing' and all parties (ESSA, consultants and the company) had performance benchmarks clearly laid out for their participation.

A preliminary assessment of the cost effectiveness of ESSA can be made in three areas: trends in terms of project performance; assessments against other business development service organizations; and on a cost/benefit basis.

To date, the performance trends of ESSA, compared to its targets, have been extremely positive. The ability of ESSA to contract more services than expected in Ghana, combined with the module approach to delivering services, has allowed a lower than expected cost per assignment. This has meant that the direct service costs have been lower per client and the project is substantially below budget, while servicing more clients than projected. In addition, ESSA staff is handling more SME clients than originally planned. While the project was to deal with 30 companies over three years, it will probably average 50 companies. In addition, ESSA's involvement has been over a longer period of time, meaning a higher client workload on an on-going basis.

It is expected that 25 clients will be handled per year with a total of four staff (including administrative). This figure is difficult to compare to other business development services (BDS) since benchmarks are not available in the current literature.[1] Even if they were, many BDS programmes deal with micro and small enterprises where the interventions are much more limited and, therefore, more clients can be handled per worker. At the other end of the scale are highly specialized caseloads such as seen at APDF, where complete financing packages and support are provided. APDF reports on the basis of projects completed during the year. On this basis, in 1997, APDF averaged slightly over two clients per investment officer. When including the full staff complement, the average was approximately 0.75 clients per worker.

BDS benchmarks provide another method to assess ESSA. Benchmarks remain extremely limited to date, for a wide range of reasons. Three benchmarks were listed in the Donor Committee Report as being indicators where value ranges for current good practices are suggested.[2] Each of the indicators relates to training and consultancy services.

- *Benchmark 1:* Percentage of direct cost recovery in training programmes. The overall average is 50 per cent with growth-oriented SMEs covering 100 per cent or more. ESSA has an average cost recovery on training of slightly over 50 per cent. This has been increasingly steadily. It should be possible to reach 100 per cent within the next year.
- *Benchmark 2:* Startup rate. The proportion of participants on a startup programme actually starting businesses afterwards should be 30–60 per cent. This benchmark is not applicable to ESSA since ESSA deals with existing SMEs, not individuals wanting to start micro-enterprises. (A more appropriate benchmark for ESSA would be the rate of implementation of changes recommended for the companies. This has been extremely high to date.)
- *Benchmark 3:* Survival rate. The proportion of businesses surviving one year after a training programme should be 80 per cent. This benchmark is also less applicable to ESSA given their client base. Survival is not the focus, but the degree of rapid expansion by companies is one indicator being tracked for ESSA.

This review of BDS benchmarks highlights the importance of beginning to distinguish within the BDS debate different types of clients and service delivery mechanisms. ESSA's approach and client base are less focused on a broad-base promotion of entrepreneurship and more on assisting existing SMEs to expand their operations.

To assess the relevance of the per client costs properly would require a cost/benefit analysis of the impact or benefit streams that emerge from each of the initiatives. Studies to date have shown that higher costs can often be offset by higher impacts generated. Given ESSA's limited history, it is too early properly to assess the benefits that are being generated. A number of case studies were undertaken in January 1998 that showed some of the potential benefits and took a preliminary look at the cost effectiveness of the services. Two cases are briefly reviewed here.

The first case involved a small company supplying wide area networks, which allow companies with branch operations to be connected with secure links that simulate private networks (at a much lower cost). The company contacted ESSA for training assistance for their technical staff. With the rapid expansion of their client base and network, the staff were having difficulty in three areas: setting up the increasingly complex company networks; solving problems within the networks; and servicing client requests. The problems were increasing rapidly and jeopardizing relations with current and future clients, and severely constraining cashflow. ESSA assisted in sourcing a consultant who was a specialist in the specific telecommunications system. The total cost of the consultancy and ESSA overhead was C$44 000. The impact of the consultancy has been substantial, and directly linked to the ESSA intervention. The gross sales of the company doubled on a monthly basis within six months. Nine full-time staff members have been added, including three women (one in a managerial position). This represents a 38 per cent increase in the labour force. With improved efficiency, costs have decreased by 10 per cent.

The second case involved a small export company which wanted to reorganize its operation and expand its product lines into value-added processed goods. The company had grown into a 60-person operation but continued to be run single-handedly by its owner. ESSA assisted in: putting in place a new organizational structure and job descriptions; recruiting personnel; preparing operations, employee and accounting manuals; and preparing a business plan. In addition, ESSA staff worked with the manager to assist in diversifying the company's products and export market. The total overhead and direct costs of the intervention was C$32 000. This assignment has already resulted in the creation of three jobs in the firm, along with approximately 40 contract jobs (30 per cent women). Sales of existing products increased by 60 per cent. New value-added export products were developed and exports have begun of these items. Sixty poor rural women have become suppliers for the value added products, representing a 400 per cent increase in net income to the group.

Both of these cases illustrate substantial benefits generated in a relatively short time, which can be directly linked to the consultancies undertaken with the firms. It will take some time before a complete cost/benefit analysis can be undertaken. However, one recognized benchmark of effectiveness is cost per job created. World Bank figures estimate cost per job created between 1980 and 1990 was US$4675.[3] For the ESSA telecommunications intervention, the cost per job created was approximately US$3300. For the exporter, counting both permanent and contract positions, cost per job created was approximately US$500.

Longer-term funding strategies

While important gains have been made by ESSA in generating revenue, the overall financial sustainability of ESSA Ghana is far more complex and was never integrated into the original Project design. While clients pay a proportion of the direct consulting fees, they are currently not required to contribute any funds towards the cost of brokering services by ESSA or the support services provided by ESSA staff. The original project documents did not address the issue of how the overall organization would become self-supporting. In fact, the inference was that it would require on-going support from some outside source to continue its operation. Neither did it address the need for ESSA to continue as an institution.

ESSA Ghana and the overall replication process for ESSA needs to begin a strategic planning process that addresses the options for financial sustainability. A number of different scenarios are presented here which could be investigated further. Each of these options requires different immediate, medium-term and long-term approaches for ESSA Ghana and the replication process.

Full sustainability

Given the experience to date, it is possible that the recovery of direct consultancy costs could approach 100 per cent. However, it is unlikely that the overall costs, including overheads, will be covered by clients in the short term without developing other methods of revenue generation. For example, a finder's fee could be charged to the consulting companies. Arrangements may also be possible with clients that would provide a two-tier system of payments for services. The initial arrangements would focus on funding the direct consulting costs by the firms. ESSA could also enter into an agreement with the companies so that, if the company is able to achieve certain agreed-upon benchmarks (i.e., increased sales or increased profitability) within a specified period, the firms will also reimburse a portion of the overhead costs. This agreement would obviously have to be based on a system of trust between ESSA and the clients, but would also tie them both to performance standards. If the targets are reached, both groups benefit from the improved company performance. In addition, the costs of ESSA have decreased substantially with increased workloads and a shift to a fully Ghanaian operation. As ESSA gains more experience (and keeps better track of time spent with various clients), it may also be possible to streamline its involvement and increase the client caseload.

Partial sustainability

The SME clients may not be able or willing to pay the complete cost of services, requiring that the operation will continue to require subsidies from some source. This will certainly be the case in the short term as ESSA tests other client-funded revenue schemes. Currently the focus has been on generating additional donor funds to expand the initiative beyond Ghana to Southern Africa, and to continue to finance ESSA Ghana. Little emphasis has been placed on finding alternative sources of funding. The current arrangement of having ESSA within the APDF institutional framework allows a sharing of costs but also limits the possibilities of building synergies with other groups. Particularly during the replication of ESSA in other parts of Africa, other routes should be explored which would allow the ESSA operations to be more completely integrated into the local framework (i.e., business associations, other service delivery centres, etc.). These alternative partnerships may allow other arrangements whereby outside resources could also be tapped to fund the overhead portion of the operation.

Phasing out ESSA

Theoretically, ESSA was designed to work itself out of a job. The intention was to build direct relationships between consultants and SMEs that would no longer require a broker to initiate or monitor. To accomplish this, ESSA provides the consultants with techniques to deal with private sector clients. They also help firms develop skills in how to manage their consultants. The ability to understand how to control assignments to get useful products was cited repeatedly by firms as a positive factor in future hiring. Firms feel confident that they now know what to demand from consultants and how to manage the process. This arrangement would be market driven and based on participation of private sector groups on both sides of the equation.

The evidence to date shows that gains are being made in individual cases in terms of direct contacts being built. Establishing when a critical mass has been reached which no longer requires an ESSA as a broker, however, is more difficult. Much of this relies on the ability of consulting companies to change their approach to supplying services. Some have been eager to change; others have not. A possibility may exist to build pockets of expertise and a track record within those companies more likely to see SMEs as an important market. ESSA is planning to give training programs to consultants to highlight the differences in servicing this market. The possible role that could be played by groups such as the Consultant Association could be explored.

Transferring the function to another institution

The final option that needs to be reviewed is to merge the ESSA function totally into an existing organization which has revenue sources and a complementary mandate. This organization could range from a business association to another business services provider. The intention would be to have the ESSA role become another line of business within an existing institution.

Results and impact

ESSA Ghana targeted two primary objectives for the pilot phase. These are:

- enhancing the profitability of the small and medium firms assisted by the project; and
- reinforcing the capacity of local consulting firms to provide services to private firms.

ESSA has developed an extensive electronic database of information on its clients. Baseline data are collected during the needs assessment phase and updates of progress are made every six months. An external monitor also verifies results to date and assists in analysing the causal lines between the ESSA interventions and the results being seen at the firm level. In terms of enhancing the performance of the SMEs, the results to date are preliminary. Eleven client firms have fully completed consulting contracts to date. Even with this small base of firms to analyse, indicators of impact at the client level are already being seen. Follow-ups are undertaken with firms every six months to assess the results achieved. Some of the preliminary results are shown in Table 11.1.

In terms of the consulting companies, the consultants represent an extremely diverse group of individuals and firms. The ability to draw general conclusions

Table 11.1 Summary of selected firm-level results to date

Expected result	Performance indicators	Results as at September 30 1998
Expanded international or export markets	Increase in export products and markets Increase in export sales as percentage of total sales	Of two export companies with completed consulting contracts both (100%) have increased sales: one service company has increased export share of sales by 50%; one agro-processing export company has diversified its products to higher value-added and increased sales by 60%
Increase in sales/revenue of client firms and suppliers	Percentage in sales/revenue	Five of 11 (45%) firms documented to date with increased sales attributed to ESSA intervention
5% increase in profitability of firms over baseline	Percentage increase in baseline	Four of 11 (36%) firms have seen an increase in profitability in the range of 10–15%
Increase in number of employees of client firms and targeted suppliers, and employee wages and earnings increase	Number of new jobs created in client firms and suppliers by gender and skill level/category Higher wages paid (outside of inflation rates)	55 in-house jobs created to date in two firms Three firms have increased salaries based on the new skill level of staff
Increase in productivity	Change in unit cost or changes in production and/or volume	Five of 11 firms (45%) have been able to decrease unit costs by 10%
Improvement in technical skills of client firms	Number of staff trained in technical skills by ESSA consultancies Training & professional development opportunities for management and staff pursued outside of ESSA training	318 people received on-the-job training in technical areas at firm level Four firms providing additional complementary training for staff outside of the ESSA consultancy (total 12 people of which 6 are women)

regarding impact within the consulting firms will be difficult, even at the project's end. From the interviews undertaken, the current consultants generally fall into two categories. These are presented here in a stylized form to give an indication of the type of spinoffs or changes that are likely by the end of the project.

The first group of consultants tends to be larger, more established consulting firms with extensive experience. These consultants have taken on many of the more complex assignments to date and have the in-house expertise to provide both the organizational and technical skills needed. The primary issues with working with these groups from ESSA's point of view are ensuring that a participatory approach is taken with clients. From the point of view of the consultants interviewed, the primary benefit of working with ESSA is the access to SMEs as clients. The work with ESSA will have some impact on these firms in terms of quality of services (i.e., understanding and meeting client needs) and possibly the breadth of services provided. Beyond this, however, there will likely be limited impact within the consulting firm. It was unclear in discussions with some of the groups whether they realized that the approach ESSA was advocating towards private sector clients was one that they needed to adopt on a more general level with private clients. The inability to differentiate services between private sector clients and other clients such as donor organizations will limit the inroads that the companies are able to make into SMEs in the future.

The second group represents smaller consultants, usually in specialized services, such as MIS, which has developed specific expertise and grown quickly in recent years. They are in the process of developing both client bases and new products to deliver to clients. The potential impact of ESSA with this group appears to be more extensive.

There is evidence of the smaller companies having made improvements in terms of skills development and strengthening market niches to the private sector. They have also begun to develop new products that are specifically marketable to the private sector, and see this group as being critical to their expansion.

Conclusions

BDS programmes should have realistic strategies for developing the scale and coverage of their operations

Most BDS programmes need to achieve an economy of scale if they hope to achieve financial viability.

This indicator, as it applies to ESSA, is more complex and highlights some of the differences between a BDS that targets microenterprises and one that targets small and medium enterprises. A limited amount of emphasis has been placed to date in the literature on SME delivery agents. While many of the issues are common, differences also exist. The ESSA case highlights some of these differences, which should be further investigated.

For micro BDS delivery agents, two factors were identified in the best practice study as being critical: a need to find ways to serve a large number of clients with a relatively low-cost service; and the large number of microenterprises, often within specific sub-sectors, that can be assisted. Both of these factors push the BDS programmes towards increasing the scale and coverage of the operation.

The ESSA experience shows that a strategy that focuses on large numbers of clients at low cost will not produce the greatest impact on SMEs. Their needs are usually more sophisticated and complex and require a less generic intervention than might be possible with microenterprises. Restructuring a 50-employee company takes more resources and diversified expertise than providing a microentrepreneur with support in areas such as bookkeeping. The costs are inevitably higher. The benefits can also be higher, however, to offset this. Little work has been done to date that actually examines the tradeoffs. The ESSA database should allow some information that will help to clarify this issue over the next year.

Effective BDS programmes produce positive externalities in addition to serving particular sets of clients

The BDS programmes should generate external benefits or public goods that are equal to or greater than the public subsidies that may be required to get the programme up and running. These can take the form of: stimulating demand for business support services; strengthening business linkages; and serving as catalysts to stimulate increased rates of learning and diffusion of innovation.

The intention of ESSA in the long term is to build direct linkages between consultants and SMEs where a brokering service is no longer necessary. There is evidence to date that this is beginning to take place. With an expanded network of consultants experienced in dealing with SMEs, the demand for the services should continue to increase without ESSA's intervention.

In terms of strengthening business linkages, ESSA has made limited progress to date. While ESSA staff made initial overtures to co-ordinate with other private sector support agencies, currently ESSA has limited contact or co-ordination with these programmes (partly due to the non-receptiveness of other service providers).

While ESSA currently serves a specific niche within Ghana, it should become more proactive in terms of ensuring that its services are co-ordinated with other agencies and that its role remains unique and useful. This does not mean taking on a role of overall co-ordination – something that the Private Enterprise Foundation is better suited to do. It does mean, for example, ensuring that clients are not 'shopping' for different programmes to try to get the best deal. This also highlights again the need to co-ordinate activities with other donor agencies. The ESSA replication process has begun to be planned in Southern Africa. At the same time, UNDP has funded an Africa-wide programme called Enterprise Africa. While it is unclear whether there will be overlap or complementarity between the two, neither group appears to be taking into account the other's activities during their planning.

Finally, in terms of acting as a catalyst for change, ESSA has clearly succeeded on this level over its first two years. Many of the clients interviewed have made fundamental changes within their companies that will impact on both their operations and their standing within their sub-sectors. The evidence of the successes is also attracting other clients. Over 50 per cent of all firms assisted to date have been found through word of mouth. ESSA specifically targets firms that are dynamic, ready to change, and have potential to make gains in the short term. These firms are not only serious about building their businesses, they also act as the new wave of entrepreneurs within Ghana. Their successes will provide support to other SMEs that are attempting to fight many of the inherent biases within the economy. Older-style companies, which are not interested in shifting from a reliance on government subsidies or benefits, are unwilling to change their practices or the lingering policies. The SMEs are promoting a truly private sector-driven economy.

Notes

1. See, *Business Development Services for SME Development: a Guideline for Donor-Funded Interventions*, Donor Committee on Small Enterprise Development, April 1997.
2. *Business Development Services for SME Development*, op. cit., p. 21.
3. See *Business Development Services for SME Development*, op. cit., p. 22.

12. Kenya voucher programme for training and business development services

THYRA A. RILEY and WILLIAM F. STEEL

THIS CASE STUDY reviews one aspect of the World Bank's Micro and Small Enterprises Training and Technology Project:[1] the use of a voucher mechanism to stimulate demand for business development services, including training, technology, and specialized management and marketing consultations. The potential demand for such services is substantial among micro and small enterprises in Kenya. Furthermore, the capability of supplying these services exists, if it can be reoriented toward serving this clientele. The voucher mechanism is designed to catalyse the development of a market for training and business development services by bringing together potential demand and potential supply.

On the basis of a pilot programme and the first phase (nearly 8000 vouchers), the voucher programme has already begun catalysing training and business development services, supplied mostly by the private sector. Future challenges are to facilitate a sustainable market for business development services among micro and small enterprises and to measure the impact of training and services on the clients.

The demand side of the market

Both the government, through its development strategy, and the World Bank, through the Micro and Small Enterprises Training and Technology Project, seek to support productivity and income growth in Kenya's Jua Kali sector. Jua Kali refers to the full range of enterprises employing between one and 49 workers in all sectors. Jua Kali literally means 'hot sun' in Kiswahili, referring to enterprises conducted under the hot sun without adequate shelter or workshop space. With weak growth of formal employment, this sector has absorbed large numbers of low-skilled workers. This chapter focuses on the project components designed to raise the skills and growth potential of Jua Kali enterprises.

Important aspects of the regulatory environment affect micro and small enterprises, and many of these have improved, at least on paper, including streamlining the Municipal Licensing Act and abolition of various acts: Trade Licensing, Chiefs Authority, Building Standards, and Power. However, the availability of affordable and appropriately sized and serviced industrial infrastructure is severely restricted. This constrains the growth of Kenya's micro and small enterprises, because lack of access to secure sites discourages optimal investment behaviour as the basis for expanding a business. Despite government efforts to provide plots to Jua Kali associations throughout the country, title to such land remains elusive. Small, growth-oriented manufacturing enterprises decry the unreliability of utility services and the small size of business premises. The project is also piloting an approach to assisting Jua Kali associations to obtain and develop secure sites.

Jua Kali sector

According to a 1995 survey of 11 012 enterprises, overall employment growth in the informal sector during 1994 and 1995 was 10–12 per cent a year.[2] The survey identified 900 000 micro and small enterprises: approximately 30 per cent in manufacturing and productive services and 55 per cent in retail and commerce.

In general, Kenya's Jua Kali sector is composed of very small firms that employ one to two people (Table 12.1), are highly vulnerable to general economic conditions, and few grow. Firms are young: 40 per cent have been in existence less than two years, and nearly 70 per cent have been in existence less than five years. Estimated new employment during 1994 was 100 000 (net of 150 000 jobs lost), with 30 per cent of growth coming from expanding rather than net new firms.

Table 12.1   Breakdown of enterprises, by size

Number of workers	Percentage of all small and microenterprises
1	56.5
2	31.1
3–5	11.2
6–10	1.1
11–50	0.2

Source: 1995 survey results from Daniels et al.[2]

In the 88 per cent of firms that employ no more than two workers, employer and employee alike receive average incomes at or below the minimum wage. These subsistence-level firms are heavily populated by women-run businesses, which tend to have lower-than-average employment and incomes. The majority of firms (about 55 per cent) are involved in retail, where incomes and employment are particularly low because the market is highly competitive and saturated. Because of their vulnerability, few of these microenterprises ever grow or graduate to become small or medium-scale enterprises.

Nevertheless, certain types of firms and subsectors have above-average levels of employment, income, and growth. One-third generate returns equal to or above the minimum wage, and 20 per cent produce returns that are more than double the minimum wage. Manufacturing makes an above-average contribution to gross domestic product per worker and employment growth (Table 12.2). Enterprises in urban areas and run by men earn above-average profits (Table 12.3). Most notable is the increase in profitability as enterprises grow in size: a 30 per cent increase in average returns per worker is associated with growth from one worker to between two and five workers.

Enterprises that are expanding generate higher incomes, are more efficient, and generate higher returns than new firms (Table 12.4). Moreover, net income per worker per month that is at least twice the minimum wage is also highly correlated with higher educational achievement of the owner and the existence of paid workers.

Target groups

The project targets two types of Jua Kali engaged in the manufacturing and productive service sectors: (a) microenterprises that employ 1–10 workers and are run by women or demonstrate the potential for growth; and (b) small firms

Table 12.2 Patterns of micro and small enterprise employment growth, by sector

Selected sectors	Total employment 1995	Percentage that have grown	Share of employment from expansion
Average all sectors	1 175 230	17.6	14.0
Manufacturing	22 423	6.7	7.8
Wearing apparel	94 111	55.2	35.5
Wood products	27 319	66.6	37.2
Repairs	137 006	31.8	26.4
Other manufacturing			
Retail			
Second-hand clothes	29 770	4.9	−5.3
Hardware, building materials, machines, tools	8680	12.6	15.2
Fuel and charcoal	63 426	27.2	19.7
Wholesale trade	8238	39.5	31.9

Source: Selected 1995 survey results from Daniels et al.

Table 12.3 Net profits per person per year in micro and small enterprises

Characteristic of the enterprise	Net profits per person per year (Kenyan shillings)
National average	33 200
By location	
Urban enterprises	85 544
Rural enterprises	16 350
By gender of owner	
Enterprises owned by women	15 552
Enterprises owned by men	63 335
By size of enterprise	
1 worker	22 458
2–5 workers	29 719
6–50 workers	3 182 832

Source: 1995 survey results from Daniels et al.

Table 12.4 Average net income per enterprise, by employment growth category

Characteristic of the firm	Average annual income per enterprise (Kenyan shillings per person per year)
Started in 1994	19 038
Expanded in 1994	21 745
Started in 1995	18 901
Expanded in 1995	52 787
Average: new start-ups, 1994 and 1995	18 980
Average: enterprises that expanded in 1994 or 1995	45 479

Source: 1995 survey results from Daniels et al.

that employ 11–50 employees. The target group consists of approximately 30 per cent of all micro and small enterprises.

To date, 62 per cent of all project beneficiaries have been women – with two-thirds seeking to start manufacturing enterprises – who are targeted on equity and poverty alleviation grounds. For existing enterprises, the screening process attempts to identify those with the highest potential, based on their level of education and assets as well as fixed business premises. Eligible microenterprises can purchase training vouchers for employees or owner-managers for 10–30 per cent of face value, depending on the type and level of training course.

Small-scale enterprises have demonstrated their dynamism (often having grown from one to two employees) and have substantial educational and financial capacity to develop their enterprises. Although they are a minuscule proportion of Kenya's Jua Kali sector – 0.2 per cent – they have demonstrated their sustainability and potential for expansion. Eligible small firms can purchase vouchers for individualized technology and other business development services at 30 to 50 per cent of cost.

About 24 000 microenterprise employees and owner-managers and 200 small firms are expected to participate in the voucher programme over four years. Nearly a quarter of all vouchers issued may be to the same enterprises as they progress from basic to intermediate and to advanced training. The project is expected to benefit about 8 per cent of all firms in the target group.

The supply side: the availability of business development services

The voucher mechanism is intended to develop a market for the broad range of training, technology, and other business development services available in the private sector. By catalysing the market through the demand side, the voucher departs from an old paradigm that:

- financed the supply side through budgetary support for public training and technology institutions. These public institutions provided a classroom-based curriculum that did not address the needs of Jua Kali. The curriculum relied heavily on theoretical, textbook-based teaching rather than practical learning. Most important, the public institutions were funded, and could remain in existence, regardless of their ability or willingness to serve the burgeoning Jua Kali enterprise market. Over the years, few have adapted their programmes to the training and technology needs of Jua Kalis.
- ignored the apprenticeship culture within the Jua Kali business community, which is an important mechanism for transferring skills and developing enterprises. During the apprentice period, a young person works at negligible wages within an existing Jua Kali enterprise to learn a skill or trade. Subsequently, the apprentice graduates to become an 'employee' or to begin his or her own enterprise. The apprenticeship culture indicates the existence of both supply – master craftworkers capable of delivering training – and demand – employees and enterprises seeking training.

In contrast, the voucher programme builds on indigenous learning and enterprise development mechanisms. The voucher mechanism has encouraged a supply response to the demand expressed by beneficiaries from a broad range of training and business development service providers, including master craftworkers, consultants, consulting firms, private training institutions, technology institutions and suppliers, and financial institutions (Table 12.5). About 110 training and business development service providers participated in the first phase of the voucher programme. By the end, effective demand will have been

Table 12.5 Details of the voucher programme

Type of voucher and recipient	Service provided	Service provider
Training vouchers	*Standardized, group learning to improve basic skills and practices*	
Start-up firms, mostly owned by women, and promising microenterprises with basic needs	• Training in technical skills • Basic management and marketing	Master craftworkers, private companies, public training institutes with adapted Jua Kali programmes
	• Training in becoming a microfinance client and organized credit and savings associations	Microfinance institutions, Co-operative Bank, Union of Savings and Credit Co-operatives
Technology and business development vouchers	*Individual assistance to solve problems or improve products, processes, and equipment*	
Small-scale dynamic firms and Jua Kali associations with special needs	• Advice on management, marketing, and technology • Development of high-potential (sub)contract opportunities	Consulting firms, technology institutions and suppliers Larger firms seeking to outsource or contract out
	• Specialized training in advanced technical skills	Master craftworkers, private training institutes, larger firms
Upgrading Master craftworkers	Vouchers for training-of-trainers	
Public training and technology institutions	Grants to retool curricula and training methods	

Note: Training is currently availabale to owners and their employees. Technicon leavers, along with unemployed or downsized civil servants, have been excluded, although they are being considered as appropriate beneficiaries because of their relatively high educational attainment and ability to self-finance (from severance benefits).

stimulated for at least 300 private sector business development service providers throughout Kenya.

The voucher programme is already enhancing the role of master craftworkers by placing millions of Kenyan shillings in the hands of potential entrepreneurs. In response to this effective demand, master craftworkers have adapted, condensed, costed, and packaged their training programmes as a product. Whereas apprenticeships take a year or more, in the voucher programme no course exceeds one month. The higher the quality of training and skills imparted, the higher the demand and the greater the voucher income earned. Experience has shown that the more successful master craftworkers have made training a profitable adjunct to their enterprise. Others have found that the provision of training is even more profitable than their business, especially after former students raise the level of competition, and some have made training their principal business. Master craftworkers are encouraged to use the voucher programme to upgrade their skills through training-of-trainer courses.

Recognizing that some public institutions might need assistance in adapting their curricula to the needs of Jua Kalis, the project also provides grants for public training and technology institutions seeking to 'retool' their offerings. Public institutions have been slow to respond, but private training institutions have sought to take advantage of this growing market by developing training-of-trainers courses for master craftworkers.

Services for microenterprises

By subsidizing the demand side, Jua Kali preferences have conditioned the form, duration, and content of instruction as well as the type of service providers. Courses for existing microenterprises and for women wishing to start a manufacturing business are short, and impart readily implementable skills and practices. Because the skills imparted are relatively basic, courses are standardized and emphasize group learning. The average cost of a course is Ksh10 000 (about US$200).

The strong preference of Jua Kali workers for appropriate, accessible training by these master craftworkers was revealed in the first phase of the project: 85 per cent of all vouchers went to buy the services of master craftworkers, and only 15 per cent went to private and public training institutions. This preference reflects the tradition of apprenticeship and the attraction for micro and small enterprises of receiving training in the type of firm that they can reasonably aspire to become, rather than in a formal training centre.

The voucher mechanism is being adapted to respond to the demand of Jua Kali enterprises for greater access to finance by subsidizing the outreach of Kenya's existing micro-finance institutions (MFIs) to this market. MFIs are being asked to package their savings and credit education programmes as training courses that could qualify for the voucher programme, thereby reaching potential clients who are willing to bear a portion of the costs. Some MFIs view training voucher graduates as good potential clients, while others are making training through the programme a condition of a loan. The Kenya Co-operative Bank is voluntarily training Jua Kali associations on how to establish savings and credit associations, as part of its business development efforts. The Jua Kali savings and credit associations will become future channels and guarantors for the Co-operative Bank's credit and savings services.

Services for small firms

The target group of small firms requires more costly specialized and individualized training and assistance as well as ongoing advice. Whereas the supply of training services for the vast market of Jua Kali microenterprises responded spontaneously, the supply of higher-level consulting and other services for small firms is being cultivated more deliberately. In the pilot phase, the project is selecting small firms that could benefit from specialized technological training and industrial attachments. In the next phase, consultants and technology institutions are being invited to apply for listing as service providers under the voucher programme. The methodology is the same as for the training programme, except that the services and voucher amounts will be tailored to the needs of the individual enterprise.

Thus the voucher methodology is being adapted to provide differentiated products that are suited to different segments of the micro and small enterprise sector. The training vouchers cater more to the basic training needs of the smaller end of the scale, which can be provided in standard training courses, while the technology and business development service vouchers cater more to larger firms with specialized needs.

The voucher mechanism: how it works

The voucher programme has four important sets of actors (as indicated in Figure 12.1):

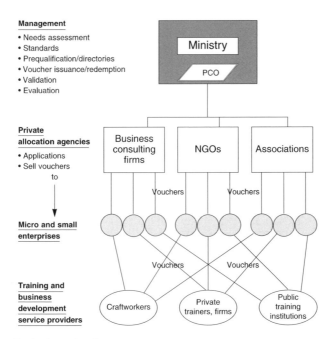

Figure 12.1 *Project mechanisms*

- a central co-ordination/management unit
- private allocation agencies
- micro and small enterprises (self-employed entrepreneurs and employees)
- training and business development service providers.

The role of the firms and service providers has already been discussed. This section addresses the role and organization of the central co-ordination management unit and of the private allocation agencies.

Co-ordination/management unit

A project co-ordination office (PCO) was established under separate management within the Ministry of Research and Technology (subsequently the Office of the President) to co-ordinate overall project activities. The PCO is responsible for the following operations.

- Assess the demand and supply sides: (a) to assess the training needs of micro and small enterprises to identify gaps in skills, and (b) to assess the availability of required skills among service providers in the public and private sectors (to support the design of a programme to upgrade their skills as trainers).
- Design the programme and pilot operations: (a) to develop the design and procedures manual and (b) to carry out a pilot programme of about 430 vouchers to test the programme's design and procedures.
- Manage a directory of prequalified trainers and business development service providers: (a) to establish standards and prequalification criteria for training and service providers and (b) to carry out procurement activities for allocation agencies and for training and service providers, including placing

171

advertisements to request proposals, validating the capabilities of service providers, evaluating proposals, and approving and prequalifying providers.

- Manage ongoing operations: (a) to market the voucher programme to service providers, specialized master craftworkers, training institutions, Jua Kali associations, and entrepreneurs; (b) to print vouchers, with watermarks and other security features; (c) to establish contractual relationships with private voucher allocation agencies (non-governmental organizations, consulting firms, Jua Kali associations); (d) to issue vouchers to allocation agencies; (e) to pay allocation agencies (about 25 per cent of the value of vouchers issued); (f) to validate vouchers to ensure that the training or service was performed; and (g) to redeem vouchers and make payments to training and service providers, following validation.
- Prepare for institutionalization: (a) to work with, and train, ministry staff at the central, district, and provincial levels to carry out project activities; (b) to maintain ongoing responsibility for quality control such as setting of standards, procurement, and audits; and (c) to co-ordinate the training provider upgrading programme.

Private allocation agencies

Kenya is a large country, and the voucher programme is designed to be implemented in a decentralized way. To achieve this, the project uses Jua Kali associations, private consultants and consulting firms, and associations of micro and small enterprises to allocate vouchers. Typically, Jua Kali and other business associations bid to become allocation agencies as a service to their clientele. Consultants and consulting firms have chosen to become allocation agencies as a way of marketing their business services to a broader clientele.

If the association or consultant is prequalified as an allocation agency, it is issued a volume of voucher applications that it can sell to microenterprises for about Kshs100 (about US$2). The allocation agent is expected to assist the firm in filling out the application (about eight pages). The voucher application provides baseline data on the enterprise for project monitoring purposes. The application is also the basis for screening and qualifying applicants. Presumably the allocation agent is in a position to verify the information contained in the application because he knows the applicant or can visit the applicant's business.

The allocation agent carries the applications to Nairobi (in the future, to the district applied technology office) and returns with vouchers that can be sold to applicants who have passed the screening process.

In the process of issuing vouchers, the allocation agent shares with the entrepreneur the directory of prequalified service and training providers and often discusses the type of business or training services that would be appropriate for the future of the firm. In this way, the allocation agency serves as a business advisory service.

The allocation agency issues the voucher once the applicant has paid the required share (presently 10–30 per cent) of its face value. When the training or service has been completed and validated, the allocation agent returns the documentation to Nairobi and receives 3 per cent of the voucher value as compensation.

Selection and validation

Selection of allocating agencies and training providers is treated as procurement under the regulations of the Ministry Tender Board. The process of recruiting,

172

selecting, and contracting begins when advertisements are placed in the national and local media and proposals are requested from agencies seeking to be considered either as allocation agencies or as training providers (but not both). Applicants are rated according to established criteria, which are applied rigorously to prequalify only applicants with demonstrated capabilities. Qualified training providers submit their courses and fees, which are averaged by type of course and subsector in order to establish standard voucher values. Field officers visit prequalified applicants to validate the information and facilities before they are entered into the directory.

Vouchers are numbered and printed on special watermarked paper with laser seals to prevent fraud. Trainees must countersign the vouchers after training to indicate their satisfaction before training providers can be reimbursed. Field inspections are used to validate that training is provided as indicated in the directory and to investigate cases in which questions have been raised. Audits indicate that the rigorous selection, validation, and security procedures have minimized the scope for collusion, although they also delay payment.

Cost sharing and prospects for sustainability

The use of vouchers to catalyse development of a market for training and business development services assumes the existence of potential demand that is not expressed because micro and small enterprises lack information on the availability of such services and because they are reluctant to pay for a service of uncertain value. It also assumes that business development service providers would be able to serve Jua Kali enterprises if those firms were willing and able to pay for services.

There is already ample evidence that consulting firms and other business service providers, which in the past have never served Jua Kali enterprises, are now packaging their services and marketing themselves to the Jua Kali market. The increased purchasing power in the hands of the Jua Kali, made possible by the vouchers, has made serving those enterprises an attractive business. The information gap is overcome by involving the Jua Kalis' own associations and allocating agencies and by sharing information through the directory of training providers and courses tailored to their needs. By subsidizing the initial contact between service providers and clients, the project enables micro and small enterprises to receive the economic benefits of training. The demonstration effect following training and business services is expected, over time, to create an environment where training and business improvements are sufficiently valued so that micro and small enterprises are willing and able to bear their full cost.

In the effort to overcome the market failures that have inhibited the emergence of business services appropriate for micro and small enterprises, the voucher programme is highly subsidized in its initial phase, with differential rates of subsidy depending on the level of training and the size of the client firm (micro or small). As the market develops and enterprises begin to value the skills, management, or technology training, the rate of cost sharing will increase. For example, with a client's purchase of a second and third voucher, the rate of subsidy financed by the project will decline, as illustrated in Table 12.6.

Already, some training providers report that some participants, after receiving basic skills training, have paid full cost to receive more advanced training because they did not want to wait the six months that must pass before they could obtain an additional voucher. However, given the project's relatively limited

Table 12.6 Cost sharing under the voucher programme

Target group	Average value of voucher	Projected subsidy for	
		First-time voucher (percentage at beginning/end of project)	Repeat voucher (end of project)
Start-up and dynamic microenterprises			
Basic skills training	Ksh10 000 (US$200)	90/50	Overhead costs only
Intermediate training	Ksh15 000 (US$300)	80/50	Overhead costs only
Advanced skills and management training	Ksh20 000 (US$400)	70/50	Overhead costs only
Small-scale firms			
Technology/BDS voucher	Ksh50 000–Ksh100 000 (US$1000–US$2000)	70/50	Overhead costs only

penetration into the target group, it is likely that an additional five years or more will be needed to catalyse development of the market for business development services to the point where significant numbers of micro and small enterprises are bearing the full cost, making this a sustainable private market.

Although conceptually the need for special programmes and subsidies should disappear as the market develops, some questions arise regarding long-term impact and sustainability:

- Is there a long-term role for the central management unit or ministry in managing the programme for first-time voucher recipients, upgrading the skills of training providers, or matching small-firm clients with appropriate business development service providers?
- If it has an appropriate long-term role, should the project be spun off as an independent agency in order to ensure that it has the incentive and independence to operate as a commercial agent, on the basis of fees, in collaboration with private sector allocation agencies and business development service providers?
- Should donors continue to finance subsidies for start-ups, the poor, and first-time voucher recipients, while requiring full cost recovery from small firms and repeat recipients?
- If continued subsidies to special target groups are warranted, could an independent agency profitably deliver those subsidies through a commission-based voucher programme?

The challenge of measuring impact

In its present form, the project has been operating for less than two years, so the achievement of sustainable impact can only be projected at this stage. The project has an active monitoring and evaluation component and has carried out two initial tracer studies. The detailed beneficiary application form provides rich baseline data for analysing impact.

Impact on enterprises

By the end of the project in 2001, the surviving beneficiary firms are expected to achieve a 50 per cent increase in income and employment, on average. In surveys of micro and small enterprises throughout the world, enterprises consistently identity 'market constraints' as key factors inhibiting their growth, including highly competitive markets for undifferentiated products, lack of customers, and low margins and profitability. Initial results of tracer studies indicate that the voucher programme has had an almost immediate positive impact on income by alleviating these market constraints. The training services provided under the project have improved the ability of beneficiary enterprises to compete, by allowing them to:

- upgrade the quality of their product, differentiate the product, produce new products in some cases, and thereby compete in less-saturated market niches
- produce more efficiently, reduce waste, and raise net income
- expand their client base through improved marketing and client services.

Training in new methods and introduction to new technologies appear to have improved efficiency and productivity and reduced production costs, thereby increasing margins. As a result, the majority of beneficiary firms interviewed attested that the voucher programme helped them to increase their income significantly and expand employment, even with no financial assistance.

Impact on institutions

During the project, about 20 public training institutions will receive upgrading grants to retool their curricula and training methods to serve Jua Kali enterprises. The project is also developing a training provider upgrading programme to allow master craftworkers and other service providers, who do not initially qualify for the project, to improve their training or service, compete in subsequent procurement rounds, and participate in the voucher market.

Over the long term, the voucher programme, if implemented successfully, is expected to develop a viable market for the provision of training, technology, and other business services to Jua Kali enterprises.

Notes

1. The project was approved by the World Bank's executive board of directors in December 1994. Since approval, it has been substantially restructured to focus on market development, eliminating certain components and conditions. The remaining training and technology components have been streamlined and now operate around a central voucher mechanism. After a three-year delay from the time of board approval, implementation began in 1998. The authors are grateful to R. Gichira (project co-ordinator), J. G. Gichohi, and the rest of the project team.
2. Lisa Daniels, Donald C. Mead, and Muli Musinga, *Employment and Income in Micro and Small Enterprises in Kenya: Results of a 1995 Survey* (Washington, D.C.: USAID, GEMINI, September 1995).

13. Matching grant schemes

DANIEL CRISAFULLI

ASSISTANCE TO SMALL ENTERPRISES (SEs) gained prominence in the 1970s, as the focus of industrial policy on large-scale industry increasingly came into question. The resulting assistance to small firms, financed and executed by the state, was an attempt to offset the privileged access to finance and other support services available to large firms and thereby improve the economy's overall growth potential.

Business development services (BDS) were viewed primarily as an offshoot of directed financing programmes and were often used as a prerequisite for access to subsidized credits. Continuing through the 1980s, these programmes emphasized the *supply* of services via public sector agencies and generally ignored issues of market creation or sustained impact. The emphasis was placed on creating a public sector supply of business development services, often forced on clients seeking access to subsidized credit. Not surprisingly, a study of World Bank lending for SEs found that these schemes were mostly 'slow to get off the ground, costly and ineffective'.[1]

By the 1990s, a new approach emerged which used a demand-side intervention to stimulate the private market for business development services. This approach combined private sector execution with a temporary subsidy – with a view toward long-term sustainability of outcomes. For basic training or small-scale consulting needs, the voucher scheme has emerged as a leading policy instrument. However, for larger and more complex firm-level projects the matching grant scheme has been adopted as the preferred model by the donor community.

The experience under these matching grant schemes has come under increased scrutiny. To what degree have they lived up to expectations in terms of providing high-quality BDS to clients? What has been the impact on private markets for BDS? Which design characteristics were likely to increase chances for success/failure?

This chapter will examine two matching grant schemes implemented in middle-income countries noted for success in structural reform and export-oriented growth, Chile and Mauritius. Analysis of schemes in two relatively similar countries allows a focus on detailed design issues. A further consideration in the choice of countries is the *ex ante* supply of BDS. Although BDS markets were apparently not well developed in either country, a reasonable supply of technical advisers was available (through local or international providers). This condition allows the analysis to focus on the effectiveness of the demand-side intervention – setting aside the issues of technical and higher education relating to formation of skilled human resources. Evidence from countries with a very low skill base (or poor access/linkage to foreign providers) confirms that conditions in the local market for BDS should be taken into consideration to avoid negative distortions (e.g., large price increases for BDS).

Despite their basic similarities, the programmes in Chile and Mauritius differ across a number of design criteria – with implications for design of programmes elsewhere. A description of the two countries' approaches forms the next section of the chapter, followed by a discussion of relative strengths/weaknesses and policy lessons of each approach in terms of cost effectiveness, transparency, and sustainability. Governance issues and the role of executing agent will be explored, including a discussion of the selection process and the agent compensation and incentive system. Finally, the implications for market creation and sustainability will be addressed, along with the agenda for monitoring and evaluation.

The Chilean approach

Chile's programme of market-oriented reforms have been widely recognized for their role in creating sustained economic growth and poverty reduction; however, the Government's pro-active intervention to support market development has received less attention. The importance of the favourable macroeconomic and legal/regulatory environment cannot be overemphasized. The relatively small size of the informal economy (an estimated 30 per cent of GDP), compared with other Latin American economies (40–60 per cent of GDP), serves as an indicator of the relative compatibility of the legal/regulatory environment with private entrepreneurship.[2]

The use of private agents for programme implementation emerged gradually from earlier state-operated schemes.[3] In 1993, a portion of the public agency SERCOTEC's activities (US$500 000) were outsourced to a leading association of manufacturing exporters. The association was charged with the responsibility of implementing both single-firm projects (FAT) and multi-firm (PROFO) projects.[4] The role of CORFO became one of regulator, with a focus on financial management, monitoring and evaluation. In 1994, a group of business associations formed CEPRI[5], which became the largest agent for the FAT programme and an important facilitator of PROFOs. A variety of other agents have been approved on a sectoral and regional basis.

General description

The FAT and PROFO programmes support a wide range of SE upgrading activities, including in the areas of financial management, marketing, quality, design, production systems, strategic planning, and environmental management. The FAT extends a relatively small level of support for short-term consulting projects for one or more firms; PROFO supports longer-term multifirm projects. The programmes are open to a broad range of SEs (with the exception of microenterprises), although the level of subsidy and activities eligible for support programme favour the participation of smaller firms.

Budgetary support for the two programmes has grown from US$0.5 million in 1993[6] to US$25.4 million in 1998, although programme funding was under review in 1998 due to fiscal tightening driven by Chile's macroeconomic situation.

Role of agents

The central innovation of the Chilean approach is the use of private sector agents for implementation of the FAT and PROFO programmes. Under the three-tiered delivery mechanism, the role of the public sector moved from direct provision of services to one of policy formulation, monitoring, evaluation, financial management, sharing of best practices, and provision of (temporary) subsidy. The second-tier consisted of the private or quasi-private agents encharged

Table 13.1 Comparison of basic characteristics of Chile and Mauritius schemes

	Chile		Mauritius
	FAT	*PROFO*	
Firm eligibility	US$80 000–US$3.4 million in sales	US$80 000–US$3.4 million in sales	All firms with at least 51 per cent private equity
Subsidy gap	US$2500 per project	US$100 000 per project per annum, or US$13 600 per firm per annum	US$100 000 per firm over life of programme
Cost sharing	If firm annual sales are less than US$1.7 million, subsidy declines from 85 per cent to 50 per cent over the course of six projects If annual sales US$1.7–3.4 million, subsidy declines from 70 per cent to 30 per cent over six projects	Subsidy decreases from max. 70 per cent in first year to max. 50 per cent in third year	50/50

with either brokering of initial use of external consultant services by SEs in the case of FAT, or cultivating group projects between firms with shared interests (PROFO). The third tier consisted of the private consultants which executed the firm-level advisory projects.

Agents were selected on a regional and sectoral basis with constrained competition. Selected agents were formed by business associations or other local non-profit groups, often in alliance with technical universities and local government. This developmental approach toward agent selection has had an ambiguous impact on programme implementation. Use of local private sector groups as agents may have brought benefits in terms of ability to convene collective action projects and promote inter-firm associativity, and creation of local capacity for brokering of firm upgrading services to outlast the period of subsidized operation. However, the increased discretionality on the part of government administrators (versus the Mauritius approach) has acted to reduce the autonomy and accountability of agents and has diluted overall transparency of the programme.

The regional structure of the programme also served to reduce transparency. Each agent negotiates its contracts on a regional basis, whether or not the agent has a nationwide presence. *Ex post* evaluations of the FAT and PROFO programmes suggest a high degree of variation between agents in terms of cost effectiveness and quality of service.[7]

The financial management system, with a focus on monitoring and safeguards to promote accountability, played a key role in independent operation of FAT agents. Following the signing of an operating agreement and bonding of the agent, funds were advanced to the agent by CORFO for the projected activity over the next quarter or semester (depending on the agent's track record). Prior to payment to the consultant, the agent required proof that the work had been completed to the satisfaction of the client firm.

FAT agents were given an administration fee of 15 per cent of the cost of the overall project, including private and public contributions – a dramatic cost reduction from previous state-operated schemes. However, this fixed fee is likely to underfund the sensitive start-up phase and overcompensate mature service providers. A more balanced regime, combined with competition between potential agents, is likely to reduce overall costs.

PROFO has retained a greater degree of centralization, with full *ex ante* review of projects by CORFO management due to the larger size and longer duration of the subsidy. The result is predictable: participants have complained of bureaucracy and delays during approval, as well as the large time commitment required to comply with CORFO requirements.

Consultants: incentives, characteristics, and management

Private consultants serve a critical function in the FAT and PROFO programmes – they provide the direct assistance to client firms. The aim of the programmes is to provide high-quality consultants to address the real needs of enterprises. Several potential tools are available to maximize the benefits provided.

The first tool is the registry of consultants, currently maintained by CORFO at the regional level. Any experienced consultant, local or international, may request registry; however, national consultants are used almost exclusively. To avoid conflicts of interest, agents are not allowed input regarding CORFO's decision to list a consultant in the registry. As noted above, CORFO is launching a national on-line registry to ensure consistent standards across regions, and to increase the pool of consultants available to firms.

The second tool is the training of consultants in techniques for managing consulting projects. CORFO has undertaken consultant training programmes in selected regions, but has not given a particular emphasis to this task.

Economic impact and sustainability

The economic argument for the FAT and PROFO programmes rests on two pillars: direct economic impact on the productivity, sales revenue, and employment of firms; and impact on the market for business advisory services. As with many other SE support programmes, monitoring and evaluation have focused on the first goal, which has more immediate tangible, political benefits. The second goal, with greater benefits in the longer term, has received less analysis.

Evaluations of the FAT and PROFO programmes undertaken in 1997 by the University of Chile were based on a survey of participating firms.[8] Partial results of the survey of FAT participants are presented in Table 13.2. Firms reported broad gains in a variety of output measures, with a reasonable portion of the benefits attributed to the FAT programme. The corresponding figures for the agent CEPRI are presented as well to exclude projects undertaken by quasi-public agents. Although data on the percentage increase in output were not collected, one may infer that the programme had a significant positive impact on firm growth.

For PROFO, there were positive returns in economic and financial (fiscal) terms. The economic cost–benefit (CB) ratio for PROFO was estimated at 1:2.4, and the fiscal CB ratio at 1:3.2. Broad benefits in firm upgrading were identified for participating firms versus a control group. No studies regarding the

Table 13.2   Impact assessment of FAT scheme

Growth in:	Total sample		CEPRI	
	Firms reporting	Attributed to FAT	Firms reporting	Attributed to FAT
Sales	65	30	73	34
Production volume	62	25	66	28
Employment	39	21	35	24
Exports	16	5	28	12
Salaries	66	11	72	11

development of the market for consulting services in Chile were available during the preparation of this chapter. However, anecdotal evidence suggests some success in creating a sustained private market for SE advisory services.

Several weaknesses in the system for monitoring and evaluation were apparent. Agents collected data from participating firms as a prerequisite for payment to consultants, introducing an important potential source of bias. Data collection is a severe challenge under any circumstances due to confidentiality concerns and logistical difficulties; however, the Mauritius experience suggests that a sustained effort by agents operating under an appropriate incentive regime is necessary to ensure adequate data collection.

The Mauritius Technology Diffusion Scheme

Mauritius is a small, open economy which experienced high rates of growth during the 1980s based on exports of garments and sugar. When growth rates began to decline in the early 1990s, the Government recognized the need to upgrade the technological capacity of firms and move into higher value-added products to support continuing increases in real wages. The Technology Diffusion Scheme (TDS) was developed in 1993–94 to address this problem.

The TDS was conceived as a temporary intervention aimed at demonstrating to firms the value of external advisory services and thus facilitating creation of a private market. Executed by a private agent hired under international tender, the programme extended matching support to single- and multi-firm projects for upgrading of enterprise capacity.

General description

The TDS supported a similar range of services to the Chilean schemes, including product quality, design, process technology and productivity enhancement – with the proviso that the project contribute to Mauritius' competitive position in international markets. Any firm with majority private sector ownership was eligible to participate, regardless of size; however, due to the nature of services supported, the main clients were in the manufacturing industry and related support services.

Simplicity in operation was a central principle in the design of the scheme. A uniform 50/50 ratio in determining subsidy levels was applied across all projects and sizes of firms. Flexibility in operation was enhanced by the wide range of projects supported. Although most projects were small, with the average less than US$10 000, TDS was able to support much larger projects of up to US$100 000 in subsidy.[9] Both single- and multi-firm projects were supported.

Unlike the Chilean schemes, large firms were not prohibited from participation. This flexibility in design allowed a natural progression of firms to participate in the scheme. During the early stage of operation, larger firms within the SE spectrum were attracted to the scheme as a result of existing consultancy relationships and greater propensity to use external advisory services. As the results of these projects were diffused, smaller firms were attracted to the scheme through a demonstration effect and the status associated with participation of larger firms. Over the life of the scheme, the average grant size declined from US$15 100 to US$9800.

A second rationale for inclusion of large firms was discovered *ex post:* the programme evaluation indicates no correlation of firm size with programme benefits (i.e., increase in sales or exports). This finding implies that the information asymmetry in the market for consulting services was true for larger firms in Mauritius as well as smaller competitors. Another benefit of large firm participation was the potential tie-in with backward linkage programmes. Finally, transaction costs associated with participation in the scheme were likely to screen out most large firms – a further argument for simplification of programme rules to permit their participation.

Total grant funding of US$2.1 million, supported under a World Bank loan, was committed during the programme's four-year implementation period (1994–98). After four years of operation, the programme had supported 225 projects in 153 firms. Including firm contributions, the cost of services provided under the TDS reached US$5.1 million. In addition, the World Bank financed US$450 000 in operational costs, representing 8.8 per cent of the cost of services provided to firms. This amount represents a 42 per cent saving in administrative cost compared with Chile's FAT programme.

Role of agent

The TDS shared the key innovation of the Chilean approach – execution by a private agent under contract from the Government. The private agent was encharged with promoting the programme to potential clients; assisting clients with planning firm-level activities; facilitating contact between firms and suitable consultants; helping clients to complete grant applications; advising client firms how to maximize use of consultancy; and administering approvals and disbursement of funds.

Instead of a proactive, developmental role for Government *vis-à-vis* the private agent, as in Chile, a non-discretionary fee-for-service relationship with explicit performance criteria was established. The agent was selected through competitive international bidding to execute the full four-year programme, subject to an annual performance review. Selection criteria for the agent focused on technical capacity to execute a firm-upgrading scheme. Local institutional development criteria did not enter into the selection process. A foreign provider offered several benefits. The temporary nature of the planned intervention was not viewed as requiring the creation of local institutional capacity (which could more easily engage in rent-seeking behaviour). The programme aimed to create a sustained private market for external consultancy services, not a permanent broker. In addition, the use of a foreign agent was viewed as improving the Government's control over the agent relationship and reducing the potential for collusion between the agent and participating consultants.

The result of the explicitly contractual and non-discretionary relationship between Government and agent resulted in a greater degree of transparency and accountability of the private agent. Although Chile's approach represented a tremendous advance over previous public sector executed schemes, the role of the state in Mauritius was streamlined one step further, allowing the public sector to focus on policy formulation, monitoring, and evaluation.

Mechanics of agent system

A supervision committee, consisting of three public sector representatives and three private business associations, was encharged with oversight of the programme by the Ministry of Industry and Industrial Technology (MIIT).[10] In addition to general supervision of the agent, the supervision committee approved all grant applications over US$50 000 and was intended to facilitate any government approvals required in the course of the firm-level projects. Individual projects were approved on an *ex post* basis by the supervision committee; however, the sole condition for the committee to refuse support for a project approved by the agent was in the case of demonstrated fraud.

With a small staff (generalist/administrator, broadly-experienced technician, and secretary), the agent managed the approval and disbursement of grants while providing assistance to applicants in the selection of consultants, promoting the programme, and collecting data for monitoring and evaluation purposes. The agent was responsible for confirming the completion of each project and delivery of the final product to the client firm. Upon this confirmation, the Ministry of Finance issued the reimbursement to the participating firm.

The key strength of the Mauritius TDS was the high degree of transparency and low level of discretionality in management. The agent approved projects on a first-come-first-served basis according to conformity with eligibility criteria and was responsible for all project activities, including administration of funds. The resulting degree of discretion on the part of the agent, supervision committee, and MIIT was very low.

Approval of projects by the agent, a key feature in ensuring the accountability and responsiveness of the Mauritius scheme, was reportedly planned to be modified under the second phase scheme currently being prepared by the Mauritius government. Increased *ex ante* review by the supervision committee would likely result in reduced effectiveness of the programme through increased politicization, bureaucratization, and delays. Any changes in programme design which could undermine the technical independence and accountability of the private agent would be highly damaging to the future of the scheme.

Consultants: incentives, characteristics, and management

As under the Chilean programmes, private consultants form the core of the Mauritius scheme through direct provision of services to client firms. The agent was charged with registration of consultants on technical grounds. Of the 204 consultants registered by the agent, 52 per cent actually provided services under the scheme. Although the agent offered assistance in the selection of consultants, 70 per cent of participating firms selected a consultant of their own accord. The agent's role in registry and selection of consultants as well as approval of projects represents a potential conflict of interest. In the case of Mauritius, the potential conflict of interest on the part of the agent was reduced by the use of a technically qualified foreign contractor with a strong interest in maintaining its international reputation. Nevertheless, this design element deserves careful consideration to ensure proper alignment of incentives to agent and participating consultants and firms.

The consultants were a mix of local and international specialists – with 57 per cent of projects undertaken by Mauritius-based experts. On a cost basis, however, foreign consultants absorbed 53 per cent of all grants, primarily as a result of increased travel costs.

The Mauritius scheme had the explicit aim of facilitating creation of a market for external business advisory services. However, the scheme was not linked to any local training programmes to upgrade consultant capability.

Interaction with local groups/associations

The scheme was designed as a free-standing programme, with a dedicated agent for implementation. The design was intended, however, to promote interaction with activities of private business associations. A key benefit in Chile of using local business associations for programme implementation was their power to promote the schemes and to convene groups of firms for joint activities. In Mauritius, this benefit was obtained through informal marketing alliances and the inclusion of three leading business associations on the supervision committee. The agent also hired local staff with a strong reputation and ties to business groups, which served to build confidence in the scheme.

The Export Processing Zone Development Authority (EPZDA) was instrumental in promoting the TDS. Over half of all projects (53 per cent) were undertaken by firms located in the Export Processing Zone. The group schemes, in particular, required extensive recruitment and preparation which were beyond the capabilities of the two-person TDS contractor. During the life of the scheme, thirteen group projects involving 37 firms were undertaken.

The agent also developed a relationship with the national development bank and private commercial banks which facilitated financing of the firm contribution under the program, as well as follow-on investment projects based on business plans.

Economic impact and sustainability

The TDS aimed to enhance the international competitiveness of private firms through stimulating the market for technology support services. The intervention was intended to 'offset the learning costs in the initial acquisition of technology services and to promote technology diffusion through . . . demonstration effects'.[11] Despite this stated objective, monitoring and evaluation of the TDS focused on direct benefits (increased sales and exports) accruing to firms as a result of participation. No systematic analysis of the market for consulting services was undertaken to assess directly the progress toward the scheme's stated goal of stimulating the growth of this market.

The TDS design supported a reasonably strong measurement of the scheme's direct impact on firm competitiveness. The letter of agreement signed with participating firms required them to disclose incremental sales and export revenues as well as indicators associated with implementation of business plans (e.g., ISO 9000 certification, increased productivity, and new product launch); importantly, the private agent was required to follow up with firms to ensure this information was properly collected. With substantial effort, the agent was able to collect monitoring information on 148 projects involving 110 firms (72 per cent).[12] The remaining firms were unwilling to submit information following completion and disbursement of projects.

The average reported increase in sales for participating firms is 49 per cent, with exports growing by 53 per cent – far in excess of expectations at project launch. The total net sales increase for the 145 projects with relevant data was US$186 million; exports grew by a reported US$106 million. Export performance for participating firms versus non-participants in sectors for which data were available was strongly positive (see Figure 13.1). Other indicators of project success were also strongly positive, with high growth in sales and exports associated with various types of projects.

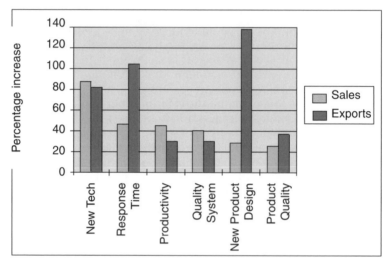

Figure 13.1   *TDS impact on sales and exports by type of project*

The impact evaluation of the TDS is based on relatively robust data, with a large sample size and appropriate incentives for data collection by the implementing agent. However, analysis of the TDS suffered from weaknesses common to studies of programmes to upgrade firm capacity, including selection bias, whereby relatively successful firms are the first to apply for programme participation; and collinearity with other factors influencing overall growth in productivity, sales and exports. However, the large magnitude of reported benefits, sectoral analysis, and evidence from interviews,[13] suggests that the impact was indeed positive. Larger firms tended to respond that they would have postponed or downsized the project had TDS support not been available. Smaller enterprises typically responded that participation in the scheme was 'a turning point' in the development of the firm. The TDS apparently had a significant and positive impact on participating enterprises.

Regarding the impact on the market for external advisory services, interviews with consultants indicated that the market for advisory services was poorly-developed in Mauritius prior to the scheme. One indicator of programme success was a reported decrease in consultant fees, reflecting increased competition and overall activity in the market. In addition, the use of local consultants increased during the life of the scheme from 40 per cent during the first year to 60 per cent in the final year. Anecdotal evidence suggests that markets for quality systems and ISO 9000-related advisory services benefited greatly from the scheme. However, no broad quantitative analysis of programme impact on the consultant market was undertaken.

Summary and conclusions

The two programmes discussed in this chapter share a basic philosophy of demand-driven, private sector implementation with an aim to facilitate creation of sustained markets for BDS. The selection process and contractual relationship between government and agent differ between Chile and Mauritius, resulting in potential lessons for the design of programmes in other countries.

Chile uses a developmental approach, working with regional and sectoral trade associations to build local agent capacity. The Mauritius approach uses a private, international contractor to administer the programme on a fully autonomous basis with a low degree of discretion on the part of both government and agent.

The developmental approach toward agents used in Chile resulted in a discretionary and non-transparent relationship between the agents and government. The Mauritius scheme offers the benefit of supporting the activities of local business associations – but without the danger of their involvement in direct execution. Acting as service providers and sources of free publicity under the scheme, local business groups extended their outreach and ability to meet the needs of member firms. In this way, the TDS encouraged the long-term creation of sustainable infrastructure for SE services.

The roles of each level of the system are clear under the TDS: government focuses on policy formulation, monitoring, and evaluation while the private agent is incentivized to provide the lowest-cost service through performance-based contracting.

The programmes also offer evidence that private sector operation of BDS support programmes, with maximum autonomy and accountability for the implementing agents, offer significant benefits in cost effectiveness versus previous state-executed regimes. In addition to reduced cost, the private operators offer increased flexibility, improved responsiveness, and a more entrepreneurial attitude in meeting client needs than the public sector providers.

Regarding sustainability, the Mauritius scheme aimed to create local BDS markets, not to build local capacity in execution of a (temporary) matching grant scheme. In Chile the view toward sustainability was muddled; the emphasis on building capacity of local agents presumed the need for a longer-term intervention. Neither scheme adequately measured the direct impact on market activity.

Financial management of these BDS schemes created proper incentives for the appropriate use of funds. The control mechanisms were not foolproof in screening out fraud, but were considered to be effective overall.

The inclusion of large firms in the programme offers several potential benefits. First, firms that are large for a given economy may still be small relative to international competitors – and benefit as much as smaller firms from participation. In addition, participation of large firms offers a demonstration effect for smaller firms and may also bring them into 'vertical' or 'backward linkage' projects.

Incentives for the oversight of consultant participation in the programme is critical to maximize the quality of services while minimizing moral hazard for participants. Clear, simple criteria for registry of consultants should focus on provision of information to enable firms to select for themselves. Schemes in which agents or the government become involved with discretionary schemes for consultant registry involve risks which need to be closely monitored.

Both programmes offer evidence of a positive net impact on economic growth and exports, although evaluation is hampered by methodological and practical difficulties. One clear lesson is that provisions for monitoring and evaluation need to be defined up front, including the incentive structure and methods for collection of data. Increased analysis will be necessary to determine the appropriate period of intervention, as well as exploring potential improvements in programme design. Evidence from Chile and Mauritius give strong indications of positive economic impact for matching grant schemes; however, strengthened impact assessment is needed better to design the interventions of the future.

Notes

1. Leila M. Webster, Randall Riopelle, and Anne-Marie Chidzero, 'World Bank Lending for Small Enterprises 1989–1993', World Bank Technical Paper No. 311, World Bank (1996): 33.
2. Víctor E. Tokman and Emilio Klein, eds., *Regulation and the Informal Economy: Microenterprises in Chile, Ecuador, and Jamaica*, Lynne Rienner Publishers (1996).
3. Enrique Roman, *Criterios de Auto-Sustentabilidad de un Sistema de Provisión de Servicios no Financieros a la Pequeña Empresa: La Experiencia del Centro de Productividad Industrial*, CEPRI, Inter-American Development Bank (1997).
4. *Fondo de Asistencia Técnica:* Technical Assistance Fund; *Proyecto de Fomento:* Promotion Project.
5. *Centro de Productividad Integral*, or Center for Integral Productivity.
6. The figure for 1993 includes only the activities of private agents. SERCOTEC began implementation of FAT and PROFO in 1992, with a budget of US$1.6 million. The SERCOTEC share of implementation has declined, but the public agency continues to administer the programme in sectors and regions not covered by private agents.
7. José Miguel Benavente, Julio Cáceres, Gustavo Crespi, and Robert Muñoz, *Impacto del Instrumento FAT en la Pequeña y Mediana Empresa*, and José Miguel Benavente, Gustavo Crespi, Jorge Katz, and Julio Cáceres, *Impacto del Instrumento PROFO en la Pequeña y Mediana Empresa*, Departmento de Economía, Universidad de Chile (1997).
8. Benavente, Cáceres, Crespi, and Muñoz, (1997) and Benavente, Crespi, Katz, and Cáceres, (1997).
9. Maximum grant support per firm was limited to US$100 000 over the life of the TDS programme.
10. Supervision committee membership included representatives of MIIT, Ministry of Finance, Prime Minister's office, and three business associations.
11. *Technology Diffusion Scheme: Manual of Policies and Operating Procedures*, Mauritius Ministry of Industry and Industrial Technology, 1995.
12. A 66% response rate of the 225 projects undertaken. See *Mauritius Technology Diffusion Scheme, Final Report*, Segal Quince Wicksteed Limited, November 1998.
13. 'An Evaluation of the Mauritius Technology Diffusion Scheme,' *New World Ventures*, September 1997.

14. Business linkages in Zimbabwe: the Manicaland Project

JOHN GRIERSON, DONALD C. MEAD and EDWARD KAKORE

Abstract

BUSINESS LINKAGES are ongoing commercial dealings between separate profit-oriented enterprises. Good business linkages result in specialization, diversification, improved efficiency and wide benefit dispersion. This chapter describes an action research project in Eastern Zimbabwe – the Manicaland Business Linkages Project (MBLP)[1], that uses an approach to enterprise development based on business linkages to respond to the realities of globalization while helping to redress historic social and economic imbalances. The focus of the MBLP is on: pinpointing specific linkage opportunities; encouraging cost-effective capacity-building based on 'buyer mentoring'; and helping with access to credit, as an alternative to direct involvement in the provision of credit or finance. The MBLP is 'minimalist' in concept and practice – the project strives to provide only the minimum assistance necessary to catalyse each business linkage. The operational focus on minimalism is intended to establish efficiency and effectiveness as the basis for sustainability. The MBLP's concept of sustainability is based on the notion that when business linkages become normal practice in Zimbabwe there will be little need for a project or institution to promote business linkages. The MBLP was markedly successful during its initial pilot phase of two-and-a-half years, having catalysed 139 ongoing business linkages.

Background

Business linkages are commercial dealings between separate profit-oriented enterprises. Business linkages are the positive result of market forces compelling businesses to seek the most efficient means of sourcing the components and services that make up their products and services. Good business linkages result in specialization, diversification, efficiency, and wide benefit dispersion (Grierson and Mead, 1995), as well as access to higher value-added opportunities in both domestic and foreign markets (Nadvi, 1998).

Zimbabwe's changing economic structure

Until the early 1990s the Zimbabwe economy was characterized by strong market incentives for vertical integration in an inefficient dualistic economy, one typified by shortages of products, services and production inputs. In recent years, steadily increasing imports have put competitive pressures on large producers, while the liberalization of import and domestic trade regulations have created many new opportunities for small enterprises. These forces have generated both pressures and opportunities for large and small enterprises to interact efficiently with one another. Such interactions – characterized as 'business linkages' when they involve multiple transactions within an established relationship – enhance overall economic efficiency while encouraging smaller enterprises run by indigenous entrepreneurs to participate in the dynamic sectors of the economy (Grierson, Mead and Moyo, 1997). All dynamic market economies are characterized by an extensive and eclectic array of business linkages. Zimbabwe is in the early stage of developing an efficient market economy. The practice of business linkages is not yet common or instinctive in Zimbabwe.

The Manicaland Business Linkages Project

The Confederation of Zimbabwe Industries (CZI) is using small business development approaches based on business linkages to help capture the opportunities generated by economic reform. The Manicaland Business Linkages Project (MBLP), one of the first projects under the CZI small business programme, is designed to respond to structural adjustment, to help redress Zimbabwe's deeply rooted social and economic imbalances and to help embed the practice of business linkages in Zimbabwe's commercial culture. As a pilot project, the MBLP has two objectives: *the impact objective*, to increase overall economic efficiency while expanding participation in the growth sectors of the economy; and *the learning objective*, to develop effective, equitable and sustainable approaches to enterprise development.

The building blocks of business linkages

There are three building blocks of business linkages: information, capacity building, and capital. While each may be needed to establish a successful linkage, in general a single organization should not attempt to supply all three (DCSED, 1998). Business linkages by their nature do much to help small enterprises address their need for capital. The MBLP builds on this strength while concentrating its activities on information and capacity-building.

Information is needed about potential linkage partners. Buyers need to know who are the potential suppliers of goods and services, and suppliers need to know who will buy their products and services. Providing this information cost effectively presents an array of challenges. The fundamental challenge is that information is expensive to collect and collate and, once gathered, is quickly out of date. The MBLP responds to this challenge by concentrating on current credible market demand. Buyers and suppliers are helped to identify current market demand and to form linkages in order to respond to demand. The project often helps broker the initial linkage relationship. Little emphasis is given to databases or other means of compiling information on potential linkage partners.

Capacity-building is sometimes needed to ensure that suppliers can meet their obligations in terms of quantity, quality, timeliness and price (Grierson and Mead, 1995). Buyers know best the specifications and scheduling of the products they require and they have a direct interest in seeing that the terms of the linkage agreement are met. It is due to this simple truth; that 'buyer mentoring' – the practice of buyers helping their suppliers – is the most effective and sustainable form of supplier capacity-building. Buyer mentoring is at the heart of the MBLP. Capacity-building assistance is usually in support of a specific business linkage relationship and is usually supplied by the buyer in the first instance. In cases where direct project intervention is justified, the MBLP either helps suppliers find assistance, or contracts support services from local specialist providers.

Finally, capital is needed to fund operations, buy equipment and build infrastructure. Business linkages help businesses address their need for credit in four ways:

- by identifying and clarifying real credit needs
- by reducing the need for credit (it is increasingly common for buyers to supply equipment or raw materials to their suppliers, thereby reducing the supplier's need for working capital from a third party)
- by the buyer providing credit directly to the supplier, and
- by improving the supplier's access to credit from financial institutions, principally through contracts and various forms of guarantee.

Reducing the need for credit, supplying credit directly, the facilitating access to credit are all forms of buyer mentoring.

The components of the MBLP's design

The MBLP has three areas of operational emphasis:

- identification of linkage opportunities
- business linkages promotion, and
- supplier capacity-building.

Identification of linkage opportunities

Opportunity identification involves helping both buyers and suppliers identify mutually profitable opportunities, and, when asked to do so, helping to broker viable linkages arrangements. The project offers four types of opportunity identification assistance:

- *Buyer Open Houses.* Open Houses give small groups of potential suppliers a chance to visit buyers who are seeking linkage partners.
- *Supplier Capacity Audits.* Supplier capacity audits assess the ability of an enterprise to supply specific goods or services, by identifying strengths and weaknesses in terms of products, production processes, financial capacity, management capacity and technical skills.
- *Feasibility Studies.* Feasibility studies examine the merits of specific linkage proposals and outline the conditions under which it would be profitable for a supplier to enter into a linkages arrangement.
- *Linkages Identification Workshops*, for buyers and suppliers, usually with a sub-sector focus.

Business linkages promotion

Business linkages promotion involves presenting the business linkage concept to Manicaland's business community. Promotional activities include:

- Media Campaigns, including brochures and leaflets, and
- the MBLP Newsletter.

Most aspects of promotional work are sub-contracted to specialist providers.

Supplier capacity building

Supplier capacity-building is intended to strengthen individual enterprises in clearly identified areas so that they can perform as reliable partners in specific linkage contracts. Capacity-building assistance is usually tied to a specific linkage contract or opportunity. As a rule, capacity-building assistance is not provided by the MBLP itself. In cases where direct project intervention is justified, the MBLP will either facilitate access to assistance for others, or, if needed, 'buy-in' training or support services from local specialist consultants or institutions. Buy-in services usually involve either specific training (for individuals or groups) or specialist problem solving (e.g. short-term provision of specialist technical, managerial, financial or marketing assistance). The MBLP is encouraged to use its 'buy-in' budget to leverage contributions from others, particularly the buyers and suppliers who stand to benefit from the services provided.

Designing for sustainability

The MBLP is an innovative attempt to introduce new and unfamiliar techniques into Zimbabwe. The MBLP's concept of sustainability is based upon the expectation that new techniques, if effective and affordable, will gradually become standard business practice in Manicaland and beyond. When business linkages become standard practice, the costs of generating them (i.e. 'information') and sustaining them (i.e. 'capacity-building' and 'buyer mentoring') are largely borne by the buyers and suppliers themselves. Hence, the quest for sustainability is based upon efficiency-motivated change in the local commercial culture, rather than on institution building or fee-for-service-based revenue generation. The MBLP's quest for sustainability has three pragmatic thrusts:

- *impact* – if business linkages work, the practice of business linkages will soon become a normal aspect of Zimbabwe's business culture
- *cost sharing* – as business linkages become standard practice, the costs involved are increasingly borne by the direct beneficiaries, the buyers and suppliers, and
- *minimalism* – external interventions (including the MBLP itself) are carefully limited; the design seeks to hold down costs by stimulating normal economic processes rather than by attempting to substitute for them.

Implementation 'principles'

- The MBLP seeks 'win-win' relationships – both buyer and seller must profit.
- The MBLP emphasises 'buyer mentoring' as the most effective and sustainable approach to developing supplier capacity.
- The MBLP is minimalist in practice, providing only the minimum necessary assistance to each client, while striving to serve as many clients as possible.
- The MBLP is strongly local – it uses Manicaland resources in the first instance, Zimbabwean resources whenever possible, and external resources only when necessary.

Activities, results and costs

Linkages in place (at 31 August 1998)

The sub-sectors identified at the outset were forestry/timber, horticulture, tourism, and furniture manufacture. Forestry-related industries represent up to

Table 14.1 Activities

Information-related		Capacity- and capital-related		
Activity	No.	Activity	No.	Comments
Business linkages promotion workshops	22	'Buy-ins' and capacity audits	18	Of which 13 were help with formulating loan proposals
Buyer open houses	27			
Media campaigns	2	Promoting buyer monitoring	Applies in all cases	Which in many cases served to pinpoint, reduce, supply 'in-kind' or otherwise 'facilitate access to' credit
Newsletter (quarterly)	On-going			

Table 14.2 Number of linkages in place x supplier sector and buyer sector

Buyer sector / Supplier sector	Timber & wood products	Construc-tion	Public sector entities	Other buyers	Total, all buying sectors
Timber harvesting	40	–	1	–	41
Silviculture	20	–	–	–	20
Wood supply	10	–	1	–	11
Construction	3	8	–	–	11
Transport	8	5	–	1	14
Protective clothing	3	1	–	5	9
Cleaning and waste removal	3	–	–	1	4
Canteens and catering	1	1	–	–	2
Farm produce				10	10
Other products & services	6	4	1	6	17
Total, all buying sectors	94	19	3	23	139

70 per cent of the Manicaland economy and account for the bulk of readily available linkage opportunities. The forestry sector lends itself well to business linkages.

Most of the 139 linkages catalysed were in the forestry sector. Sixty-seven per cent of these – 94 of 139 linkages – involved contracts where the buyer was one of only a few large local timber companies. Overall, when measured according to *buyer*, the project's focus sectors are different and less diverse than originally projected. In contrast, sector activity when measured by *supplier sector* is both more eclectic and more diverse than originally expected.

Table 14.3 Costs

Output measure	Projected	Actual
Number of linkages	64	139
Cost/linkage	US$4000	US$1360
Net jobs created		1250
Cost/job		US$150

The human dimension

The following mini-case studies are included to give a human face to the numbers set out above. The vignettes that follow include both forestry-related activities, to emphasize the MBLP's principal economic sub-sector, the linkages in other sub-sectors, to highlight the flexibility of the linkages approach. The MBLP was actively involved in the formation of all of the business linkages reported below.

Box 14.1   Timber harvesting

Mrs Munhundiripo and Mrs Kaneta have recently begun harvesting timber for a large timber company based in Manicaland Province. Neither has previous experience in the timber industry. Both of them have chosen to start their forestry careers as entrepreneurs and their business careers as foresters. Both businesses harvest logs on contract, using chainsaws to fell the trees and oxen to drag the felled timber to the roadside, where it is then collected and transported by other separate small enterprises. Both women hope to expand their enterprises and eventually to replace their oxen with tractors. Mrs. Munhundiripo now has 41 employees, including 11 women. Mrs. Kaneta's enterprise employs 35 men.

Box 14.2   Commercial cleaning

Mr. Mdokwani, who trades as Industrial Housewife, provides office-cleaning services to commercial buildings including banks and the management offices of large companies. Mr. Mdokwani has a staff of 36, one industrial carpet cleaner and nine industrial floor polishers. Industrial Housewife currently has 11 contracts, several of which were obtained through the good offices of the project. Mr. Mdokwani has a number of operational problems, including equipment breakdowns and cash flow difficulties related to inflation and increases in the mandated minimum wage. The project is helping him to address these problems. He hopes to expand his services to include medical waste management and municipal solid waste management.

Box 14.3   Rural road construction

Mr. Njunga, the managing director of Shumba Construction and Engineering, is a qualified engineer and former civil servant with many years' experience overseeing road construction and maintenance. Mr. Njunga's decision to leave government service and create Shumba Construction coincided with a large local timber company's decision to out-source all road maintenance work on their timber estates. The timber company sold their heavy equipment to Mr. Njunga under a hire-purchase agreement and gave him a long-term contract for road maintenance, Shumba Construction's long-term contract provides a stable revenue flow and ensures that Mr. Njunga can make the hire-purchase payments. At the end of the contract Mr. Njunga will own most of his capital equipment.

Evidence of impact

Linkages and mentoring: increasingly common practice

Existing linkages are under increasing pressure as Zimbabwe's economy takes a severe downturn. Markets are contracting and input prices are increasing. High inflation means that the real value of nominal stocks of working capital are declining, while bank interest rates are steadily rising. Suppliers run the risk of having their profits squeezed through more stringent terms with their commercial partners. Yet, in spite of these pressures, there are no reports of either suppliers being forced out of business, or of buyers abandoning business linkages and again taking on non-core functions themselves. Business linkages continue to be seen as an efficient way of dealing with a difficult economic situation.

Among suppliers, there has been vigorous growth in both numbers and scale. If there is a broad generalization that can be made it is that most businesses are doing satisfactorily, with some doing very well. Most suppliers are facing and managing their business problems, though many are struggling to meet their commitments in a deteriorating economic climate.

Many new jobs have been created, in part because the forestry sector enjoyed a long period of steady growth. Encouraging the practice of business linkages has made this growth more efficient, which in turn has stimulated further expansion. The net employment effects of new linkage formation are unknown. However, there is clear evidence of strong employment growth in project-assisted businesses, and overall indications of new employment growth due to sector growth.

There is evidence of widespread acceptance of business linkages as a profitable and efficient way of doing business. There is no longer any need to promote the linkage concept among many of the major businesses in Manicaland. It is now accepted policy, mandated at the highest company levels. Increasingly, the issue is not whether to move forward with business linkages, but how to do so as rapidly and efficiently as possible. One of the clearest indicators of the acceptance of linkages is the degree to which the buyers recognize that it is in their interest to help make linkages work – even when this requires mentoring. It is now widely acknowledged that no one gains when a business linkage fails. In more and more cases the buyers offer advice, 'credit in kind' and training to their suppliers. This mentoring is done to help ensure that the suppliers complete their work in a timely and efficient manner. Buyer mentoring in the form of training is usually precisely targeted on a specific current need, a recognized characteristic of successful and cost-effective training.

Balancing factors: keeping business linkages in perspective

In business, a degree of failure is normal and should be recognized as such. Nonetheless, it is necessary to understand the reasons behind failures and to modify design and practice accordingly. Assessment of apparent failures in forming linkages suggests three principal causes: inadequate information and poor communications; slow decision-making on the part of the buyer; and limited specialization (capacity) on the part of suppliers.

Business linkages help established businesses do better. Those businesses most capable of significant growth are often the ones that have been in existence for some time. Established enterprises have often mastered the basic techniques of their core business, and are thus well placed to grow and to improve efficiency further. Established businesses are more likely to enter business linkage arrangements and they are more likely to become good business linkage partners.

New linkages must come from different buyers and sectors. The prospects for new linkages with current buyers are limited. While there are undoubtedly still some opportunities for further linkages with these buyers, the obvious opportunities have already been grasped. Future growth in linkages in Manicaland will most likely come from other firms in the forestry sector, or in other sectors.

The issue of power imbalance is important and must be addressed. When a large buyer makes purchases from a small supplier, the buyer generally has overwhelming power to dictate the terms of the contract. This can result in exploitation of small suppliers. A number of techniques are commonly mooted to ameliorate the effects of the power imbalance:

- Multiple buyers: If a small supplier can sell to several different customers, the supplier will be less dependent on the terms offered by any single buyer.
- Education of buyers: Forward-looking buyers recognize that it is not in their interest to exploit their suppliers. Suppliers need to earn a fair return. There is an educational role to play in ensuring that buyers understand this.
- Assistance with costing and pricing: A major weakness of small suppliers is that they do not know how to cost and price their products and services. An outside agency can help them determine reasonable and competitive prices.
- Maintaining a bilateral relationship: Addressing the power imbalance issue must be done in ways that do not unduly constrain the efforts of buyers and suppliers to form linkages. The basic rule is a simple one: ensure that the linkage remains essentially a bilateral arrangement between buyer and supplier.

Conclusions

Lessons learned

Two key lessons have emerged from the first phase of the MBLP:

- The driving force must be economic. An attitude of charity on the part of the buyer, or of entitlement on the part of the supplier, can alter the focus, diminish the degree of win-win motivation and potential, and hinder the emergence of business linkages as a commercially rewarding business practice (Mead, 1998).
- Cost-effectiveness is a key part of the equation. There is no likely source of long-term external support for linkages 'projects'. Therefore, short-term external resources must be used carefully and efficiently. In general, this means avoiding costly 'integrated' approaches and instead placing stress on providing only the bare minimum of useful and necessary assistance.

The challenge ahead

The Manicaland Business Linkages Project was fortunate to have been launched at a time when the Manicaland economy was healthy and growing. The early successes of the project owe much to the fact that several large enterprises viewed linkages as an effective approach to restructuring and an efficient way to grasp expanding market opportunities. However, due to the recent downturns in both the Zimbabwe economy and in many of Zimbabwe's export markets as well, both buyers and suppliers now face stagnant markets, unfavourable shifts in relative prices and scarce and expensive credit.

The challenges facing the MBLP now are essentially two: to help ensure that existing linkages survive and to seek out new growth sectors and new opportunities. In the years ahead the MBLP will help the Manicaland business community test whether business linkages are an efficient, equitable and sustainable tool for business development in both good times and bad. As the MBLP responds to these challenges it will have to find the balance between two often conflicting forces. On the one hand, as a demand-led economic activity, it must follow the market. On the other hand, consistent with the logic of business linkages, it must seek specialization and efficiency. If it is to balance these competing realities the MBLP will need to determine both real market demand and the range of needs that the project can reasonably be expected to address. The ultimate measure of the MBLP's success will be the degree to which business linkages eventually become a normal and natural aspect of Zimbabwe's commercial culture.

References

DCSED (Donor Committee for Small Enterprise Development) (January 1998) 'Business Development Services for SMEs: Preliminary Guidelines for Donor-funded Interventions'. DCSED Secretariat, World Bank, Washington, DC. Processed.

Grierson, John, Donald C. Mead and Sam Moyo (August 1997) 'Business Linkages in Zimbabwe: Helping Shape "Win–Win" Economic Structures'. *Development in Practice*, Vol. 7, No. 3, Oxford.

Grierson, John and Donald C. Mead (May 1995) 'Business Linkages in Zimbabwe: Concept, Practice and Strategies'. GEMINI Working Paper No. 50. PACT Publications, USA.

Mead, Donald C. (June 1998) 'Small Enterprise Growth through Business Linkages in South Africa'. Report to USAID and Harvard University under the EAGER/PSGE research project. MSU, East Lansing, MI. Processed.

Nadvi, Khalid (March 1998) 'International competitiveness and small firm clusters – evidence from Pakistan'. *Small Enterprise Development*. Vol. 9, No. 1. London.

Zimconsult (May 1997). 'Evaluation of the Small and Medium Enterprise Development Programme' (ZIB-028). Harare. Processed.

Terms used in the chapter

Business Linkages	Ongoing commercial relationships between separate profit-oriented enterprises.
Mentoring	A relationship in which a person, business or organization provides on-going advice or support to another. In *buyer mentoring*, an enterprise buying goods or services assists the supplier, to help ensure that the supplier will be able to fulfil the expectations of the linkages agreement. Buyer mentoring is a *bilateral relationship* – only the buyer and the supplier are involved, there is no third party.
Sub-Contracting	An arrangement whereby one enterprise enters into a formal agreement with a separate independent enterprise to supply a product or service, according to an agreed price, quality, quantity and delivery schedule.

Note

1. The Manicaland Business Linkages Project (MBLP) is a bilateral (Zimbabwe-Norway) business development project implemented by the Manicaland Chamber of Industries of the Confederation of Zimbabwean Industries (CZI).

15. Global experience in industrial subcontracting and partnerships

ANDRÉ DE CROMBRUGGHE and J.C. MONTES

The theme and its relevance to BDS

THIS CHAPTER FOCUSES on lessons learned from the United Nations Industrial Development Organization's (UNIDO) programme to promote subcontracting and partnership relations of SMEs with large enterprises, and among themselves.

The various linkages that the small and medium enterprises (SMEs) can establish among themselves and with large and state-owned enterprises, are essential factors for their growth and competitiveness. The organization of these linkages is crucial both up-stream with the suppliers and sub-contractors, and down-stream with the distribution and marketing channels.

Industrial subcontracting and out-sourcing are modern and efficient ways to organize industrial production. New forms of industrial subcontracting, here called 'industrial partnerships', are based on the complementarity between the large contracting and assembling enterprises and the various specialized sub-contractors and suppliers, and on the necessity of involving them from the very early stages of the production cycle (design, testing and prototype). Moreover, SMEs frequently co-operate closely with each other in order to complement their activities within the production cycle, by entering into production associations or clusters, and increasingly through networking arrangements. These new forms tend to become more stable, more lasting, with a more equitable distribution of responsibilities (risks and profits) between the various partners. In fact, such subcontracting and partnership linkages enable the SMEs to concentrate on their field of specialization.

In order to increase the chances of success, these linkages often call for other complementary forms of linkages, such as the provision by the main-contractor of special raw materials, specialized equipment, moulds, technical assistance, training, know-how and licence agreements; and even in some cases equity participation or joint investments. Here the traditional subcontracting relationship has become a full-fledged partnership.

While large enterprises are geared by their managerial and marketing strategies and mechanisms towards all forms of industrial collaboration with other enterprises, small and medium enterprises are not equipped to promote such collaboration, and thus deserve special attention and assistance in this area. It is evident that SMEs, particularly in the prevailing context of global out-sourcing, are most in need of support services, given their limited expertise in the matter of foreign markets and their generally higher risk aversion compared to large transnational corporations. Institutional support mechanisms are thus needed that will help them to acquire the necessary information on, and access to, upgraded technology, sources of finance, new markets, foreign licences, etc. and to establish long-term industrial co-operation agreements. It is also SMEs that attach particular value to the neutrality of international organizations as impartial advisers and intermediaries. By contributing to the development of the SME sector, such assistance will also further the overall industrialization process.

As indicated in the UNIDO Medium-Term Plan, 1996–2001, the networking of small and medium enterprises among themselves and with large manufacturing firms, through production linkages, is an indispensable dimension of industrial resilience and competitiveness. In the period covered by the plan, UNIDO will further strengthen and integrate its related services in terms of:

- policy analysis and advisory services concerning approaches to bring about and promote local sourcing by large industries
- assistance to small-scale suppliers in upgrading their technical and commercial skills and their capability to meet quality requirements, and
- support in building up technical information systems on networking potentials (for example, through subcontracting and partnership exchanges – SPXs).

Subcontracting, supply and partnership relations between industries of various types and sizes, especially between large and small enterprises, is a feature of every modern industrial economy. Because industrial subcontracting and similar forms of linkages between small and large industries are so complex and so important for the development of the SMEs, that act as subcontractors or suppliers, special programmes for the promotion of industrial sub-contracting, supply chain management and partnerships, need to be undertaken.

The object of the UNIDO programme is to reinforce the capacity of SMEs in developing countries, as well as in countries with economies in transition, to increase their production and employment, to upgrade their manufacturing processes and products, to improve their productivity and international competitiveness, to encourage import substitution and to promote the export of manufactured products from the SME sector. This programme also contributes to the optimal allocation of industrial resources and thus to national industrial growth and integration. At the same time, it contributes to the international redeployment of manufacturing facilities and the transfer of industrial technology and know-how to the SME sector in developing countries.

The service

Institutional mechanisms: subcontracting and partnership exchanges (SPXs)

Subcontracting and partnership exchanges (SPXs) are technical information, promotion and match-making centres for industrial subcontracting and partnership agreements between main contractors, suppliers and subcontractors, aimed at the optimal (the most complete, rational and productive) utilization of the manufacturing capacities and capabilities of the affiliated industries. SPXs should be driven by the private sector and organized as non-profit industrial associations run by qualified entrepreneurs. In effect, the exchanges appear not only as the meeting points and the instruments of regulation between the supply and the demand of industrial subcontracting orders, but also as instruments of assistance to both partners, and particularly to the small and medium supplier or subcontracting enterprises.

UNIDO provides technical assistance to developing countries for establishing and operating SPXs. To this end, it assists in setting up a roster of subcontractors, suppliers and main contractors. The SPXs act as centres for technical information, match-making and promotion as well as clearing-houses for industrial subcontracting and partnership inquiries and opportunities. They have a number of core functions, including:

- the collection, analysis, storage and organization for rapid retrieval of information and data on the existing production capacities and capabilities of industries, especially SMEs
- the identification of subcontracting, supply and partnership inquiries or offers from large foreign or domestic buyers and main contractors and their dissemination to potential subcontractors/suppliers/partners
- assistance to potential subcontractors/suppliers/partners in organizing production clusters and associations and in negotiating agreements with main contractors, which could be their own governments.

In addition, as recommended by two UNIDO expert group meetings on 'Industrial Subcontracting and Partnership Exchanges and Policies', the new generation of SPXs act as centres of multi-disciplinary assistance and information for subcontractors and suppliers, in fields such as:

- technical support (product design, technology, equipment, innovation)
- quality management, standards and certification
- marketing strategies and analysis (including participation in international fairs and business promotion forums)
- access to credit, financial facilities and incentives
- management (rehabilitation, financial management, stock control)
- legal advice (legal contracts, codes of conduct, reconciliation or settlement of disputes)
- human resource management (training).

This assistance and information is provided either directly by the SPX in the form of surveys, advice, training, awareness seminars and industrial fairs, or by referring the enterprises to the relevant specialized institutes.

UNIDO recommends legal statutes and standard terms of reference for the establishment of autonomous subcontracting and partnership exchanges under boards of directors (or management boards), to be operated as a not-for-profit private sector association.

Necessary conditions for the establishment of an SPX are: existence of a potential subcontracting market in the country (including a critical mass of manufacturing units); the existence of potential stakeholders, from both the public and private sectors, who share the principles of the SPX operation; and potential and commitment to create a capable and sustainable operation.

Methodology, tools and software

In the framework of its programme, UNIDO has been surveying, designing and developing standard instruments and methods for the development of industrial subcontracting, supply and partnership relations. It has been working on:

- policy issues and industrial legislation
- guidance on the creation and operation of SPXs
- computer programs for database management (UNIDOSS) – see below
- subcontracting nomenclatures and terminologies
- legal statutes for establishing autonomous SPXs
- legal guidelines and model contracts for establishing subcontracting agreements
- guidelines on the organization of subcontracting fairs

- brochures, demo-diskettes, power-points and videotapes for awareness building.

UNIDO has developed a new version of the coherent computer software called UNIDOSS (UNIDO Subcontracting System), which is available in English, French and Spanish. UNIDOSS is protected by a licence agreement which is granted free of charge to SPXs established by UNIDO in the context of a technical assistance project.

The basic functions of the UNIDOSS software are:

- the registration of manufacturing capacities and capabilities of industrial companies, based on detailed questionnaires and surveys
- the classification of these companies according to a set of given industrial nomenclatures, such as products, sectors, manufacturing processes and equipment, and
- a search of subcontracting and supplying enterprises according to a very large set of criteria (including an exhaustive analysis of the registered machinery and its technical characteristics) to match them with inquiries from buyers and contractors.

UNIDOSS software also enables the printing of targeted mailing and facilitates an organized follow-up of inquiries. In addition, it allows economic analyses to be carried out on specific sub-sectors and areas, on enterprise deficiencies and required remedies, on technological and quality assessments and on investment and marketing strategies.

Related government policies and programmes

UNIDO also advises governments on how to create a favourable environment and to develop policies and programmes for the promotion of industrial subcontracting, supply and partnership using the following means.

- Industrial legislation, including:
  - incentives to encourage large enterprises to decentralize their production through out-sourcing and subcontracting operations (including 'spin-offs')
  - decrees to improve inter-enterprise credit schemes and terms of payment
  - tax regulations to de-penalize the SMEs that act as subcontractors and suppliers
  - customs regulations to encourage international subcontracting and out-sourcing operations.
- Public procurement policies aimed at providing special facilities or access for SMEs.
- Appropriate Government policies and programmes on 'indigenization' to promote local sourcing and subcontracting by large national or foreign industries and to negotiate with the latter production programmes for increasing the local content of products manufactured under foreign licence.
- The international promotion of capable and reliable subcontractors and suppliers, which is a strong incentive for foreign companies to establish manufacturing facilities in the country.
- Supply (or vendor or partnership) development programmes between main contractors and groups of subcontractors and suppliers, for upgrading their technical and commercial skills and their capacity to meet quality requirements.

The outreach of the programme

Between 1984 and 1997, some 54 SPXs were established in 30 countries with UNIDO assistance (see Table 15.1). In Latin America 32 SPXs have been created in 14 countries, applying a common methodology. Moreover, a regional Latin American network among these SPXs has been created, enabling the participating countries to benefit from the complementarities and synergies created by such an extensive network (ALABSUB – Asociacion Latino Americana de Bolsas de Subcontratación). To date, a total of 12 joint subcontracting exhibitions (Subcontrato Latino Americana) have been held since 1991 in the participating countries. A similar SPX and regional co-operation network has been established in the Arab region (Algeria, Egypt, Jordan, Tunisia, Morocco). More recently the programme has been expanding to a number of economies in transition as well as to a number of sub-Saharan African countries.

In total, approximately US$7.5 million of technical co-operation funds have been spent since 1984. Of the 54 SPXs established, a total of 45 are currently operating (rate of survival: 83%). The total number of companies registered in these SPXs is nearly 15,600. Table 15.1 also reflects the recognition that there is a strong correlation between the level of economic development and the size of

Table 15.1 Subcontracting and partnership exchange (SPX) programme. Countries covered – 1984 to 1997

Countries benefiting	Source of finance	Number of SPX(s) established	SPX(s) currently operating	Number of companies registered
1. Algeria	UNDP/Donor	3	3	804
2. Argentina	Donor	5	3	1190
3. Bolivia	Donor	2	2	540
4. Brazil	Donor	4	4	780
5. Chile	Donor	1	1	2710
6. Colombia	Donor + Self	5	5	1687
7. Costa Rica	Donor	1	1	170
8. Côte d'Ivoire	Self	1	1	46
9. Cuba	Donor	1	1	62
10. Czech Republic	EU	1	1	156
11. Ecuador	Donor	1	1	274
12. Egypt	Donor + Self	1	–	–
13. France	Self	1	1	150
14. Guatemala	Donor	1	1	127
15. Iraq	UNDP	1	–	–
16. Jordan	SIS	1	1	370
17. Kenya	UNDP	1	–	–
18. Madagascar	UNDP	1	1	75
19. Mauritius	W.B.	1	1	75
20. Mexico	Donor	8	8	1193
21. Morocco	UNDP	3	2	600
22. Paraguay	Donor	1	1	418
23. Peru	SIS/Donor	2	1	655
24. Poland	UNDP	1	–	–
25. Slovakia	EU	1	1	156
26. Tunisia	UNDP	1	1	1450
27. Turkey	SIS + Self	1	1	550
28. Uruguay	Donor	1	1	500
29. Venezuela	Donor	2	1	750
Total		54	45 (83%)	15 488

subcontracting opportunities in a given country. In terms of sub-sectoral coverage, the industrial sectors where subcontracting is most important are metalworking industries, the mechanical, electrical and electronic industries, plastic and rubber, and the textile and clothing industries. Furthermore, subcontracting in industrial services is becoming increasingly important.

SPX: frequently asked questions

The following is a list of questions most frequently asked about subcontracting and partnership exchanges:

- where to set up an SPX? (The institutional set-up of the SPXs)
- how to finance and manage an SPX? (The modalities of financing and management of SPXs)
- which services are offered by SPXs?
- what are the minimum staff requirements for SPXs?
- what are the premises, the facilities and the equipment required?
- who are the clients/end-users?
- how long do SPXs live?
- what are the main industrial sectors covered by SPXs?
- what results should be expected from an SPX?
- an example, please?
- what is covered by a UNIDO Project for establishing a SPX?

Where to set up an SPX?

Let us recall that an SPX is first of all a non-profit manufacturers' association enjoying full autonomy, supported/sponsored by public authorities and professional organizations, but driven by the private sector and run by a team of qualified engineers specially trained for this purpose.

Experience has shown that SPXs incorporated in ministries of industry and public organizations are monopolized by the state, cut off from their industrial basis, and hence bound to disappear. The formula of hosting the SPX in a ministry or public organization should be considered only as a transitory start-up stage before being transferred to the private sector, preferably on an autonomous basis.

SPXs incorporated in private sector institutions such as chambers of commerce and industry, federations of industry, professional or manufacturers' associations, can survive when accorded the necessary recognition and operational autonomy. They are then considered as a specialized service provided by the chamber of federation to its affiliated/member companies.

But the full autonomy of SPXs is the most sustainable form of institutional set-up. It is then an industrial association with an autonomous budget and operational structure, managed by a board of directors (or national council) which should be composed of the representatives of all the public and private sector organizations/institutions/associations that are involved in, or interested in industrial subcontracting, supply, and similar forms of inter-industry linkages. In addition, the affiliated enterprises themselves should also be well represented on the board, and possibly even take the leading role.

For this reason, UNIDO has proposed standard 'legal statutes for establishing an autonomous SPX', as a standard instrument, to achieve the required sustainability of the SPXs.

How to finance and manage an SPX?

Here also, experience has shown that when the funds are provided exclusively by one source of financing, the SPX dies. An SPX financed exclusively by the government becomes a government department and is quickly isolated from its industry basis. The same applies to SPXs fully subsidized by international aid programmes.

On the other hand, an SPX financed exclusively by the affiliated enterprises, under the false assumption that it is a profit-making activity, will soon be superseded by other activities which generate more profit, and will abandon the specific activities related to subcontracting promotion (which is not in itself a profit-making activity).

Therefore, in accordance with the tripartite participation proposed for the board of directors, and with the legal statutes proposed by UNIDO for autonomous SPXs, the financing proposed should include:

- state or public institutions, in recognition of the contribution to the national economy (at least 10 per cent of the budget, and ideally not more than 50 per cent)
- professional associations/industrial federations, in recognition of the contribution to the development of the private sub-sectors of industry (at least 10 per cent of the budget)
- the affiliated enterprises themselves, in recognition of their contribution to their own productivity, competitiveness and growth (affiliation or registration fees should amount to at least 10 per cent of the budget);
- in addition, SPXs should provide various fund-generating services (to non-members as well as members) such as:
  - participation in industrial subcontracting/supply fairs and business forums/ meetings training seminars and conferences
  - training seminars and conferences
  - marketing surveys and missions (national and international)
  - sectoral studies on investment requirements and incentives
  - technology and quality (ISO 9000) audits and assistance
  - legal assistance in relation to contracts, fiscal matters, etc.

But the SPXs should not receive commissions on contracts awarded. A success fee, no matter how desirable, remains a difficult proposition to implement, as firms are not always willing to disclose the business achieved, or may lead the SPX to put priority on big prospective contracts and leave aside smaller operations.

In fact, this survey has revealed that, on average, the operational budget of SPXs is financed almost equally by the four components mentioned above (with 25 per cent each).

Which services are offered by SPXs?

The SPX should provide a range of services in different functional areas. The services could be grouped under five major themes:

Database. The SPX should establish, maintain and regularly update a comprehensive computerized database of industrial enterprises in the country, according to internationally accepted terminologies and procedures. This information service should be made available to domestic and foreign main contractors and clients interested in examining subcontracting and partnership opportunities.

Match-making. The SPX should collect and analyse incoming inquiries from main contractors or client enterprises for subcontracted products, services, supplies and industrial co-operation, by identifying and selecting the suitable companies. The SPX should also process incoming requests for know-how, technical co-operation and partnership agreements from local subcontractors and suppliers trying to identify domestic and foreign potential partners.

Promotion. The SPX should promote, through any relevant channel, products and services of local companies capable of acting as reliable subcontractors or suppliers for suitable markets.

In this respect the SPX should:

- organize the participation of groups of subcontractors/suppliers in specialized fairs
- arrange for meetings with and presentations to potential customers
- design, produce and disseminate promotional documentation and audiovisuals
- organize mailing and direct marketing campaigns and promotional initiatives for specific ranges of products and services
- publicize the national subcontractors/suppliers to the global market through the extensive use of the opportunities offered by the information technologies (e.g. creation of Web site dedicated to the SPX and the subcontracting companies).

Consultancy. The SPX should provide advisory services to enterprises on issues specifically relevant to industrial subcontracting and partnership, such as product and process innovation, interpretation and application of international standards and certification procedures, costing, marketing, assistance on technology transfer and legal agreements between main contractors and subcontractors. Additionally, sector studies and market surveys should be conducted regularly to explore potential areas and market niches for the development of subcontracting and partnership relations.

Training. The SPX should identify critical areas for training subcontracting personnel and organize seminars, study tours and courses to disseminate advanced management techniques and methods specifically relevant to subcontracting and partnership, such as production management, industrial costing, marketing for purchasing, value analysis, total quality management and certification procedures, product and process innovation, and legal agreements between main contractors and subcontractors.

What are the minimum staff requirements for SPXs?

- One executive manager, an industrial engineer with an MBA, (with nine years of experience)
- One or two graduate industrial engineers (with five years of experience)
- One or two secretaries/typists (bilingual) (with two years of experience)

The SPX staff should be able to respond with precision and rapidity to requests from industry, provide reliable solutions, propose new alternatives and practical innovations. Accordingly, the SPX staff should receive remuneration and career development prospects which are appropriate to their professional qualifications and experience, otherwise they will be offered more attractive (and better paid) jobs in industry and will leave the SPX after having received an excellent training (both on-the-job and formal) and exposure to the needs of industry.

What are the premises, the facilities and the equipment required?

The SPX should have three furnished offices and one meeting room within the host institutions, at least two personal computers, Internet and e-mail connection, photocopy machine, two or three telephone and fax lines. In addition, at least one vehicle should be made available to the SPX for the plant visits.

Who are the clients/end-users?

Each SPX will provide a complete range of services to small and medium industrial sub-contractors and suppliers in the respective countries and will provide information services to large domestic and foreign enterprises acting as main contractors or purchasing enterprises as well as to other SPXs, chambers of commerce and industrial federations of industries, industrial promotion agencies, foreign trade offices, etc. operating in the sub-region and worldwide.

How long do SPXs live?

SPXs are like enterprises: they live and they die. Some have a very long life, (some of the first established in the 1960s are still alive) and some die after a few years. Others can be reborn and have a second life after some years.

Some argue that SPXs have fulfilled their temporary functions and can disappear when all the industrial enterprises of the area covered by the SPX come to know each other. This may be correct in some cases, but usually it is not, because:

- the manufacturing facilities and capacities of the enterprises keep changing all the time
- new enterprises with new technologies and processes enter into the market and are willing to undertake operations under subcontract
- new export markets become accessible through the SPX (In 1997, on average, some 30 per cent of the inquiries received by SPXs were from foreign companies)
- new forms of enterprise collaborations appear (partnerships, strategic alliances, market and licence agreements etc.) for which the SPX can play a unique and privileged role.

Therefore, the *flexibility* or *adaptability* of SPXs to changing conditions and environment are a critical condition of their survival or sustainability.

What are the main industrial sectors covered by SPXs?

The industrial sectors where subcontracting and supply chain management apply are, by ranking order of importance: (a) the metal-working industries; (b) the mechanical, electrical and electronic engineering industries (it is well known that the whole manufacturing process in the automobile, the electronics and aeronautics industries relies on subcontracting); as well as (c) the plastic and rubber industries (d) the textile clothing and leather industries, and to a lesser extent (e) the wood-working, ceramics, glass and chemical industries. Furthermore, sub-contracting in industrial services is becoming increasingly important (repair and maintenance, testing and quality control, financial accounting, computer ser-vices, R&D, marketing, packaging transportation, etc.). Therefore, newly set up SPXs should start operating in the metal-working and engineering industries and move progressively to the other industrial sectors as the SPX strengthens in overall capacity to fulfil its functions and enlarge its participating industries.

What results should be expected from an SPX?

Results expected from an SPX performing well, after a three-year take-off period, could be estimated at least as follows:

- 500 enterprises visited and registered by the SPX (an additional 100 per year up to 700–800 enterprises)
- 200 successful interventions (or consultations) per year (successful means to the satisfaction of the main contractors)
- 50–100 national contracts concluded per year (worth approximately US$3–8 million)
- 25–50 international contracts concluded per year (worth approximately US$2–5 million).

An example, please?

In the early 1980s, an SPX was established in Lima, Peru, with the assistance of UNIDO within the Socieda Nacional de Industrias (SNI), and served as one of the pilot SPXs in Latin America. After nine years of existence, the Lima SPX gained momentum and appeared already as a dynamic example: more than 2000 enterprises were visited; 885 of these enterprises were affiliated to the Lima SPX; around 1570 successful interventions were registered (to the satisfaction of the main contractor); around 1290 national contracts were concluded (worth approx. US$66 million); and around 285 international contracts were concluded (worth approx. US$2 million).

What is covered by a UNIDO project for establishing an SPX?

UNIDO assistance in establishing SPXs through technical co-operation projects involves:

- short-term specialized expertise in all aspects related to the SPX (institutional, operational, management, computerized software, enterprise auditing, mar-keting and fairs, legal aspects, etc.)
- specialized and on-the-job training
- applying the whole package of UNIDO methodology and tools
- participation in international fairs and business meetings, and
- networking with other SPXs and industrial promotion agencies.

A comparison of the financial estimates shows that UNIDO's initial contribution in technical co-operation (initial investment in a standard project of US$200 000) is rapidly transformed into an effective and profitable promotion of industrial development in the country.

The impact (or performance criteria) of SPXs

The ultimate indicator of achieving the purpose of establishing and operating an SPX is a contract resulting from its match-making facilities. However, it is generally recognized that it is impossible for the SPXs to obtain comprehensive and up-to-date information, and sometimes even any information at all, on the contracts concluded and their value, for reasons of confidentiality, because firms are usually not willing to reveal certain aspects of their business activities or those of their clients). It should also be noted that, from an evaluation made upon completion of a regional project for 'The Promotion of Industrial Subcontracting and Partnership between France and Arab countries', it takes a long time (1 to 3 years) for a partnership project to mature. This evaluation also revealed that only a small proportion (9 per cent) of those projects under negotiation are actually concluded.

A survey conducted in 1994 indicated that, on average, 80 per cent of the companies registered in SPXs had been consulted at least once during the year, and that 40 per cent of these consultations had resulted in a signed contract; thus, on average, 37 per cent of the companies registered in an SPX had concluded at least one contract in 1993. A similar survey conducted on 1997 results indicate that, on average each registered company in an SPX had been consulted at least twice (219 per cent) in the course of the year, and that 21 per cent of these consultations had resulted in a signed contract; thus, on average, 66 per cent of the companies registered in an SPX had concluded at least one contract in 1997. However, as mentioned above, the results are not fully significant since they are based on 50 per cent of the replies.

Most of the inquiries made to SPXs are generated through:

- organization and participation in fairs (showing available subcontracting capabilities or, reversibly, displaying the requirements for the manufacturing of parts by large contractors
- personal contacts (staff of SPX visiting plants and establishing databases on industrial capabilities to facilitate match-making)
- awareness building through conferences, seminars, workshops
- market analysis and research and supply development programmes by the SPXs for large main contractors and clients.

Conclusions

As a result of UNIDO's long and well-established experience in relation to this programme, as described above, and as illustrated in the *Practical Case Studies on Industrial Subcontracting and Partnership* (this publication available from UNIDO on request) conducted by UNIDO SME Branch in 1997 on selected national and international agreements in 14 countries, one can conclude that:

- Industrial subcontracting and supply chain management, including the associated supply development and up-grading programmes, are recognized as major instruments for the development of the SMI sector and as an efficient tool to increase both industrial production and employment in the SMI sector, to increase the rate of utilization of installed industrial capacities and of existing specialized skills, to produce better quality products at a reduced cost, to contribute to a reallocation of industrial resources, and thus to an overall industrial growth and integration.

- Subcontracting and partnership exchanges (SPXs) play an instrumental role in the promotion of long-lasting industrial subcontracting, supply and related industrial partnership agreements. In the Evaluation Report completed by UNIDO Evaluation Section in 1996 on this particular programme, it was acknowledged even in the first paragraph of its executive summary that SPXs are the most appropriate institutional mechanism to promote these industrial linkages, which do not occur spontaneously. And when established according to the principles and conditions defined by UNIDO in its technical assistance projects, these SPXs are cost-effective and sustainable instruments, with a direct and practical impact on industry.
- The globalization of the economy fully applies to industrial subcontracting and supply chain management, since enterprises are now searching for out-sourcing and supply opportunities world-wide, in almost all sectors of industry and services, in a constant search for increased productivity and competitive-ness, evidenced by an ever-increasing share of subcontracting and supply relations within international trade flows. Through this programme, UNIDO's ultimate aim is to encourage and support modern industrial linkages to further economic development on a global basis.

16. Clusters and network development in developing countries

GIOVANNA CEGLIE and MARCO DINI

Introduction

THE GUIDING PRINCIPLE of UNIDO's approach towards SMEs is that small-scale manufacturing enterprises can play a key role in triggering and sustaining economic growth and equitable development in developing countries. However, this potential role is often not fulfilled because of a particular set of problems characterizing SMEs that are related to their size. Individually, SMEs are often unable to capture market opportunities that require large production quantities, homogenous standards, and regular supplies. By the same account, they experience difficulties in achieving economies of scale in the purchase of inputs (such as equipment, raw materials, finance, consulting services, etc.). Small size also constitutes a significant hindrance to the internalization of functions such as training, market intelligence, logistics and technology innovation – all of which are at the very core of firm dynamism. Furthermore, small scale can also prevent the achievement of specialized and effective internal division of labour which, according to classical economic theory, fosters cumulative improvements in productive capabilities and innovation. Finally, because of the continuous and fierce struggle to preserve their scarce profit margins, small-scale entrepreneurs in developing countries are often locked in their routines and are unable to innovate their products and processes, and look beyond the boundaries of their firms to capture new market opportunities.

Through networking, individual SMEs can address the problems related to their size and improve their competitive position. On account of the common problems they all share, small enterprises are in the best position to help each other. Through horizontal co-operation (i.e. with other SMEs occupying the same position in the value chain), enterprises can collectively achieve scale economies beyond the reach of individual small firms and can obtain bulk-purchase inputs, achieve optimal scale in the use of machinery and pool together their production capacities to satisfy large-scale orders (Pyke, 1992). Through vertical integration (with other SMEs as well as with large-scale enterprises along the value chain), enterprises can specialize in their core business and give way to an external division of labour (Marshall, 1990). Inter-firm co-operation also gives rise to a collective learning space, an 'invisible college' (Best, 1998), where ideas are exchanged and developed and knowledge is shared in a collective attempt to improve product quality and occupy more profitable market segments. Lastly, networking among enterprises, providers of business development services (BDS) and local policy makers can help to shape a shared local development vision and give strength to collective actions to enhance entrepreneurial strategies.

This chapter is an attempt to reflect upon UNIDO's experience in promoting business development services focused on networking as a strategy to develop small-scale enterprises. The following section, 'Origins of the cluster/network-based approach', provides the rationale for the approach. 'From theory to practice' illustrates real cases of networking development projects drawn from some of the countries where the approach is currently being implemented. The section entitled 'Methodology' emphasizes the key components of a methodology that have emerged as a result of a five-year-long experience in project implementation. A concluding section reflects upon some of the key 'Lessons learned' and highlights what emerge as the most significant issues that might prove useful to consider in further applications.

Prior to a closer examination of the main elements of UNIDO's experience, a working definition for the concept of 'networks', 'clusters' and 'networking' needs to be introduced. In this chapter the term 'network' refers to a group of firms that co-operate on a joint development project – complementing each other and specializing in order to overcome common problems, achieve collective efficiency and conquer markets beyond their individual reach. The term 'cluster' is used to indicate a sectoral and geographical concentration of enterprises which, first, gives rise to external economies (such as the emergence of specialized suppliers of raw materials and components or the growth of a pool of sector-specific skills) and second, favours the rise of specialized services in technical, administrative and financial matters. Such specialized services create a conducive ground for the development of a network of public and private local institutions that support local economic development, promoting collective learning and innovation through implicit and explicit co-ordination[1]. And lastly, 'networking' refers to the overall action of establishing the relationships characterizing both networks and clusters. In this chapter, therefore, networking development services indicate those services aimed at promoting the development of clusters and networks.

Origins of the cluster/network-based approach

In spite of the potential benefits for the enterprises, evidence shows that inter-firm co-operation and the other features of successful clusters do not always emerge spontaneously. Three factors are among the main ones significantly hindering this process: the significance of the transaction costs that need to be borne to identify suitable network partners and to forge relationships; the imperfect market functioning for the provision of crucial inputs for networking development, such as information and innovation; and the high risk of 'free-riding' that is faced especially in contexts where the legal framework to back up joint endeavours is relatively underdeveloped.

The available literature vividly bears out that the intervention of an 'external agent' that acts as a catalyst to facilitate the emergence of clusters and networks can greatly reduce the significance of the above factors. Among cases of developing countries, Navdi (1995) provides interesting examples of successful interventions aimed at fostering co-operative relations within SME clusters drawn from the experience of Brazil, Mexico and India. Along the very same lines, Humphrey and Schmitz (1995) describe the main features of the Chilean PROFO (*Proyectos de Fomento*) programme consisting of a carefully designed set of public incentives, which has stimulated the establishment of approximately 450 SME networks with significant results in terms of increase in SME profitability and sales (Dini 1998).

Taking stock of these experiences and of the general reflection on the clustering and networking phenomena, UNIDO has promoted a new technical assistance programme for SMEs. This is characterized by an emphasis on the promotion of efficient systems of relations between enterprises, and between enterprises and institutions, which allow enterprises to overcome their isolation and reach new collective competitive advantages beyond the reach of individual small firms. The programme[2] also emphasizes the development of local institutions to act as facilitators of the networking process, or 'system integrators'. These should support the emergence of a joint entrepreneurial vision involving the whole business system – composed of firms, their suppliers, buyers and support institutions – and be able to enact that vision through common development projects. Indeed, it is this emphasis on the whole business system – and not on the individual enterprise – that constitutes the main difference between networking programmes and other traditional technical assistance programmes.

From theory to practice

In order to illustrate UNIDO's experience and its crucial aspects, the following cases have been selected which exhibit some of the more significant features of the projects implemented over the last five years. The case of Honduras represents a project that evolved from the creation of SME networks into the establishment of a specialized institution (CERTEC) acting as a networking promotion agency. Considerations on diffusion and sustainability of impact, as well as on funding mechanisms of networking BDS, will be made here. The case of Nicaragua illustrates three main points: first, how, as a result of its successes with network brokering, a project has achieved significant influence on policy-making at the national level; second, the importance of capacity-building of local BDS providers, and third, how the principles of economies of scale and scope inform the delivery of support services. The case of Mexico highlights a project promoting vertical integration arguing for the direct involvement of large-scale manufacturers into suppliers' upgrading efforts. And finally, the case of Jamaica presents an example of entry at the top institutional level (whereby the effort to bring about cluster-based development lies at the operational core of the national SME support agency) and a case of creation of specialized service centres (for garments, fashion, furniture, etc.).

Honduras: evolution of a networking project

In 1993 the Honduran Government requested UNIDO to design and implement a technical assistance project for the development of the SME sector. Due to the unsupportive institutional environment which characterized the SME sector at the onset of the project, the project focused directly on the enterprise level, relying on a group of eight national consultants with engineering and management skills under the guidance of the local UNIDO director.

Initially, the national consultants[3] concentrated on identifying groups of enterprises with similar characteristics and growth constraints and helped them to establish common development projects. The client base was constituted by micro and small enterprises with an average staff between two and 15. The enterprises were selected based on either personal knowledge of the consultant or through the assistance of the local producers' associations (AMPIH: Asociación Nacional de Mediana y Pequeña Industria de Honduras and ANDI: Asociación Nacional de Industriales) or through other local institutions such as INFOP (Instituto Nacional de Formación Profesional), the local training institute. Following a visit to the enterprises selected, weekly joint discussions ensued, organized by the consultant, to support the group of entrepreneurs in analysing their problem, identifying common solutions and outlining a common workplan.

The workplan envisaged a division of tasks among network members and often group saving schemes to establish a common fund to finance common activities.

The consultants are assisted in the implementation of the workplans, calling upon other local BDS providers to provide specialized inputs. Among the institutions which most actively participated were PASI (Programa de Apoyo al Sector Informal) for the provision of credit, and INFOP for the provision of training.

Over its five years of operation, with an investment of approximately US$680 000 (contributed by the Government of the Netherlands), the project has established 33 networks with common development projects involving some 300 enterprises. Common projects focused on, for instance, joint purchasing of raw material, joint establishment of shops to retail finished products, launching of new production lines, product or process specialization, sharing of large orders (including public procurement), and creation of new enterprises which complement existing production facilities. It should be noted that the assistance given by the project to the networks has consisted entirely of technical assistance, while no funding of working capital or investment whatsoever was granted. On the financial side, the project acted only as an intermediary between the networks and the financial institutions to help the enterprises meeting the requirements for obtaining loans. One example of a network developed by this project is described in Box 16.1.

Box 16.1   Emasim: Metalworking network

Emasim is a group of 11 enterprises in the metalworking sector in Tegucigalpa. Their average employment is four workers. At the beginning of the project, the entrepreneurs were invited to participate in a training course at INFOP to improve their technical capabilities. It was through this course that the entrepreneurs started to get to know one another better and, with the help of a project consultant, began analysing their problems while searching for common solutions.

The consistent supply and cost of raw materials was identified as the most urgent problem. In response, a common raw material supply centre was created, a common loan obtained from PASI and an internal revolving fund established to be used by members of the network as working capital. Based on the progress achieved through this initiative, the network members expanded their co-operation to the production level, by exchanging tools, identifying and sharing large orders (for instance in metal construction and maintenance works at supermarkets and banks) and examining ways to complement their production processes. In order to diversify production and target new market segments, the network decided to invest collectively in new larger equipment and establish a separate independent enterprise to manage the new equipment and provide services to the network members. Among the quantitative results registered in this network, it can be noted that, to date, collective sales have increased by 200 per cent (in comparison to the total individual sales prior to network establishment), employment increased by 15 per cent and fixed assets by 98 per cent.

In most cases, the collective projects have launched new businesses for the networks, increased the revenues of the participating enterprises, and generated new employment. A recent in-depth evaluation of six networks, selected from among the 33 mentioned above, showed a positive trend for all basic performance indicators. For instance, comparing the data at the beginning of the project with the present data, sales increased between 35 and 200 per cent, employment has increased between 11 and 50 per cent and investment in fixed assets has increased between 10 and 100 per cent.

In 1996, the idea of charging a fee to the networks for the service provided to them was introduced, for two reasons: to increase the resources available to the project for enlarging and extending the activities and, more importantly, to ensure a more active/convinced participation of the entrepreneurs. The fee is determined on the basis of the work plan decided upon by the consultant and the group. It varies, depending on the time requested from the consultant and it is stipulated in a simple contract signed by the network and the broker, which is reviewed and renewed yearly. The fee normally increases each year.

As the project implementation advanced, two interlinked themes emerged, namely: how to increase the impact of the project by creating additional networks – thus benefiting more entrepreneurs – and by accelerating their development process; and how, over time, to guarantee the sustainability of the networking promotion effort.

In an attempt to address the first theme, a three-point strategy was adopted: First, the project consultants started training other 'network brokers' in order to diffuse network creation capabilities and multiply results. New network brokers were selected from locally active institutions (especially entrepreneurial associations) and from other technical assistance projects. More and more local institutions are currently demanding the service of training other network brokers. Second, the project consultants invested time in drafting a network development methodology to facilitate the transfer of knowledge to new brokers in order to accelerate their learning process. At the same time, working instruments were devised to assist and facilitate their work. One such instrument is described in Box 16.2. Third, the scope of networking was increasingly broadened to include: the development of vertical networks involving relations between small

---

Box 16.2   The Network Evaluation Tool (NET)

As a result of the network development experience acquired in the Honduras project, the Network Evaluation Tool (NET) was developed. This tool is structured on the basis of a matrix which intersects network development indicators with network development stages in order to measure the level of network development. The development indicators used are: group cohesion, group organization, capacity of problem analysis, capacity of strategic planning, production and organization changes, changes in economic variables and relations with the external economic environment. The development stages, as described in the methodology chapter, are: promotion and motivation, strategic planning, pilot projects, strategic projects and self-management. At each intersection of development indicators and development stages, the results the network should achieve are described. Achievement, partial achievement or non-achievement of the results is translated into scores that, at the end of the application, indicate the level of network progression. This score is then represented graphically, permitting the assessment of a network's evolution over time and comparisons with other networks for benchmarking purposes. The tool is also a useful instrument to assess constantly and redesign the network development methodology. It provides feedback to network brokers on their own work so that they, in turn, can accordingly adjust the services rendered to the enterprises.

enterprises and larger ones; and the development of clusters where the emphasis shifted from the pure entrepreneurial strategy of the horizontal; networks to a strategic vision of local development involving local institutions and local governments.

In an attempt to address the second theme of long-term sustainability, a process of project 'privatisation' was implemented. A foundation was established whose employees are the team of national consultants and whose members are local private and public institutions. The foundation, called CERTEC (Centro de Recursos y Tecnologia), started working within the UNIDO project in 1997. After one year of operation, during which US$60 000 in revenue was generated, representing more than 50 per cent of total annual costs, the institution became independent from UNIDO and is now managing its own budget and strategy.[4]

Finally, two elements of the Honduras experience are worth highlighting. First, it should be stressed that the type of BDS provided evolved from direct assistance to the enterprises to higher level functions of training other intermediaries (network brokers), improving the intervention methodology and devising new integration modalities. This resulted in a substantive multiplication effect. For example, between 1997 and 1998, CERTEC trained 71 brokers who have since organized 59 networks/clusters with the participation of 1200 enterprises.

Second, consideration should be made of the type of funding requested by a BDS provider such as CERTEC. The financing of an institution like CERTEC has to draw from a combination of public and private funds. In the case of CERTEC, a tripartite funding is envisaged for the next years of operation, namely: service fees, i.e. funds generated by the sale of services to the enterprises (networking services) and to institutions (associations, local and central government for services such as training network brokers); membership fees; and public funds which, in the case of CERTEC, will be contributed by an international donor.

As will be mentioned in the final section, 'Lessons learned', the investment of public funds in institutions such as CERTEC is justified by the fact that CERTEC aims at implementing development measures for the SME sector, which is populated predominantly by enterprises that are not, as clients, in a position fully to fund the operating costs of the organisation. Pushing CERTEC to survive under pure commercial conditions would entice CERTEC to look for wealthier clients, thus giving second priority to the demands of small enterprises for whose promotion the institution was created.

Nicaragua: broadening the scope of networking

The Nicaragua project started in 1995 with PAMIC (Programa Nacional de Apoyo a la Micro Empresa which has, since 1998, become INPYME, Instituto Nacional para la Pequeña y Mediana Empresa) as the counterpart. During the first phase of the project, the strategy has been similar to the one described in the Honduras case. Some 20 networks (horizontal) were created (one example is described in Box 16.3) by a team of seven national consultants assisted by short-term international consultants.

The main difference *vis-à-vis* the Honduras case is that the Nicaragua project has had, since the beginning, a public counterpart. Due to this distinction, three consequences have emerged. First, the project has had an easier entry into local policy dialogue and formulation. As a result, the project has had leverage in

Box 16.3 EcoHamaca: Handicraft hammock sector

EcoHamaca is a network of 11 enterprises operating in the handicraft hammock production sector. While the network members all compete with one another in the local market, they are trying to collaborate in an attempt to break into foreign markets. Prior to UNIDO's assistance, none of the local producers had direct exporting experience. Through the work of the project the producers were assisted in standardizing their production in order collectively to reach quantities suitable for export, and at the same time improve the quality and design of the products and the pricing systems. The group selected an ecologically friendly strategy and therefore focused on changing the wood used for the poles (from cedar wood, which is close to extinction, to other more abundant exotic species) and the dyeing substances from chemical to natural ones. This strategy proved to be successful since it permitted the group to penetrate important markets like the EU and USA. To date, the producers have exported on eight different occasions to destinations such as Sweden, Finland, USA and Peru and over 3000 hammocks are exported on average every month. In order to consolidate results and further common work, the group has acquired legal status and has hired a manager whose tasks presently include the identification of more formal training schemes for the workers, the research of other technical and financial assistance inputs from a variety of local SME support institutions, and strengthening their marketing strategy. EcoHamaca now has a presence on the Internet.

proposing the networking strategy as a key SME development strategy. Networking promotion has now become one of the main axes of government approach for private sector support. Second, the project has also played a more prominent role in inter-institutional co-ordination and has had greater access to local people and resources (channelled through the counterpart). Third, the Nicaraguan project, from the onset, displayed a much clearer prospect of sustainability. The long-term prospect is that the project, with its team, will be taken over by the counterpart and it will become one of its strategic branches. At the moment, however, the project is maintaining its autonomy in operational terms and is managed independently, although in close consultation with the counterpart. This will guarantee that the project team acquires the necessary skills and experience, ensuring the needed maturity in its dialogue with the counterpart and with the public sector in general.

The project (which has now entered its second phase of three-year duration, with a budget of US$1.3 M financed by the Government of Austria), as in the Honduras case, is now diversifying its activities to include, in addition to the promotion of horizontal networks, the training of new network brokers, the promotion of industrial integration along production chains (SME/large enterprises subcontracting, with emphasis on supplier upgrading) and the promotion of industrial districts (in Nicaragua the term 'industrial district' is used to mean clusters as defined in the introduction to this chapter). This evolution has come about quite naturally, while realizing that economies of scale and scope can extend beyond the boundaries of horizontal networks. As exemplified in Box 16.4 on Masaya, the task is to find 'the right equilibrium' in the scale and scope of the joint action, and to aim the common development projects to achieve maximum efficiency and return. In Masaya, this has translated into a progressive evolution of the scale of the common project from networks to sector to cluster to national level, as described in Box 16.4.

Box 16.4 Masaya handicrafts

Masaya is a town south-east of Managua with a strong handicraft tradition. One of the main local products is hammocks. Initially, the project assisted networks of hammock producers to upgrade their products for export (see Box 16.3 'Eco-Hamaca' above). While implementing the network's projects, it became evident that the main factor influencing hammock prices was the cost of the cotton yarn used as raw material. After studying the relationship of the cost of cotton yarn to quantities purchased, it became clear that the best prices could be obtained for quantities greater than those required by the single networks, i.e. co-ordinating the purchase of yarn at the level of the whole hammock sector of Masaya. The brokers, therefore, focused on creating a local purchase centre offering raw material to a large number of Masaya hammock producers.

Another important factor that was identified for improving the performance of the hammock sector was design. In response to this, the project is working towards improving design according to market trends, and creating new products (for instance hanging chairs, deckchairs, cribs, etc.). The design of the new products, in order to be successful, is being done in co-operation with the wood and furniture sector. At the same time, since the most interesting market for this line of products is the export market, the need has arisen to build up an export promotion strategy. The resulting launch of the common brand, 'made in Masaya', is being developed to promote local identity accompanied by activities to increase the quality of local products. This brand will be extended to all handicraft products from Masaya, and therefore to the entire cluster.

Finally, other initiatives will have a national dimension. For instance, actions to facilitate export transactions which are part of the export strategy for Masaya, will obviously extend their effect to all Nicaraguan enterprises.

The conclusion emerging from the experience in Masaya is that the concepts which guide the implementation of network/cluster-based projects are demand orientation and creative solution design. Brokers should look at the entire business system, tap all available resources, and design the intervention in order to take maximum advantage of economies of scale and scope.

Mexico: promoting vertical integration

In the second half of 1997, the Mexican Confederation of Industrial Chambers (CONCAMIN), the Fundación para la Transferencia Tecnológica a la Pequeñas y Medianas Empresas (FUNTEC), the United Nation Development Programme (UNDP) and UNIDO, gave birth to the Program of Industrial Integration (PII). Through a flexible and decentralized set of initiatives, the PII aims at stimulating and supporting local projects to promote networks of SMEs as well as sub-contracting networks between small- and large-scale enterprises.

The two projects initiated in the states of Chihuahua and Jalisco, over the first six months of the programme, are focused on this second feature[5] – aiming at increasing the competitiveness of local SMEs by stimulating a deeper and broader integration with the multinationals established locally.[6] In both

Chihuahua and Jalisco, the participating entrepreneurs cover one third of the operating costs; another third has been contributed by the state government while the remaining third has been funded by the PII.

Both projects are in the process of establishing two technical centres (Centres for Suppliers Development) with the following aims: helping enterprises to identify sub-contracting opportunities; co-operating with the technical personnel of the lead-firms on the definition of support programmes targeted at up-grading the capabilities of the identified sub-contractors; and identifying and channelling technical support, training and loans (when required) from locally available institutions to the subcontractors to assist them in meeting the needs of the main contractors.

While both centres are still in their initial phase, some lessons can, nevertheless, be derived from the experience gained during their design and initiation.

- Despite the well known scepticism that many foreign multinationals, and especially *maquiladoras* firms, have towards local producers, the fact that lead-firms are playing an important role in both centres in terms of direct (financial) support and sensitization of other partners, proves that in Mexico large-firm openness towards establishing linkages with small firms is improving.
- The benefits that a centre for supplier development presents for the client enterprises are twofold. First of all, such a centre can co-ordinate the demand for the goods and services of the main-contractors. It becomes possible, therefore, to achieve significant economies of scale that not only lower the prices of production inputs but that can also justify new investments by the subcontractors to meet the demands of a pool of lead firms. Second, such a centre can co-ordinate supply and to help establish horizontal networking among subcontractors, since it can provide an efficient measure to fulfil an intermediate position that is frequently missing in the supply chain.
- In spite of the advantages previously mentioned, the idea of a centre implies a collective action by the main contractors which can often be extremely complex and characterized by significant transaction costs, which are often high enough to freeze or to radically slow down the development of any collective project. It is precisely the reduction of such transaction costs that justify the existence of a PII whose main added value is, therefore, to speed up the decision-making process at the enterprise level, minimize the time wasted in negotiations and promote the emergence of a consensus.
- The experience of the Mexican project indicates that a support measure focusing on subcontractors has the best prospect for maximizing its impact when the lead firms participate not only in its funding, but also commit their own technical personnel to the selection of the potential subcontractors and design of the support initiatives. This type of participation ensures not only that the initiatives are genuinely demand-led but also the transfer of the knowledge base accumulated by the main contractors to the subcontractors.
- Lastly, it needs to be noted that, in spite of numerous similarities, the two centres initiated in Jalisco and in Chihuahua are profoundly different from the traditional subcontracting exchange schemes that operate in many countries with the aim of linking the demand and the supply of subcontracting services. The centres in Jalisco and in Chihuahua do not operate on the idea that the main obstacle to the creation of such links is an information failure (which is at the basis of traditional types of subcontracting exchanges). While instruments

that tackle the information gap are used (like the creation of databanks on demand and supply) the centres concentrate mainly upon technical support initiatives trying to address the basic problems of capacity failure and difficulty in establishing relationships based on trust.

Jamaica: an example of institutional networking

The Jamaica project is another example of entry at the institutional level. The project, which was initiated in 1994 (the second phase started in 1997 for a duration of three years; the total budget for the two phases is approximately US$1.5M contributed by the United Nations Development Programme – UNDP), was requested by the Jamaican Government to assist the public development agency, JAMPRO, in implementing a support strategy for the local SME sector.

The productivity centre, located within JAMPRO, is the focal point for project implementation. Unlike the other projects described, the activities of the Jamaican project are implemented directly through the staff of the productivity centre. There are two main features of this project to be noted: institutional capacity-building and network promotion. Institutional capacity-building consisted of strengthening the capabilities of the productivity centre to act as a networking promotion agency, and creating specialized centres, co-ordinated by JAMPRO, to provide 'real services' to the SMEs. As a result of the project, the productivity centre is now performing the following functions: identifying SME needs and designing the public institutional answer to meet these needs; networking and co-ordinating actions with other local institutions active in SME-related fields (such as HEART, the national training agency, community colleges, University of the West Indies, vocational schools, specialized service centres, etc.) favouring streamlining and specialization of services; acting as an information hub on issues related to SMEs, acting as network broker. Specialized centres have been created/upgraded (mainly within existing institutions) by the project in fields such as garments and fashion, furniture, food processing, handicrafts and in the metalworking sector. The centres provide technical services to the entrepreneurs (see Box 16.5 as an example) and act as 'second level' networking institutions also linking the entrepreneurs with other service providers for services they do not offer.

Box 16.5   Network support system for the fashion industry

An institutional support network has been established involving educational, training, and technical institutions to help the Jamaican SMEs operating in the fashion sector. At the heart of the network is the JAMPRO Design Centre and, through its fashion division, offers the following services: information on fashion trends, advice to manufacturers on design improvements using CAD systems, linkages between manufacturers and local and foreign designers, and information on suppliers of inputs for the fashion industry. Other important actors in the networks are the two apparel technical centres – one in Kingston and one in Montego Bay – to provide training and technical assistance to producers in areas such as computerized pattern-making and grading, product development, and flexible manufacturing systems. These centres have both the functions of diffusing best manufacturing practices and stimulating SMEs to network for joint purchase of raw material, joint marketing, etc.

What should be emphasized about this project is that the entry at the top institutional level has guaranteed highest local ownership of the initiative and, in turn, good prospects of sustainability. Moreover, JAMPRO is ideally positioned to articulate a coherent structure of services for the SMEs, playing the role of system co-ordinator. The challenge of this project is now to help the support institutions to study and implement a coherent fee structure to recover at least part of the service costs from the client enterprises.

Methodology

On the basis of the experiences described in the previous section, and UNIDO's current overall involvement in cluster/network-related projects (including projects in 11 countries), it is possible to draw some conclusions on the methodological steps and principles which characterize UNIDO's networking initiatives. Four phases, which also represent distinct intervention levels, need to be distinguished: the promotion of networks; the restructuring at the firm level; the improvement of the institutional environment; and the improvement of the dialogue between the public and private sectors. These phases do not require strict adherence. On the contrary, as the case studies amply demonstrate, their sequencing and relative importance must be fine-tuned in accordance with the surrounding environment.

The promotion of networks[7]

The central element for the development of a network is the creation of a sufficient level of trust through a process of mutual learning, which can be suitably stimulated and guided by an external agent (the network broker) trained to perform such a function.

In somewhat simplified terms, it could be argued that the mutual learning process has the following two features. First of all it is an *empirical* process based on trial and error within which theoretical and conceptual elements necessarily play a limited role. In order to create a relationship based on trust, entrepreneurs need to be exposed to an interactive process starting with 'role assignment' leading to 'criticisms based on the analysis of the results' and finally 'reassignment of responsibilities' within which they can assess, empirically, the capability and commitment of their partners. Second, the process is an *incremental* one because it is assumed that, lacking any previous experience with trust, the group needs to act gradually; it will therefore start by undertaking initiatives with low risks for the participating enterprises and only subsequently shift to more complex ones as mutual trust increasingly builds.

In practical terms, through UNIDO's experience in the field, five different phases have been identified for the establishment of an effective and viable network of enterprises: promotion and motivation; strategic planning; pilot projects; strategic projects; and self-management (Rabellotti, 1998).

The promotion and motivation phase initially consists of a set of promotional initiatives which need to be launched to contribute to: the identification of a critical mass of SMEs sharing similar growth constraints, their sensitization to the benefits of networking; and the emergence of groups and of group leaders. In this first stage, the network brokers normally organize large and open meetings to introduce the principles of networking and to indicate their possible applications. As a result of this promotional initiative, entrepreneurs group around issues (problems and/or opportunities) that they have in common. There appears to be no such thing as an optimal selection criterion for enterprises to be part of the same network. The entrepreneurial characteristics that appear to be most conducive to collective actions, and which needs to be stimulated by the network brokers, are a willingness to learn and an openness to discuss and develop relationships with other people. Similarly, there appear to be no general rules concerning size or location of the groups. Nevertheless, it should be noted that limited numbers and geographical concentration reduce co-ordination costs. The viability of a collective project depends, in other words, on the trade-off between the critical mass of enterprises which is necessary to sustain the joint action and, inevitably, its co-ordination costs.

Once groups have emerged, it becomes possible to move to the strategic planning phase, which involves the following elements: analysis of common problems and opportunities; establishment of a common workplan; and group organizational structure. For the identification of common problems and opportunities, it is necessary that the network brokers carry out an in-depth analysis of the growth constraints of the enterprises and of their causes and that they do not rely exclusively upon the perception of the entrepreneurs. Often, the entrepreneur is biased towards short-term needs, for instance shortage of working capital, not realizing the causes of those needs which could be, in the case of working capital, inappropriate cash-flow management. A crucial component in delineating a group work plan is to reach a consensus concerning a definition of the evaluation criteria of the collective action to be applies in the short-, medium-, and long-term. Such criteria need to be both quantitative (like those described in the Honduras case) and qualitative, and be easily understood, computed and, needless to say, be in line with the objectives that the group has selected.

The strategic planning phase opens the door for the implementation of a pilot project phase through which co-operation should start bearing concrete results to the participating enterprises. In general, the projects undertaken over this phase are of a commercial and/or promotional kind: joint participation in fairs, joint purchase of raw materials, design of a collective catalogue, etc. The idea is to generate visible results (although of a short-term nature) in order to engender optimism and trust, and consolidate the network's willingness for furthering co-operation.

When successful, pilot projects are expected to give way to strategic projects – those focused on specialization and complementation at the production level. Strategic projects commonly involve one or more of the following components: an increase in the degree of specialization by process and by product of the network members; the provision of common facilities also through the creation of new enterprises (as in the case of EMASIM described above); or the launch of new product lines and common brands (as in the case of EcoHamaca, also described above).

The final stage of the network-building exercise, the self-management phase, coincides with the group of enterprises earning greater autonomy from the network brokers and the capability of independently carrying out further joint activities. Self-management is not always an easy step and it has been observed that networks often tend to lean on the broker's assistance for a longer time than initially envisaged. In order to avoid dependency, two rules apply. The first is that the workplan established by the network members and the broker must have a specific time frame and must not continue for an undefined time period.

In this way, the network knows from the beginning that it can count on the broker for only a limited period of time and must use this time wisely. The second rule is that the fees that are normally charged to the network for the assistance given by the broker, and which are quite low at the beginning, must be progressively increased to encourage network autonomy and, from the broker's point of view, allow investment in new target beneficiaries.

The last element, which is worth stressing in such a process of enterprise network establishment, is the role and profile of the network leaders. In the initial phases of group establishment, the network brokers are the real leaders. As groups mature, the function of the network brokers must shift towards softer co-ordination and a progressive transfer of responsibilities from network brokers to entrepreneurs must be ensured. Often, in order to balance the reduction of the assistance by the broker, networks contract a manager to assist in the implementation and up-grading of the workplan (see the EcoHamaca case as an example).

Restructuring at the firm level

In addition to engendering a collective competitive advantage, network creation also often brings about a transformation within the individual member enterprises aimed at adapting their production and organizational capabilities to the requirements of the common objectives. If, for instance, the network embarks upon process specialization, whereby the network members subcontract each other, the individual enterprises will be pushed to improve their internal organization to respect the quality standards, production schedules and pricing levels decided by the group. Group pressure will stimulate individual enterprises to commit fully to implementing the necessary improvements and will sanction members for failing to accomplish common objectives.

While networks can generate positive changes in the individual enterprises, the opposite also holds true: enterprise restructuring can greatly contribute to improve network prospects. Therefore, the objective of individual improvements should also be kept in mind by the network broker, who should help to orientate the efforts of the enterprises and liaise with the various BDS providers operating in the surrounding environment.

Improving the institutional environment

There are two types of BDS institutions that are involved in the network programmes of UNIDO: the institutions that are direct actors in project implementation (which have a primary and proactive role) and those that have an indirect role (which support the implementation of actions designed by the first type of institutions). The cluster/network brokers and the networking unit belong to the first type of institutions. The cluster/network brokers play a pivotal role at the level of direct assistance to the enterprises. They are the agents (institutions and consultants) who facilitate the generation of the networks as described above. The networking unit is the actor that plays the strategic role within the networking projects: it bears the responsibility of designing and promoting the networking strategy in a given country; identifies the sectors/regions to address, depending on their potential; carries out extensive awareness-building among the small-scale enterprises and the local institutions; trains network brokers; manages the available funds, searching and implementing a sustainability strategy; monitors the development and impact of the networking initiative; and provides feedback to the various actors involved.

At the beginning of a networking project, the functions of the networking unit and of the network/cluster broker are usually assumed by the same institution/ team of professionals. As the scale of activities of the project increases and there is a need for specialization, the two functions are progressively split and assumed by different actors, as described in the case of Honduras.

The external institutions, on the other hand, essentially support the realization of the networks' work plans requiring a wide range of technical and financial services. It is the task of the networking unit to ensure that networks can draw the assistance they require from within the environment that surrounds them. In a relatively weak institutional environment, this task often implies upgrading the capacity of specialized service centres or, in some cases, even bringing about their establishment, which the case of Jamaica illustrates.

Improving the dialogue between private and public sectors

Finally, a fundamental component of a networking/cluster project concerns the establishment of co-operative relations between the public and the private sectors. The aim of such relations is to promote the emergence of a co-ordinated industrial policy and identify, develop and implement coherent actions to support the entrepreneurial effort.

In each of the UNIDO projects described, the creation of a public/private project advisory committee, on the participation in existing co-ordinating bodies such as the National Committee for Competitiveness in Nicaragua, has contributed to sensitizing policy makers to the benefits of clusters and networks, thus favouring the internalization of the key principles of networking development within the strategy of public SME support agencies. At the same time, this co-ordination also allowed the projects to convey to the policy makers issues of concern to the private sector (such as reforestation policies in Nicaragua to guarantee a regular supply of raw material to the local furniture sector; banning illegal imports of leather goods in Honduras; and improving credit access to the SME sector in Nicaragua). On each of these issues, the projects have contributed to elaborating proposals for the consideration of the public decision-makers.

Lessons learned

The experiences gained during five years of UNIDO's involvement in network/ cluster-related projects permit certain conclusions to be drawn. The nine 'lessons learned' presented below do not purport to be a *summa* of prescripts to apply in networking projects, but rather a selection of some observations that may prove useful in designing future projects:

- An important principle in the design and provision of networking development services is demand orientation. In UNIDO's experience, project strategies must be flexible and vary from network to network and from cluster to cluster depending on the nature of the constraint/objective of the client base. One important requirement is that the intervention must be designed after a thorough analysis of the client base needs as well as of the surrounding economic environment from which resources can be tapped to satisfy those needs.

Consideration should be made of the type of demand orientation used in these projects. While projects are initiated on the basis of a beneficiary's demand, beneficiaries should be helped in formulating these demands based on an analysis of their growth constraints and of the causes of those. In this sense, demand orientation is not passive but proactive, with the brokers playing an important role in helping the strategic planning process of the enterprises. Especially in developing countries, where small enterprises have a weak capacity to develop a strategic response to market challenges, this approach has proven to be the most suitable in UNIDO's experience.

- Three principles guide UNIDO's work with respect to networks, namely, they need to be: business oriented; production grounded; and targeted at SMEs. Business orientation refers essentially to two components: first, networking must aim at visible improvements in the economic situation and prospects of participating SMEs; and second, it must grant the group a new competitive advantage which the enterprises alone could not reach. While the first point might seem an obvious one, it has been repeatedly observed that networking can often be interpreted as pure exchange of information, or as an end in itself, rather than as a means to achieve concrete economic advantages. In the Honduras case, for instance, it took great efforts to change network meetings from social events to business talks. A further step is to translate business talks into action and ensure that the actions are profitable and lead to positive structural, as opposed to temporary, changes in the enterprises. The second point emphasizes the fact that, while other technical assistance schemes promote the network concept as purely applied to groups of enterprises participating in the same activity, in UNIDO's approach a network should also have a further scope. Although common activities are useful – as in the case of joint training, which reduces the fixed cost of training – in UNIDO's experience networks should also aim at generating a new competitive advantage translating into the generation of new business within which the networks do not fulfil their whole potential (as in the case of EcoHamaca, where the participating SMEs were able to enter the export market thanks to the joint action).

The second principle, focus on production, points to the importance of process and product innovation and structural improvement, as opposed to, for instance, an increase of sales resulting from an occasional participation in a fair. While activities like information exchange and joint participation in fairs are important parts of a network workplan, they are not the end objective of UNIDO's approach, which is rather to improve the business prospects for the SMEs – producing long-term changes in the production capability and organization. It might surely be argued that a new market opportunity stemming, for example, from the joint participation in a fair, might spur the creation of networks and the development of co-operative relationships among members. In UNIDO's experience, however, such a transition rarely occurs automatically. In some projects, the networks have been exposed to market opportunities (especially for export) which they could not fulfil due to a lack of organizational capabilities and productive capacity. Supporting a network, therefore, should involve not only the search for new market opportunities, but also provide the assistance required to restructure the network's production organization to respond to new markets in a timely manner, with the right quantities and quality.

Finally, the focus on SMEs refers to the fact that, even though networks may involve other partners (such as large-scale firms, retail chains, etc.), the primary beneficiaries need to be the SMEs. For instance, in the case of Mexico, while multinational industries are among the main actors involved in the project, the focus is clearly on supplier development and local development.

- Networking is a multidimensional concept and does not only apply to enterprise. Institutional networking, networking between private and public sector, country networking (as in the case of the joint learning programme outlined below) are equally important concepts in UNIDO activities. The idea is to specialize and co-operate to the maximum extent, so that each actor in the economic system can dedicate itself to core functions and perform them to the best of its abilities. In practice, this principle translates into the natural evolution of the networking units which, as described in the cases of Honduras and Nicaragua, specialize into strategic functions, decentralizing the implementation functions to other network brokers after an initial period when they centralize all such functions. By the same token, this principle implies a suitable division of labour among network brokers and BDS providers, whereby the network brokers do not pretend to solve all the problems of the enterprises, but help the enterprise to identify other service providers that may be of assistance – as is the case in Jamaica, where JAMPRO is working towards diffusing the specialized function to other institutions.

- The key resource in networking initiatives is the people involved (policy makers, brokers, other service providers). With this in mind, it is important to discern four factors that can increase the likelihood of project success: people's ownership, empowerment, skills, and incentives. At all levels, project actors must:
  - own the project, and feel it is in their interest to execute it. To this end, it is important adequately to invest in raising awareness, at all levels, to involve local actors in project design, and encourage their continual feedback for improving project implementation.
  - be empowered to act. In other words, all the actors involved must have the leverage, credibility and resources to play their role. If, for instance, counterpart institutions do not have credibility *vis-à-vis* the beneficiaries, project activities will not have the desired impact.
  - have the right skills to act. In addition to an appropriate academic and professional background, the skills of network brokers must encompass such invaluable 'extra-curricular' skills as the capacity to build teams, deep knowledge of local social rules and an openness to establish contacts. Network brokers must possess a rare combination of technical background, business mentality and 'social sensitivity' to produce market-feasible projects for collective benefit.
  - have the right motivation and incentives. The issue at stake here is that, in addition to the leverage and skills to act, network brokers must also have the right motivation to look for clients and help them improve their business. UNIDO's experience indicates that appropriate incentive schemes can enhance brokers' motivation and channel their efforts into projects that hold the possibility of higher impact and longer-term gains for the networks. However, what types of incentives work best in achieving the desired results, and what types of results should be encouraged? On the latter issue, while incentives anchored to the financial gains of the networks assisted may seem to be a sound idea, there lurks the danger that this could bias the choice of projects/firms, leading network brokers to select relatively 'easy'

targets (i.e. larger enterprises) or promote relatively short-term activities with quick returns rather than longer-term but more structural changes. In UNIDO's experience, the incentives must be anchored not only to financial performance of the networks but to more comprehensive criteria involving qualitative assessment. The qualitative assessment is made based on the achievement of the objectives indicated in the workplans agreed upon by the network broker, the network, and the overall project co-ordinator (depending on the particular case, it can be the UNIDO project manager or the director of the project counterpart).

Regarding the nature of the incentive, in UNIDO's experience the most effective incentive for network brokers has been training – such as the study tours discussed below. Study tours, and the possibility to learn about successful experiences of other countries and regions, have proven to be, especially among young professionals, a very positive stimulus to improve performance. A less tangible, but effective motivator, is simply the existence of a framework that allows network brokers to work together and exchange ideas, thus fostering a sense of teamwork. The positive atmosphere created when such teamwork is encouraged and the sense of 'not going it alone' not only applies to enterprises in a network but is also key in supporting, encouraging and motivating the brokers.

- The importance of investing in people has been emphasized in the point above. What warrants further expansion is one of the critical ways to support these key actors through providing the necessary training and exposure to best practices. The importance of continuous training, as well as the need to diffuse information related to best practices to orientate networking agents' decisions, is most important. In UNIDO's experience, the kind of training that has emerged as valuable and effective, in transferring knowledge of the 'nuts and bolts' of networking, is to rely heavily on concrete cases of successful networks and clusters and let networking agents hear directly from other agents who have implemented successful networking projects. To this end, UNIDO has elaborated on the idea of the 'joint learning programmes' aimed at giving first-hand exposure to cluster and network agents from developing countries to successful cluster/network experiences. To date, this programme has run in the Emilia Romagna region of Italy and focused on the experience of Italian industrial districts. This programme will be expanded to the overall European experience by inviting other countries to participate. A second programme is being planned in Chile based on the Latin American network/cluster promotion experiences. In addition to this specific training, a series of working tools, such as the 'NET-tool' (see the Honduras case) are also being systematized to facilitate the work of the network brokers and accelerate the transfer of knowledge to new networking agents. Other instruments are being developed, such as a practical manual for network brokers and a set of monitoring and evaluation indicators for networking projects. All these instruments are constantly evolving and are meant to stimulate creative thinking rather than impose rigid boundaries.
- A combination of private and public investment appears to be the best way to finance networking development services. The main elements that appear to militate against an exclusive reliance on the market is that networking development services aim at balancing some market failures, as described in this chapter's introduction, and therefore the market cannot be expected to cover their costs entirely. Such a realization should not, however, lead one to

believe that networks need to rely entirely on public funding. The elements that diminish the appeal of exclusive reliance upon public funding are first, the limits it is likely to impose upon the accountability of project managers to market feedback and therefore clients' satisfaction; second the fact that clients' co-financing ensures selectivity of clients on an objective basis (or, from another angle, less discretionality by the service provider in targeting one or another beneficiary). Finally, the balance between private and public funding need not be the same over time. As the initiative progresses and the impact becomes more visible, it normally changes in favour of a higher market share.

- Evaluation criteria for networking development services need to be carefully designed, as seen in the Honduras example. While quantitative evaluation indicators are always auspicious, there are three aspects to consider: the scarcity of reliable and comparable data on the performance of small firms; the understandable unwillingness of the entrepreneurs to release confidential data about their businesses; purely quantitative measure often fail to take into consideration results like institutional building as well as indirect results such as those resulting from the work of second (or third, etc.) generation brokers. On the other hand, in spite of the difficulties related to quantitative measurement of service impact, gathering objective data is essential not only for evaluating the return on the investment made by the donor but also to disclose the possibility of charging private sector beneficiaries who, understandably, require to know with a certain degree of objectivity what benefits they can expect from buying certain services. In UNIDO projects, a combination of both qualitative (related to the specific objectives of clusters/networks workplans) and quantitative criteria (or the type mentioned in the country cases) is used for evaluating networking development services.

- The introduction of the elements of market cost recovery should be pursued as early as possible in order to avoid the beneficiaries becoming accustomed to full subsidies and the risk that the enterprise becomes dependent on the service provider. Progressively increasing the share of the cost that enterprises have to cover is one a way to reduce such a risk. It is the task of the network brokers to lead the networks towards a process of self-management (as described in the Methodology section) and to develop an autonomous capacity to identify new collective strategies, implement the joint projects and liaise with SME support institutions. By the same token, in UNIDO's experience, the long-term impact of networking development projects may be endangered unless networking institutions/cluster-brokers can free themselves from dependence on the continuous assistance provided by UNIDO and develop an autonomous 'strategic thinking' capability to improve and continually upgrade their services in line with the dynamics of the entrepreneurs.

- And last, there is no single and pre-defined path to be followed in the implementation of cluster/networks promotion initiatives that can be effortlessly replicated across countries, regions and industrial sectors. Cluster/network support initiatives need to be flexible and in tune with the characteristics of the environment where SMEs operate. While the elements that comprise the intervention are always those described in the Methodology section (network, firm, institution, and policy), the 'dosage' and 'sequence' need not be the same for all projects and all countries. A bottom-up approach, centred on fostering an entrepreneurial vision and supporting local actors' initiative to realize it, appears to be the best in UNIDO's experience.

References and bibliography

Beccattini, G. (1990) 'The Re-emergence of Small Enterprises in Italy' in Sengenberger, Loveman & Piore.

Best, Michael H. (1998) 'Cluster Dynamics in Theory and Practice with Application to Penang', UNIDO report.

Best, Michael H. (1990) The New Competition: Institutions of Industrial Restructuring, First Harvard Press, Great Britain.

Brusco, S. (1982) 'The Emilian Model: Productive Decentralisation and Social Integration' *Cambridge Journal of Economics*, Vol. 6, No. 1, pp. 167–184.

Dini, M. (1998) 'Proyectos de Fomento – Chilean Experience Promoting the Implementation of SMEs Networks' paper presented at the UNIDO Joint Learning Workshop, Bologna, 28/9–3/10/1998.

Goodman, E. Bamford, J. and Saynor, P. (1989) *Small Firms and Industrial Districts in Italy*, Routledge, London.

Humphrey, J. and Schmitz, H. (1995) 'Principles for Promoting Clusters & Networks of SMEs', UNIDO Discussion Papers, No. 1, Vienna.

Marshall, A. (1990) *Industry and Trade*, Macmillan, London.

Navdi, K. (1995) 'Industrial Clusters and Networks: Case Studies of SME Growth and Innovation', UNIDO Discussion Paper, Vienna.

Piore, M.J. and Sabel, C.F. 91984) *The Second Industrial Divide: Possibilities for Prosperity* New York: Basic Books.

Pyke, F. Becattini, G. & Sengenberger, W. (1990) 'Industrial Districts and Inter-firm Co-operation in Italy' Geneva: International Institute for Labour Studies.

Pyke, F. (1992) 'Industrial development through small-firm co-operation' ILO: Geneva.

Rabellotti, R. (1998) 'Helping Small Firms to Network in Small Enterprise' *Development Journal*, Vol. 9, No. 1, pp. 25–34.

Schmitz, H. (1990) 'Small Firms and Flexible Specialisation in Developing Countries' *Labour and Society*.

Sengenberger, W. Loveman, G.W. Piore, M.J. (1990), 'The Re-emergence of Small Enterprises: Industrial Restructuring in Industrialised Countries' ILO: Geneva.

UNCTAD (1994) 'Technological Dynamism in Industrial Districts: an Alternative Approach to Industrialization in Developing Countries': United Nations: New York.

Notes

1. This definition takes into consideration Humphrey and Schmitz, 1995.
2. The term 'programme' here indicates a technical assistance framework implemented through country projects.
3. In the projects described in this chapter, the consultants promoting networks/clusters are also called 'network/cluster brokers'. The terms 'consultant' and 'broker' will therefore be used interchangeably.
4. Revenues have been generated by selling services to the networks and to client institutions, especially for training of network brokers. It should be noted that, while, as mentioned above, the fees paid by the networks do not entirely cover the cost of those services, the fees charged to institutional clients fully cover the cost of the service plus a certain amount of overheads which are used to subsidize the other services only partially covered.
5. According to the document programme, 12 projects will be initiated over the three years of the Programme.
6. Multinationals in Mexico have very little interaction with local subcontractors. In the case of Chihuahua, for example, the integration level (which is slightly higher than the national average and has grown over the last years) reached barely 3 per cent in 1997.
7. This section will focus primarily on horizontal networks of enterprises.

17. Nurturing entrepreneurs: incubators in Brazil

RUSTAM LALKAKA and DANIEL SHAFFER

INTRODUCTION

BUSINESS INCUBATORS, evolving from experiences with other business development services, have the purpose of assisting the new venture creation process. Their numbers world wide have increased from 200 a decade ago to over 2000 today. Due to the significance of technological innovation and entrepreneurship in shaping the future, this chapter looks at technology business incubation centres (which have common features with the 'innovation centres' in Europe) as a means of commercializing technologies and developing high value-added products, processes and services.

Objectives and method of study

The chapter presents a case study of two Brazilian technology business incubation programmes. The first of these is the Incubadora de Empresas de Base Tecnologica (Incubator of Technology-based Enterprises) in Belo Horizonte, Minas Gerais State, sponsored by the Biominas Foundation. The second is sponsored by the ParqTec Foundation in Sao Carlos, Sao Paulo State and houses two programmes under one roof: CINET – Centro Incubador de Empresas Tecnologicas (Incubation Centre for Technology Enterprises) and SOFNET, a facility with a computer lab for enterprises in the computer software field.

Ventures incubated by Biominas and ParqTec are generally knowledge based, requiring well-educated and trained staff, many of whom are faculty and graduates from local universities. They also require special attention in raising venture capital, sourcing technology, protecting intellectual property and marketing, nationally and internationally. The two programmes were selected because they represent a range of experience, one (ParqTec) being the oldest and the other (Biominas) among the newest in Brazil. They are comparable in their public–private sponsorship and location in cities with sound technical infrastructure. Both are integral parts of larger regional economic development initiatives, providing information, public relations and marketing services that help the state governments to promote their development goals.

The purposes of the study are two-fold: first, to gain an understanding of the technology incubation system in Brazil through the experience of Biominas and ParqTec; and second, to field-test a rapid assessment approach to the evaluation of incubation programmes, looking at their practices, effectiveness, sustainability and stakeholder satisfaction. Good practices are identified, for adaptation to enhance the performance of incubators elsewhere.

The work for this study involved several elements: a literature review of previous incubator evaluations; a comprehensive survey questionnaire completed by the managements at both incubators; participation in September, 1998 at the annual meeting of ANPROTEC, the National Association of Institutions Promoting Advanced Technology Ventures; visits and on-site interviews in Belo Horizonte and Sao Carlos with sponsors, managers, tenants, graduates and other stakeholders; and follow-up by telephone, facsimile and the Internet. This study was informed as well by the first-hand experiences of the authors in planning and establishing incubators and other business development service (BDS) mechanisms in 25 countries.

Business incubators in the global context

Incubators first appeared in the industrialized countries in the early 1980s, where they are now reaching maturity. In contrast, those in industrializing countries are of more recent origin. Their numbers are growing rapidly in China, Brazil, Turkey, South Korea, Taiwan and Indonesia as well as in many of the countries in transition to more open market systems. The UNDP-UNIDO-OAS-sponsored assessment of incubators in seven industrializing countries indicated that around 26 000 jobs had been created by the 78 incubators studied (Lalkaka and Bishop 1996). Developments in some industrializing countries are in Appendix 1.

Incubators generally provide affordable work space, shared facilities, counselling, training, information and access to external networks for entrepreneurial groups, thereby helping to promote venture creation and economic development. Some incubators target clusters of knowledge activities, such as biotechnology and computer software, but most have mixed tenants. This focused help to selected early-stage firms has been shown to increase their chances of survival (three- to fourfold in the U.S. compared to those starting outside the incubator), providing benefits to the entrepreneur, enterprise, community and the state.

Incubators in Brazil

Brazil now has 74 business incubators, mostly in the south and south-east, with the objectives of economic development, technology commercialization and employment-generation. Some 614 small enterprises are located in the incubators and employ 2700 persons, of whom 29 per cent are women. The tenants are in computing software (33%), services (17%), electronics (14%), biotechnology and chemistry (9%), mechanics (8%), food products (5%), and other categories. The incubators have graduated 226 companies. They have 407 affiliated companies that work in their own premises.

The incubation industry is well supported by the Service for Support to Micro and Small Business (SEBRAE), with ANPROTEC serving a networking role. Further, banks and other mechanisms provide funds and also support *bolsistas* – student interns assigned to work with incubator firms. More than 30 universities in Brazil, covering one-fifth of total college students, participate in incubator projects, mainly in technological fields. Among the largest sponsors of incubators are federal-state agencies (52%) and private not-for-profit/for-profit organizations (40%) of total). For instance, the Federation of Industries Sao Paulo (FIESP) runs a dozen business incubators as its contribution to entrepreneurial venture development.

Framework for performance assessment

The majority of incubation programmes worldwide can be characterized as 'public–private partnerships' in which initial (and often continuing) financial support is received from the state bodies. Many governments consider them as part of the business infrastructure, and the evidence indicates that the annual taxes and other benefits from regional economic development more than offset the capital and operating cost subsidy. The private sector participates when it sees that the programme will lead to greater business opportunities and promote spin-offs.

The ability of a BDS (such as an incubator) to replace the resources it consumes and become financially sustainable can be shown by an analysis of the flow of funds in and out of the system over at least five years. Sustainability implies the ability to continue achieving positive outcomes and the durability of the benefits achieved. Effectiveness can be expressed in terms of all the benefits derived by the whole system in relation to the use of all resources and the overall satisfaction of those involved. Outreach depends on the replicability of the embodied concept and the means of reaching larger numbers of enterprises. The metrics and criteria of assessing BDS performance require common understandings by donors and governments, as well as by the businesses they serve.

As business incubation programmes are a fairly recent phenomenon, the history of their evaluation is similarly short, beginning in the late 1980s. These initial studies evaluated incubation largely in terms of the number of new jobs created and the success or failure rates of incubated businesses. There were early attempts to evaluate incubation in terms of costs and benefits.

A study by the Southern Research Council focused on best practices and tools from 50 incubator programmes (Tournatsky, et al., 1995). Safraz Mian (1997) has proposed a model for assessing university technology business incubators in terms of an 'integrative framework' that examines programme sustainability and growth, tenant firms' survival, and contributions to the sponsoring university's mission.

Good measures of performance of an incubation system are the medium-term benefits accruing to small businesses, sponsors, local community, region and nation (Figure 17.1). The overall system assessment requires that donors make

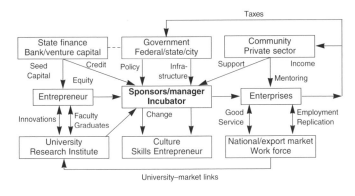

I. Impact/outreach
1. Enterprises created
2. Survival rate of enterprises
3. Jobs generated (6 years)
   A. in incubated/affiliated terms
   B. in graduated firms
   C. indirect jobs
4. Entrepreneur/enterprises reached
5. Replication of 'pilot' model
6. 'Extra-curricular' activities

II. Effectiveness
7. Employment per net $ subsidy
8. Taxes paid per net $ subsidy
9. Income, sales & exports generated
10. Research commercialized
11. Disadvantaged groups addressed
12. Incubator expansion

III. Sustainability
13. Revenue surplus (6 years)
14. Services cost recovery
15. University–business relations
16. Stakeholder satisfacation
17. Tenant/graduate satisfaction
18. Changes in culture
19. Enhancement of skills
20. Leveraging state policies
21. Enhanced self-esteem

Figure 17.1 *Assessment of incubator impacts, effectiveness and sustainability*

provision for – and pursue – the collection of the needed information by the management team, on firms in the facility and those leaving, as well as other parameters. While some of the coefficients can be readily calculated, others require complex social benefit–cost estimations.

Institutional analysis of Biominas and ParqTec

Main characteristics

The locational, implementation, governance and management factors of the Biominas and ParqTec incubators are reviewed below. The main characteristics are summarized in Table 17.1.

Table 17.1   Characteristics of Biominas and ParqTec incubators

	Biominas	ParqTec
Start of operations	1997	1984
Building	Custom-built	Renovated
Gross area, sq m	2850	1417
Rentable area, sq m	1080	550
Tenants, numbers		
Resident	5	15
Affiliates	30	33
Graduates	1	21
Business survival rate	100%	82%
Tenant concentration, %		
Biotechnology	60	–
Informatics	–	20
Mechanical	–	47
Others	40	33

Incubators need to be sited where there is a strong business infrastructure, with available scientific talent, good living conditions, and positive government and community support. On these counts, both the Biominas and ParqTec incubators have good locations. Both plan major technology parks linked to the incubators.

Biominas: Minas Gerais (MG), the second largest industrial state with its capital at Belo Horizonte, has traditional strengths in minerals, mechanical and automotive manufacturing, and now in biotechnology. MG has an impressive technical infrastructure, with universities such as UFMG, Vicosa, Ouro Preto and Uberlandia; research institutes Rene Rachou, FUNED and CETEC; support agencies such as FAPEMIG and SEBRAE; and a vibrant private sector, with BIOBRAS as a world-class insulin producer.

Biominas incubator occupies a prime site of 10 000 sq m of land adjacent to the publicly-funded, multi-disciplinary research laboratory – CETEC. It is a custom-built building with excellent biochemical laboratories.

ParqTec: The city of Sao Paulo is Brazil's major business hub. Some 230 km to the north-west is the city of Sao Carlos, population 200 000, which has the distinction of having the highest density of PhDs in science/engineering – one for every 230 inhabitants. Industry is concentrated on consumption goods and mechanical appliances. It has two public universities and private learning centres, laboratories for cattle and animal protein development, and over 70 enterprises

230

in aeronautics, informatics, new materials and robotics. Fundacao ParqTec de Alta Tecnologia houses the CINET and SOFNET incubators, together with related facilities.

Business planning and implementation

Biominas: The sponsors began operations in 1994 in vacant laboratory space provided by CETEC while the new facility was being planned. This was a good move as it helped prepare both the prospective tenants and future incubator staff while giving advance promotion. During this period five biotech-related companies were assisted. Three of these are now tenants in the new incubator and the others are affiliates.

The new building layout was designed by local architects, and the business plan was prepared by an expert mission under UNDP auspices. Thereafter, advice was provided by Prof. Adelaide Baeta of UFMG. The driving force has been Dr Guilherme Emrich and Ms Patricia Mascarenhas of the Biominas Foundation, and Mr Mauricio Borges, planning secretary of the municipality. The main delay was in mobilizing the significant funds needed for new building construction. operations were started in the custom-built facility in June 1997. It currently has five resident members occupying about 40 per cent of the space, and 30 affiliates. It is planned to serve 15 to 20 tenants in future.

ParqTec began operations in 1984 by nurturing tenants in the physics laboratory of USPSaoCarlos. Then, a house was rented downtown, and in April, 1990 the incubator moved to its present site in an industrial area close to downtown Sao Carlos and equidistant from the universities. The champions driving the process have been Prof. Sylvio Goulart Rosa and Prof. Milton Ferreira de Souza.

The investment in Biominas (about US$1.9 million) is high because of the new construction and the extensive, common bio-tech lab facilities being provided. ParqTec began in a renovated space, costing under $400 000. The alternative approaches were warranted by the nature of the businesses being incubated. Both need to review their space allocations in order to increase the rentable space in relation to the gross building areas.

Incubator sponsors and objectives

Biominas and ParqTec are sponsored through partnerships with government at the city, state and federal levels and with local universities, research institutes and private businesses. Both were developed on local initiatives with significant national support. The sponsors have contributed financially and continue to be actively involved in supervising the operations and mentoring the tenant-businesses. Such involvement is not usual in other industrializing countries.

At both incubators the objectives are:

- creation of new business opportunities, employment and products with high added value, and
- developing entrepreneurship in technology-based businesses.

For promoting investment and bio-technology transfer in Minas Gerais, Biominas works closely with the MG State Government, Belo Horizonte municipality, and agencies such as FAPEMIG, CNPq, SEBRAE and EMRAPA.

Fundacao ParqTec has overarching responsibility for its incubators as well as technology promotion for Sao Carlos city. While enterprise development is the primary purpose, job creation and technology commercialization are significant concerns.

Governance and management

Biominas incubator is a unit of Biominas Foundation, headed by a superior council with members including SEBRAE, university community, state government, and incubated companies. An interesting function of Biominas is to help procure imported equipment and supplies for its member companies, at an average service charge of 5 per cent. It derives an income while the companies avoid bureaucratic delays and benefit by a tax deduction on a temporary 'gift', as the equipment stays nominally on Biominas books until it is fully depreciated.

The management team comprises the executive director with overall responsibility for the Foundation, and the manager who supervises the incubator. A laboratory co-ordinator oversees the use of the shared lab facilities.

ParqTec incubator is also not a separate legal entity, being part of several programmes organized by Fundacao ParqTec. A high council oversees an executive board which manages the incubator, business school, business modernization, research and advisory centres. The high council is advised by an advisory committee. Management consists of five people: general manager, technical manager, computer specialist, and two librarians. In both incubators the teams are well trained in the country and on visits abroad. Remuneration is comparable to salaries paid in the private sector.

In our interviews, the managers rated the levels of their relationships with local government as 'very co-operative', with universities as 'co-operative', and with private sector as 'neutral'. They claim that their competitive advantage *vis-à-vis* other business development services in the region is in providing affordable space, conference rooms, computing facilities, better interactions among the tenants/affiliates, and ready access to government agencies, finance institutions and external networks of professional services. These linkages and facilitations contribute, in large measure, to the success of technology incubation in Brazil.

Services and client base

While Biominas and ParqTec incubators differ in their history and the types of enterprises incubated, they share a professional comprehensive approach. The process of incubation starts with entrepreneurial groups applying for admission. Those who meet the selection criteria are admitted. Some must leave when their space and service needs 'out-grow' those being provided, or when there is evidence that they will not develop a viable business.

Services provided

Many of the individuals entering Biominas and ParqTec are university faculty, graduate students and researchers who have no prior business experience. The personalized services provided by the incubator management help raise their confidence and reduce their isolation. Both incubators offer a range of counselling, training and support services, as well as shared facilities such as use of reception, meeting rooms, parking, security, telephone, and their promotion efforts reach beyond the incubators to scientists and entrepreneurs in the communities.

Biominas' most used services are help in business plan development, technology sourcing and securing licences and permits from government agencies for pharmaceutical products. Facilities provided on a cost recovery or fee basis include: fax, photocopying, electricity, long-distance telephone, wet lab space and equipment, temperature-controlled storage for raw materials/products, and special areas for washing and sterilization.

ParqTec covers, in the base rent paid, use of common facilities, electronic and computer laboratory, technical information centre, and mechanical workshop. Counselling services are offered (at subsidized rates) in the areas of accounting, legal issues, marketing, financial and tax administration, registering of trademarks and patents, and visual communication. To the larger business community, ParqTec offers technological and marketing services, and assists in organizing trade fairs, commercial networks and participation in the CCT – Centro de Commercializacao Tecnica of SEBRAE – Sao Paulo.

To summarize, essentially the types of support provided to tenants in both cases are:

- help in translating concepts to business plans, accessing finance and tackling government regulations
- access to external professional networks, and linkages to the academic and business communities
- assistance in commercializing research from universities and research institutes
- a supportive environment to build confidence and synergistic relationships among the tenants
- work space, shared services, common lab, Internet access and telecommunications facilities
- the credibility created by the incubators' reputation.

In addition, Biominas and ParqTec assist the city and state agencies in promoting their development goals.

Markets served

Both have a number of women beneficiaries: owners of two tenant firms (out of five) and the Biominas Foundation's executive director are women. At ParqTec Foundation, the manager is a woman, and there are two women-owned enterprises, and at least two among graduated firms. Profiles of a tenant at Biominas and a graduate from ParqTec outline the kind of support provided (Box 17.1).

Biominas has focused on the incubation of firms in the fields of biotechnology and fine chemistry. Current tenants and the graduated enterprise are involved in the development and marketing of diagnostic kits for uroculture, production of hydroxyapatite for bone repair, specialized packaging for pharmaceutical products, and consulting in biotech commercialization. The alliance with Biominas has helped DIAMED, a Swiss-based, medium-sized company in medical diagnostics, to adapt and enter local markets (Judice and Diniz, 1998).

ParqTec has assisted tenants in incorporation, patent application, trademark registration and proposal writing. Its tenants and graduated firms are involved in the production of opto-electronic products, digital sound processing technology, industrial process controllers, chromatography columns, time delay switches for safety and energy conservation, automotive alarms, software applications,

Box 17.1 Biominas incubator tenant: CEPA Biotecnologia

CEPA Biotecnologia entered Biominas in February, 1995, at which time it had six employees and no revenues. Utilizing technology licensed from Suma Laboratories, a Cuban firm, CEPA produces diagnostic kits for uroculture and distributes a variety of medical supplies. It entered the Biominas incubator in order to scale up its production process, and to get assistance in licensing and registering its products with the Brazilian Health Ministry. By mid-1998, CEPA had a payroll of 30 employees and average sales of 150 000 reals/month, (about US$1.54 million/year).

The availability of certifiable laboratory facilities in the incubator had greatly reduced the initial capital investment needed by CEPA, which otherwise would have had to build its own facilities elsewhere. And the excellent infrastructure of the incubator made it possible to get new products to market more quickly.

ParqTec Incubator Graduate: Opto Eletrônica, S.A.

Opto Eletrônica (Opto) is one of Brazil's outstanding examples of a successfully incubated enterprise based on technology transfer from the university community. Today, São Carlos-based Opto employs 100 people and, during 1997, had revenues of US$9.1 million from the sale of optical and electro-optical products. Opto mirrors are widely used in commercial laser scanners, and Opto has captured a 30 per cent share of the world wide market for 'cold light' reflectors used in dental chair lamps. In addition, it produces and markets patented laser measuring and positioning systems, microscopes for ophthalmologic surgery and anti-reflective coatings for eyeglasses.

Opto was founded in 1985 by members of the faculty of the Institute of physics at the University in São Carlos. The CINET incubator provided legal assistance for incorporation and the filing of patents, and a convenient initial business location. After about one year, Opto 'graduated' and now occupies a 7200 sq. m. site. Opto products today are exported to the US, China, Italy, Korea, and many countries in Latin America. In addition to its facilities in São Carlos, Opto has a commercial office in São Paulo and a subsidiary in the US at Northbrook, Illinois.

process simulation training, Internet/intranet networks, low-wattage transmitters, microterminals for automation, test equipment for automatic braking systems, and consulting services in ecology, environment management, medical equipment, and computer security applications.

Sources of seed capital and venture financing

Most of the seed capital used by incubated enterprises comes from the personal savings of entrepreneurs, supplemented by government grants, subsidized technical assistance, and loans or investments from relatives and friends. There is no established venture capital in Brazil.

Biominas Foundation is now actively involved in developing new sources of private venture capital. It expects to gain access in 1999 to seed capital funding through the Interamerican Development Bank.

ParqTec Foundation: Major sources of funding for its incubated enterprises are the entrepreneurs' own resources and seed grants from the State of Sao

Paulo under the RHAE and PIPE programmes. ParqTec is working to establish a revolving loan fund utilizing credit from the Interamerican Development Bank. For the longer term, SEBRAE-Sao Paulo is working on the establishment of a US$30 million venture capital fund.

Sources of support for Brazilian incubators are SEBRAE (40% of respondents) followed by city governments (17%), CNPq (14%), FINEP (8%), FAP's (8%), and others (Guedes and Filartigas, 1998 survey). Funding for SEBRAE comes from a set aside portion of federal payroll taxes. Its mission is to support SMEs through activities that include regional development initiatives, research studies and assessments of geographic regions and economic sectors, business training and roundtables, and funding for incubation programmes. According to SEBRAE-MG: 'We subsidize the operating costs of the incubators and monitor their performance in our role of a social and economic accelerator. The return expected is that the incubator be successful in providing the conditions for small enterprise development.'

Biominas and ParqTec Foundations, along with their respective incubators, are well integrated with major SME support programmes in Brazil. There appears to be a consensus at all levels in support of business incubation as a tool to promote economic development through the cultivation of tech-based SMEs.

Financial viability and outreach

Estimates of income and expenses

Biominas: Due to limitations on leasable space, it is unlikely that the incubator could become financially viable solely on the basis of tenant rents and fees for services in the near term. After one-and-half years of operation, about half of the rentable space remains vacant as management is being selective in its choice of tenants. Repayment is scheduled to begin in 1999 on the US$540 000 loan from FINEP used in the construction of the new facility. This will impact the cash flow.

Interviews with stakeholders point to continuing support for Biominas. Biotechnology is an economic development focus for Belo Horizonte, and Biominas serves as a visible 'flagship' for this. Under normal conditions, state agencies would continue their funding; it is problematic whether they could continue present levels in the face of a severe economic crisis.

Estimates of income and expenses for the two incubators are shown in Table 17.2. Such data are hard to collect in most countries. Annual revenue from services (in relation to total) is considered low. Support through the partnership with SEBRAE constitutes more than half of revenue, on average.

Both Foundations plan to achieve greater financial self-sufficiency through the development of technology parks. Biominas has initiated the feasibility analyses and business planning for a biotech-related park adjacent to the existing incubator-CETEC complex.

The São Carlos Science Park is on a 172 000 sq. m. property that it owns in a prime industrial location. Planning and design for the first 3500 sq. m. building has been completed along with a master plan for the balance of the property. The first structure will house the ParqTec headquarters as well as incubator modules for 64 additional tenant enterprises. The master development plan also includes industrial sites for lease to technology-based enterprises as well as two multi-tenant buildings and a convention centre, designed to establish São Carlos

Table 17.2 Pro-forma income and expenses at ParqTec and Biominas Incubators (All figures in US$,000. Rate R/$ = 0.84)

	ParqTec			Biominas	
	1996	1997	1998	1997	1998
Revenues					
Rental income	24.4	38.6	39.4	28.9	81.7
Fees from tenants	2.1	2.1	2.5	3.1	12.9
Utilities cost recovery	9.2	18.5	18.5	–	–
Partnership with SEBRAE	139.4	62.2	239.4	186.0	186.0
Total revenue	175.1	121.4	299.8	218.0	280.6
Expenses					
Manager	27.7	38.6	32.9	36.0	54.0
Admin assist/tech adviser	0.0	0.7	4.5	10.0	5.0
Lab co-ordinator	–	–	–	7.0	13.4
Receptionist/secretary	0.8	2.5	4.2	7.3	14.3
Other professionals	22.8	26.8	33.4	37.9	48.4
Fringe benefits	5.9	8.4	10.9	–	–
Sub-total staff	57.3	77.0	85.9	98.2	135.1
Bldg. maintenance/cleaning	31.9	70.6	70.6	8.0	17.5
Utilities/telephone (net)	18.5	24.4	23.5	30.8	48.4
Travel & promotion	1.3	0.8	20.2	3.2	3.2
Supplies	0.7	1.3	0.7	4.5	9.3
Audit & legal	9.1	9.1	20.2	3.2	4.9
Insurance	5.0	3.8	4.7	–	–
Publications			56.3	–	–
Interest/debt repayment	–	–	–	30.4	39.7
Total expenses	123.7	187.0	282.1	178.3	258.1
Operational surplus (deficit)	51.4	(65.6)	17.7	39.7	22.5

as the 'Capital of Technology' in Brazil. ParqTec has organized a week-long technology fair in Sao Carlos every year since 1986.

Cost effectiveness and stakeholder satisfaction

The evaluation methodology in this study uses a combination of qualitative descriptions, quantitative analysis, and stakeholder perceptions. The stakeholders interviewed for this purpose were the public and private sponsors as well as the incubated enterprises themselves.

Businesses incubated and jobs created

An approach to evaluating the effectiveness of incubation programmes is to look at the number of businesses incubated, the success rate, and the number of jobs created by incubated firms. As noted, both incubators have to recruit more tenants and affiliates aggressively as well as increase the through-put of graduating businesses.

The figures in Table 17.3 should be considered as preliminary, as it is often difficult to get data from privately-held firms on sensitive topics such as sales, payroll and taxes. At ParqTec, the tenant firms have 69 employees while 17 (of the 21) graduated firms have 168, making a total of 237 direct jobs.

Table 17.3 Jobs and taxes, 1997 (approximate), US$

	ParqTec	Biominas
Jobs (tenants and graduates)*	237	92
1997 payroll	$1 854 000	$1 030 040
1997 sales	$9 846 990	$2 558 320
1997 payroll taxes payable	$463 500	$258 510
1997 corporate taxes payable	$590 820	$153 500
Total taxes	$1 054 320	$412 010
Initial investment in incubators	$383 000	$1 940 000

*This includes current tenants plus the one graduate tenant at Biominas and 17 graduated firms at ParqTec for whom information is available. Taxes are estimated at 25% on payroll and 6% on sales

As ParqTec has been in operation at its present location since 1990, it has more results to evaluate compared to Biominas, which has been operating only since July, 1997 in its new permanent facilities. The 1997 estimate of public capital and operating subsidy for ParqTec, and the personal and corporate taxes payable, would be approximately as follows, based on the limited data available:

Total jobs (with employment multiplier of 1.5*)	357
Capital cost subsidy per year (20-year straight line depreciation)	$19 150
Operating subsidy per year (average of last three years)	$147 000
Capital and operational subsidy per year	$166 150
Total subsidy over seven years	$1 163 050
Subsidy cost per job (excluding jobs in affiliates)	$3258
Estimated payroll & corporate taxes by tenants & graduated firms	$1 054 320
Return on public investment as taxes per year	$6.34 per $ subsidy

*Indirect employment multiplier based on ranges for similar economic activities in the US

The subsidy per job should decline at ParqTec as more firms graduate and continue to expand, and as additional incubator space becomes available. For mixed-use incubators, which typically have much larger areas and fewer services for tenants, the subsidy cost per job can be much lower. A point to note is that while the investment is made once, the jobs continue, and it is useful to think in terms of 'job-years' in the stream of benefits.

1997 taxes realizable from sales and payroll of ParqTec tenants and graduates could be about six times the subsidy.

Stakeholder perceptions of programme effectiveness

Biominas: Interviews were held with stakeholders serving on the superior council, representing the MG State, Municipal Prefecture of Belo Horizonte, and SEBRAE. They expressed satisfaction with the progress of the programme, and felt that it is meeting their expectations. One person was particularly pleased with the speed with which enterprises making pharmaceutical products were able to get licences from the Health Department.

In their view, the challenges facing Biominas are:

- Formalization of Policies and Procedures: There is a need to establish formal internal rules and operating procedures for tenants as well as for the relationship with non-tenant 'associated enterprises'.
- Raising Operating Revenues: For the future, Biominas needs to take steps to induct more tenants and increase its operational income. Further, it has to develop sources of venture/seed capital for its tenants.
- Establishment of a Biotechnology Park: Belo Municipality is very interested in the establishment of the biotechnology-focused park to provide graduating enterprises with space to relocate and attract other technical ventures.

ParqTec: The institutional stakeholder representatives interviewed expressed satisfaction with the progress of the ParqTec programme to date. They said that it is meeting their expectations, but that faster growth is required for it to realize its potential. The challenges cited as most important were:

- Expand through development of the São Carlos Science Park to include an innovation centre, incubation space, a rapid prototyping centre, ceramics lab, and convention centre.
- Develop Better Access to Early-Stage Venture 'Seed' Capital: The lack of a Brazilian venture capital community and a traditionally low savings rate make it difficult for enterprises to attract venture capital.
- Maintain and Strengthen Regional Support: ParqTec-CINET must strengthen public–private support in the region for incubation, as well as for important collateral programmes such as the High Technology Fair.

Performance evaluation by incubator tenants and graduates:

Biominas: Representatives of the present enterprises and the one graduate were asked to evaluate the effectiveness of the incubator as well as the advantages and disadvantages in being tenants. Everyone interviewed felt that the programme was of value to them. The major benefits expressed were: help in dealing with bureaucracies resulting in faster permits; valuable assistance in marketing and faster time to market for new products; excellent infrastructure and labs; interaction with other tenants; and legal assistance.

ParqTec: The incubator tenants and graduates interviewed expressed satisfaction with their experiences. The major benefits cited were its: good location for a startup venture; access to facilities such as labs., telephone, Internet, and fax service; valuable marketing assistance received; legal assistance for incorporation and patent development; and business training on site.

To summarize, the ParqTec and Biominas incubators studied have had positive impacts and outcomes on their respective city and state economies in nurturing entrepreneurs and creating sound enterprises with good survival rates. ParqTec has generated employment with public subsidy of around US$3258 per job, without including jobs in affiliates. The estimated return in the form of taxes could be about $6 per dollar of public subsidy.

The linkages to universities and research institutes have resulted in commercialization of some technologies. The sponsors and tenants at both incubators have expressed satisfaction with the results achieved, particularly the help in marketing, business planning, and securing government permits. Both are helping their government sponsors in promoting technological development, together with other social aspects such as reinforcing the cultures of entrepreneurship and university-research-business co-operation.

That being said, Biominas and ParqTec have the major challenges ahead of enhancing their operational effectiveness through innovative activities and creative financing, increased occupancy and higher fees for quality services, with more affiliate companies and anchor tenants, in order to reduce dependence on state subsidies.

Both also need continuously to raise the skills of their management teams through interaction with ANPROTEC and, on a selective basis, with the international incubator community. They have to implement information systems which will provide the data required for monitoring, bench-marking and evaluating performance. To move towards self-sustainability, both should accelerate work on developing their technology parks.

Success factors and lessons learned

While difficult to quantify, the social and economic impacts of incubators are becoming manifest the world over. Nevertheless, the quality of these systems shows variations from country to country, and even within the same country. Due to the imperatives of culture and context, good practices in Brazil are not necessarily applicable in another situation. They can, however, be identified and adapted for use elsewhere.

Pre-requisites at national level

The threshold requirements for success are a stable macro-economic environment, relatively open markets, and government policies friendly to technological entrepreneurship. The Brazil incubator programme began to expand rapidly only after the country's economic situation was stabilized after 1993. Political, business and technology leaders have to agree on bold goals for the creation of knowledge-based enterprises, and expand the incentives for research, innovation and risk-taking. The regulatory framework has to stimulate markets for new goods and services, in consultation with local communities and small businesses. Commensurate investments are required in transport and communications infrastructure, technical education and entrepreneurship development from school onwards, engineering and management consultancy, quality assurance and environmental preservation.

Donor interventions

There have been significant inputs by the World Bank and donors to strengthen technology development in Brazil, but little direct assistance to the incubator programmes. These have been initiated at local level, and sustained by the national development agencies. The domestic sponsors have provided the 'patient money'. As contributions toward building the national infrastructure for technological innovation, governments in industrializing countries (with participation by international donors) should help secure the building space and preparatory costs of the incubator. Further, the working capital for initial operations (on a declining scale over three to six years) also needs to be earmarked up front, in order that the managements can properly run the facility and proactively assist the tenants. This pattern of donor intervention has been successful in Uzbekistan and Indonesia.

Good incubation practices

The ten good incubation practices emerging from the Brazilian experience are outlined below.

- *Identifying strong sponsors and a clear mission:* Both Biominas and ParqTec have proactive promoters and wide-ranging support from the state as well as the private sector, university, banking and civil society. Both are being utilized to promote investment in their respective cities and states, to mutual benefit.
- *Selecting good locations and planning functional buildings:* The Belo and Sao Carlos locations provide the business infrastructure in proximity to knowledge centres. Buildings are of good quality to attract tenants.
- *Building a dedicated, trained management team:* Success depends to a significant extent on the business experience and networking capabilities of carefully selected local managers. The Brazilian managers have been well trained and properly remunerated. The people in top management at both Foundations are women.
- *Selecting good entrepreneurial tenants:* People with innovative concepts, analytical and inter-personal skills, and strong growth potential, are not easy to find, as Biominas now knows. Good practice calls for a transparent process for their selection, a flexible means for graduation, and pre- and post-incubation support.
- *Mobilizing investment and working capital for the incubator and its tenants:* Brazil has a variety of financing sources for incubator and tenants. However, the incubator boards must move progressively towards better recovery of operating expenses, say two-thirds on average (up to 100 per cent and more at for-profit incubators).
- *Adding value through quality services for tenant companies and affiliates:* The rationale of incubation is not just bricks-and-mortar but the counselling, training, information dissemination, and synergy together with external networks of finance and support. Tenants at Biominas and ParqTec have rated these services highly.
- *Creating linkages to the professional and business communities:* In Brazil as in other industrializing countries, many of the incubators are linked to technical universities as the main sources of technology for commercialization, faculty expertise, graduate students, documentation and laboratory support.
- *Monitoring performance and assessing impact:* A SEBRAE representative sits on the governing board at both incubators to monitor the use of state funds. Sponsors have themselves to blame if they do not participate, self-critically, in overseeing the progress of their interventions or do not insist upon the collection of complete data.
- *Promoting industry associations and international relationships:* ANPROTEC is playing an important role in compiling statistics, exchanging experiences, and linking up to the international community. To promote internationalization, Biominas is now attracting high-tech foreign companies through its incubator.
- *Planning strategically for the future:* The changing pattern of work, exponential technological change and globalization of trade now require that

incubators – and the businesses they serve – plan purposefully for the future if they are to survive and prosper.

Conclusion

The ParqTec and Biominas incubators have demonstrated success in a number of areas. They have launched new enterprises, developed linkages with universities and research centres, secured broad-based support from the private and public sectors, and met the expectations of stakeholders. Both contribute to the development initiatives of their respective city and state governments, as well as to their tax revenues.

ParqTec and Biominas are typical of most incubators in Brazil and elsewhere in their reliance on high levels of public subsidy. This leaves them vulnerable should subsidies be reduced or eliminated as a result of economic crisis or changes in policy. Faced with calls for government austerity, it is imperative that Brazil's incubators actively develop new sources of service and rental revenues to supplement public subsidies.

The problems for further research are essentially in the areas of information gathering and defining the metrics, both the quantification and interpretation of costs and benefits, at the micro- and macroeconomic levels. Few programmes have adequately built into their management systems the routine accumulation and analyses of data on the success or failure of their graduates, and indeed of the service facility itself. Yet it is precisely these longer-term outcomes that validate (or invalidate) the usefulness, impacts and sustainability of business incubation and other SME development programmes.

Appendix 1: Incubator developments in selected countries

China: Among industrializing countries, the largest programme, with 100 incubators, is in China. From a modest beginning in the late 1980s with assistance from the United Nations Development Programme, the incubators have graduated over 200 enterprises, expanding their contribution to economic restructuring. Difficulties have been encountered, such as insufficient assistance to tenant companies, low levels of local technological development, and weak incubator management. Incubators in China are generally non-profit, state-owned corporations, reporting to the provincial/municipal science and technology committees and local economic development zone. While the Ministry of Science and Technology's TORCH programme provides policy guidelines, the management is left to the local agencies. Most entrepreneurs come from adjacent universities and technical institutes. The local government often offers free land to help to reduce capital costs, while flexibility in leasing for commercial purposes raises operating revenues. Eight incubators have been transformed into international business incubators, where small foreign high-tech companies will be facilitated to enter the complex Chinese market, while Chinese tenants are helped on joint-venturing and exporting.

Uzbekistan: As the government forces the pace of transforming its 70-year command system into a market economy, the business incubator programme is helping to overcome the hindrances encountered by self-owned businesses, including problems of cumbersome registration, high taxes, inadequate banking, materials procurement, and access to credit and business services. With political support at the highest level and initial UN assistance, three pilot incubators were started at Tashkent and Samarkand in mid-1995. Over 200 jobs have been created. In 1996 the Republic Business Incubator Network was initiated and has been expanded to 23 incubators serving 365 tenant businesses and creating 3000 jobs, with a turnover of about US$5 million. The programme is also being used effectively to leverage small-enterprise-friendly policies. Uzbekistan provides a good example of strong state support and effective donor intervention.

South Africa has had for many years a network of facilities called 'hives of industry', established by the Small Business Development Corporation. An incubator has now been started in Johannesburg by South African Breweries to help provide alternative livelihoods for their laid-off employees. The technology incubator at Technikon Natal, Durban will empower communities. State agencies – NTSIKA and KHULA – are establishing three local industrial parks comprising incubators and multi-tenant buildings.

Malaysia: The large state investment of US$80 million in the new Technology Park Malaysia near Kuala Lumpur has been 'corporatized'. The core facility is an innovation-incubation-enterprise complex, with dominance in ICT. The integration of support facilities includes a proto-typing center, quality control lab, recreational facilities and a small in-house venture capital fund. A dozen incubation variants are operating in Malaysia, mainly linked to universities.

Indonesia: Starting with UNDP assistance in 1994, three pilot incubators were established in Java: at PUSPIPTEK tech-park, Serpong; a regional incubator at Solo; and an industrial incubator at Surabaya. By osmosis, seven more began, many as 'out-wall incubators' which also provided out-reach services to businesses in their own premises. Then, government decided to establish a major national programme, with many more incubators at universities in the out-lying islands. The programme is now in jeopardy when it is most needed.

Egypt: The Social Fund for Development of the government of Egypt has initiated a network of incubators as a component of its extensive employment generation programmes. A business incubator at Tala in the Nile Delta started operations in March 1998 with eight tenants, and another eight being inducted. The plan is to operationalize up to 15 incubators by 2000 (including biotechnology and information technology incubators at Mubarak Science City). The implementation is being undertaken by the Egyptian Incubator Association, an NGO set up for this purpose.

References and further reading

Guedes, M. and Bermudez, L. (1997) Science Parks and business incubators in developing countries – Lessons from Brazil, in *The Economics of Science Parks*, IASP/AURRP.

Guedes, M. and Filartigas, G. (1998) *Survey of Brazilian Business Incubators*, ANPROTEC, Brasilia.

Judice, V. and Diniz, C. (1998) 'Strategic Partnerships and Incubation in the Latin American Environment', XV IASP Conference, Perth, Australia.

Lalkaka, R. (1997) 'Convergence of Enterprise Support Systems: Emerging Approaches at Asia's Technology Parks and Incubators', AURRP 12th International Conference, Monterey, California.

Lalkaka, R. and Bishop, J. (1996) *Business Incubators in Economic Development*, UNDP, New York.

Mian, S. A. (1997) 'Assessing and managing the university technology business incubator: an integrative framework, *Journal of Business Venturing*.

Molnar, L. A., et al. (1997) *Business Incubation Works.* Athens, OH: NBIA Publications.

National Business Incubator Association (1996) *A Decade of Success (1985–1995)*, D. Adkins and *Annual Survey Report (1998)* Athens, Ohio.

Shaffer, D. and Gordon, R. S. (1991) *The potential value of USAID sponsored business incubation and seed capital programs*, USAID, Washington DC.

Tournatsky, L. G., et al. (1995) *The Art and Craft of Technology Business Incubation.* Athens, OH: NBIA.

UNIDO (1997) Discussion Paper No. 3, 'Lessons from international experience for the promotion of business incubation systems, Rustam Lalkaka.

18. Russia: The Volkhov international business incubator

IDA F. S. SCHMERTZ

Abstract

The management and financial challenges of a business incubator are immense, particularly in a region of Russia where human and financial resources are scarce and political, economic and regulatory barriers are considerable. The Volkhov international business incubator (VBI) combines the characteristics of the traditional small business incubator with the objectives and methodology of empowerment or microenterprise incubators, plus the functions of a business services centre and a training centre. A particularly important component is its equipment leasing programme, which is of great benefit to clients who are otherwise unable to access credit, and to the incubator which derives a large part of its income from interest payments. It has now attained 75 per cent sustainability, despite the current economic crisis.

Introduction

THE VOLKHOV INTERNATIONAL business incubator was founded in 1995 by the city of Volkhov and by the Alliance of American and Russian Women to support the development of small businesses in the Volkhov region, with a particular emphasis on women-led businesses. Volkhov is a city of 60 000 people on both banks of the Volkhov River, 130km north-east of St. Petersburg. It is the site of the first Soviet hydroelectric plant and the first Soviet aluminium factory, both still more or less operational. Until recently, it was a closed strategic city, largely because it is an important railroad hub.

The incubator offers secure office and production space for rent; business training; computer training; office services; business consultation; a programme for women's empowerment in business; access to credit for qualified small businesses, sole proprietors and agricultural enterprises; plus a wide network of commercial, non-profit and political contacts among Russian and international agencies and organizations.

The incubator is located in an 1800 sq. m. building, contributed rent-free for 49 years by the city of Volkhov. It is managed by a Russian staff and overseen by a board of trustees. The board consists of senior incubator staff, four local entrepreneurs, representatives from two St. Petersburg financial institutions, and two representatives of the Alliance of American and Russian Women.

The incubator received funding under a three-year co-operative agreement with the United States Agency for International Development New Business Programme, 1995–98. To sustain its small business development activities, the incubator charges fees for training and services. It offered free business consultation until October 1998, when it instituted fees for that activity also, in view of the need for financial viability during the economic crisis.

The incubator's need for earned income to become financially viable, and clients' difficulty in accessing credit has led the staff to develop a programme to lease equipment for light manufacturing, agriculture and services to small businesses in the Leningrad *oblast*. The incubator was the first non-profit organization in the entire Russian Federation to be granted a leasing licence from the Ministry of Economics in Moscow.

The incubator's training and services are open to any business from Volkhov and neighbouring regions, as well as the incubator tenants. Individuals are welcome to come to the incubator to enquire about products and services. After an initial interview with potential clients, the staff determine whether they qualify for a training programme; whether they simply wish to purchase office services; whether they should be referred elsewhere; whether they may apply to become incubator tenants; or whether they may be candidates for equipment leasing. In the latter two cases, clients are required to develop an appropriate business plan, either on their own or in consultation with the staff consultant on business planning.

Clients for the leasing programmes are small businesses engaged in farming, light manufacturing or services, 80 per cent of whom are start-ups, new entrepreneurs based in the city of Volkhov, and neighbouring towns and regions.

How the Volkhov business incubator differs from traditional incubators

The aim of a business incubator is to grow profitable businesses and create jobs. Businesses are expected to graduate from an incubator after approximately two years incubation, and then to survive and prosper in the community. The primary task of incubator staff, which in the US usually number two to three people, is to service and nurture tenant businesses.

Microenterprise or 'empowerment' incubators have the additional challenge of incubating businesses in economically depressed regions, where business owners may require additional support services and where the goal may include invigorating the local economy or strengthening minority or gender-based business ownership, as well as creating profitable businesses. This approach requires additional skills, and may incur additional costs.

The city of Volkhov, at the time when the incubator was launched in 1995, could be characterized as an extremely depressed, socialist municipality. Enterprises large and small were shut down or simply not paying salaries; no new businesses or jobs had been created; no municipal services had been developed or upgraded. Trading had sprung up in the streets. There were few computers, no computer training or sales, no e-mail, few fax machines, no business services. What small businesses there were could get no access to credit. There was no particular help or attention to women, despite the fact that they constitute 80 per cent of the unemployed. The idea of the incubator was greeted with scepticism or bemusement by most city officials, potential staff, potential tenants and future clients. They viewed the undertaking as a charity, not a business, run by well-meaning but naive Americans, with only a superficial understanding of how things operate in Russia.

Today, the incubator is operating with 11 business tenants and four in the pipeline. Three former tenants have graduated, two relocated in the city. The staff are now highly regarded and valued by entrepreneurs, officials and residents, and the VBI as an institution has earned a reputation in the region and throughout Russia as a serious and important contributor to the development of small business in a provincial town and as a model participant in the market economy.

Much more is expected of VBI because of its context than would be expected from a traditional Western incubator. The incubator has major social and economic objectives that do not encumber traditional Western incubators. It serves as a catalyst for entrepreneurship and business development for the entire community. The intended outcome is that individual citizens in the region and the local city administration develop a stake in the success of a market economy.

The incubator is also a training ground for basic international business practices, including finance, accounting, management, marketing, computing, communication, human resources, customer services and common office practices. This entails formal courses, conferences, seminars, consultation, counselling and day-to-day interaction between staff and clients.

In addition, the incubator is the only institution in the region to focus on women-led businesses, to offer a women's business empowerment programme, to encourage and support women to start and manage businesses, and to offer credit and leasing to women entrepreneurs. It is also the only institution in the region that offers credit and equipment leasing to small businesses at reasonable interest rates and for long periods.

Outreach

The incubator philosophy is to offer a service for everyone. However, in 1995 and 1996 the task was not simply to recruit clients, but to introduce them to the basic concepts of a business incubator and the fundamentals of running a private, profitable business. Local residents were invited to public forums, sponsored by the mayors of Volkhov and other cities in the region, to learn about the incubator and its services and to talk informally with the staff. The local press ran articles about the incubator and eventually the incubator placed paid advertisements regarding specific services. Local and national TV and print media frequently cover seminars or events at the incubator, as well as interviews with the staff. Poster advertisements are positioned at strategic locations. Finally, there is an extremely active personal network of staff and incubator clients. The most effective outreach is done by satisfied clients, face-to-face or over the telephone. Marketing the incubator continues to be a daily preoccupation.

The result of this outreach is that, as at 1998, the incubator helped establish 50 new businesses, creating 190 new jobs. It helped to sustain an additional 70 businesses and 260 jobs. Other indicators of outreach include:

- The incubator currently rents office or production space to 10 tenant businesses, 60 per cent of whom are women.
- The incubator has sponsored 120 training programmes and seminars; and 1494 people have participated in the courses.
- Consultants have worked with 2749 individuals, including 1115 women and farmers to assess their business ideas and help them develop business plans.
- The VBI developed the Women's Business Support Programme, a special 10-week course to help women overcome fears connected with opening and running a business; 57 women have participated, of whom 22 have started their own businesses.
- Over 4400 clients have used the office services, including fax, xerox, graphic design, marketing products, etc.

Leasing programme

This programme offers the only credit available to small businesses and start-ups in the region. The business consultant works with clients who apply for equipment leasing to help them complete and refine a business plan. The plan is then subject to rigorous scrutiny and analysis by the VBI financial officer to determine whether the business can support interest payments. The analysis is followed by site visits, further assessment of the business and the client, and input from all members of the incubator staff. The final step entails a review by the credit committee, which consists of senior staff and members of the board of trustees.

Leases are offered for two years, and require equal monthly payments of interest and principal. At the end of the period, the client owns the equipment. The maximum lease amount was raised recently from US$25 000 to US$60 000, and interest rates were raised from 35 per cent to 60–90 per cent annually, in roubles, in view of inflation during the economic crisis. Interest rates are based on those of the Central Bank. In addition to the business plan, the incubator requires that the client registers the business with the municipal and tax authorities; a 12.5 per cent up-front payment on the equipment; and full insurance coverage in the name of the incubator.

As at the end of 1998, the incubator had 56 lease agreements with 48 clients, at an average of under US$10 000 a lease. An extremely popular arrangement with selected clients is the lease buy-back agreement. In a lease buy-back, the incubator may purchase title to the client's building, equipment or transport to provide working capital which could not be obtained otherwise. The client then repurchases the equipment over time, as with a regular lease.

Table 18.1 demonstrates that women play a significant role in the VBI leasing programme, constituting nearly 50 per cent of the leasing clients and over 50 per cent of the dollar volume of all leases. Women held all the leases in the manufacturing sector but less than half the leased equipment in services, trade and agriculture.

Table 18.1 VBI leasing clients

Activity	Number of leases			Revenue to incubator		
	Total	Women-led businesses	Women-led businesses as % of total	Total ($)	Women-led businesses	Women-led businesses as % of total
Agriculture	6	2	5	44 723	8138	2
Production	4	4	9	37 514	37 514	9
Services	13	6	14	182 156	142 856	32
Trade	21	9	20	176 213	45 525	10
Total	44	21	48	440 606	234 033	53

Annual turnover among VBI tenants, loan and leasing clients ranges from $3000 to $600 000. Incomes range from less than $500 to $50 000, and the number of employees from two to 50.

General market context

The competition for incubator services in the regional market is low to nil, depending on the service. The incubator is the only organization in the region with private or public sector donor support. Some St. Petersburg and local banks are said to provide credit to small businesses but, if so, the clients the incubator serves do not have access to such services. Business training is offered by several fine institutions in St. Petersburg, but these are financially beyond the reach of

Box 18.1   Client networks

Incubators are particularly important for fostering working relationships among incubator tenants. One example is the incubator's work with a tenant auditing firm. The firm's owner, Margarita, acquired about 15 sq. m. at the incubator to service three clients. After several months in the incubator, and participating in general tenants' meetings, she acquired three additional clients among the tenants. Today, nearly all the tenants rely on her bookkeeping services.

Margarita also participated in the meetings of the Volkhov Business Association. Established through the initiative of the incubator, it is the only independent, non-profit organization in the region. Her comments and recommendations in those meetings brought her additional clients, most of whom are also leasing clients of the incubator. During the year her business grew significantly. She has tripled her space and employs four additional people.

One of Margarita's new employees, Irina, moved to Volkhov one year ago. As an unemployed woman, she participated in the incubator's Women's Business Support Programme. This led her to undertake research for establishing a credit union, primarily for women entrepreneurs – the first in the region. At the same time, she enrolled in the incubator's computer course for professional bookkeeping certification, and for practical training, she interned with Margarita's auditing firm. As a result of these combined experiences, she will serve as the sole staff person for the Volkhov Business Association. The Association and the incubator will co-sponsor the credit union.

incubator clients, or probably 95 per cent of the population of the *oblast*. Evidence of competition in office services is beginning to emerge: in September 1998, the post office in the centre of the city began to offer copying services at half the cost of the incubator.

Despite substantial rhetoric and lip service, Russian government support at any level for the development of private, small business has been non-existent. On the contrary, federal and *oblast* governmental actions have tended to support large business at the expense of the small entrepreneurs.

There are international providers in St. Petersburg and other major metropolitan areas of Russia. However, the country is vast and donors and providers are few, particularly in provincial areas. There is no question that their number could be multiplied many times over without encroaching on each other's territory or competing with the private sector. Opportunities to support small business in Russia have barely been tapped, and to date the impact has been infinitesimal. In the long term, leasing and credit to small businesses promises to be an immensely lucrative market. It will be really effective, however, only when an institutional infrastructure serving small business can be encouraged and when regulatory and tax barriers can be lessened.

Taxes, regulation and other constraints

Taxes in Russia are burdensome to the extent that it is difficult or nearly impossible for a small business to understand and adhere to all requirements. The cost and time factors alone are prohibitive. In addition, the entrepreneur must pay 100 per cent of salaries to off-budget social funds, pension funds and other special funds, *plus* 30 other federal, regional and local taxes. Clearly, the sum of these taxes places an unbearable financial and regulatory burden on small businesses.

Another burden is the requirement for government approvals. Local government regulatory entities require approvals, certificates and fees for the components, ingredients and production of nearly every product: computer placement in offices, electric systems, fire systems, etc. Licences are required to produce mayonnaise; to bake bread (a separate licence for each type of bread); or to produce a line of knitwear (a separate licence for each style). Approvals and licensing fees usually involve bribery or direct extortion, above the official cost of the licence.

In addition, in many cities and towns, criminal groups collect more money than the tax inspectors or the regulatory entities. This is an obvious additional burden.

Finally, it is not unusual for small businesses to confront negative attitudes from local government authorities. Some authorities are more interested in supporting municipal and government enterprises than they are in promoting the development of private enterprise. Entrepreneurs confront outright hostility or hidden negative barriers on the part of municipal authorities, who often view private business as competitive.

It is not an exaggeration to say that in Russian provincial towns and cities there are no financial institutions to support the development of small business; government structures have other priorities; and effective non-profit or international organization support is concentrated in major metropolitan areas.

Financial sustainability

Financial sustainability is difficult to forecast because of current financial and economic developments in Russia: the implosion of the banking system, the absence of a federal economic programme, devaluation of the rouble, and imminent hyper-inflation. Like other private institutions in Russia, the incubator has had to cut expenses drastically to live within its means. The staff have agreed to a substantial cut (up to 80 per cent in dollars, 60 per cent in roubles) and lay-offs are inevitable. In spite of this, the incubator is aiming at financial self-sustainability and even financial self-sufficiency, when the leasing fund can be capitalized at US$2 million. The currently available capital pool is US$666 000. (Financial sustainability, *samaokypaemost*, means that the incubator can function on income from operations, plus additional capital investment in the leasing programme and grants for non-income-producing programmes. Financial self-sufficiency, *samafinansirovaniye*, will have been attained when revenues from an expanded leasing programme and incubator services cover all operating expenses.)

The incubator started with a grant of US$900 000 over three years from USAID, of which US$400 000 was used to capitalize the credit and leasing programmes. (Also, almost $1 million was spent in the US on direct and indirect expenses, equipment and travel. An additional $2 million was contributed in cost sharing.) Monthly operating expenses in 1997–98 were US$18 000–20 000. During the current economic crisis, these have been reduced to US$7000 a month and are expected in 1999 to continue below US$10 000 a month, unless additional investment can be obtained.

In 1999, the incubator will be 75 per cent financially self-sustainable at that reduced level. Incubator earned income will be derived 54 per cent from interest

Table 18.2 Incubator earned income, 1998, compared to forecast income (average exchange rate 12.5 roubles to the dollar)

Category	9 months 1998		1998 forecast	
	Roubles	US$	Roubles	US$
Income	998 340	124 792	1 389 752	111 180
Expense	409 546	51 193	808 662	64 693
Net income before tax	588 794	73 599	581 090	46 487
Profit tax	175 605	21 950	212 755	17 020
Property tax	30 094	3762	32 975	2638
VAT				
Road tax	32 930	4116	29 826	2386
Land tax	855	107	2130	170
Net income	349 310	43 664	303 404	24 273

payments on leases, 12 per cent from tenants' rent payments, 8 per cent from training and 2 per cent from office services. A grant programme will contribute 25 per cent of incubator revenues next year. In the spring of 1997, the US Russia Investment Fund and the VBI signed a loan agreement for US$250 000 at 5 per cent interest to enlarge the capital pool for leasing. Projections for 1999 assume that the loan will be operational at that time.

The incubator aims to maintain services during the economic crisis by adopting a flexible strategy. Training programmes and business services will be modified, deleted or added, based on demand. Prices will be raised or lowered, based on inflation, costs and competition, but always with an eye to producing revenues sufficient to sustain the activity. The training programme, for example, focuses on computer courses, including professional bookkeeping courses on computer, because demand is greater and the fees can be higher than for traditional business training. All graduates are hired by firms in the region immediately upon graduation. The incubator has discontinued its micro-loan programme which offered loans of up to US$10 000 in co-operation with Baltiisky Bank. Bank fees, regulations and required promissory notes up front to cover incubator guarantees, make this programme unprofitable and excessively time consuming.

To date, the incubator has experienced only one default from a client who had accepted credit beyond her ability to pay. However, additional defaults can be expected in the leasing programme during the current economic crisis.

The need for incubator services and programmes continues to be immense. Demand for leasing is expected to increase during (and perhaps because of) the current economic crisis. Clients and potential clients with cash are eager to invest their savings in hard goods, particularly transport, with the assistance of leases from the incubator. Retail and wholesale trade, particularly in food products, continues. Local production is expected to increase. But plans for an expanded leasing programme in terms of a larger capital pool, will probably be put on hold pending the outcome of the current economic crisis.

Impact and achievements

Federal data indicate that the number of small businesses throughout Russia has declined over the past few years, and the decline is accelerating during the current crisis. In Volkhov, the number of registered small businesses that pay taxes in the city has increased from 540 to 1420 over the past three years.

Volkhov is the only city in the region that can claim such an increase. The incubator has been a factor in creating a climate where entrepreneurship is encouraged and supported.

The VBI has also made a difference to the appearance of the city and the leisure pursuits of its residents. The first modern café in town and the first youth entertainment centre would not have been established without the incubator.

The mayor has established a municipal department for small business to 'compete' with the incubator in supporting small business. The director of the department works closely with the VBI to spotlight small business and to attract support from other levels of government. It has led to more accurate data gathering, discussion at cabinet meetings, and tender offers to small business to rent municipal property.

Other achievements of the incubator include the following:

- A 'Non-commercial Business Partnership' became the first independent, voluntary association to be established in Volkhov, as a result of the VBI initiative. It meets regularly, has united 80 small businesses, and is a registered organization with a governance structure modeled on the incubator. The partnership has worked with the mayor on local business issues, has lobbied on behalf of small business at the *oblast* and local levels, and is hiring a part-time director and seeking additional funding.
- The VBI and the Partnership lobbied successfully at the *oblast* level to reduce the tax on transport leasing from 20 per cent to 2 per cent on both the lessor and the lessee. As a result, transport is expected to become the incubator's most popular leasing programme.
- Representatives from dozens of Russian cities have travelled to Volkhov to visit the incubator and to participate in VBI training programmes, to learn how to replicate the VBI and promote small business development and women's entrepreneurship in their localities.
- The first credit union in the region is being established with the support of the VBI.
- The VBI was awarded first place in the Federation-wide competition of business incubators, held in Moscow, December 1997.
- The VBI was instrumental in conceiving and establishing the Russian National Association of Business incubators, with the intention of replicating incubators in Russia and establishing relationships with incubators internationally.

19. AMKA, Tanzania: Export Marketing Development Services

ALAN GIBSON and LEON TOMESEN

Introduction

AMKA (THE SWAHILI WORD FOR 'AWARENESS' OR 'AWAKEN') is a Tanzanian NGO specializing in export- and marketing-oriented business development services (BDS) to small and medium-sized enterprises (SMEs) in Tanzania. Its origins lie in an export development programme developed by Traidcraft Exchange (TX), a UK-based 'fair trade' promotion NGO, which has worked with Tanzanian enterprises since 1987. On the basis of this work, AMKA was formed in 1994 to[1]: Increase the incomes and numbers of Tanzanians (employees and/or producers) involved in exports . . . [and] increase the value of agricultural output in Tanzania via exports . . .

AMKA undertakes a range of activities targeting the SME sector. These form a complementary market/export-focused portfolio of services and can essentially be divided into two categories: training and advisory services; and trade promotion and intermediary services.

The rationale for, and significance of, AMKA stems from three related arguments.

- In an era of increasing global market liberalization, developing economies need to encourage more outward-looking, market-oriented behaviour among SMEs.
- While the overall macro framework for export development is of paramount importance, this is a necessary but not in itself sufficient step to stimulate enhanced SME performance in export markets. Overcoming constraints – such as inadequate networks and asymmetrical information – requires *active* intervention.
- Active support based around principles of *fair trade*[2] is more likely to have a positive impact on poorer and more disadvantaged groups.

The organization

The current situation

The development of indigenous institutional capacity has been a key priority for AMKA and a crucial element of donor support. This includes:

- organizational capacity: the structure of the organization, its people, culture and strategies
- managerial capacity: AMKA's capability to manage its operations, based on management systems; and
- financial capacity: key sources and financial resources.

Organizational capacity

Structure: AMKA operates from a modest but well equipped office in the capital, Dar es Salaam. Its operations are guided by a board of trustees of eight members, including two representatives of TX[3] and with one donor (the Department for International Development – DFID with an observer status. The organization has no separate divisions or departments. The tasks and responsibilities of the general management have been laid down in the project memorandum. The division of responsibilities and tasks between the two senior staff members of the organization is not strictly specified, and based on agreement.

People: AMKA has three staff in total. Two are senior staff, one managing director (MD) and one business adviser (BA). The secretary has multiple roles (secretarial work, office management, computing, bookkeeping, etc.). From the outset, staff development has been encouraged, predominantly through technical assistance by TX. The MD has considerable authority and experience. The qualifications and joint experience of the board members appear to be well-suited to AMKA's objectives.

Culture: The most striking aspects of the culture of AMKA are: a shared commitment to the values and mission of AMKA; a high degree of mutual respect and co-operation between the AMKA management, the trustees and the donor; and staff diligence. The dual aim of being both developmental and business-like is reflected in a culture that is more 'informal' than 'corporate'.

Strategy: AMKA is currently at a crossroads as it considers how best to pursue its main goal of improving marketing and export performance among SMEs. It may continue its current role of market facilitator, providing a mix of training and advisory and trade/intermediary services. It may split into a market *facilitator*, a not-for-profit organization concentrating on developing marketing services and technical assistance (AMKA Trust), and a market *player*, a commercial company that will buy and sell products originating from SMEs in local, regional and export markets (AMKA Trading). The debate on AMKA's future direction had not been concluded by the end of 1998.

External relations: in its first four years, AMKA has established a credible reputation with government and with NGOs in Tanzania, with ATOs and other overseas buyers, and with its partner group of producers and intermediaries.

Managerial capacity

In addition to its critical human resource base – its staff – AMKA's capacity and capability to manage its operations is based on its management systems, the elements of which are:

Work plans: AMKA prepares detailed annual operational plans of activities. These include planned institutional development, purchases, client numbers, technical assistance by TX, product development, reporting, etc. On the basis of annual plans, the trustees approve annual budgets. Work plans are used as a framework for forward planning but do not restrict flexibility and innovation. Trustees and AMKA management share a prudent approach to growth and risk.

Time sheets: The project memorandum includes a detailed list of targets and time inputs of AMKA staff and TX support needed to achieve these targets.

However, attempts to introduce time sheets have not been successful in that there is no real information on how AMKA's human resources are being used.

Client tracking/database: The system of recording the clients' profile, services assessed and impact on clients is still rather rudimentary.

Financial management: AMKA has basic financial systems in place in relation to overall funds. However, these do not allow any analysis of costs and revenues for specific services to be undertaken.

Financial capacity

AMKA's main source of income is from one donor, DFID, which approved a four-year grant of US$557 053 in 1994 to help form the organization[4]. However, dependence on DFID grant funding has been reduced from 94 per cent in 1994/5 to 40 per cent in 1997/8, partly replaced by funds from other donors. The proportion of internally generated funds has increased from 5 per cent in 1994/95 to 41 per cent in 1997/98. Table 19.1 provides evidence of consistent progress by AMKA towards reduced dependency on external funding, mainly from funds generated through charges for consultancy work for ATOs.

Table 19.1   AMKA funding*: 1994/95–97/98

	1994–95		1995–96		1996–97		1997–98	
	$	%	$	%	$	%	$	%
External funding								
Grants from DFID	75 000	94	57 500	81	48 000	57	27 750	40
Donations (other donors)	870	1	3040	4	2070	24	13 450	19
Sub-total grants	75 870	95	60 540	86	50 070	81	41 200	59
Internally-generated funds								
Producer charges/fees	1140	1	4570	6	7440	9	4480	6
Other income (office support)	110	0	630	1	4460	5	630	1
ATO charge	2760	3	3110	4	1440	2	8640	12
Consultancy	0	0	1810	3	2130	3	14 650	21
Bank interest	60	0	55	0	270	0	220	0
Sub-total internal funds	4070	5	10 175	14	15 740	19	28 620	41
Total	79 940	100	70 715	100	65 810	100	69 820	100

*Average exchange rates used to calculate dollar equivalent figures

Positive factors

- *Strong initial focus on institutional development:* Institutional development has been given great importance and AMKA has been viewed as more than a delivery mechanism for services, both by itself, but also by its key donor (DFID) and its main partner and capacity-building resource, TX. DFID funding has been used to establish and run the organization, including capital investment and funds for staff development. Thus the development of a strong board, good institutional relationships and an environment conducive to the development of people, products and systems has been encouraged.
- *Building on leadership and developing ownership:* AMKA staff are well qualified. However, much of the success and drive for AMKA comes from the

personality and experience of the MD[5]. He has created a working environment and management style that is appropriate for both AMKA's present mandate and the socio-cultural environment in Tanzania. AMKA's aims are shared among all key stakeholders; trustees play an active and effective role in the strategic guidance of AMKA and its staff; and the donor and external advisers are involved in strategic planning.

TX's role has changed since AMKA's inception. In the first two years, capacity-building (staff development, introduction to networks, service design, and administrative development) were to the fore. In the latter period, TX support has moved more to market information and research and trade facilitation; i.e. support from TX has thus moved to the provision of specific services and allowed AMKA to develop greater control over its direction. In general, the relationship between AMKA and TX has moved from dependence to a partnership. The relationship has been generally productive and the two parties have agreed to work with each other in the future.

From a total budget of US$555 053, as much as US$316 250 (more than 50 per cent) was allocated to TX to establish AMKA as an organization, recruit trustees and staff, institute operational plans, office systems and management and financial controls, and provide training and consultancy support and market information. Not all of this is institutional development investment *per se*; some is related to ongoing service delivery. Moreover, the scale of support should decline as AMKA is able to follow its own initiatives. Also, obviously TX – located in a high-income country – has a relatively more expensive cost base than AMKA and this distorts relative contributions. For an organization of three people with 18 regular clients, the *worth* of such a relatively high investment in technical assistance can certainly be questioned.

Challenges

AMKA now faces a number of challenges. Its current approach is characterized by two underpinning tensions:

- an approach building on fair trade principles, poverty alleviation objectives and other considerations, which would lead to clients who are generally from producer groups, co-operatives and parastatals (with many poor employees/members) and to partnerships with ATOs; an approach which seeks to work with those with most business potential – perhaps individually owned SMEs and commercial buyers who may be seen as less representative of the poor
- on the one hand, acting as a facilitating organization working with market-based organizations where the chances of financial sustainability are limited, and on the other hand, being a direct player in the market, buying, selling and competing with other organizations where there could be more opportunity for financial sustainability.

These dilemmas pose considerable challenges. First, how to achieve a balance between promotional work in those areas where market mechanisms are inadequate or have failed, and maximizing outreach through working with existing SMEs with greatest business potential. Second, to what extent can AMKA play the role of market player (a role it does not play currently)? NGOs that have taken this route have generally not been very successful. Furthermore, even if it becomes a market player, to what extent does this compromise its wider development role? Against this, many of the existing supposedly market structures (especially intermediaries) are clearly dysfunctional. It is highly questionable if they can ever be helped to improve performance.

The proposed split of AMKA into a developmental/promotional arm and a direct trading entity arm might be one way to resolve this issue.

Strengthening internal systems

The present management system includes a staff manual, and personal and human resource management. However, the manual does not cover the conduct of day-to-day operations, it is not regularly updated, and is not a key prompt for the way operations are conducted. If AMKA needs an updated operations manual setting out approved processes, layouts, checks etc., including dealing with buyers and suppliers, the 'institutional memory' of AMKA – presently in the heads of the staff, especially the MD – has to be formalized. There may be problems in overly-formalizing an essentially small organization but without this, institutional learning is diminished.

Some limitations in the current systems are related to clients and the market, but there is also a relative paucity of information on costs and revenues. AMKA primarily sells services to SMEs for a fee. This defines the close and transactional relationship with its clients. The present system does not allow for monitoring of the costs of the different services being delivered. There is no record-keeping of time spent on direct revenue-generating activities and non-fee earning activities. Also, the time spent by AMKA and TX staff in the preparation and conduct of workshops, seminars, trade fair participation and field visits is not priced. The challenge clearly is to think more about what services can be delivered at what cost and for what clients. Improved systems could provide AMKA with a measure of its performance, helping towards greater sustainability and business-like behaviour. AMKA is aware that it is not enough just to do the job, without adequate systems for record keeping.

Widening the management base

As with any BDS organization, a key strength of AMKA is also its weakness; namely that much of the organization is personified in one person, the MD. And like any small business, this raises a key concern over succession, especially given his possible retirement within the next few years. The possible establishment of AMKA Trading next to AMKA Trust would emphasize further the importance of addressing this management issue.

The services

The current situation

The AMKA product offer

AMKA's export- and market-oriented approach aims to improve business performance by increasing efficiency and turnover through better access to new markets (domestic and foreign). AMKA's services (see Table 19.1) is focused on pre-export and on-going support to small-scale producers and intermediaries. The service range is effectively a complementary service to facilitate the entire business process; production, marketing and the logistics of getting export produce to markets. These comprise:

- *Training and advisory services:* provision of training in small business development skills (e.g. marketing, quality control) and business planning for export. Training is delivered around specific products in a seminar/workshop environment. AMKA undertakes quarterly follow-up visits to all producers for, among other purposes, product development. Other technical assistance and consultancy services are provided according to specific requests.
- *Trade promotion and intermediary services:* AMKA acts as a facilitator between producers and buyers. It provides export market information and research, assistance to producers needing export facilities (communication; documentation; banking and shipping) and develops linkages between producers and trade organizations (buyers). AMKA helps producers and intermediary organizations to participate in trade fairs, and also provides ethical and quality standard audits of producers for external buyers.

In reality AMKA also regards buyers as its clients and provides services to them, including fees for products and market/product consultancy.

Revenues and costs

Comparison of revenues against costs for different products is limited by the lack of an in-house system for measuring direct costs on products. From the range of products that AMKA offers to its clients, it is clear that there are few (if any) activities in which revenues from clients are greater than direct costs.

- *Training workshops and seminars:* the costs for training workshops varies from US$3200 for 15 participants to US$10 000 for 40 participants, excluding the preparatory inputs and time by AMKA staff and facilitators from TX. Considering that presently a fee of US$30 (Tsh20 000) is charged per participant, this activity recovers only around 15 per cent of direct costs. Internally generated funds from producer charges and fees have constituted, on average, 7 per cent of the total budget during the last three years.
- *Trade fair participation:* for this, AMKA relies heavily on grants from other donors, such as USAID and the Tanzania Gatsby Trust Producers pay a token fee of US$75 (Tsh50 000), while the real cost is, on average, close to US$25 000 for an average of 14 participants. This implies a cost recovery rate of less than 5 per cent.
- *Counselling and diagnostic health checks:* 'One-to-one' BDS (i.e. services delivered to SMEs individually during quarterly field visits) are provided free of charge. The present MIS does enable cost calculation for such services.
- *Consultancy:* There is a steady increase of internally generated funds from AMKA consultancies, mainly from ATOs, amounting to 21 per cent of its overall income in 1997/98. Again, there is no possible cost calculation for consultancy; it clearly is generating a considerable surplus.
- *ATO charges:* These charges are fees billed to other trading organizations for intermediary services carried out on their behalf (e.g. verifying adherence of producers to fair trade principles and follow-up on trade agreements). These charges have contributed increasingly to the internally generated funds (from 3 per cent in 1994/95 to 12 per cent in 1997/98).

Other services in AMKA's portfolio, particularly when acting as a broker between producers and buyers, are essentially free; there is no fee or commission to producers for these services.

AMKA has not given a high priority to pricing its services. Most of its internally generated revenue clearly derives either from consultancy services or charges to other trading organizations and not to the indigenous SME producers.

Table 19.2 Delivery of key AMKA services

Service	Description	Number of clients
Business development workshops	Seven undertaken	82 producers, 10 intermediary organizations and 5 NGOs/government institutions
Trade fairs	Four organized	56 producers
Follow-up visits	Quarterly to provide one-to-one advisory and counselling services	To all clients (currently 18)
Support services	Trouble-shooting, monitoring fair trade practices, introduction of new suppliers, co-ordination of producers	–
Market research	Primary and secondary data collected on the market potential of Tanzanian products in international markets	–

Product development and client–product mix

AMKA's products have developed with the support of TX. Currently, these are usually not differentiated according to specific client need but tend to be relatively generalized. Similarly, AMKA offers a range of comprehensive services to almost all clients; so that it has an in-depth relationship with a relatively small client base.

The competitive environment

There are few organizations in Tanzania that provide the kind of services that AMKA offers. Such might include the Board of External Trade (BET), FAIDA, a donor project funded by the Netherlands government, and the Tanzania Business Centre (TBC), a USAID-funded project. Donors distort the market with subsidized projects that affect continuity and supplier and consumer expectations and actions. 'Demand' for AMKA's subsidized services remains strong, mainly because of the effectiveness of its service delivery and its good contacts with partners. Clients would like AMKA to expand services further and there are also plans for AMKA to expand into Uganda, but only on a project basis.

Although there are differences in approach between AMKA and its three competitors, intended beneficiaries, geographical coverage and available expertise, there is a great similarity in both training and advisory services; as well as in trade promotion and intermediary services. FAIDA and TBC in particular have greater access than AMKA to (grant) funds and specialized expertise. The relations between AMKA and FAIDA and TBC have been lukewarm; with BET a more constructive relationship has thus developed. Sooner or later the organizations will have to aim for higher levels of financial sustainability.

Product marketing

Training and other products are promoted through newspaper advertising, radio and TV, the international newsletter of TX, leaflets distributed in the UK, trade fair participation and a catalogue. It is clear that AMKA's products and services are well known to its present partners, but less so to SMEs, commercial service providers, and other potential clients in the public and private sectors. The challenge for AMKA is to promote its present and future services more aggressively to attract a much broader clientele.

Positive factors

Through its activities, AMKA has established a good reputation. Its array of services is clearly in demand not only by existing clients but also by others. Its developing close linkages with a small number of key partner institutions, and providing a wide range of services to them, has brought success.

Challenges

A range of challenges face AMKA in relation to its services, and more directly to cost recovery.

- *A more aggressive approach towards pricing:* AMKA's approach to pricing is evolving and there is some evidence that clients will pay a higher price for quality services. Producers participating in other trade fairs are willing and able to pay much more than is currently being charged. How much the market will bear for different services is currently not clear. Where no charge is made to producers for services, the rationale needs to be explicit.
- *Improving financial information systems:* Currently, AMKA does not really know the contribution or level of subsidy from different services. Consequently, it does not know where resources should be allocated. For example, considerable time and money is spent on one-to-one advisory services for producers on many issues at no cost; the scale of subsidies here should be clearer.
- *Defining and marketing products:* Currently, AMKA does not break down its different types of expertise into services which have a wider appeal, rather than just to its core group of partners; it seeks to provide a broad range of support for a small number of clients. Ultimately, AMKA has to know where its core competence lies and stick with this. Similarly, in an increasingly competitive environment, AMKA has to position itself in relation to the 'offer' from other organizations.
- *Scaling-up – clarifying subsidies for services:* Some of AMKA's services have more revenue-earning potential than others. There appears to be scope for higher fees in some types of services. Currently, however, most services to producers are subsidized to a level of over 80 per cent and AMKA's internally generated funds comes from the higher margins it can charge for services to ATOs. In order for AMKA to scale up, therefore, either the scale of funding must increase and/or it must focus its efforts on products and clients where it can earn revenue. There are three core subsidy-related issues where further clarification may be helpful:
  - o Which services warrant subsidies, why and how much?
  - o If subsidies are justified for some services, how long should this be for particular clients? (unless it is envisaged that producers/SMEs should

benefit from permanent subsidy (provided by external funds), and relationships with them should move to zero subsidy).

○ Which services should be offered at a commercial rate (direct cost plus a margin)?

Learning (appropriately) from regional and overseas experiences

Interesting developments are taking place in the field of small producer support. Imaginative approaches by business development services providers to achieve scale and cost-effectiveness have proliferated in recent years. It may be helpful for AMKA to learn from and capitalize more on the results of innovations and experiments elsewhere.

The clients

The current situation

AMKA maintains, to a limited extent, data on clients' profiles, services delivered and impact. However, there is no systematic and comprehensive database. The information should be viewed accordingly.

Identity: who are the clients?

AMKA effectively works with two groups of clients; SMEs in Tanzania, and overseas buyers, largely in two sectors: food-processing (non-farm) and handicraft production. The client base is varied in terms of the structure of the organization, the number of employees, activities and main products. The size of client enterprises ranges from four to 446 employees. Client enterprises have a variety of ownership structures; producer groups (groups of self-employed people), co-operative societies, private limited companies, parastatals, and associations. Not all owner-managers of enterprises receiving AMKA support are themselves poor, but there are many poor employees of producers.

Initially, AMKA focused on developing intermediaries – co-operatives and associations that could, in turn, deliver services to producers. Because of the weakness of these intermediaries and the difficulty in improving them, AMKA has moved towards providing more services directly itself.

Outreach: how many?

AMKA's audits do not allow a precise assessment of its outreach, particularly in terms of small-scale producers. However, AMKA currently works with at least 18 clients, and has worked with up to 23, providing training, advisory services, logistical support and trade introductions. AMKA also works with 18 export buyers on a regular basis (providing trade introductions, contract management, etc.), and has some contact with a further 100 buyers.

The impact of interventions on clients

Among the key indicators used to measure the effectiveness of AMKA's assistance are:

- number of SME clients (reaching new markets)
- number of employees/producers
- revenues/incomes (from exports/new markets).

Although not all targets have been met, AMKA has made a significant contribution to improved SME performance. Performance against measurable indicators for changes in the clients' situation resulting from AMKA's interventions include sales contracts directly attributable to AMKA: the target was to increase the value of sustainable exports from Tanzania attributable to AMKA to the value of US$700 000 p.a. There are problems ascertaining the exact level of sales attributable to AMKA; some organizations had previous relationships and not all their export sales can be attributed to AMKA alone; others have provided figures to AMKA that comprised both exports generated on their own and those generated through AMKA's interventions; and others have not been able to generate any orders from AMKA. As given by AMKA and by clients, a recent evaluation gave some different figures of the impact this agency has had on promoting export sales over a four-year period.

External evaluation would place the value of export sales generated in the range of US$1.1 million to US$1.2 million over four years. AMKA insists that export sales attributable (directly and indirectly) to its interventions amount to US$3.9 million over four years and an additional US$800 000 increase in local sales. The most accurate indicator of real economic impact would be value-added, essentially meaning profits plus wages. When multiplier effects are taken into account, total value-added is likely to be in the region of US$1.2–1.5m, equivalent to US$2–3 for every dollar of support from development agencies.

Contracts indirectly attributable to AMKA: the target here was to increase exports indirectly attributable to AMKA to 45 per cent on base. Since no clear records are available, and no clear base-line figure was obtained as a standard, it is impossible to arrive at even a qualified estimate on this indicator. The figures in the paragraph above include both directly and indirectly attributable sales.

Increase in number of employees and producers within AMKA's partner organizations: the target was to increase the number of employees with 10 per cent on base and the number of producers with 12 per cent on base. With regard to *permanent employment*, all but two organizations experienced negative growths in of between 14 and 63 per cent, which led to the loss of 437 jobs. The two that grew generated 11 permanent jobs. These figures need to be seen in a context of considerable upheaval and restructuring resulting both from increased competition and retrenchments in advance of privatization. Moreover, given that the environment now seems to be more stable, some of these partners may be able to create more permanent jobs as they grow in response to increased business.

While permanent employment declined, AMKA clients experienced an increase in *casual employment* of 12 per cent. This represented an increase of 17 jobs. All but three organizations experienced significant growths in casual employment ranging from 54 to 100 per cent. These figures need to be treated with some caution as this form of employment varies from low to high business seasons. The general trend, however, shows that AMKA clients are using more casual employees than they were at the beginning of the project period.

The biggest impact of AMKA on employment was in *producer self-employment*. The producer base of 75 per cent of the clients grew by between 25 and 1492 per cent. There was an average growth of 43 per cent which created a total of 749 self-employment opportunities. AMKA can also be said to have contributed to the sustaining of a significant proportion of the 1757 self-employment opportunities that existed at the beginning of the project period.

Increase in average real income of employees and producers: The average real income of AMKA clients grew modestly by between 2 and 6 per cent, against a target of 10 per cent on base. Presently AMKA clients have an average monthly business income of Tsh8240 (US$14). The growth in incomes did not match the growth in sales, mainly due to a large increase in the cost of raw materials. Many of them who had previously relied on raw materials from their farms now had to buy them. Costs, in some cases, increased by 150 per cent, diluting the gains made by increased sales.

Business practices: there was no evidence of AMKA clients investing in business any more than their non-AMKA counterparts. In general, business expenditure was limited to replacing tools and working capital.

The growing competition from liberalizing markets has affected AMKA clients and distort the figures, especially those for employment.

It may be too early to make any authoritative assessment of the impact of the AMKA's work. This depends on the supplier–buyer relationship, the market performance of products and the ability of suppliers to continue to provide appropriate products.

Gender issues

Focus on gender issues is promoted by AMKA as part of its fair trade principles. Approximately 20–30 per cent of client intermediaries employ women. Although women are specifically mentioned as direct beneficiaries of the project, the data available do not allow an estimate of female participation in producer groups, nor is it clear how far AMKA pursues this objective.

Positive factors

AMKA has had a positive impact on the Tanzanian economy generally, and on producers/SMEs specifically. Businesses were saved, others were introduced to exports for the first time, or increased export sales. One to two thousand individuals and households have benefited from increases in incomes and savings and created employment opportunities, mostly in the form of self-employed producers. AMKA has worked with some 18 buyers in 11 countries overseas, and it has been instrumental in forging at least 40 relationships between buyers and producers. Although the impact on priority groups such as the poor cannot be quantified, it is likely that a considerable proportion of the producers, in particular, are from poor backgrounds and their incomes have risen as a result of AMKA's intervention.

Challenges

Developing a client information system for AMKA's needs

Of the 13 main targets of AMKA, the achievements of eight could not be established by a recent evaluation team due to weaknesses in company records, absence of reliable base-line data and flaws in financial record-keeping. There are many questions on present and potential clients of AMKA, to which no answers can be given. For example: what are the basic characteristics of intermediary organizations and producers? How can client information be used more effectively in product marketing and development? What impact data would AMKA find useful for its own purposes?

Developing a client information system for funding agencies

As long as AMKA benefits from donor grants, it clearly has an obligation to be accountable for the wider impact of its activities. While AMKA may be mainly concerned about client fees and feedback, donors would be more interested in the impact on intermediaries, producers and the backward linkage to agriculture. AMKA acknowledges the importance of measuring impact: the challenge now is to address *what* should be measured, *how* and *at what cost.*

Deciding on criteria for client selection and geographical coverage

The current client portfolio has been arrived at through a process of trial and error. AMKA inherited clients from TX's earlier work in Tanzania, among which were a number of parastatals. Further selection of clients was predominantly based on adherence to fair trade practices (fair prices for producers, ethical business principles, and focus on poverty alleviation). Selection of clients through diagnostic work proved difficult. Among the key questions now confronting AMKA are:

- To what extent should clients be self-selecting or restricted by criteria such as fair trade practices or sector? Self-selection would allow AMKA to develop a demand-led process with prospective clients but this might be at the expense of other objectives.
- Should the focus be on new and start-up businesses – spreading outreach – or on enterprises that already have some export experience? AMKA seems to have had a greater impact in terms of turnover with organizations that had exported before than with organizations that had not. These organizations are not only larger but already had existing export relations with a number of ATOs and commercial organizations. Against this, if AMKA works only with existing players, to what extent is it extending services to previously-excluded groups?

Conclusions and implications

Since its formation in 1994, AMKA has established itself as a key resource for export-related services in Tanzania. In a period of difficult economic change, AMKA has achieved most of its targets. In particular, it has created significant export market opportunities for SMEs, which have had a substantial impact on employees and producers. From this experience, a number of specific achievements and lessons can be highlighted, as well as other issues relating more broadly to BDS.

Achievements

AMKA's accomplishments can be seen at three levels:

The development of a strong institutional capacity: this is manifested, for example, in the high level of competence among staff; and tangible sense of ownership; and the excellent networks it has created, built on its good reputation.

The development of growing financial autonomy: AMKA has built an institutional capacity that has reduced its dependence on external donor funding to less than 60 per cent. Although the proportion of funds coming from SME fees is relatively small, diversifying away from donor funds is a notable achievement.

The development of significant positive impacts: impact analysis suggests that AMKA has started to make a real difference to the organizations with which it has worked. Organizations have strengthened their exporting effort and, overall, jobs and incomes are increasing as a result of AMKA's work.

Issues

Three underlying issues remain unanswered to date.

Can export promotion services be offered in a cost-effective and sustainable manner? Some export services do appear to be inherently expensive. For example, participating in trade promotion events and supplying information on export market trends (involving travel and communication) both require considerable resources. On the evidence of AMKA's experience, there seems little chance of their approaching financial sustainability. It is difficult to see relatively cheap ways of providing these services. There are two competing arguments here to which no clear answer emerges. First, it is argued that difficulties in export networks, and information at a local and international level, are so great that only substantial and continued external investments can overcome them. Moreover, the potential benefits from access to lucrative markets may make high costs justifiable. Second, it is argued that the focus on exports is actually inappropriate; small enterprises develop through learning and growing in local and then national markets before the export challenge is taken up; by encouraging businesses to short-circuit the normal business development and learning process and go straight to exports they are left dependent on subsidy-supported services.

Facilitator or player: should BDS organizations move beyond support? Although currently AMKA has not set up its own trading arm, this is one preferred course of action. Knowing the market, with good contacts and appropriate skills, and having been encouraged to think and work in a business-like way, setting up directly in business may be the logical next step for BDS organizations. Indeed, AMKA's decision to work directly with producers rather than with intermediary organizations (co-operatives and associations) because the intermediary structures were simply not working does suggest the need for more active intervention. However, there are complicating factors here, not least the danger of distorting markets by intervening 'unfairly'; the extent to which other developmental objectives are sacrificed in the process; and the general experience of failure when NGOs have attempted to set up in business. Certainly, in some very competitive economies, it would be difficult to justify this step; in others – especially perhaps in Africa, where economies are characteristically less efficient – it may be a justified, if still risky, step to take. Even in this last scenario, involving the existing private sector or supporting a staff 'spin off' may be lower risk options.

Can social and business objectives be married? Every aid-funded intervention is really a union of social, economic and environmental objectives. In the case of AMKA, there is a very explicit pursuit of fair trade objectives. A fair trade approach would tend to guide organizations to a particular form of client and often towards an ATO rather than a commercial buyer. An approach which aimed to be more demand-led would seek to be more open in choice of clients and buyers so that benefits are increased. In AMKA's case it remains to be seen how effective are efforts to combine social and business objectives.

Notes

1. Quoted from Department for International Development Project Memorandum, July 1995.
2. Fair trade generally means trading relations which aim to treat key stakeholders – employees, owner-managers, buyers etc. – in a way that is fairer than in 'normal' commercial arrangements.
3. Recently the representation of TX has been changed to observer status; they will attend board meetings as and when desired.
4. The Ashden Trust provided initial funds for a feasibility study and registration.
5. Stephen Matee, whose background is in marketing and exporting.

20. Marketing micro and small enterprise products in Latin America

LENE MIKKELSEN

Introduction

IT HAS BEEN ESTABLISHED that access to profitable markets is a key factor that determines the long-term success for all businesses. Small and microenterprises, however, often suffer from a number of constraints, such as inadequate technology, geographic isolation, lack of raw materials and saturated local markets. By providing a way to overcome these constraints, marketing service providers play an essential role in developing the businesses of small and micro-producers. These specialized intermediaries facilitate access to profitable markets, whether through direct sales or via brokering or subcontracting. In addition these intermediaries offer a variety of ancillary services, and although the demand for these services may vary depending on the targeted sector and market, this study will show that ancillary services often prove just as essential as market access.

Based on three cases studies of marketing service providers, dealing with handicrafts, non-traditional agricultural products, and household goods, this study will focus on the possibility for short and long-term sustainability of marketing services. The study will discuss the impact that ancillary services have on the ability for partial or full cost recovery and for institutional sustainability, and the business strategies adopted by each marketing service provider.

Marketing intermediaries and their function

To producers wishing to penetrate new markets, or improve their position in the current market, the use of an intermediary may offer various advantages, such as significant reduction in marketing costs, provision of important consumer feedback, and access to a larger client base. The time-consuming tasks assumed by marketing service providers include identifying new clients or markets, consolidating existing ones, sourcing good raw materials, or figuring out how to ship various kinds of goods to different destinations by various means of transportation. From working in specific sectors, marketing service providers often become experts on relevant issues, such as consumer preferences, new trends and designs. This expertise translates into important feedback for the producers in terms of what to produce and how. In addition, the use of marketing intermediaries may shorten the value-added chain considerably by limiting the number of actors. Both producers and consumers are interested in keeping the chain short and reducing the costs of bringing the goods to market.

What are marketing services?

For the purpose of this chapter, marketing services are characterized as services related to different stages of sale, distribution and market penetration. When offered as a package by the same service provider, production-related services may also be included. The various services may be offered separately, and then may not necessarily be characterized as marketing. The variety of marketing services can be divided into an input phase, or the phase prior to production, and an output phase – which is the phase after production.

Marketing services in the input phase

The input phase includes activities such as technical assistance or training, product development and design, provision of raw materials, or credit for production.

- Training and technical assistance are services for which it is perceived that there is a large need, and consequently many institutions providing business development services offer technical assistance or training in some form. Whether provided to groups or to individuals, training for which there is a demand, and which helps the entrepreneurs develop their skills or their businesses, may be provided for a fee. A number of demand-driven training programmes claim high levels of cost-recovery.
- Product development and design are services that are especially important where products or markets are constantly changing, such as in the case of handicrafts. These services may be provided through advice or suggestions for change or development of a product, which makes it difficult to measure the exact cost or benefit. In other cases, outside consultants may be brought in for shorter periods of time, and thus the exact cost may be calculated.
- Access to raw materials is limited for many small producers. By grouping together, or by developing special arrangements with buyers or marketing service providers, purchases can be made in bulk at lower prices. Some marketing service organizations provide raw materials instead of credit, with a surcharge or interest fee.

Marketing services in the output phase

The output phase includes activities such as quality control, packaging, transportation, and market information.

- Quality control can be performed at different stages of production and delivery. Marketing intermediaries exercise quality control independently of production and may thus enforce consistent quality standards. Depending on the product, performing quality control objectively and critically can be a very time-consuming and expensive task, and should be priced accordingly. One example is the time involved when examining handicrafts from different producers that must comply with certain pre-set standards.
- The need for packaging and transportation depends very much on the nature of the product, and the final destination. These are functions that could be separated into isolated cost-effective functions (one of the case studies will show how one organization is attempting to let producers take over the separate function of packaging).
- By making available information on prices, consumer preferences, competition, new raw materials, and potential markets, the marketing service provider adds transparency to the market, and gives the producers the opportunity to make intelligent decisions about future production.

Table 20.1 summarizes examples of activities performed by marketing providers. The three sectors represented in the matrix correspond to the case studies.

Table 20.1   Examples of ancillary services by sector

	Handicrafts	Agricultural produce	Textiles
Input phase:			
Technical assistance/training	– production techniques/ technology – cost management	– seeding, harvesting, natural fertilizers etc. – technology – cost management – production techniques	– use of new machinery/ technology (software for pattern design, fabric cutting machinery, etc.) – cost management – production techniques
Product development and design	– changing colours, shape, form, materials according to trends – introducing new designs	– developing quality seedlings for organic growth	– introducing new models and materials according to trends – developing new patterns
Raw materials	– selecting and providing required quality – buying in bulk	– providing seeds/ seedlings	– buying fabric in bulk – providing required quality
Financial services	– provision of raw materials in advance – advance payment for production – invoice guarantee	– provision of raw materials – advance payment for production – invoice guarantee	– provision of raw materials – advance payment for production – invoice guarantee
Output phase:			
Quality control	– setting standards before production – rejecting non-compliance, low-quality	– checking quality in terms of size or freshness	– setting standards before production – checking quality, conformity, sizes
Packaging	– providing uniform and attractive presentation of handicrafts – preventing damage to fragile goods	– providing uniform presentation – preserving freshness	– providing uniform presentation – bulk packaging
Transportation	– providing bulk transportation	– bulk transportation – refrigerated storage and trucks	– providing bulk transportation
Market information/ penetration	– identifying new buyers – participation in trade fairs –market research	– identifying new buyers – market research – information on prices – contacts to buyers	– identifying new buyers – market research
Paperwork/legal assistance	– exportation logistics – taxes/customs	– certification of organic products – exportation logistics – taxes/customs	– exportation logistics – taxes/customs

How should marketing services be provided?

Given the wide differences in products, producers, and economic sectors, it is difficult to develop generally applicable guidelines for providing marketing services. A set of principles for good practice has been established for how best to deliver non-financial or business development services to micro, small and medium enterprises[1]. These principles are in general applicable to marketing services, and include:

- providing the service in a business-like and demand-led manner
- aiming at long-term sustainability
- specializing in a service or related set of services, and
- providing sub-sector-specific services (tailoring programmes to specific needs).

The first two principles are related to the issue of sustainability, and the last two to the development of a strategy.

Sustainability

The long-term sustainability of the services provided depends on the level of cost recovery. The service of buying and selling, or brokering, can generally be provided in a sustainable manner, using a simple mark-up mechanism. But some of the ancillary services may be less viable, such as training or the provision of market information. These activities are often subsidized, for a number of reasons: clients may be unwilling to pay because they do not foresee any short-term benefits; clients may have limited ability to pay, or past practices by service providers may have created a situation where these services are expected to be provided free. By charging fees, service providers can enhance cost recovery as well as obtaining important feedback about the demand for the service – the client's willingness to pay is an indicator of the relevancy of the service.

The combination of services, or an integrated service package (of which some services are profitable and others not), may therefore prove less profitable, and may narrow the margins of the marketing service provider. Providers may choose to provide unprofitable services to their clients, and then cross-subsidize with revenues from more profitable services.[2] Unless the provider calculates costs and revenues for each service, however, the level of cost recovery or profitability of these activities can only be estimated. Full cost recovery for integrated services may be difficult to obtain, at least in the short term, but business interests can be compatible and complementary with development needs on a long-term basis, and as markets develop, higher levels of cost recovery can usually be reached.

Market strategy

Even if financial profitability is not readily obtained in the short term, marketing services must be provided in a manner that guarantees long-term access to markets on the part of small producers. This implies developing a strategy based on the particular demands of a specific market, whether local, regional, or international, which then determines which services are necessary to assist producers in meeting that demand. Such demands may be identified by the marketing service providers through an exercise such as a sub-sector analysis. A sub-sector analysis is used to map out various players in the chain of events from producers to consumers within a sub-sector, and identify where the constraints to meeting market demands exist[3]. The marketing provider may then try to seek possible solutions to specific problems, such as shortage of raw materials, lack of storage facilities or market information, through the provision of integrated marketing services. This approach also seeks to find ways to capture more links in the value chain of the economic activities in which small producers are engaged, to the producers' benefit.

270

Which services to provide, how, and for whom, are questions the marketing service provider addresses when defining its own strategy. Strategies serve to reach certain goals, such as profitability or social development. Successful providers of marketing services, like successful businesses, aim to develop unique strategies which allow them to reach these goals. Aiming to assist small and micro producers in increasing their production and sales, service providers may choose to provide services at all levels, from the provision of raw materials, to quality control, to transportation of the goods, and meet all needs of the targeted clients. Institutions aiming for higher levels of cost recovery may adopt a minimalist strategy, in which a limited number of clients are provided with a small number of critical services, for which cost-covering fees are charged.

Case studies

The three case studies presented in this chapter have all to a certain extent followed the good practice guidelines listed earlier. The services of all three marketing organizations are focused on specific sub-sectors, and they are specialized to meet the demands of their clients. All three case studies show that when working with low-income producers, institutions may choose to provide certain services without full cost recovery, at least in the short term. This is not to say that the institutions do not have goals of reaching sustainability in the long term. All three organizations have been successful in providing a long-term commercial outlet for their clients' products through effective strategies of market focus, and through a careful determination of which services are required to ensure that producers penetrate the market successfully.

Colombia – Serving the local market

Created in 1983, the objective of Promotora de Comercio Social (PCS) was to provide marketing services to approximately 1000 micro and family enterprises. PCS was one of four projects carried out by the IDB to increase the sales of small and microenterprise products in Colombia. While the other three projects failed, PCS has managed to stay in business, and it is currently planning to extent its services to other parts of Colombia.

PCS works with a large number of low-income producers, providing them with a market for high volumes of low-price products. By following a strategy of local market focus, PCS has been able to position itself very well. It has built up a network of buyers – mostly department stores and supermarkets – both locally and nationally, and in addition occasionally obtains subcontracting assignments from the local textile industry. Instead of working with just one product or sector, PCS has used a methodology of diversity, both in terms of products and services provided, and currently provides practically all of the services needed by producers in four or five sub-sectors.

Marketing services. PCS generates its income through the provision of two main services to micro and family enterprises: by buying goods directly from the producers, and reselling at a price that is low enough to be competitive in the market, while still high enough to allow for a certain margin; and by subcontracting, where PCS participates in bidding processes, competing for large orders from the local government or department stores. When receiving an order, PCS assumes all responsibilities for the required quality, quantity, and timely delivery. It then subcontracts the work to a number of microentrepreneurs.

Additional services include the design and development of new products, packaging, and technical assistance related to cost management and quality improvement. Another important service is that of quality control. A sample of all merchandise passes through the PCS building for final acceptance, and sometimes the whole order passes through. Although these services are costly, they are all currently offered for free, which seriously affects the overall economic situation of the institution. Working with low-income micro and small producers, PCS views the provision of free services as necessary because of the interdependence between producers and broker, something that must be provided in order to get the required quality and quantity they need to secure a sale. With sales, PCS can then cover the cost of these free services.

The services provided by PCS are divided into programmes according to sector: food products, manufacture, leather, handicrafts, and miscellaneous (i.e. jewelry, seasonal ornaments, etc.). The majority of PCS's suppliers are micro-enterprises with fewer than 10 employees, and between 1996 and 1998 the total number of enterprises grew from 400 to 1000, representing a total of 4250 people, of which about half are women. Formalization is not a prerequisite for working with PCS, and close to 50 per cent of the enterprises are informal.

Financial services. PCS offers financial services in the form of an advance payment of up to 50 per cent of the total order (used for buying raw materials). To finance these operations, PCS uses a low-interest loan from the IDB to set up a revolving fund, and the interest income from this fund is transferred to PCS. This is a very important service for the entrepreneurs who cannot pay up-front large amounts for raw materials or transportation, and all the entrepreneurs currently use this service. The service has also proved important to the PCS, generating sufficient income to increase the overall surplus.

Performance. Fifteen years of effort have been put into developing certain levels of production quality and quantity, a solid market basis, and business relationships with various buyers, the result of which is current net sales of US$3.4 million. PCS has been able to cover operational costs since 1994. It managed to cover administrative costs fully in 1997, generating profits of US$93 485. Greater surpluses are projected for 1998 and 1999. The operational and administrative costs of offering complementary services are very high, however, and the margin between total income and total costs is approximately 3 per cent.

PCS applies an average sales markup of 11 per cent (calculated as the difference between the buying and selling price), but most of that markup is eaten away by costs incurred before reselling the product. PCS guarantees the producers a minimum price, and then resells the product, adjusting the markup to whatever it can charge while remaining competitive: PCS operates with a 15.5 per cent mark-up on handicrafts, whereas manufacture carries a mark-up of only 7.9 per cent. Costs are not calculated by sector, or by service, so PCS has no knowledge of profit levels by sector. Management has an intuitive sense that some sectors are more profitable than others, but in fact they cannot measure the degree of cross-subsidization. A more accurate costing system could enable PCS to operate based on where they are losing and gaining. Along these lines, PCS is currently planning to introduce a specific service fee for packaging, since this service represents a clear value-added for the producers, and is easy to calculate.

PROARTE[4] is a private, for-profit company, which serves as a commercial intermediary between approximately 100 Nicaraguan artisans and international buyers. Originally founded as an NGO in 1993, PROARTE made the transition to becoming a private for-profit company in 1996. Perhaps more profit-oriented than PCS, the services provided by PROARTE are oriented towards securing sales in the international market or maintaining good relationships with current buyers. PROARTE's first contacts were alternative trade organizations (ATOs), or the so-called 'sympathy market' in Europe, but realizing that this market could prove very limited in the long-term, they have moved on to other international buyers, mostly commercial wholesalers that are identified and courted mainly at international trade fairs. Commercial wholesalers open up access to a much larger market, but also operate with stricter terms and imply different risks.

Market and product focus. Quality handicrafts are produced in many developing countries where labour is fairly cheap, and the PROARTE answer to that challenge has been to concentrate on producing what is uniquely theirs: traditional Nicaraguan pottery and hammocks. The focus on this line of production has enabled PROARTE to position itself with certain international buyers, who recognize the products and the quality when visiting PROARTE on a yearly basis at the same fairs. PROARTE works mainly with family enterprises and microenterprises with fewer than five employees. Most are low-income artisans, and 30 per cent are women. The criteria for selection of producers are based on type of product, quality, design, price, and capacity for scale. PROARTE does not guarantee any continued affiliation with its organization, but lets its own standards and demands decide who will be its clients. PROARTE will set standards for the products it needs, and upon buying it rejects products that do not meet quality or standard requirements.

Ancillary services. Acknowledging the fact that its suppliers cannot otherwise access the types of services needed to ensure the continuity and quality in production, PROARTE offers some ancillary services. PROARTE checks the quality when buying the goods, administers transportation and customs formalities, provides good quality raw materials, carries out market studies, provides some product development, and participates in international trade fairs. The latter is a very costly activity, but may be a wise investment in the long term, since the international market pays much higher prices for goods.

Performance. The cost of PROARTE's marketing services is covered by a markup of approximately 50 per cent on all goods. A differentiated mark-up mechanism could be introduced, estimating which products are most popular and could potentially render the highest margin. With effective calculations of costs of marketing the product, PROARTE would then have knowledge of which product lines are most profitable, which are most costly, and consequently which product lines to focus on.

Founded with the help of grants and soft loans, PROARTE is today not dependent upon subsidies, but still receives limited assistance for specific purposes, mostly for covering costs in connection with its participation in international trade fairs. PROARTE has also received financial support from the Nicaraguan government as an incentive for exporters of non-traditional products. If PROARTE manages to hold on to its position in the international market, and can continuously develop their products and designs according to the demands of this market, both PROARTE and its artisans should be able to benefit from a very profitable market. In the long term, even costly participation in international trade fairs may be covered by the PROARTE budget, and be considered a wise investment in developing new markets.

El Salvador – developing a market niche

Sociedad Cooperativa de Productores y Exportadores del Salvador de R.L. (PROEXSAL)[5] is a co-operative which was created in 1994 with the purpose of serving as a marketing channel for member producers. PROEXSAL works very closely with CLUSA, an NGO that provides technical assistance to small producers wishing to cultivate organic or other non-traditional agricultural products. CLUSA works very intensely with the producers, preparing them for the stage where PROEXSAL gets involved in the marketing of their products, at which point CLUSA phases out its services and technical assistance to the producers. PROEXSAL develops services at strategic points in the distribution chain, including packaging centres, refrigerated storerooms, and refrigerated trucks. The co-operative's strategy, however, is gradually to turn many of these functions over to its members. Where PROEXSAL originally had to supply seedlings for the production of organic fruits and vegetables, producers have now invested their own money in greenhouses to cultivate the seedlings for sale. PROEXSAL has invested in the construction and operation of packaging centres, from which deliveries of goods are made to chains of supermarkets, hotels or restaurants. Producer groups in some areas are beginning to assume the costs and management of the centres, with the understanding that PROEXSAL will pay them a higher price for treated and packaged products. The next activity possibly to be taken over by the producers could be the refrigerated transportation system, which represents another value-added activity.

PROEXSAL markets non-traditional agricultural products, mainly organic fruits and vegetables. Organic products enjoy an expanding market in El Salvador due to the presentation of the products and increasing consumer awareness, and the majority of sales are to hotels, restaurants and medium-to-high price supermarkets. PROEXSAL carries out market studies, participates in product development, and trains supermarket personnel on how to handle organic vegetables properly. Yet another service of value to the producers is the channeling of market information back to producers from buyers, who are invited from the capital to visit the packaging centres and co-operatives in order to talk with the producers and share ideas and information on demand, quality, etc.

Performance. At present PROEXSAL generates sufficient income to cover all its costs, and currently has a net profit. PROEXSAL is charging different prices for its services, dependent on whether the services are directed towards the domestic or international market. It charges a 25 per cent commission on gross sales for its services, which include market information, refrigerated transportation, refrigerated storage, quality control, distribution and sales, and recovering payment from buyers. For exports, all of PROEXSAL's income comes from a variable commission charged per unit sold. This commission covers market information, assistance in contract signing, follow-up on the operation, export logistics, quality control, and recovery of payment. Through the use of fees and commissions, the clients become aware of the cost of the services, and consequently of the value of the service provided.

Since PROEXSAL is a co-operative, the clients are also the owners. The way the system is designed, the objective of PROEXSAL is not only to provide marketing services, but also eventually to let the clients take over the operational responsibility for the ancillary services, as was done with the production of seedlings, and which is projected for the packaging centres. PROEXSAL's use of a transparent pricing system, and the producers' willingness to pay, shows that the services are relevant and that producers perceive a gain from the service.

PROEXSAL has grown rapidly, generating annual sales between US$418 000 and US$680 000 in each of the last three years, and projecting increasing annual sales in 1999. From 1995 to 1996, PROEXSAL experienced an increase in sales of more than 600 per cent, accompanied by an increase in administrative costs of 137 per cent. The following year, however, PROEXSAL experienced a sales decrease of 38 per cent due to the failure of a projected production programme, but still an increase in administrative costs of 23 per cent. The level of growth of administrative costs was adjusted to a mere 1 per cent from 1997 to 1998, and projected performance is based on an effort to reduce the growth of administrative costs while increasing growth in sales.

Conclusions: Good practices in the provision of marketing services

Developing strategies

Even if full cost recovery or profitability may not be readily obtained in the short term, evidence shows that marketing services can be provided in a manner that promises a long-term market access for the producers. That implies developing a marketing strategy based on the demands of a particular market, be it local, regional, or international. The PCS case shows that it is possible to penetrate the local market very successfully, if marketing services focus on meeting the demands of local consumers in terms of quality and price. On the other hand, for lack of a domestic market for handicrafts, PROARTE focuses on the international market. PROARTE has benefited from being exposed to the international trend-setting of the larger US and European trade fairs, and each exposure has led to greater security in making decisions about what to produce and for whom. PROEXSAL identified a not-yet exploited local niche market for organic fruits and vegetables.

The institutions themselves have developed strategies for providing marketing services, setting priorities for what which goals they want to achieve. PCS's goal was to reach a large number of low-income producers and provide them with a market for high volumes of low-price products, a goal which they have successfully achieved by following a sound strategy of positioning themselves in the local market. PCS has put less emphasis on obtaining any substantial level of cost recovery, although it is in the process of generating modest surpluses. The strategy of PROARTE, on the other hand, has been to penetrate the international market, with the final objective of generating profit while at the same time providing low-income producers of handicrafts with access to a profitable market. PROARTE operates with full cost recovery but, with more attention to the level of profitability for each product or service, could generate an even greater surplus. PROEXSAL has developed a strategy aimed at providing a number of services to a limited group of producers. The time-phased approach adopted in the partnership with CLUSA results in a decreasing intensity of services, and the gradual take-over of responsibilities by the producers.

The need for ancillary services

In the three case studies the importance of ancillary services was clearly shown. When working with small enterprises, and especially microenterprises, the provision of integrated services has been shown to be one effective way of facilitating market access. Although buying and selling represents market access, and may be a profitable business for the marketing provider, often other less viable ancillary services are necessary for the producers to obtain long-term success in the market. By aiming to overcome constraints in accessing markets, the marketing service providers facilitate production and sales, and at the same time capture certain value-added activities.

Careful measurement of cost and profit

Both PROARTE and PCS are generating their income from a general mark-up system when reselling the products; in the case of PROARTE a mark-up of 50 per cent on all goods, whereas PCS apply a different mark-up, depending on the product. The two institutions are trying to recover costs through their calculation of mark-ups, which is easier than charging the producers a fee. The result is that both the institutions and the producers are in the dark regarding the real costs of the services provided, which perpetuates the situation of unwillingness to pay on the producer side. They will not understand why they should suddenly be required to pay for a service, nor understand the level of payment. On the provider side, decisions on which services to provide or focus on are made based on estimates.

By carefully calculating actual costs and margins of bringing specific goods to market or providing a specific service, the marketing service provider can make decisions on which services or products to focus on in the long term. Introducing such calculations can be costly and strenuous, however, especially if the service provider is working with a number of different products or services, as is PCS. Those who do not introduce such calculations, or improve their mechanism for such calculations, may not be able to progress towards sustainability.

Immediate or short-term cost recovery may be difficult to obtain, but on a long-term basis full cost recovery should be aimed for, and can be reached. Marketing companies seem willing to bear *some* costs, at least for a time, hoping that sales will eventually increase sufficiently to cover not only the operational, but also the administrative costs. Alternatively, services can be developed, and then separated to stand alone. In the case of PROEXSAL, the production of seedlings as input was separated from the other services, and is now a cost-effective service provided on a fee-for-service basis. PCS is planning to isolate the packaging into a separate service for which the producers must pay a fee. Thus, learning the true price of the packaging service, the producer may decide that PCS is not competitive in its prices, and may seek to have packaging done elsewhere. The producers may even suggest taking over packaging themselves, as is the plan for the producers at PROEXSAL.

Sustainability

Long-term success for marketing service providers may depend on their ability to develop focused market strategies and position themselves well in a given market, but long-term success also depends on institutional sustainability, which is linked to the ability to generate sufficient income to cover all costs –

operational and administrative. It may often be the case, however, that a service provider chooses to continue providing a service which produces losses, covering these through cross-subsidizing from another more profitable service or unrelated activity. The mix of services will depend on the goals of the service provider – social or for-profit or both – and will influence institutional sustainability. The ability to generate profits determines the continued presence in the market of a service provider.

Many institutions have relied on donor resources, but since continued support of this type cannot be guaranteed, institutions in Latin America and the Caribbean are innovating to develop alternative financing mechanisms. All three marketing service providers analysed in this chapter started out with donor assistance, but have a vision which instead links the long-term sustainability of their institutions to the profitability of their operations. They all generate surpluses, although they have all struggled for several years to reach relatively modest levels of profitability.

Notes

1. Committee of Donor Agencies for Small Enterprise Development: *Business Development Services for SMEs: Preliminary Guidelines for Donor-Funded Interventions*, January 1998. Goldmark, Lara, Sira Berte and Sergio Campos: *Preliminary Survey Results and Case Studies on Business Development Services*, IDB, 1997.
2. This is a strategy used by other types of business development service providers, as well as marketing service providers. See Goldmark, Chapter 23.
3. Lusby, Frank, 'The Subsector/Trade Group Method: A Demand-Driven Approach to Nonfinancial Assistance for Micro and Small Enterprise. GEMINI Working Paper No. 55. Maryland, 1995.
4. The discussion of PROARTE is based on case study in Goldmark et al. (1997), and on the presentation made by PROARTE at the IDB Conference: Foro Interamericano de la Microempresa, March 1998.
5. The PROEXSAL case study is based on an analysis for project preparation by Lara Goldmark, SDS/MIC, Inter-American Development Bank, 1998.

21. Business development and technology improvement services in India

SANJAY SINHA

Introduction

THE SMALL INDUSTRIES DEVELOPMENT BANK OF INDIA (SIDBI) is a major development finance institution charged with the responsibility of promoting the flow of funds to small-scale productive enterprises both directly and via the formal commercial banking sector. However, in practice the cost structure and operational mechanisms of the bank have meant that SIDBI's funds have tended to levitate to the upper end of the financing scale, leaving the microenterprise sector (with investment less than Rs500 000/US$12 000) relatively unattended by the formal sector.

Recognizing this, SIDBI has for several years been making a special effort to assist the microenterprise sector through its promotion and development programme (P&D), which incorporates elements of both financial and non-financial services. P&D addresses the issue of the promotion of 'tiny' enterprises (investment of less than Rs25 000/US$650) by opening a line of credit through (usually) NGO-operated semi-formal financial institutions, better known as microfinance institutions (MFIs). For the more organized microenterprises (investment in the range Rs25 000–500 000/US$650–12 000), in a developing country situation such as India's, SIDBI has recognized that stimulating the flow of funds requires a more comprehensive approach, including numerous components of technical support ranging from the development of entrepreneurial skills to promoting the transfer of technology from technical research institutions to entrepreneurs.

SIDBI's P&D programme for microenterprises has grown organically over the past five to seven years. It attempts to be progressive and innovative and its components have developed in response to lessons learned from experimentation, observation of similar programmes in India and elsewhere, and dialogue with partner organizations and collaborators such as the Swiss Agency for Development and Co-operation (SDC). As a result, although it has undergone regular modifications based on new experience/information, it has not, so far, been consciously cast into a specific framework, though substantial lessons have been learnt. These lessons are sufficient to facilitate the development of a strategic framework for the provision of cost-effective and (largely) financially sustainable business development/technology improvement services (BTS) to microenterprises.[1]

SIDBI's business and technology services

Objectives

According to SIDBI's Development Report[2] the aim of its promotional and development initiatives is to 'improve the inherent strength of small scale sector on the one hand as also employment generation and economic rehabilitation of the rural poor, on the other'. As explained in the introduction, this chapter covers only the BTS intended for the more organized, formal sector microenterprises.[3] Such services form a sub-set of SIDBI's P&D activities and their objectives – though not specifically differentiated in the Development Report – can be characterized as follows: to accelerate the growth of employment and incomes in small towns and villages of India by promoting the organized microenterprise sector through

- augmentation of the availability of finance for the establishment of such enterprises
- professional support for such enterprises – including information, training, management support, technology improvement and transfer.

Methodology and content of SIDBI's BTS

Those specific components of SIDBI's P&D initiatives, which are characterized in this chapter as comprising BTS for organized microenterprises, are summarized in Table 21.1. Specifically, the

- Rural Industries Programme (RIP), which facilitates the establishment of 'viable and self-sustaining enterprises in rural and semi-urban areas' through the provision of comprehensive enterprise development services and business counselling, ranging from entrepreneur motivation and activity identification through informational, technology support and analytical skills, to credit mobilization and marketing support. The services are provided either by professional consultancy organizations or by not-for-profit development agencies (or NGOs). Coverage is limited to between one and three districts[4] per initiative in order to focus the energies of the service provider and maximize the efficacy of the programme.
- Entrepreneurship Development Programmes (EDPs), which 'aim at training various target groups in entrepreneurial traits', including information, motivation and guidance for setting up their own enterprises. Currently, these are conducted for relatively homogeneous groups such as rural entrepreneurs, women and scheduled caste/tribes. EDPs are (usually) conducted by publicly funded enterprise promotion institutions such as state-level institutes for entrepreneurship development, management or technology institutes, or NGOs with an enterprise orientation. Programmes are usually of six weeks' duration, with participants drawn from within the state or a cluster of districts surrounding the venue of the programme.

- Technology Fund, which consists of a moderate sum of money (of the order of Rs 1 million/US$25 000) presently set aside for individual initiatives for technical study tours by entrepreneurs, short skill training courses for microenterprise workers or other financial support for technology transfer. Sanctions are provided by SIDBI's state-level branch offices to individual microenterprise units working together with the advice and support of an RIP implementing agency.
- Marketing Fund, which is intended to provide either loan or grant support to both small and microenterprises for undertaking market research, market planning, product improvement, advertising/catalogue preparation, participation in trade fairs/exhibitions, establishment of showrooms/warehousing

facilities and training of marketing personnel. The aim is to enable enterprises to increase their sales turnover in domestic or export markets, on the one hand, and to finance larger corporations in providing support services and/or infrastructural facilities for improving the marketing capabilities of the small sector, on the other. The fund is managed by the marketing finance and development department of SIDBI, and proposals are channelled to them by the branch offices.

- Skill-cum-Technology Upgradation Programme (STUP), which is designed to strengthen the managerial skills and technical competence of entrepreneurs through an enhanced awareness of process improvements, technical developments and self-assessment by entrepreneurs of their enterprises. Industry-focused programmes of two to six days are undertaken by institutions such as Indian institutes of technology, regional engineering colleges, Indian institutes of management, and the Institute of Hotel Management and Catering.
- Cluster Technology Upgradation programme (CTUP), which involves the identification of process technology and systemic needs of clusters of similar industrial units by technical consultants. These needs are then addressed through unit-specific interventions co-ordinated by the consultants and financed through grant-cum-loan financial support by SIDBI.

Table 21.1   SIDBI's business and technology services for microenterprises

Service	Description	Coverage	Provides by
Rural Industries Programme (RIP)	Comprehensive enterprise development services and business counselling	Usually 1–3 districts	Professional business consultancy or non-profit development agency [NGO]
Entrepreneurship Development Programmes	Training for development of entrepreneurship skills	Provincial or sub-provincial	Publicly funded entrepreneurship promotion agency or NGO
Technology Fund	Finances for technology transfer or technical skill development	Provincial or sub-provincial	SIDBI branch office usually under advice from RIP agency
Marketing Fund	Finances for marketing or market support initiatives	National	SIDBI Marketing Finance and Development Department; proposals through branch offices
Skill-cum-Technology Upgradation Programme (STUP)	Technical skill development and technology transfer	Local or sub-provincial	Local institutes responsible for technology adaptation transfer
Cluster Technology Upgradation Programme (CTUP)	Environment/pollution technology related services to clusters of enterprises	Local or sub-provicial	Technical consultants

Efficacy and impact of BTS

An indication of the efficacy and impact of the BTS emerges from an evaluation of SIDBI's P&D programmes in the Eastern Region of India and from experience of monitoring various components of P&D in other parts of the country.[5] The progress and impact of BTS are discussed here separately for each component.

Rural industries programme

In a period of nearly four years, from its inception up to the end of March 1998, RIP has been gradually introduced in 36 (out of over 600) districts located in 11 of the 25 states in India. The 23 implementing agencies engaged in the programme had, by March 1998, helped to establish some 5000 enterprise units. Nearly 50 per cent of the promoted units were concentrated in the one state of Andhra Pradesh, where services were provided by Andhra Pradesh Industrial and Technical Consultants Ltd (APITCO). Another 25 per cent were claimed to have been promoted in Orissa, where the service providers were an NGO and a private consultancy, and another 10 per cent in Bihar, where a professional training institute was involved. It is apparent, therefore, that the number of units promoted in each of the other eight states – where implementation had started more recently – was relatively small.

An evaluation of the RIP in Andhra Pradesh, commissioned by SIDBI, and a later review undertaken by SDC showed that:

• project investment in these units ranged from US$30 to US$12 000, but the average was less than US$400.
• the average time taken by each unit to generate a cash surplus was relatively low, at just three months, and 76 per cent of the units were still generating profits some two years later.
• while APITCO had provided some support to each of the entrepreneurs, in a vast majority of the cases the professional support could not be deemed to be crucial in the establishment of the unit. Most of the enterprises had utilized assistance under existing government-sponsored microenterprise development of poverty alleviation programmes. Since such programmes operate with numerical targets, most of the units would have been established even without APITCO's intervention.

The Eastern Region evaluation (covering the state of Orissa and Bihar among others) also showed that:

• since many of the enterprises were established as part of an existing employment generation programme, the RIP service providers were, at best, providing reasonably good post-implementation and follow-up services.
• Support by the service providers at the pre-implementation and project financing stages was either negligible or unnecessary.

Yet the evaluation showed that assistance and advice in obtaining credit was regarded by entrepreneurs as the most important support for establishing new units. Of the four most important factors – credit support, project selection, production training and marketing – only the last had received any significant attention from the service providers.

It is apparent that the RIP implementing agencies were, by and large, not providing the comprehensive business development services envisaged under the programme. Indeed, monitoring feedback from the programme in the Northern and Eastern regions of the country has shown that most service providers have either not fully understood their role in the programme or have taken the path of minimum effort. Thus they have tried to garner the start-up financial support and performance fees paid by SIDBI (discussed below) without necessarily serving the needs of the programme.

Entrepreneurship development programmes

By March 1998, the number of EDPs sponsored by SIDBI amounted to around 750. Some 50 per cent of these were focused on rural youth and another 25 per cent specifically on poor women. The experience with the EDP in the Eastern region indicates a success ratio – in establishing enterprises – of the order of 50 per cent (with a range between 10 and 80 per cent). A wide range of differences between the EDP-providing institutions occurs in terms of skilled trainers, content and organization of the training and, most importantly, follow-up as well as in the financial commitment of the training institution. Some institutions have tried to cut corners in the practical content of their programme and follow-up. Others, however, provided a complete range of high quality training and motivation services and achieved a good success rate.

Technology fund

This is, potentially, a highly useful but underused support fund. Although the fund was created some three years ago, the number of technology support activities sanctioned has been extremely small (fewer than 10) and utilization has been around 25 per cent. This is attributable to its low profile implementation by SIDBI, resulting in very few personnel of RIP service providers and, by extension, entrepreneurs (covered by RIP) being aware of its existence. Support activities undertaken include training in fruit processing for rural women entrepreneurs in Bihar, and a study tour from Malda district in Eastern India to Surat (on the west coast) to identify appropriate silk weaving machinery.

Marketing fund

The Marketing Fund has become increasingly popular as it has become better known and, by March 1998, 76 proposals worth Rs145 million (US$3.5 million) had been sanctioned – nearly 95 per cent as loans. The bulk of this is for setting up showrooms and retail outlets and for other marketing, distribution and sales promotion activities. However, due to problems in completing collateral and other administrative formalities, less than a third of this (US$1.1 million) had actually been utilized. Case studies of activities promoted by the Marketing Fund show that it has:

- been instrumental in helping rural handicraft enterprises in various parts of the country to find urban markets, both by facilitating participation in fairs and exhibitions in cosmopolitan cities – Delhi, Mumbai, Bangalore – with large markets of upper class consumers, and by establishing modern showrooms in smaller cities like Patna (the state capital of Bihar), where such facilities did not exist before
- enabled the establishment of a brand and home delivery marketing of spices, honey and jams to urban households
- facilitated marketing links between a large honey trader and processor in Mumbai with small rural producers in Bihar.

Skill-cum-technology upgradation programme

SIDBI had sponsored around 400 STUPs covering some 9000 participants all over the country until March 1998. These covered diverse areas like product/process technology, quality control, industrial design, export management, computer applications and working capital management in homogeneous industry clusters like fruit/food processing, leather goods, ready-made garments, plastic processing, welding, foundries and packaging. Evaluations of the programme – all over India as well as in the Eastern region – show that, by and large:

- participants find STUPs relevant and useful in disseminating 'state of the art' knowledge of technologies affecting their industries, although
- there is a need for the technical institutions to sharpen their focus on disseminating practical techniques through interactive methods rather than just imparting theoretical knowledge, and that
- if the programmes were conducted on a part-time basis, to enable entrepreneurs to spend a part of each day in running their units, the attentiveness of the participants and utility of the programmes would be greatly enhanced.

Cluster Technology Upgradation Programme

Since its formation in 1990, SIDBI has undertaken CTUPs in some 20 different homogeneous clusters in different parts of the country. While, in the initial years, interventions in clusters such as the salt industry in Kutch, the machine tool industry in Rajkot and the rubber industry in Kottayam, were not very successful, important lessons were learned. Emerging from these lessons, the programme was re-oriented to ensure that interventions were based on careful demand assessments by technical consultants. Over the past three years, the programme has focused on some 10 industry clusters, incorporating modernization studies of around 450 units and resulting in technological improvements in over 200 units so far. Information available on the impact of the programme indicates significant improvements in profitability (for the bicycle industry in Ludhiana, brass and bell metal industry in Assam, and the lock industry in Aligarh). As a major benefit, the foundry cluster at Howrah (in Calcutta) reports a drastic reduction in pollution levels and movement towards conforming with local pollution control norms.

Financing mechanisms and cost effectiveness assessment of services

A broad indication of the financial mechanisms used and the present status of cost-recovery in SIDBI's BTS is provided in Table 21.2.

Cost effectiveness of the RIP

The work of the service providers – referred to by SIDBI as the implementing agencies – involved in the RIP is funded in two ways. During the first year of the agency's operations in any district SIDBI pays start-up expenses (the subsidy referred to in Table 21.2), of the order of US$2000 per district, to cover initial overhead and professional costs. From the second year onwards, the agency is expected to 'earn' its expenses by way of performance incentives (fees for provider's services) paid by SIDBI at the rate of US$36–120 per unit for investments ranging from up to US$700 to over US$4800.

Table 21.2   Financing mechanisms for SIDBI's BTS

Service	Financing mechanism	Status of cost recovery
Rural Industries Programme	Start up grant by SIDBI (first year only) 'Performance incentive' for establishment/follow up of enterprises	Subsidy to service provider Fees for provider's services yield 70–100% cost recovery, but constitutes subsidy to enterprise
Entrepreneurship Development Programmes	Potential entrepreneur pays small registration/training fee Additional expenses paid by SIDBI	Less than 20% from trainees
Technology Fund	Loans/grants for technology transfer Grants for skill training	Less than 10% since most assistance is in grant form
Marketing Fund	Loans for marketing infrastructure/trade fairs Grant for market research, pilot marketing, branding, publicity	80–90% in the form of loans at commercial interest rates
Skill-cum-Technology Upgradation Programme (STUP)	Training/technology transfer fees charged to entrepreneurs; additional expenses borne by SIDBI Loans for modernization	35% cost recover achieved in 27 sample programmes at commercial rates
Cluster Technology Upgradation Programme (CTUP)	Loans for technology improvement/pollution control Grants for technical advice	More effort required to generate demand for this socially beneficial service

SIDBI's total expenditure on the RIP up to March 1998 amounts to US$59 000, consisting of $10 500 by way of start-up expenses and around $48 500 in performance fees. Though service providers have claimed incentives for the promotion of around 5000 enterprises, SIDBI has paid out only 26 per cent of these claims so far. While some of these claims are still under assessment, monitoring experience shows that no more than 35 per cent of these claims will eventually be paid as there are serious questions about whether the implementing agencies really played a serious role in the promotion of most of these units. On this basis, the cost effectiveness of the RIP can be assessed as in Table 21.3.

Table 21.3   Cost effectiveness of the RIP

	Average per unit/ enterprise promoted	Total for all RIP activities
Units claimed to have been promoted		5000
Claims likely to be accepted	Proportion: 35%	1750
Performance fees likely to be paid	US$39	US$68 250
Start-up expenses disbursed to implementing agencies		US$10 500
SIDBI's monitoring costs (estimated)[6]		US$12 850
Total expenses incurred by SIDBI	US$52	US$91 600
Capital invested in the units promoted	US$740	US$1 295 000
Expected annual production in the units promoted	US$1500	US$2 625 000
Expected (minimum) return on investment	100%	
SIDBI's investment as a proportion of annual returns	7%	

285

It is apparent that, even allowing for the large proportion of units for which the claims are not acceptable to SIDBI, the average investment made by it in the enterprises promoted is not a significant proportion of the net annual income of the enterprise. RIP, therefore, appears to be a highly cost-effective programme.

EDPs

The financing of EDPs is undertaken directly by SIDBI with the training institution. Each institution is expected to recover from trainees 15–20 per cent of the overall cost of the EDP. It is apparent from Table 21.4 that, in effect, SIDBI spends $137 per trainee who either establishes a unit or already operates one.

Table 21.4 EDP costs

Training programmes, no.	750
Average expenditure on EDPs	US$1190
Total expenditure on EDPs	US$895 000
Trainees, no.	14 000
Operational units, no.	6500
Expenditure per unit established	US$137

Although a few of the entrepreneurs trained through EDPs may be the same as those assisted under RIP, this is rare and, indeed, the average investment in rural enterprises established through EDPs is likely to be far lower – around US$300–500. In this situation, the investment of $137 per successful trainee may be relatively high but it is adequately compensated by the higher average returns on investment (200–500 per cent) in these smaller microenterprises, and makes the exercise worthwhile.

Technology fund

As indicated earlier, the utilization of this US$25 000 fund has been just 25 per cent and it has not needed any replenishment since its creation three years ago. Virtually all assistance has been in the form of grants for skill training and technology transfer. The efficacy of these grants is highly variable, but is usually considerable when utilized for technology selection or transfer by serious entrepreneurs. On other occasions it has, unfortunately, been sourced to finance NGOs' supply-led skill training programmes – such as that for fruit processing in Bihar – leading to very little follow-up action.

Marketing fund

It is apparent that, with more experience than that available for the Technology Fund, the Marketing Fund has evolved into a more business-like venture. Total disbursements from the fund amount to US$1.1 million (though sanctions are nearly US$3.5 million) of which only 12.5 per cent consists of grants. As discussed earlier, this has become an effective means of facilitating market promotion. However, monitoring experience also suggests that it is used more productively when utilized by private sector initiatives than by NGOs with a (sometimes) questionable commitment to efficiency.

STUPs

The design of STUPs involves maximizing cost recovery from participants and financing the deficit by SIDBI in two ways:

- release of individual programme-based grants to specific training/professional institutions conducting each course. Such programme-based provisions have averaged US$1100 over the past two years.
- provision of lump-sum corpus grants ranging from US$24 000 to US$54 000 (average US$40 000) to identified institutions with the requisite experience to provide some three to seven STUPs (and one to two longer small industries management programmes) each year. The idea of such grants is to enable the training institution to fund deficits (after cost recovery from participants) out of income from the corpus.

The institutions conducting STUP courses are asked by SIDBI to recover, in participant fees, as much as possible of the costs. While some institutions take this request seriously and market their courses actively, others – accustomed to the *ancien régime* of subsidized technical education – are yet to take this seriously. As a result, cost recovery varies from a high of around 100 per cent for one institution and around 70 per cent for another, to just 10–25 per cent for others, resulting in an average cost recovery of US$46 per participant. Thus, sample data indicate that, on average, institutions have recovered from participants 35 per cent of the average US$1700 cost of conducting STUPs. By and large, there is a direct link between the practical orientation of the institution – in terms of meeting the needs of participants – and cost recovery.

SIDBI also encourages the training institutions to promote links between entrepreneurs and commercial banks to facilitate the utilization of the knowledge gained by the latter from the training. However, information on the results of this facilitation is not collected and it is therefore impossible to assess its impact.

CTUP

Under the CTUP, SIDBI pays fees to technical consultants for reviewing the modernization needs of clusters of industries and then provides loan-cum-grant assistance to individual units for implementing the recommended measures. Over the 20 clusters covered so far, SIDBI has spent roughly US$380 000, resulting in technological improvements in some 200 enterprises – mostly larger units in the small industry sector. Where clusters of organized microenterprises are involved – such as in the bicycle parts industry in Ludhiana and shoemaking in the north-east – small focused interventions have resulted in substantial benefits. Thus, in the case of the bicycle parts cluster as many as 41 enterprises are reported to have gained from SIDBI's support, amounting to US$18 000 (average: $440 per enterprise). Of these, 18 utilized loans from commercial banks and SIDBI for undertaking improvements, and another 23 implemented the recommended measures with their own resources. The net increase of 21–53 per cent of sales resulting from these measures amounts to an increase in turnover of the order of US$150 000 per annum (or more than eight times SIDBI's initial investment).

A strategic framework

According to a recent study, there were nearly 25 million microenterprises in India in 1990 employing some 45 million workers. While many of these are in the formal microenterprise class not covered by the scope of this chapter, there were as many as 900 000 units with six to nine workers, employing over six million people.[7] Based on this information, it can reasonably be estimated that the market of formal sector microenterprises for SIDBI's BTS is enormous – of the order of three million enterprises employing around 15 million workers. Given India's size as a country, and the extent of the poverty problem, the potential benefits to the spread of effective BTS are substantial.

The above discussion of the cost effectiveness of SIDBI's support to formal sector microenterprises indicates a pattern of growing experience in providing focused BTS to this sector. However, it also indicates a varied experience in which each component of the BTS has been separately identified and implemented, largely piecemeal. Thus, while some of the individual components have yielded results, others have not been so effective. None has yet reached substantial numbers relative to the size of the sector.

Thus, although formal enterprise training could clearly be beneficially linked to entrepreneurs identified under the RIP, the linkage with EDP has not, up to now, been officially recognized by SIDBI. Similarly, STUPs and CTUPs have also not been directly organized for RIP-assisted enterprises.[8] Finally, service providers have not, so far, been encouraged to guide RIP enterprises to use the facilities of the marketing fund.

What the figure essentially shows is that the RIP could form the basis for SIDBI's efforts in providing BTS, with all other components clearly linked to it. In this situation, RIP service providers would be directly responsible for ensuring appropriate utilization of the BTS and for improving the access of entrepreneurs and enterprises to all its components. Clearly, this has substantial implications for the competence, approach and commitment of the RIP service providers, on the one hand, as well as for the resources and support to be provided by SIDBI, on the other. By extension, there are also specific implications for the design of the other components of BTS and for the institutions engaged in their implementation. These are considered in the following section.

Lessons for good practice in BTS

The lessons for good practice in the implementation of BTS emerging from evaluation, monitoring and direct RIP implementation experience can be considered in the context of the analytical framework shown in Table 21.5.

First, the discussion in the previous section indicates the need for making strategic improvements. It clearly establishes a linkage between all the components of BTS and RIP, tilting – in the context of Table 21.5 – the range of services offered in the direction of the wide ranging from the limited services presently offered by many service providers.

Table 21.5

| | | Implementation (skills, resources, systems) | |
		Good	Poor
Range of services offered	Wide-ranging	Success	– need to change implementation arrangements
	Limited	– make appropriate strategic improvements	Failure – discontinue the programme

It is apparent that, for this purpose, the design of some components would have to be recast in order to fit them together in one strategic framework. Thus,

- EDP would most appropriately be limited to formal enterprise training when conducted for RIP enterprises, with follow-up undertaken by the service provider, and
- STUP and CTUP support would be facilitated by the sector-focused RIPs – silk production and processing, honey production/processing and floriculture – now being implemented in the Eastern Region.

Second, good service providers have to extend themselves beyond moral support, informal marketing advice and assistance in completing forms for loans or subsidies. These constitute no more than the minimalist effort necessary to garner SIDBI's performance incentive.

Good practice extends to proactive involvement in feasible activity identification, choice of technology, capital (including credit) mobilization and post-implementation follow-up with marketing advice, and such (apparently minor but potentially disastrous) issues as working capital management.

The skills required by the service provider for this purpose include:

- the ability to undertake activity and microeconomic feasibility analysis
- knowledge of the focused sub-sector(s) and the basic technologies available within it
- understanding of financial issues and the appraisal requirements of banks
- basic management skills and appreciation of the practical realities of business
- exposure to, and understanding of, the needs of markets
- an analytical approach to production/productivity and quality issues, and
- a concern for environmental issues.

Experience shows that this list of qualities, though apparently formidable, is nevertheless essential for successful and mutually beneficial implementation of the BTS. To the extent that the list is formidable, it emphasizes the perception that BTS is not an activity to be entrusted to the average organization with mediocre skills and, usually, poor motivation systems. It is, on the other hand, an activity that can be successfully carried forward by professional organizations with experience of the specific microeconomic sub-sectors promoted. Inevitably, this experience and knowledge needs to be combined with a motivated and entrepreneurial approach to service provision.

Thus, with small changes of approach, the strategic framework for SIDBI's BTS set out in the previous section, can present a fairly cohesive picture. However, the reorientation in the methodology of implementing the programme signalled by the new sub-sectoral focus of RIP activities needs to be accompanied by the choice and encouragement of appropriate service providers in order to enhance programme efficacy. For this purpose, a reorientation within SIDBI from the mind-set of risk-averse programme 'controllers' to entrepreneurial 'innovation catalysts' needs to be initiated. Institutional morbidity within India may retard this process in the short term but, in the long term, insistence on a quality-oriented and innovative approach will, undoubtedly, yield substantive benefits to a large and well-dispersed set of micro-entrepreneurs.[9]

Notes

1. These will, henceforth, be referred to as business & technology services (BTS).
2. SIDBI, 1997. SIDBI Development Report: Promotional and Development Initiatives for Small Industries. Lucknow: Small Industries Development Bank of India, October. Much of the narrative of this section is obtained from this report, interpreted by the author based on experience with the programme.
3. The distinction made here is between individual microenterprise financed by mainstream financial institutions and the specific poverty-focused components for 'tiny enterprises' – such as the Micro-Credit Scheme and Mahila Vikas Nidhi (Women's Development Fund) implemented through non-formal micro-finance institutions (MFIs). Programmes such as the Small Industries Management Appreciation Programme (SIMAP) intended for the larger units of the small enterprise sector are also excluded here.
4. An area with an average radius of 100 km and population of around three million.
5. Various exercises undertaken by the author's institution, EDA Rural Systems Private Limited – a development consultancy company based outside New Delhi.
6. Estimated generously, 15 per cent of the costs paid to SIDBI's regional monitoring agencies during the past three years.
7. EDA, 1996. India: Microenterprise Country Paper for the Asian Development Bank. Gurgaon India: EDA Rural Systems.
8. Although it may be argued that, in the absence of clusters of similar enterprises supported under the RIP, STUP and CTUP have been inappropriate programmes for establishing such a linkage.
9. The assistance of my colleagues Ramesh Arunachalam – who undertook the Eastern Region evaluation – and Frances Sinha in providing insight and comments on this paper is gratefully acknowledged. Other work for SIDBI has been undertaken by various EDA teams including, in particular, Ashok Kumar, Rajesh Mishra, Tanmay Chetan and Shipra Goyal.

22. A market-based approach to BDS: the FIT project

JIM TANBURN

Abstract

This chapter outlines experiences gained in providing BDS through private-sector channels, tailored as closely as possible to the market demand for specific services. The objectives have been to formulate services which could be provided profitably, and to stimulate provision of those services by entrepreneurial providers. Services are listed for which small-scale entrepreneurs are willing to pay the full cost; early experiences in commercializing these services are also described. The chapter draws on lessons learned in Africa, Asia and Europe.

Introduction

THE FIT PROJECT[1] started in 1993 to ask the question: how can business development services (BDS) be offered to small enterprises in ways that are financially sustainable, and even profitable? The importance of financial sustainability has been underlined by the success in recent years of methodologies for the provision of financial services to small enterprises; these methodologies have shown that entrepreneurs are willing to pay for services that are closely tailored to their needs. FIT therefore set out to determine how this insight might be applied in the field of BDS. It focused in two specific areas, around which this chapter is structured:

- what BDS are in demand? How can these services be defined and developed, so that they closely match the perceived needs of entrepreneurs? (the 'micro' level)
- how can these services be offered, so that the prospects for sustainability are maximized? (the 'meso' level)

In order to keep as open a mind as possible on the types of BDS in demand by small-scale entrepreneurs, a very broad definition was adopted by FIT; this flexibility ensured that innovative possibilities could be explored. Thus, any non-financial support service needed by an enterprise in its operations was included; the definition was not limited, for example, only to those services that enable an enterprise to develop and grow.

Most of the experience reported here was gained in Africa, but related insights and lessons from Asia and Europe are also included; many of the principles developed through this work seem to be applicable to business development work anywhere, since they draw as much as possible on the fundamental commercial realities of running a small enterprise. Indeed, the challenge has been to find ways of working within the private sector, rather than in parallel with it. This seems to be the key to achieving the scale and dynamism required.

What BDS are in demand?

The design of many projects is based on a survey of perceived needs among entrepreneurs. There may also be a set of methodologies which have been successful elsewhere, and which are now to be adapted to local conditions. Generally, there is also a partner organization already in place, with its own views on project design. It is therefore, in practice, not easy to launch a project with a completely open mind about what services may be in demand. In particular, and while it is vital to understand the perceived needs of entrepreneurs locally, major surveys of perceived needs can suffer from the following drawbacks:

- it is very difficult for entrepreneurs to give a view on whether or not they would like (and even pay for) services that they have never seen before; such a survey will therefore not reveal much about the potential for innovative BDS developing economies can change rapidly, and the evidence suggests that the priorities of entrepreneurs depend on the macroeconomic conditions at the time; a survey is only a 'snapshot' at one particular moment, and a project built too rigidly on its findings may find that it lags behind perceived needs surveys often adopt a certain definition of BDS, unintentionally excluding some innovative support services with high potential.

Similarly, if the project already has a methodology that has been successful elsewhere, experts must then make a link between the expressed or observed needs, and the existing methodology; the subsequent project may then need a mandate to 'educate' the target group on the need for this methodology. This can apply even to the basic format; for example, many owners of very small businesses are sceptical about the desirability of formal training, and projects often have to work hard to convince such people of the merits of investing their time and energies in such training.

This is important, in that training is the most important single BDS in terms of development financing, and it is often provided in quite formal ways. Indeed, BDS generally seem to have clear roots in services developed for larger companies in industrialized economies; while some modifications have been made along the way, formality still prevails. FIT therefore decided to adopt a different sequence in identifying BDS:

- starting with a completely clean sheet of paper, FIT listened very closely to entrepreneurs, in order to discover exactly what they considered to be their constrains, and what types of BDS they might be willing to pay for, in addressing those constraints
- starting points identified in this way were then developed through dialogue, drawing cautiously on ideas and experience in BDS provision by the for-profit private sector in other countries
- the services identified through this dialogue were then marketed on a pilot basis; initial offers were partially subsidized, on condition that the entrepreneur clients gave feedback on the design of the service
- the design of the service was then modified as quickly as possible in response to this feedback, so that it could conform more closely to what entrepreneurs wanted to pay for.

This change in approach brought with it some rather profound shifts in the way of working. For example, entrepreneurs were no longer beneficiaries, carefully selected to receive largesse; they became discerning (and often supportive) clients. No longer was it so easy to probe into every aspect of their lives in the quest for impact; after all, they had purchased a service, and had no obvious obligation to reveal every personal detail as well. On the other hand, communications became much easier; entrepreneurs have little idea what is meant by terms such as 'cost recovery' or even 'sustainability', but they can readily relate to the aim of making a service profitable.

The services that emerged from this process had their roots in one of the following areas:

- services that entrepreneurs were already providing to each other, on an informal basis, and which no one had thought to formalize
- services already provided within the private sector, often formally, but which had been largely ignored by development agencies
- services already provided by the private sector in industrialized countries, but not generally seen yet in some developing countries.

Examples are given below of services in each of these categories.

Can informal BDS be formalized?

A close examination of services that entrepreneurs already consider to be of value revealed that they intuitively felt that they would benefit from increased contact with other entrepreneurs, particularly those enjoying some success, and based outside their immediate locale. Often, they did not have a clear idea of what the likely benefits of that contact would be, but demand was certainly strong.

There were many 'clues' to this; for example, one of the few BDS already provided by associations of small businesses is the chance to visit other groups and associations, for the exchange of experience, ideas, knowledge and contacts. This was remarkable, in that associations in Africa often seem to have their roots in mutual support and social gatherings, rather than in the provision of BDS. Another indication came from development agencies providing micro-finance; one of the requests most commonly articulated by their clients was noted to be the chance to visit other clients, elsewhere.

FIT therefore offered the chance to visit other businesses, to explore whether this could form the basis for a new industry, tentatively named 'business tourism'. Experience has now been gained with over 1400 trips in six countries in East and West Africa. Entrepreneurs are willing to pay the full cost of such trips, providing that the format and marketing are right, and that costs are contained. It has become clear that an external agency can add value here, since otherwise entrepreneurs find it difficult to go outside their immediate locale.

It is also clear that, as with micro-loans, such visits are of interest only to the smaller enterprises; larger enterprises have their own networks (Rotary, Chambers of Commerce etc.) through which to achieve such exchanges. It is also clear that, when they need to, entrepreneurs with small businesses can find the sums required to make such tours viable; demand is strong for tours costing $100–200 per person. The aim of this work was not simply to create a new business opportunity, but rather to define a profitable service which also had substantial development impact. Willingness to pay is important, but FIT also looked at the impact that these visits achieved. Actually, similar visits have been used for many years in agricultural extension, albeit in highly subsidized ways, so it seemed reasonable to suppose that some impact could also be achieved through the promotion of business tourism.

External evaluations have indeed found a wide range of benefits among visiting entrepreneurs; the most frequently cited included new production processes (including safer working practices), new product designs, new sources of spare parts, improved relations with customers and employees, and increased self-confidence (Hileman, 1995). Eighty per cent achieved greatly increased sales (more than 45 per cent improvement), spending the extra profits on business expansion (58 per cent), school fees, clearing debts, getting married, land or livestock. On average, each employed 2.5 additional staff.

In addition to business tourism, there are many services provided informally, and which could perhaps be provided more formally in the longer term. For example, entrepreneurs depend on information and advice gleaned from family, friends, suppliers and customers (in small enterprises, the four groups often overlap considerably). The information and advice provided is often of poor quality, relating only to short-term needs and generic areas rather than to specific problems and opportunities (Allal et al., 1997).

FIT has therefore experimented with the facilitation of forums in which entrepreneurs can communicate more effectively with customers and traders. For example, a sequence of meetings was set up between groups of metalworkers and groups of farmers in western Kenya. Seven months after the sequence had started, a range of innovative, agriculture-related equipment had been designed, and sales were strong; on average, each participating enterprise had sold new types of equipment, worth $700 (KIC-K, 1996).

This experience showed that small-scale entrepreneurs can be innovative, designing and developing new and improved products which their customers want to buy. A key constraint in this process seems to be the lack of opportunities for constructive communication with those customers, on product design and the optimum quality–price mix. When those opportunities are provided, small enterprises can respond effectively (Tanburn, 1996). The process has now been formalized as a new service termed 'user-led innovation' (ULI); it is presented as a new training 'product' for existing for-profit trainers in the private sector. These trainers are profiled in the following section.

Existing BDS: More formal but still neglected

Many BDS are provided to small enterprises by the private sector, but have not been incorporated into project design on a widespread basis. The traditional apprenticeship system, for example, probably provides more vocational training than all of the formal institutions combined, in many countries, but only a few projects have sought practical ways in which to enhance that existing system. Similarly, FIT has found, through detailed surveys in Uganda and Zimbabwe, a thriving private sector, providing training to small-scale entrepreneurs on a for-profit basis in a wide range of skills.

In Uganda, FIT identified 160 independent trainers and 89 small-scale private training institutions. In Zimbabwe, 90 small training businesses have been identified; cross-checking with a DFID-supported study (Bennell, 1997) revealed an additional 32. An active effort was needed to find these trainers; they often advertise only by word of mouth, as they cater for training needs in their immediate locale. They may also be apprehensive about the time-consuming registration requirements, should they enter the mainstream training sector. As a result, the numbers reported above probably understate the size of the sector.

These 'back-street' training companies offer a wide range of courses, covering both business management skills (accountancy, marketing, import–export trading, clearing and forwarding, business planning and administration, etc.) and vocational skills (hairdressing, tailoring, hotel and tourism, food production, woodwork and metalwork, etc.)

More courses were found in Uganda than in Zimbabwe; this might be partly because public sector provision is less developed, and partly because the regulatory environment in Zimbabwe does not make life easy for the smallest trainers. Also, there is apparently rather less management training on offer in Zimbabwe, but proportionately more training available in computer-related skills. The lower offer of management skills may again be because the large-scale, formal training sector is more developed in its offer of management training in Zimbabwe, than in Uganda.

Meanwhile, the offer of computer training in Uganda is hampered by a number of factors (not least the quality of the electricity supply). The focus in Zimbabwe on dress-making and tailoring skills is remarkable, whereas Ugandan trainers are offering a much broader range of vocational skills. Tanzania has more of a spread of vocational skills, and indeed a greater emphasis on vocational skills generally.

Because of the existence of this training capacity, FIT has not launched any training services aimed directly at small enterprises. Instead, it has offered training-of-trainers (ToT) courses to the private trainers, and these experiences are described later (under 'Strengthening existing private sector BDS providers').

BDS already provided elsewhere by the for-profit sector

It might be imagined that BDS provision in industrialized countries can offer useful insights and pointers for providers in developing countries. FIT therefore made a preliminary study of BDS provision in the UK, with financial support from DFID (Tanburn, 1998). One of the most outstanding observations from this study was the contrast between publicly funded BDS providers in the UK, and donor-funded provision in developing countries.

This contrast is not limited to the UK; a comparative analysis of support for service providers in the Netherlands and Zimbabwe, for example, noted a greater emphasis in Zimbabwe on financial sustainability (van den Berg, 1995). Publicly funded BDS provision in industrialized countries has often been designed with different objectives in view, and may not always be considered to have been particularly successful, even in its home environment (Havers, 1998).

The study tour did note, however, a large number of other BDS, provided in the UK on a commercial basis; they included:

- publication of magazines, aimed at growing small enterprises, and generating revenues through the sale of advertising to larger companies, and/or diversification into contract publishing and other services
- organization of regional, multi-sectoral exhibitions for small enterprises
- support services provided as part of franchise packages.

All of these services probably have the potential to be introduced commercially in developing countries. The service selected by FIT for pilot introduction was that of the publication aimed at the small enterprise market, in terms of both information and advertising. The very wide range of publications in industrialized countries, catering for the marketing and information needs of small enterprises, is impressive. These publications include both specialist trade journals and free (or low-cost) publications carrying a large number of classified advertisements.

Meanwhile, small enterprises in developing countries can face formidable constraints in both obtaining commercially valuable information, and in reaching new markets. In particular, the cost of reaching new markets can be very high, mainly because there are few established channels through which to do so. Those channels (national newspapers, television, etc.) are also rarely focused sufficiently on the target groups they need to reach.

In several countries in Africa, FIT has therefore reviewed demand for both information and for advertising among small enterprises; in all cases, demand has been found to be strong. Entrepreneurs report that the chance to advertise outside their existing customer base (and to include helpful information, for example on how to find their business) is of great interest. Similarly, larger companies selling goods and services into the small enterprise sector appear very interested to purchase advertising focused at the target group, since they often have no way to do this at the moment.

FIT is therefore launching, or planning to launch, advertising papers in four countries; early sales of advertising have been encouraging. In general, the papers are following a similar format. Large copy advertisements are sold to larger enterprises at rates that are similar to those of national newspapers (but offering more specific targeting); these sales generate most of the publication's income. Smaller classified advertisements are available at much lower cost. The papers are distributed throughout the local business community; where a cover price is charged, it is only minimal.

One important feature of these operations is that they are not commercially viable through the contributions of the target group alone. Large companies wishing to access the target group as a potential market become the chief source of revenue. Since this group is acting on a commercial interest (rather than out of philanthropy, for example), it seems reasonable to assume that they will continue to fund the venture, for as long as it provides them with an important service. It seems fair, therefore, to include this type of funding within the category of 'sustainable'.

Clearly, however, there are many other BDS which could be offered commercially, and which could assist large numbers of small enterprises to grow, and so to employ more people. Some of these services would probably be introduced by the private sector in due course; a major role of the development agency in this case is to accelerate the process. At the same time, the service can be designed so that developmental concerns are also reflected in its delivery. The key factor to bear in mind here is that a very large number of people are involved in small enterprises; services which cater exactly to their needs are therefore tapping into a large (and still largely unreached) market with great commercial potential.

How can BDS best be provided, to achieve sustainability?

Most of the experiences outlined above were gained while working through NGOs, but a number of limitations were experienced in this approach.

- Many NGOs have rather focused outreach and target groups, for example geographically within a specific town or province; 'scaling up' BDS to national and even international level therefore becomes difficult. In addition, few yet aim to develop and deliver innovative BDS products as part of their core mandate.
- The running costs and culture of NGOs may be influenced (albeit unintentionally) by relations with external funders and other collaborators, and are not necessarily very close to those of most small enterprises locally.

- NGOs are perceived by entrepreneurs to be non-profit, receiving substantial external funds (which are often reported in the newspapers, and therefore widely known about). Many entrepreneurs feel strongly that such organizations should not be charging substantial fees for their services, but should rather be passing on the largesse from which the NGO itself is benefiting.

These arguments – and particularly the last one – seemed to provide a compelling rationale for exploring other vehicles through which to deliver services to small enterprises. After all, the NGO format originated in industrialized countries, where the dispensers of charity wanted to be sure that their generosity was not being abused through the enrichment of one company or individual. In developing countries, the same format reassured donors and their constituencies, not least because it related closely to their experiences at home. In addition, it was considered sensible to provide core funding to deserving organizations, and non-profit status made such core funding much easier to justify. Recently, however, the soporific effect of such funding has been widely noted.

Indeed, the world of SED has changed in many respects, and the time is therefore ripe for reviewing the ways in which services are delivered to small enterprises. In this context, it is interesting to note that NGOs offering financial services are also examining ways in which they can operate more within the private sector; for example through the establishment of banks. So FIT also started to address the question: how might the improved provision of BDS be stimulated through other means, and particularly through the private sector? Might not donor funding be provided to private service providers, to deliver measurable services? Thus, contracts would be strictly performance-based (as they are already with consultancy firms), rather than containing elements of core funding. They would also be designed with an exit strategy in view, probably articulated in the form of a business plan, showing the point at which the BDS was expected to become profitable.

Experiences gained in this search are outlined below, under two headings:

- the introduction of a new BDS product (i.e., not previously seen in the country) on a commercial basis
- the strengthening of existing private sector BDS providers

Introducing a new BDS product on a commercial basis

The introduction of a new BDS on a commercial basis carries the potential of building on local entrepreneurial talent. But the availability of temporary subsidies carries with it the danger that this introduction displaces existing initiatives within the private sector. An important first step, when introducing a new service, has therefore been to mount a thorough search for anyone who is already offering a similar or related service. This search can actually be a part of the search for a local partner or entrepreneur, with whom the service can be introduced.

To this end, FIT has advertised extensively in national papers for partners; it has also run competitions for people with the best ideas for new services. It has undertaken extensive searches through word of mouth, and by contracting local companies which seem likely to have related interests (e.g. local travel agencies, in the case of business tourism).

In all of this, FIT has moved away from the appearance of a 'project office' and more towards that of a foreign investor – looking for opportunities to invest in BDS which can ultimately be commercially viable. An important point to note about this approach is that it requires a funding agency that is not insistent on seeing its name and support credited at every opportunity. Commitment by the funding agency to the basic concepts involved is therefore vital to success.

The search for a local partner with whom to launch a new service has generally been formulated as a joint venture between the project office and the local entrepreneur (or company). In this context, the following criteria have been used.

- The partner should be sufficiently interested in the venture to provide a substantial proportion of the start-up capital required (25 per cent, say), either in cash or in kind.
- The partner should also be bringing expertise, contacts, infrastructure and other elements that the development agency does not have, and could not otherwise readily access.
- The partner should also have a good track record of business success and integrity; it should not be entering the joint venture as a failing business looking for a lifeline, but rather as a successful business looking for opportunities for expansion.
- Ideally, the partner should also be a small enterprise; costs are likely to be lower, and understanding of the sector to be higher.

Once launched, joint ventures can also require considerable management inputs from the project office, although the external financing required can remain quite modest (US$40 000 per venture may be sufficient). These funds represent the input required to persuade a local entrepreneur to enter a new sector with a new service. Once the joint venture becomes profitable, returns on the investment can (potentially) be used to launch new ventures and services; it is expected that the services themselves may also be replicated through franchising to other local entrepreneurs. FIT continues to implement this approach on a pilot basis in a number of countries.

Strengthening existing private sector BDS providers

As outlined above, FIT has devoted some time to trying to identify for-profit service providers locally (excluding those accessing public funds in one form or another). As a result of these searches, FIT is working with existing private sector trainers of small enterprises, in Uganda and Zimbabwe. In both these countries, the trainers have expressed strong demand for support in upgrading what they were able to offer to small enterprises. FIT has therefore offered training-of-trainers (ToT) courses in two 'products': rapid market appraisal (RMA) and user-led innovation (ULI).

Both courses are short, and show entrepreneurs how to become more market-oriented in their businesses; RMA covers the basics of market research for individual entrepreneurs, while ULI provides a setting where groups of entrepreneurs meet with groups of their customers. Despite their very modest incomes, trainers have been willing to pay around US$40 per ToT course in Uganda; initial evidence suggests that some have then been able to market their new products on a commercial basis to local entrepreneurs.

The interface between this part of the private sector, and development agencies, has not always been straightforward. For example, mixing private-sector trainers and NGO trainers in the same ToT courses has led to complications, because of the different educational standards and financial expectations. Similarly, development agencies providing technical support for ToT courses may require trainers to provide extensive monitoring reports post-training. Meanwhile, private sector trainers are just trying to make a living, and have neither the time nor (often) the skills to measure the impact of their training. Again, willingness to pay is an interesting, and perhaps necessary, proxy indication of impact.

The most remarkable feature of these training businesses is their low financial scale; independent trainers in Uganda were found to be earning US$80–160 per month from their training activities, while training institutes paid US$40–80 per month to their predominantly part-time trainers. The range of incomes found in Zimbabwe was rather larger, but trainers at the bottom end were earning very little, even by Ugandan standards. This is a clear contrast with trainers paid by development agencies, often in the range of US$100–200 per day. The factor of approximately 20 between the cost levels of private trainers and development trainers might correspond to the level of cost recovery achieved by some projects, of 5–10 per cent.

The quality of the training provided is very variable, and the sector probably attracts its share of rogues. But strong government regulation (as in Zimbabwe) probably only drives some of the private sector trainers 'underground'. The provision of highly subsidized, high-quality training (and even the paying of 'sitting allowances' to trainees) probably has a negative effect on the sector, too. As if to confirm that, a higher concentration of Ugandan training businesses was found in towns that had little non-commercial training; on the other hand, fewer private sector trainers were found in towns that were better covered with publicly funded training.

FIT is now working in both countries to develop networks of for-profit trainers, through which to strengthen their capacities; possible services include:

- ToT courses in new skills and training methodologies
- refresher and upgrading courses
- group advertising of training services
- certification of training courses that meet agreed standards
- publication of a directory of private sector training facilities
- facilitation of resource-sharing among institutes (e.g. secondment of part-time trainers).

Conclusion

This chapter outlines work in progress; hopefully it conveys some of the experience of offering BDS in new ways (at least as far as development work is concerned). Tailoring BDS totally to the perceived needs and demand of people in small enterprises, and then offering those services through for-profit channels, may require a different approach to development work. Employers' organizations may be able to play a particularly important role here, since many count existing and potential service providers in the private sector among their members.

While lessons can be learned from the success of methodologies in the field of micro-finance, there is a strong case in BDS for focusing for the time being on the identification and development of innovative services, rather than on institutions providing a range, or 'package' of services; in micro-finance, on the other hand, the focus is generally more on the creation of strong institutions.

If this in approach can be achieved, the potential is there, finally, to reach millions of small enterprises with the support services that they urgently need. Many questions remain to be answered, but the evidence does suggest that this approach is possible. More work is now needed, to fill the gaps and to define methodologies that can be followed, to achieve good results in different environments. The author is particularly keen to hear from anyone who is interested to collaborate in working towards the goal.

References and bibliography

Allal, M. K., Dixon-Fyle, M. Engelhard, S. Seegers, F. Bonnet, J. Kratzheller and K. van Elk (1997). 'Research on the role of information in the growth of small and microenterprises and on the relative efficiency of information sources'. ILO Geneva/Tool Foundation/Royal Government of the Netherlands.

Bennell, Paul, (1997). 'Vocational education and training in Zimbabwe: The role of private sector provision in the context of economic reform.' Institute of Development Studies, University of Sussex, UK.

Bennell, Paul, with Shane Bendera, Emrode Kimambo, Sixtus Kiwia, Faustin Mukyanuzi, Willy Parsalaw and John Temu (1998). 'Vocational education and training in Tanzania in the context of economic reform'. Final Report from the VET Study Group.

Havers, Mark (1998). 'Enterprise development – the irrelevance of western models'. *Small Enterprise Development Journal*, Volume 9, Number 2 – June 1998.

Hileman, Milena (1995). 'An evaluation of the PRIDE/FIT Exchange Visit Programme'. Nairobi, Kenya.

KIC–K (1996). 'Participatory Technology Development of farm tools in the Kisumu area: Final evaluation report'. Kenya.

Mbeine, Enoth and Gavin Anderson (1998). 'Sustainable training of micro and small enterprises through grassroots training businesses'. Paper for BDS Workshop 'How sustainable can BDS really be?', Harare, September 1998.

Tanburn, Jim (1996). 'User-Led Innovation: Enabling MSEs to develop improved technologies.' FIT Working Document, ILO Geneva.

Tanburn, Jim (1998). 'Study tour of commercial BDS providers in the UK'. ILO Geneva.

Van Bussel, Peter (1998). 'Business Support and the Importance of the Business Network'. *Small Enterprise Development Journal*, Volume 9 number 4.

Van den Berg, 1995. 'The support system for SMEs: Comparative analysis of the systems in the Netherlands, France and Zimbabwe'. Masters Thesis.

Note

1. 'FIT' started as an action-research project, jointly implemented by the ILO and a Dutch NGO called Tool; financing was provided by the Government of the Netherlands. More recently, the insights gained have been replicated with funding from other agencies, including the Government of Austria and UNDP.

23. The financial viability of business development services

LARA GOLDMARK

BUSINESS DEVELOPMENT SERVICES (BDS) is the term used to cover a broad array of services, excluding finance, that are offered to small businesses and microenterprises in order to improve their management, production, or marketing functions. This chapter and the research on which it is based focus specifically on microenterprises, defined as enterprises with fewer than 10 employees. The major service areas that will be discussed are training, information, technical assistance (in the form of consultancies or business counselling), legal and accounting services, marketing, and technology access (making available the use of machines to microenterprises). These services are analysed for two reasons: to reflect current practice in the field; and to explore which services are financially viable when offered to small businesses and microenterprises.

This chapter is based on earlier research conducted by the author, including a survey of 182 business development services providers operating in Latin America and the Caribbean region and 10 case studies. Cases were selected initially because the services offered appeared to have some potential for viability, or used new and creative delivery and cost-recovery mechanisms. By the end of the research a few of the cases were discovered not to represent 'best practice' in all aspects of their operations; however, the lessons learned through studying these cases are considered just as valuable as those learned by studying model success stories, and the cases have been included as examples to demonstrate important points.

The research was based on interviews conducted with entrepreneurs, practitioners, donors and academics, on-site institutional and market analyses of each case study, and second-hand information on numerous other business development service programmes.

The credit connection

Earlier research found that business development services offered in conjunction with credit often faced low demand, while stand-alone services were more likely to enjoy greater popularity among entrepreneurs. There are several probable reasons for this. First, credit programmes frequently offer sector-wide, management-oriented training or technical assistance which is out of tune with entrepreneurs' needs. The content of these services is tailored to the needs of the credit programme, i.e. to encourage entrepreneurs to improve their accounting records or credit management. Second, credit programmes reach only credit clients. The client market for business development services overlaps with, but is not the same as, that of micro-credit. (The 'overlap' clients of several BDS programmes analysed, i.e. clients demanding credit and business development services from the same institution or programme, represented less than 30 per cent of the total number of BDS clients). Potential BDS clients may not currently be using credit at all, or they may use credit from another financial institution or from a source such as buyers or suppliers. In any case, evidence shows that BDS providers offering sector-specific products are usually more attractive to clients than financial service institutions, except where the services sought relate to credit management, such as accounting or business plan preparation.

Why so much emphasis on sustainability?

The intense focus that has been placed on the institutional and programme sustainability of development projects in recent years is due to a number of reasons. First, the spread of capitalist principles throughout the world has affected even the most isolated governments and donor institutions. The view that market forces are positive and should be used to stimulate growth and development has spurred a wave of 'market-based' development projects and initiatives, including demand-led interventions. Examples include the Social Investment Funds in Latin America, which respond to demand from poor communities for social and productive infrastructure; bidding processes in Chile and Colombia whereby state training institutions compete with private contractors in a surrogate market created by the government; and voucher training programmes for microenterprises in Paraguay and Ecuador.

With donor funds becoming scarcer, institutions that can finance their own operations, completely or partially, possess a major advantage. This is true for two reasons: these institutions will survive the 'dry spells' when donor assistance is not available, and be able to protect themselves from funding 'shocks'; and donors are looking for strong institutions that will continue their work after project funds are exhausted. In any case, most institutions, whether for-profit or non-profit, aim to diversify their funding sources.

Institutional sustainability has become an important success indicator in some development fields. Willingness to pay even a symbolic fee on the part of small businesses and microenterprises (MSEs) shows that the services being offered are relevant and that the provider has gained credibility in its sector or area of operation. Since the quality of services is hard to judge before use, increasing levels of cost recovery are thought to show that MSEs have experienced gains in profitability and productivity through using the services, and thus repeat clients are willing to pay higher prices to access the services. New clients, if they have talked to former clients, may be willing to pay higher prices from the start, or may need to receive 'discounts' until they experience the benefits first-hand. Thus, steadily increasing cost recovery, along with a growing client base, can serve as an indicator of success, and as a proxy measure for impact, i.e. the clients would not keep coming back or refer others to the programme unless they had benefited from the services.

The appearance of a number of institutions that seem to espouse successfully a 'double mission' (social and for-profit) has led donors and practitioners to seek to emulate these models. For micro-finance institutions, sustainability is equated with successful growth past the break-even point, allowing the institution to cover all operating and financial costs through interest income earned. Progress towards sustainability corresponds to growth in outreach. Thus, donors and practitioners argue that there is no trade-off between serving the poor and reaching financial self-sufficiency, since a sustainable institution will, by definition, reach larger numbers of poor micro-entrepreneurs than an unsustainable one.

For other types of development programmes, sustainability may be defined not in an institutional sense but in a market context. For example, projects that encourage the use of solar panels in rural communities without access to electricity hope to stimulate the creation of sustainable markets for renewable energy sources. This implies that consumers, suppliers, repair technicians, and financing intermediaries will continue to interact in such a way that renewable energy use will continue to grow long after the development project is completed. In such a case, the institution that acts to catalyse this market development may not be sustainable, although the new institutions that emerge as the market grows should be.

The viability of business development services

In BDS, the term sustainability can be used to refer to the service provider or institution, to the service itself, and in some cases, to the businesses assisted or created through the provision of the services. This chapter focuses primarily on the financial viability (i.e. potential for profitability) of specific services, although the important issue of the institutional sustainability of BDS providers is also addressed. Institutional sustainability varies, depending on management choices. Institutions may offer a range of services, some of which are profitable and some of which are not. Many cross-subsidize from one service to another or from one client group to another.

For a BDS provider aiming to serve MSEs, the single most influential factor in determining the provider's institutional sustainability is the service mix. Some services are clearly financially viable. These services can be offered in a commercial or a developmental setting. In developmental settings, the revenues earned through these services may finance a number of complementary services which are less viable but are believed to have a beneficial impact on participating enterprises, or on the market as a whole. In non-developmental settings, the services may be offered with a pure profit motive.

The profit margins for BDS usually, though not always, shrink as the size of the businesses served decreases. A classic example is management consulting, which is an immensely profitable business when the clients are Fortune 500 companies. Management consulting to microenterprises, on the other hand, is not profitable at all. The size rule does not always apply, however. For example, technology access services face their strongest demand from the smallest of micro-enterprises, which cannot afford to buy their own equipment. Larger enterprises may use the services for a short period of time, or may not need them at all.

Examples of services that have proved to be viable at the microenterprise level are marketing (as in intermediation or brokering), technology access, accounting, and legal services. Those that are not viable may exhibit the characteristics of public goods which make them less viable at every level of enterprise size (e.g. information), or they may suffer from market imperfections characteristic of the environments in which microenterprises operate, such as lack of reliable information about the quality and benefits of services (e.g. training and technical assistance). Given project experience in the field, it seems unlikely to expect that training, technical assistance, or information services for microenterprises will ever achieve total cost-recovery through up-front user fees. It is worth exploring how far cost recovery can go, however, and aiming for at least 20–50 per cent recovery of direct costs.

Service providers wishing to offer non-viable products to MSEs have adopted the following approaches to cover costs:

- cross-subsidize from larger to smaller clients
- cross-subsidize using revenues from more profitable services
- obtain income through an unrelated income-generating activity (the so-called 'car wash' approach, though most institutions prefer to sell services that are more related to their market expertise; for example, the sale of research publications or consultancy services to donors or practitioner institutions wishing to replicate the institution's methodology)
- find a supplier or buyer who is willing to underwrite all or a portion of the cost of service provision because this actor will benefit from the improved perform-ance of the MSEs, and
- use donor or government funds.

Many institutions use several of these strategies at once. The challenge is to maintain an accurate costing system so that management can make intelligent decisions about the use of revenue flows, maintaining the desired equilibrium between short-term financial health, long-term sustainability, and the achieve-ment of the institution's goals. For example, using revenues from a first, viable service to subsidize the provision of a second, unviable service, may jeopardize the viability of the first service unless a significant proportion of the revenues are set aside for reinvestment. Reinvestment in the service provider's own institu-tion is important in the short term to maintain the provider's competitiveness in the market, and to ensure long-term sustainability.

Table 23.1 gives the reader an idea of which service areas have the potential to be viable, with explanations of the cost-recovery mechanisms used and examples of the case study institutions using these mechanisms to achieve these outcomes. A discussion of the services used and the important issues and factors which determine viability in each case follows.

Marketing services

Marketing, when it involves intermediating, subcontracting, or brokering goods, is a business development service which seems likely to be viable. Much like credit, the intermediation of goods is certainly a viable commercial activity when working with large businesses. Some marketing enterprises specialize in the sale of finished microenterprise products, while others focus on the provision of raw materials. It is important to note that the intermediation of goods produced by microenterprises is often accompanied by other less viable services, such as technical assistance and the provision of market information. These ancillary services may be necessary to ensure the delivery of quality products on time, or they may be offered because the intermediary wishes to assist the microenter-prises in gaining access to a new, more profitable market.

Some intermediaries are created with the explicit goal of helping small busi-nesses sell their goods, recognizing that these entrepreneurs are often exploited by larger market actors. Others, like many co-operatives, work with producers of different sizes. Studies have shown that in some sectors, groups of small pro-ducers have an advantage over large producers, since they can respond more flexibly to market demand. In other sectors, large producers possess a clear

Table 23.1 Estimated cost-recovery levels of selected business development service programmes serving microenterprises

Service type	Cost-recovery mechanism	Estimated cost-recovery level (%)	Examples	Number of clients (annual)
Marketing	a) mark-up on goods bought and sold	a) 105 115 102	a) PROEXSAL PROARTE Promotora del Comercio	1000 100 1000
	b) commission on sales	b) 103	b)PROEXSAL	500
Technology access	fees for machine services	a) 206* b) 35*	a) INSOTEC b) Fundacion Mac	130 700
Accounting and legal services	fees for services	>100	COFIDE Centre, Peru	2000
		>100	SEBRAE-Bahia, Brazil	6000
Training	a) fee for services	a) > 50 23	a) IDB Voucher Programme IDEPRO	6000 5000
	b) built into marketing margin	b) >100	b) Promotora del Comercio	900
Technical assistance	a) fee for services b) built into marketing margin	a) 19* b) 0–20* c) 12–15	a) IDEPRO b) CLUSA c) Technoserve	700 2200 unknown
Information	a) fee for service b) advertisement fees	a) 32* b) 25*	a) INSOTEC b) IDEPRO	unknown 9000

*Direct costs only.

advantage because economies of scale enhance profit margins. In either case, producer co-operatives or associations can improve the small producer's relative position, either by providing processing facilities on a larger scale in order to compete with larger actors by providing bulk purchasing services, or by acting as a flexible market agent.

Just how profitable marketing services for microenterprises should be is difficult to estimate. How much narrower are the margins when one works with microenterprises? For example, administrative and operating costs for a company purchasing goods from many small producers will probably be higher than those of a company with several large suppliers. A company serving small producers will also have to factor in some extra quality control and perhaps a higher rate of late deliveries. The decision to provide complementary services without recovering their full cost (for example, training), may further decrease already narrow profit margins. The small producers' lack of access to credit may force the intermediary to offer advances, while international buyers may not pay for several months. Thus, the parent company may need higher amounts of working capital. In addition, such companies – whether co-operatives, associations, or NGOs – are often severely undercapitalized, which reduces their own flexibility in the market place.

Of course, profitability will vary by sector, region, and type of cost-recovery mechanism. Some marketing intermediaries do not buy or sell products, charging only a commission and leaving the production risk to the microenterprises. Others cover costs through a pre-set resale margin. In every sector, certain key principles may dominate marketing practices, for example the need for constant innovation in design in the handicrafts sector, the advantage that can be obtained by the processing or packaging of agricultural products, and the use of new technologies to add value in manufacturing. In addition, overall lessons, such as the importance of defining a target market or pricing products properly, can apply to all sectors. Still, clear lessons for marketing intermediaries working with microproducers have not been disseminated. The question of how best to structure an institution that aims to earn a profit while improving the access of microproducers to profitable markets remains one that practitioners are still struggling to address. Another study under way as part of the BDS research mentioned earlier is addressing just these issues. A survey of over 200 marketing intermediaries has been designed to gather data on their cost and capital structures as well as on the microproducers they serve and the additional services they offer.

Three case studies prepared for this chapter analysed the sustainability of marketing intermediaries selling the products of low-income microentrepreneurs: a Nicaraguan handicrafts exporter, an agricultural marketing co-operative in El Salvador, and a Colombian intermediary selling leather, textiles, and household wares, primarily in the local market. All three institutions had received assistance from international donor organizations during their start-up period and in the first few years of operation. However, all three envision the long-term sustainability of their institutions to be linked to the profitability of their operations, rather than donor support. Below, two of the three cases are briefly analysed with respect to the viability of their services. The third is discussed in the training section.

PROARTE, a Nicaraguan handicrafts marketing company, works with about 100 microentrepreneurs, ranging from very low-income artisans in isolated communities to more sophisticated small business owners who sell to several buyers. PROARTE was created as an offshoot of a credit programme in 1993, since then growing to become a private, for-profit company. Since December 1997, PROARTE has been operating free of major subsidies, although occasionally the manager and staff obtain sponsorship from international donors to attend trade fairs in Europe and the United States. Also, PROARTE's shareholders are international donors, some of whom will eventually want to divest.

PROARTE was able to reach institutional sustainability relatively rapidly through a minimalist strategy of providing only the essential services necessary to get its producers' goods to market. When possible, PROARTE has co-ordinated with other local development efforts to make sure its producers receive training and other types of assistance. PROARTE has also enforced strict quality-control standards and at times has had to discontinue its work with producers who could not deliver on time or whose products were consistently below quality standards. However, PROARTE's challenge in the future will be maintaining its foothold in the international markets. The company will be required to innovate frequently in design and keep up with market trends, interpreting these trends in order to find products that its producers have the skills to make, or adapt products which they are currently making. Keeping up with trends in faraway markets can be costly, but PROARTE must do so in order to remain competitive.

PROEXSAL is a national agricultural producer co-operative formed in El Salvador in 1994 to market its member's products to local and international buyers. The company benefited from a small grant at start-up and is expected to receive additional donor funding in 1999. The company plans to operate free of all subsidies after 2001. PROEXSAL works in tandem with CLUSA, a technical-assistance NGO working with producers in transition to organic or other non-traditional crops. A new value chain is created through the CLUSA/PROEXSAL intervention, including the sourcing of inputs, growing techniques, post-harvest treatment, packaging, and distribution. The co-operative plays an important incubation function, helping to create packaging centres at key points in the distribution chain. PROEXSAL (with help from international donors) invests in the packaging centres and trains local producers to operate the business. Over time, the producers take over the operating costs of the packaging centre and slowly buy the business from PROEXSAL. This is an example of an additional service which currently is not profitable for PROEXSAL. However, in the long run the packaging centres will play an important quality control function, making PROEXSAL able to adopt a more minimalist role with experienced producers, offering its ancillary services only to new groups.

PROEXSAL's financial indicators are typical for an intermediary working with small producers. The co-operative has grown rapidly – annual sales increasing from US$418 000 to $680 000 over the past three years. Administrative costs, however, have at times grown faster than sales, and the co-operative is under-capitalized and over-indebted. The extra services required to maintain quality can be costly, especially when initiating work with new producer groups. Right now, no standard indicators or benchmarks exist with which to measure the efficiency and general financial health of marketing companies working with small producers. This is an area in need of further research in order to provide guidelines that could be used in evaluating these types of institutions and in designing financing packages which provide incentives for healthy, efficient growth.

Technology access services

Technology access providers charge microentrepreneurs for access to the most up-to-date equipment in their sector. For example, Fundacion Mac in Cali, Colombia offers computerized design, cutting, and finishing services to micro-entrepreneurs in the textile sector; INSOTEC offers buttonholing, computerized embroidery, and other finishing services to clothing manufacturers in four cities in Ecuador (Goldmark and Londoño, 1997). As shown in Table 23.1, technology access services have yielded direct cost-recovery levels as low as 35 per cent and as high as 206 per cent, depending on the market context and the strategy of the institution providing the services.

INSOTEC has pursued an aggressive cost-recovery strategy in order to further institutional sustainability. The institution's leadership believes that market positioning and the quality of the services are more important to clients than service fees. Data from 1997 show that INSOTEC's technology access services have achieved cost-recovery levels high enough to cover all indirect costs and allow for reinvestment in the institution's research and development functions. INSOTEC invests strategically in the development of services which appear to have profitability potential after an initial trial period. If the service is tested in one city and does not attract a sufficient number of clients to reach its break-even point within a few months, it is dropped. Each of INSOTEC's four business development service centres operates as a separate cost centre and is required to pay to the central headquarters in Quito a monthly fee which is meant to contribute to research and development costs, and to cover administrative and technical assistance services provided to the centres by headquarters.

Fundacion Mac, on the other hand, has pursued a much more costly strategy and been able to recover only about 35 per cent of the direct costs of its technology access services so far. Fundacion Mac believes in the importance of offering a complete package of services to its clients, which includes access to all the latest technology in design, cutting, and finishing. The organization has been recognized for the role it plays in the development of the local textile sector and receives significant donations from both international donors and local corporations, more than enough to cover its operating deficit. Thus, the service mix it provides is decided not by the profitability of each service but by Fundacion Mac's desire to provide its clients with access to the latest equipment and techniques. Costs are not allocated by service, nor are they considered separately from Fundacion Mac's parallel training services.

While INSOTEC achieves a much higher cost-recovery rate than Fundacion Mac for its technology access services, both institutions offer additional business development services to their clients – such as training and technical assistance, which are far less profitable. A subsidy analysis of two of INSOTEC's service centres showed that while a few individual technology access services remain profitable even after accounting for all hidden subsidies, the multiple service centres do not. This is a typical constraint faced by non-marketing BDS providers. Technology access services may be extremely profitable, but rarely will they be able to finance fully the entire institution's operations. Another challenge faced by INSOTEC, in addition to the sustainability question, is the need to innovate constantly. As the technology offered by INSOTEC becomes more accessible in the market place, service profitability declines and INSOTEC is pressed to come up with new services, offering access to new equipment which local MSEs cannot currently obtain in the local market.

Accounting and legal services

These services are usually available from private, for-profit providers (often individuals) in microenterprise markets. Quality varies widely, however, and some BDS providers play a brokering role, stamping qualified professionals with some type of 'seal of approval', or housing their offices within the programme's premises to ensure that services will be readily available to their clients. Two examples of these are COFIDE's Business Development Centre in Lima, Peru, and SEBRAE-Bahia in Brazil.

Since in both of these cases the service providers were private entrepreneurs, data on the profitability of their businesses were difficult to obtain. Rather than achieving financial viability, the challenge for these services seems to be the development of market incentives or systems where providers offer microentrepreneurs a high-quality service, in a transparent and fair manner.

Training

Training is the service which, in the past, was most frequently packaged with credit for microentrepreneurs. Many microfinance institutions initially believed that training aimed at improving the performance of microentrepreneurs' businesses would generate returns, if not through fees, in the form of higher repayment rates. Experience has demon-strated, however, that integrating training services into a credit programme's activities increases transaction costs for both clients and the microfinance institution, without clear evidence of the expected benefits (Gulli, forthcoming).

Decades of saturating microentrepreneurs with obligatory training or training, which is packaged so as to seem 'free' to the entrepreneur, has made training very difficult to sell in some markets. A pilot programme financed by the IDB in Paraguay has demonstrated that micro-entrepreneurs do demand training, and will in fact line up to obtain vouchers which reduce, but do not eliminate, the out-of-pocket cost of short training courses offered by private institutions in areas such as electronic equipment repair, hairdressing, catering and baking, and paying business taxes. Since 1995 the programme has trained 19 486 entrepreneurs and microenterprise employees. Vouchers are allocated to micro-enterprise owners, who may then use them or distribute them to employees. Each voucher covers US$20 of the cost of any six-session course, and prices range from US$25 to US$75. Course content changes rapidly, in line with seasonal market fluctuations. Since 1995, over 500 different courses have been taught. The course content is so specific, and so immediately applicable, that trainees can usually earn back their investment within a month. Most courses are taught by small business owners, and involve hands-on demonstrations and practice sessions.

A measure of the subsidy that has been allocated to the private institutions operating with voucher revenues showed an average of about 50 per cent annually, ranging from 20–70 per cent genuine cost-recovery by the institutions (i.e. out-of-pocket fees collected). In the long term, the vouchers are supposed to fade away and what will remain is an information infrastructure detailing the availability of different courses, course prices, and the popularity of each institution (currently measured by the number of vouchers redeemed per month). If the vouchers are set at a fixed monetary amount which does not change, inflation will effectively reduce the amount of subsidy each year as course prices rise.

The third example in the matrix under training services, Promotora del Comercio, is a Colombian NGO which buys and sells products made by local micro-entrepreneurs. The institution's total assets are US$1.4 million, and in 1997 sales were over US$3.4 million. However, compared to its sales, Promotora earned a tiny profit of only US$93 000 in 1997. The profit margin in past years has been equally narrow, and before 1995, negative. Promotora's mission is to help microentre-preneurs access local markets, and the programme provides free business development services as a complement to intermediation.

In the matrix, cost-recovery for Promotora's training services is listed as greater than 100 per cent. This is technically true, since the programme recovers more than 100 per cent of its total costs through the mark-up on microproducers' goods. The figure is deceptive, however, in the sense that Promotora does not account separately for the costs of providing additional services. A review of the programme's financial records shows that the narrowness of the profit margin is partly due to the additional services offered by Promotora, which the institution would probably not have to provide if its producers were larger and more sophisticated. Even within the programme, there is cross-subsidy between the larger producers and the smaller, less-experienced entrepreneurs who require more intensive assistance.

Linking training to marketing services is a traditional approach, which has been used frequently, in manner similar to the credit linkage. The advantage of using a marketing link is that training services are more likely to reflect the demand of the ultimate consumer, and thus to provide microentrepreneurs with immediately applicable skills and information. The problem with building fees into a marketing margin, however, is similar to that of embedding costs into an interest rate. In both cases, there is no opportunity for microentrepreneurs to send and receive 'price signals'. Institutions such as Promotora may want to continue building fees into their margin, because this is a convenient way to recover costs. However, both the institution and the producers would benefit if costs were transparently measured and communicated, and the percentage of the marketing margin that included service fees was calculated separately. This approach would also facilitate the gradual phasing out of services in cases where producers improve their skills or reliability to the point where quality control or training are no longer needed, or need not be as intensive.

Technical assistance

Technical assistance is a more costly service than training because it is delivered on an individualized basis and because it frequently involves advanced technical knowledge on the part of extensionists or counsellors. Like training, this service suffers from a history of being linked to credit and offered without a visible fee. For years in many Latin American countries, government extension services have offered free technical assistance to small agricultural producers, believing that the eventual economic benefits of such services outweighed the costs. Such services were usually linked to rural credit programmes. Today, technical assistance to agricultural producers can command a fee in markets where *all* providers of such services charge fees; however, cost recovery levels are still minimal.

CLUSA, a technical assistance provider to small agricultural producers in El Salvador, in the past did not charge for services unless the producers were relatively well off. What the organization called a sliding scale was essentially a scale with '0' at one end and '20 per cent' at the other, for selected clients. Recently, however, CLUSA held a meeting with a group of producers who had received services for several years and were seeing marked increases in their incomes as a result. The producers stated that they would be willing to pay 25 per cent of the direct costs of the service. Technoserve, a CLUSA competitor, has maintained a strict policy of charging fees in recent years, both up-front and linked to marketing efforts. Cost recovery is only about 12–15 per cent of direct costs, however.

IDEPRO offers an individual counselling service to micro-entrepreneurs whom it recruits through door-to-door canvassing of businesses. The service is also expensive to provide, although less so since counsellors may be young business school students. IDEPRO's counselling service recovered 19 per cent of direct costs in 1997.

Information services

Information services for microenterprises have rarely been seen to recover a substantial portion of their costs. INSOTEC's information service does not solely target microenterprises. Instead, the service is accessible to micro-entrepreneurs, small and medium businesses, associations and co-operatives, and other development organizations. Clients access the materials in INSOTEC's

Quito library for a fee. The institution is currently developing new information products which will specifically target MSEs. These new products are not expected to recover their full costs.

IDEPRO offers an innovative information service to micro-entrepreneurs in six Bolivian cities. The institution has developed a partnership with a national newspaper, which publishes IDEPRO's insert every other Friday. The insert contains general information relevant to the microenterprise sector, and IDEPRO sells advertisements to microentrepreneurs who are looking for buyers, suppliers, or other business partners. Advertisements are sold to larger clients at a higher price. The newspaper that publishes IDEPRO's bulletin has doubled its sales on the days the insert is included in the paper. Cost-recovery, based on revenue from advertisements, is currently at 25 per cent of direct costs. IDEPRO pays the newspaper to format the insert; the newpaper publishes the insert for free. The market trend, however, seems to indicate that an aggressive strategy by IDEPRO, possibly involving both advertisement sales and negotiation with the newspaper, should yield at least 100 per cent recovery of direct costs.

Conclusion

The viability of business development services clearly varies widely by type of service. It seems that characteristics of each service market, including past practices of development institutions, determine a possible cost-recovery range for each type of service. For example, both marketing services and technology services have the potential to be viable services which can even support the provision of other, less viable ancillary services. For this to be true, however, the business development service provider must be committed to an aggressive cost-recovery strategy and must be willing to prioritize the most viable services provided. At the other end of the spectrum, individualized technical assistance services and training may be the least viable services at the microenterprise level. Information services also seem to have little potential for financial viability, although one institution has developed an innovative cost-recovery mechanism which indicates that at least a 'respectable' level of cost-recovery can be achieved (25 per cent).

Possibly as important in determining service viability is the service provider's business strategy, defined as market positioning and the setting of institutional priorities. In the case of technology access services, an institution that was concerned with maximizing cost-recovery generated six times the cost-recovery percentage of an institution providing similar services. One aspect of market positioning includes the decision to play a frontier role in providing access to new technology or opening new markets or imparting new skills, versus the decision to rely on tested methodologies which may be easier to disseminate among a large or less experienced cadre of employees. The more unique the strategy adopted, the more difficult it is to copy and thus the longer the BDS provider should be able to retain its competitive advantage. A BDS provider that successfully positions itself in the market should be able to reach, at a minimum, the upper limits of the cost-recovery ranges defined for each service area in Table 23.1.

Based on the examples discussed, there does not seem to be any correlation between the scale of operations and service viability. The existence of economies of scale in BDS is improbable in general, due to the customized nature of many of the services. Also, in some cases, working with a smaller number of producers can be to a BDS provider's advantage. For example, a marketing intermediary wishing to guarantee quality and performance may prefer a stable base of 200 clients to a flexible, shifting base of 2000. The case analyses showed that each service's break-even volume of operations will vary according to several factors, such as local market characteristics, delivery mechanisms, clients' sub-sector, client, and other aspects related to institutional strategy.

The importance of measuring profitability by activity has been highlighted throughout the chapter. It may be even more important to measure cost-recovery when institutions offer non-viable services. Although an institution that does not measure its positive profit margin carefully may miss the opportunity to learn important lessons, an institution that does not measure its *negative* profit margins is risking its own existence. Activities that make the overall positive profit margin narrower must be identified and minimized where necessary.

Some key indicators, such as the percentage of direct cost recovery, are useful for comparisons across regions and types of institutions. The inclusion of indirect costs is critical when measuring overall institutional sustainability; however, the measure may highlight institutional differences which are unrelated to service viability. Many of the institutions studied were found to have extremely high fixed costs, in some cases left over from decades of working with donor or government resources. There is a need for more concrete benchmarks, specific-ally with respect to the financial and business performance of BDS providers. For instance, information about appropriate levels of administrative costs for marketing companies could help evaluate the efficiency of intermediaries work-ing with small producers. This information could serve to develop financing packages aimed at providing incentives for efficiency and genuinely increasing institutions' chances of reaching long-term sustainability.

Blurring the lines between BDS 'programmes' and BDS 'enterprises'

In theory, there should be a clear difference between donor-supported BDS programmes, designed to compensate for market imperfections, and private sector business services that are offered by for-profit entities at cost-covering prices. In practice, as donors press business development service providers to become more sustainable, the two start to look more and more alike. For ex-ample, INSOTEC competes with private businesses in offering some technology services, although the institution has a strategy of seeking out new services and abandoning those that are being taken over by the market. PROEXSAL and Promotora del Comercio both compete with private intermediaries, although admittedly these private intermediaries do not provide customized services and market feedback designed to benefit the smallest producers. In cases where BDS providers are competing with private enterprises, important indicators to watch carefully would be prices charged for services (to avoid unfair competition) and measures of performance of the microenterprises purchasing the services.

On the other hand, a failure by BDS providers to reinvest in themselves clearly leads to decreased benefits for future clients. One clear example of this is the story of Manos de Uruguay, an NGO which was supported by the IDB in the late 1970s. Over the past 20 years, Manos has enjoyed recognition throughout Latin America as a successful handicrafts exporter working with low-income women in rural areas. At its peak, in 1984, Manos provided an outlet for the products of 1200 women, organized into local co-operatives. Over the years, however, Manos did not reinvest in itself, opting to distribute short-term benefits as quickly as possible to the rural women involved in the project. A graph of the institution's total assets over time shows an increase during the execution of the original IDB project, followed by a steadily falling slope (Mikkelsen et al., 1997). The institution is now experiencing financial distress and works with fewer than 300 artisans. Manos staff did not regard their institution as a business, and thus did not value its financial health. This neglect eventually endangered the institution's capacity to continue carrying out its social mission.

Similar examples abound all over the region. The principles involved in an attitude shift are similar to those now widely understood in microfinance. Although clients are poor, if a service allows them to increase their incomes, they will be willing to share a portion of this increase with a service provider whom they understand to be responsible for this increase, and who they hope will be in existence in future.

References

Goldmark, Lara and Rosario Londoño, (1997), 'Technology access services for microenterprise.' Microenterprise Unit, Inter-American Development Bank, Washington, DC.

Gulli, Hege, (forthcoming) 'Microfinance and poverty,' Microenterprise Unit, Inter-American Development Bank, Washington, DC.

Mikkelsen, Lene, *et al.* (1997), 'IDB Support to the Handicrafts Sector: 1965–2001.' Microenterprise Unit, Inter-American Development Bank, Washington, DC.

24. Measuring BDS performance – a summary framework

MARY McVAY

Introduction

IN AN ERA WHEN microfinance programmes are reaching a significant scale and becoming increasingly self-sufficient, BDS programmes are faced with the challenge of demonstrating that 'credit is not enough' to realize the full economic and social potential of the small and microenterprise sector. Intuitively, theoretically, and by anecdote, BDS programmes are emerging as an important complement to micro-finance. However, the development of best practices is hindered by the lack of standard performance measures that can help practitioners assess objectively what works and what does not, in different programmes and different contexts. This chapter presents a preliminary framework for measuring the performance of business development services.

This framework proposes a set of indicators and methodologies for collecting and reporting performance information for BDS programmes focused on microenterprises. It is offered as a first step towards establishing 'best practices' indicators that can be widely used by business development practitioners, and as such, comments and suggested modifications from practitioners are welcomed. Although the framework has implications for establishing best-practice standards, at this stage it does not contain implicit performance standards, nor should it contain biases towards any particular type of BDS or implementation methodology. The particular level of performance that is appropriate for each type of BDS may be established later. In addition, there is no attempt at this stage to prioritize the importance of various indicators. Rather, the framework proposes a wide range of indicators, based in practice, that should capture a wide range of benefits. The framework is summarized in Table 24.1, followed by a detailed description of each category of indicators.

The framework provides indicators according to common goals and objectives observed to be important to BDS practitioners and donors:

- reaching large numbers of people (Scale)
- reaching under-served markets, particularly the poor (Outreach)
- improving people's live through poverty alleviation and enterprise growth (Impact)
- doing so at the least cost possible (Cost-effectiveness), and
- ensuring that services and benefits continue in the long run (Sustainability).

In addition, the framework is organized around four groups of players that practitioners and donors typically analyse:

- the 'customer' being served or benefiting from the service – usually entrepreneurs or farmers
- the service providers who directly interact with the customers to supply the service; these may be private businesses, government agencies, non-governmental organizations or co-operatives
- the service facilitator, who designs and develops the service, and raises and manages funds to do so. This player is usually a non-governmental organiza-

Table 24.1 BDS performer measurement framework: a summary

Player Goal	MSE customer	Direct service provider	Service facilitator	Market place
Scale	• Cumulative number of entrepreneurs or farmers *acquiring* the service through commercial transactions • Number acquiring per year • Same, annual growth rate	• Cumulative number of entrepreneurs *providing* business development services directly to microentrepreneurs (or farmers) • Same for NGOs or government institutions • Number of 'copycat' providers	None: scale is measured at the MSE and provider level	None: scale is measured at the MSE and provider level
Outreach	• % owned by women • % poor • % with other barriers	• Number of service delivery locations	None: outreach is measured at the MSE and provider level	• Geographic spread of services
Impact	• % of MSE customers who *use* the service as intended • % of MSE customers who *benefit* as intended, and the extent of those benefits, when applicable • satisfaction level (scale of 1–5) • % repeat customers • % of MSE customers reporting standard business benefits, percentage change in these (profits, assets, etc.) Timeframe of analysis	• % of *providers* acquiring facilitative services who *use* them as intended; • % of *providers* acquiring facilitative services who *benefit* as intended • Satisfaction level (scale of 1–5) • % of *providers* who report standard business benefit, percentage change in these, and timeframe of analysis	None: impact is measured at the MSE and provider level	None: impact is measured at the MSE and provider level. If there is a practical indicator, displacement affects could be assessed here
Cost-effectiveness	• Total transaction costs to acquire and use the service	• For private sector or co-operative providers: Up-front investment costs to provide the service • For non-profit providers: service provision costs to be included in facilitator indicators	• Cost per MSE customer *acquiring*, annual and cumulative • Cost per MSE customer *using*, annual and cumulative • Cost per MSE customer *benefiting*, annual and cumulative Cumulative and last year's cost per person who increased sales, profits, assets, employees, number of customers, product or service lines, or who reduced costs • Same for providers	None: Cost-effectiveness is not measured for the market level
Sustainability	• Payback period: average amount of time it took for an entrepreneur's or farmer's investment in the BDS to pay for itself in increased income, as reported by the entrepreneur/farmer	• Annual profits or cost-recovery of the BDS and facilitative services provided, broken down by activities ranging from pure facilitation to direct service provision • Institutional independence of service provision and facilitation		• Comparison of number of people serviced to programme costs • Number of copycats

Compiled by Mary McVay, Marshall Bear, Candace Nelson and Joan Parker; October, 1998

315

tion or government agency, but there is no reason why it need be so. Sometimes the 'facilitator' is also the 'provider,' depending on the service delivery channels being established. These two functions are separated in the framework, however, to reflect the many programmes that have both players, and to indicate the different roles that have implications for sustainability

• the 'market', by which is meant the general population of people exchanging goods and services whose businesses might be affected by the introduction of the service into their commercial lives. Often, BDS programmes attempt to demonstrate the commercial viability of a service, for example, in the hope that others will copy it throughout the market.

The framework examines relevant goal categories for each player being assessed, or each level of analysis. In Table 24.1, the goal categories are on the vertical axis and the player is on the horizontal. The boxes in the body of the matrix contain the summary of the proposed indicators for each goal category and beneficiary level. A general discussion of the issues arising from the framework is followed here by a more detailed discussion of each of the indicators.

General issues in BDS performance measurement

There are many challenges in assessing the performance of BDS programmes, which the framework has attempted to address.

General BDS indicators vs. service-specific indicators. On the one hand, it is useful to have general BDS performance indicators in order to capture the benefits of multi-service programmes and to compare the performance of different services. On the other hand, service-specific indicators would capture the benefits of particular services more accurately. The aim has been to establish a general framework with some general indicators, into which service-specific indicators can be placed. Service-specific indicators should emerge, as significant numbers of programmes report their performance indicators within the context of the framework. For example, the impact section asks BDS programmes both to *define* and *report* the 'benefit' of their programmes, such as increased sales resulting from a subcontracting service.

Assessing institutions vs. assessing products and services. Many BDS programmes are still in their product development phase. They are trying to scale up, and a few are developing strategies for sustainability. As a result, some of the performance indicators relevant to the more developed field of microfinance do not capture the benefits of BDS programmes. Indicators have therefore been selected that are relevant for the product development phase of a programme, in particular indicators that reflect customer satisfaction and expected programme outcomes, rather than broad impact and longer-term sustainability. For example, a technology access provider in Latin America assesses the operational cost-recovery of one service, but does not assess the cost of new services development and promotion. At the same time, the framework assesses cost-recovery and sustainability at a range of levels. In this manner, the framework reflects small steps that the field is currently making toward financial sustainability, and, as BDS programmes mature, it will reflect increasing levels of sustainability.

Level of analysis: 'enterprise', 'provider', 'facilitator' and 'market'. In microfinance programmes, the primary process in performance assessment is analysing the operational efficiency and financial sustainability of the microfinance institution. Very few BDS programmes engage in this type of performance assessment.

One reason is the difference in institutional arrangements often involved in BDS programmes. These arrangements obscure the unit of analysis for assessing key variables such as scale, cost-effectiveness and sustainability. For example, if an international non-profit organization works, over a period of three years, with 50 co-operatives to assist them in managing oil presses, each of which serves hundreds of microenterprises, which institutions can be expected to become financially sustainable? The microenterprises, yes, the co-operatives, yes, but the BDS provider? No. Yet, some international BDS providers work with similar co-operatives and market their handicrafts, indeed, hoping to earn a profit. Thus, performance expectations depend significantly on programme design and content. This framework gets around this issue by defining the levels of analysis as clearly as possible, and, in particular, differentiating between 'microenterprise or small business (MSE) customers'; 'BDS providers' who directly service those customers; and 'BDS facilitators' who provide temporary assistance to providers and facilitate the market for BDS services. The 'provider' and 'facilitator' are sometimes the same organization, but this framework encourages BDS organizations to differentiate between these roles in order to apply appropriate performance indicators to each function and, in particular, to separate sustainable from unsustainable activities.

Quantitative or qualitative indicators. Many BDS programmes, particularly programmes that focus on structural changes such as gender relations, or policy changes, use qualitative indicators to assess performance. However, quantitative indicators are more easily compared across programmes and in different programme contexts. There has been an attempt to accommodate qualitative programme indicators by allowing BDS facilitators to define their objectives in either quantitative or qualitative terms, and then to aggregate the percentage of beneficiaries that are realizing those outcomes. At the same time, the framework tracks some standard quantitative indicators, and, over time, additional common indicators may emerge as more programmes report their outcome goals and results.

Scale

Information on scale, like several of the other indicators, is mostly of interest to facilitators and donors, who are interested in reaching the largest possible number of microentrepreneurs and farmers through commercial transactions, and who want to see the growth of a com-petitive market for services.

The proposed indicators are the following, including (in brackets) the level that is being measured, and some indication of the methods used.

- Cumulative number of entrepreneurs or farmers acquiring the service through commercial transactions – paying a fee for services or selling products through a service provider (customer level). The cumulative number of enterprises using the service is divided by the number of years the programme has been in existence. This helps to compare older programmes with younger ones more fairly.
- Number of entrepreneurs or farmers acquiring the service through commercial transactions per year of service provision (customer level).
- Annual and cumulative number of enterprises providing business development services directly to entrepreneurs or farmers (provider level). If there is a BDS facilitator who works through separate providers, then the providers

who paid a fee for services, or sold goods or services through the facilitator, must be tracked annually since the beginning of the project or programme. The providers then track the microentrepreneurs or farmers who purchased services or sold goods or services through them since the project or programme began. In tracking providers, the facilitator should distinguish between commercial enterprises, co-operatives and non-profit institutions (NGOs or government agencies).

Table 24.2 Examples of scale indicators in use

Organization, programme, location	Indicator and results
ApproTEC, Kenya: product development training	76 clients trained in product development for a fee
ApproTEC Kenya: water pump programme	2000 farmers purchased water pumps through 3 manufacturers who were trained by ApproTEC
EnterpriseWorks (ATI) oil press programme in Tanzania	8570 enterprises acquiring services, including machine manufacturers, oil press purchasers, and sunflower seed suppliers
IDE, designers and manufacturers of water pumps in Bangladesh	Over 2 million farmers purchasing water pumps for irrigation
SEWA, Vegetable Vendor's Co-operatives, India	4578 vendors pay membership fees for advocacy services
IDB/GAMA/CEPAE, Paraguayan Voucher Training programme in vouchers	4530 individuals trained for a fee; 32 providers cashing
MEDA/PROARTE, company marketing crafts in international markets, Nicaragua	100 craftspeople selling crafts to PROARTE

- Annual and cumulative number of NGOs or government institutions providing business development services directly to entrepreneurs or farmers (provider level).
- Number of 'copycats' (market level). Methods still need to be developed to measure those who began providing a BDS because they observed another provider, but did not benefit directly from the BDS programme.

One of the key issues that arise out of this is how can BDS providers be persuaded by facilitators to track the number of their customers? Some programmes provide service providers with incentives to track. For example, ApproTEC provides brand-name quality control plates for its machines (which are inspected randomly). Each has a serial number which reflects the identity of the manufacturer. When the manufacturer needs additional plates, he must report the customer list to ApproTEC, who in turn knows the number of customers roughly corresponds to the number of plates previously issued. Additional methodologies such as this need to be identified for other services.

Outreach

Measuring the number of people who acquire the service may not be enough. This indicator concerns to what extent services are reaching specific target populations, for example, women, the poor, ethnic populations that have faced discrimination, rural people, and others who face barriers to self-employment.

Market forces may encourage the development of services towards more mainstream customers, but donors and facilitators are also interested in using public funds to expand the flow of services to reach people who would otherwise not have access to market services. The proposed indicators include:

- the percentage of entrepreneurs and farmers using a BDS who are women (customer level). This means that either the individual purchasing the service is a woman, or the enterprise is 50 per cent or more owned by a woman
- the percentage who are poor, defined in the context of the national economy or standard of living (customer level)
- The percentage who are facing another barrier to self-employment (customer level)

Table 24.3   Examples of outreach indicators in use

Organization, programme, location	Indicator and results
ApproTEC, Kenya: product development training	29% of trainees are women; tracks % in lowest business bracket
IDE water pumps in Bangladesh	85% of farmers purchasing pumps rent or own less than 1 hectare of land
MEDA/PROARTE, crafts marketing company, Nicaragua	30% of businesses are women; all but one with fewer than 5 employees; all rural; all businesses within the bottom 2 quintiles of national income range
WWB survey of BDS programmes	64% of clients are rural and in the bottom 20% income level

- whether the programme is reaching: a community (neigh-bourhood or village); a city or town; a state or district; a nation; or an international community (marketplace level). The agency will use the loose definitions provided to describe their geographic outreach.

Impact

Impact provides information about how many people are changing their business practices as a result of using a business development service. It is notoriously difficult to measure. Rather than attempting to measure household or individual impacts on income and well-being, this framework looks at enterprise-level changes which contribute to household-level change. In addition, rather than surveying entrepreneurs and collecting objectively verifiable data, this framework asks entrepreneurs to articulate how the BDS has assisted them, and to what extent. Thus, the indicator functions as both a proxy indicator for impact and a tool for gathering customer feedback that will assist the facilitator to design better commercial services. The assessment of in-depth impact in this framework is left to occasional programme evaluations and the long-term development of improved impact measurement tools.

Impact measurement should be of interest to providers as well as to donors and facilitators. BDS providers want to offer services that are in high demand, that people use and from which people benefit as the programme expects, and which will keep their customers returning for additional services. The proposed indicators are used for tracking both MSE customers, as they experience BDS services, and BDS service providers in their relation to facilitators.

- Customer satisfaction: survey with results on a scale of 1-5, and percentage of clients that are repeat customers.
- Service-specific use: percentage of customers using the service as intended (as defined by the BDS provider).
- Service-specific benefits: percentage of customers benefiting from the service as intended, and an indicator of the extent of the change (see Table 24.4).

Table 24.4   Hypothetical impact report, Product Development Training

Customer report, 1997	Number	Percentage	Average % change*
NUMBER ACQUIRING (from SCALE)	1000	100	
SERVICE-SPECIFIC USE			
Use 1: Conducted market research	800	80	25
Use 2: Made new or improved product	500	50	N/A
Use 3: Changed production process	800	80	
Total reporting at least one use:	800	80	
SERVICE-SPECIFIC BENEFITS			
Benefit 1: Sold to new customers	500	50	50
Benefit 2: Increased prices	300	30	
Benefit 3: Reduced costs	100	10	
Total reporting at least one benefit	600	60	
GENERAL BUSINESS BENEFITS			
Increased profits	500	50	10
Increased sales	600	60	30
Increased assets	200	20	10
Increased employees	200	20	75
Increased customers	100	10	25
Increase product/service lines	500	50	15
Decreased costs	100	10	10
Total reporting at least one standard business benefit	700	70	
Percentage that are repeat customers (from scale report)			50% (500)
Average customer satisfaction rating (on a scale of 1 to 5)			4.2
Average time lapsed between service provision and impact measurement:			14 months

*Change that customers attribute to BDS service, average of customer responses.

- General business benefits: percentage of customers reporting an increase in profits, sales, assets, employees, number of customers, product/service lines, and/or decreased costs. The extent of these benefits as measured by the average percentage change in these indicators that customers attribute to the BDS.
- Timeframe: the BDS provider will state the timeframe of their analysis: how much time has elapsed between BDS service provision and the impact data collection.

One problem with the methodology is that it relies heavily on self-reported financial data. Customers want to please the surveyor, and MSE customers also often find it hard to estimate 'percentage change'. Yet, the level of effort and expense involved in verifying business financial data is overwhelming for most BDS providers.

The proposed indicator is based on impact indicators currently in use by typical BDS programmes (see Table 24.5).

Table 24.5   Examples of impact indicators in use

Organization, programme, location	Indicator and result
AppoTEC, Kenya: Akili training programme	USE: 81% developed new products. BENEFITS: 35% increase in income compared to –4% in control group; 70% reduction in no. of entrepreneurs that are poor; 9% increase in employees compared to –11% in control group; PERCEIVED VALUE: 19% of increased sales due to new products
ENTERPRISEWORKS (ATI) oil press programme in Tanzania	USE: 47% proven sustainable enterprises; BENEFITS; Total monetary benefits $3.5 million; income gains per enterprise $653 per year
IDB/GAMA/CEPAE, Paraguayan Voucher Training Programme	Average number of trainings purchased by micro-entrepreneurs, 2.5; business owners increased productivity, lowered costs, increased sales.
ILO,SIYB, global	USE: 30-60% of people trained start a business. BENEFITS: 80% are still in business one year later.
SERCOTEC, Chile, cluster networks	USE: 75% made expected changes in processes, products, sales strategies, and financial management
K-MAP consulting services, Kenya	BENEFITS: 106% increase in employment, 292% increase in assets, 189% increase in employment

Cost-effectiveness

Whether a programme makes a wise use of funds, and how much it costs to access services is equally of interest to donors, to MSE customers, and to BDS providers and facilitators. The aim is to create the greatest impact on MSE customer businesses for the least cost. The proposed indicators are given here, with some indication of how they are calculated (see Table 24.6, based on the data from Table 24.4, with 'Cost per impact unit' calculated in the last column). Note that the indicators selected differ significantly from standard cost-benefit analyses, which can be challenging to calculate and are generally as open to manipulation as is the simpler approach outlined here.

- Transaction costs per MSE customer to acquire the service (customer level). (Total programme costs are divided by each impact indicator, in this case the number of customers acquiring the service.)
- Transaction costs per BDS provider, if a private sector businesses (provider level).
- Net, cumulative programme costs per cumulative MSE customer acquiring, using, and benefiting from the business development service, tracked separately (cost per number acquiring; cost per number using; cost per number

Table 24.6 Hypothetical cost-effectiveness report, product development training

Customer report: 1977 (A separate, cumulative report would also be compiled)	Number	Percent	Average % change*	Cost per impact unit (US$)
NUMBER ACQUIRING (from SCALE)	1000	100		
TOTAL PROGRAMME COSTS				300 000 (total costs)
USE				
Use 1: Conducted market research	800	80	25	375
Use 2: Made new or improved product	500	50	N/A	600
Use 3: Changed production process	200	20		1500
Total reporting at least one use:	800	80		375
PARTICULAR BENEFITS				
Increased profits	500	50	10	600
Increased sales	600	60	30	500
Increased assets	200	20	10	1500
Increased employees	200	20	75	1500
Increased customers	100	10	25	1000
Increase product/service lines	500	50	15	600
Decreased costs	100	10	10	3000
Total reporting at least one standard business benefit	700	70		430
Percentage that are repeat customers (from scale report)			50% (500)	
Average customer satisfaction rating (on a scale of 1 to 5)			4.2	
Average time lapsed between service provision and impact measurement				14 months

*The change that customers attribute to BDS service, average of customer responses.

benefiting) (facilitator and provider tracked separately, if different institutions).

- Last year's net programme costs per new or repeat MSE customer acquiring, using and benefiting last year (facilitator and provider tracked separately, if different institutions).
- The same, for the number of MSE customers increasing their sales, income, assets, number of customers, number of product or service lines, or reducing costs (facilitator and provider tracked separately, if different institutions).

Transaction costs are defined here as the financial and non-financial expenses an MSE customer (or private sector BDS provider) invests in order to acquire and use the BDS service. A methodology needs to be developed for assessing the transaction costs of MSE customers and private sector BDS providers. This may include a range of costs, such as the time required to attend training courses, or cash required to purchase sunflower seed to operate a press, in addition to the actual cost of training or purchasing the oil press. Costs should be reported in one currency and deflated to a single year.

Facilitator programme costs should be the most inclusive definition possible: cumulative, start-up and recurrent, international and local, fixed and variable, overhead as well as direct service provision, research and development, etc. Costs of the BDS facilitator or providers will be net of fees collected by non-profit institutions. The costs of private sector entrepreneurs acting as service providers will not be included.

The proposed cost-effectiveness indicator is a compilation of indicators tracked by typical BDS programmes, such as those given in Table 24.7.

Sustainability

Sustainability is an indicator of whether business development services will be available to customers in the long term. It has several layers. To what extent are the costs of different programme activities, ranging from BDS facilitation to direct BDS provision, recovered? To what extent are services being provided by institutions that are independent of subsidy? Is there a competitive, growing market for BDS? In addition, from the entrepreneur's or farmer's point of view, how quickly is the investment in the service paying for itself and will it be a profitable investment? Clearly, sustainability is an issue for all actors: MSE customers, BDS providers, BDS facilitators and donors.

Financial sustainability is the key indicator used to assess micro-finance institutions. However, BDS practitioners have often resisted this type of analysis. Why? Because there are activities required to develop and facilitate BDS provision that are heavily subsidized and, some argue, are likely to remain so. At the same time, substantial progress is being made in sustainability of direct service provision. The indicator described below attempts to resolve this debate by assessing sustainability at different levels customer, provider, facilitator, and market.

Table 24.7   Examples of cost-effectiveness indicators: in use

Organization, programme, location	Indicator and results
Technoserve, Santa Valley	Benefit to cost ratio, 24.95
IDE water pumps, 4 countries	Net present value of benefits US$190m for a US$4.5m investment
ACA/AFE training in Senegal	Cost per enterprise trained, US$150
IDB/GMA/CEPAE, Paraguayan Voucher Training Programme	Cost per person trained, US$19.50
ATI oil presses in Tanzania	Cumulative cost per cumulative enterprise acquiring service, US$152; annual cost per newly assisted enterprise US$128. Benefit:cost ratio 4.65

- Payback period: average amount of time it took for an entrepreneur or farmer's investment in the BDS to pay for itself in increased income (customer level).
- Annual profits or cost-recovery of the BDS facilitator activities, broken down by activities ranging from pure facilitation to direct service provision (provider and facilitator level).
- Type of institution providing a service (whether subsidized facilitators or commercial enterprises) broken down by activity ranging from facilitation to direct service provision (provider and facilitator level).
- Number of MSE customers, compared to net programme costs, over time (market place level).
- Number of 'copycats', service providers that entered the market without assistance from the BDS facilitator (marketplace level). (A methodology still needs to be developed for identifying and measuring 'copycats'.)

Table 24.8 Examples of sustainability indicators in use: cost recovery in each part of ApproTEC's service for oil press dissemination: non-adjusted values

ACTIVITY	Institution	Commercial? Temporary?	Cost (US$)	Recovery (US$)	Recovery (%)
Business opportunity identification/market research (facilitator)	ApproTEC	Temporary, non-commercial	N/A	N/A	N/A
Technology design and development (facilitator)	ApproTEC	Temporary, non-commercial	94 882	0	0%
Selection, training and equipping of manufacturers (facilitator)	ApproTEC	Temporary, non-commercial	7548	4000	53%
Marketing and promotion (facilitator?)		ApproTEC, on-going non-commercial	142 744	14 667	10%
Machine manufacturing (provider)	Independent enterprises	On-going, commercial	Ksh.19 500 per machine	Ksh.23 500 per maching	Ksh.4000 or 121%
Machine distribution (provider)	Independent enterprises	Yes	Ksh.23 500 per machine	Ksh.26 500 per maching	Ksh.3000 or 113%
Oil pressing business	MSE customer	Yes			
Impact monitoring (facilitator)	ApproTEC	No	6191	0	0%

To illustrate the different levels of sustainability, the activities involved in developing and delivering the BDS to the entrepreneur can be broken down in a table (see Table 24.8, which takes as an example Approtech's oil pressing programme in Kenya). For each activity, the table indicates the institution carrying out the activity and whether the activity is intended to be commercial or subsidized, temporary or on-going. Then, for each activity, the previous year's costs and revenues are listed and compared as a percentage. The most facilitative, subsidized activities may not recover any costs. In contrast, entrepreneurs providing a BDS should be making a profit. Institutions will define their own 'steps' according to their programmes and their capacities to break down costs. All programme costs incurred in the previous year should be considered, including estimates of overheads, which may be under a separate activity such as 'management'.

Figure 24.1 is a hypothetical example of what it might look like to compare annual programme costs (net) to annual entrepreneurs acquiring services. Since most agencies collect both data sets, the indicator would be easy to apply. If a service is becoming sustainable, then over time, more people would continue to be served as net programme costs, or subsidies, decline.

Conclusion

Performance measurement is the biggest challenge facing the BDS industry. This framework is a preliminary attempt to present best practices currently in use, with many of their flaws still in place. The Microenterprise Best Practice Project